THE TUC
AND
EDUCATION
REFORM
1926–1970

CLIVE GRIGGS

WOBURN PRESS
LONDON • PORTLAND, OR

First published in 2002 in Great Britain by
FRANK CASS PUBLISHERS
Crown House, 47 Chase Side, Southgate
London N14 5BP

and in the United States of America by
FRANK CASS PUBLISHERS
c/o ISBS, 5824 N.E. Hassalo Street
Portland, Oregon, 97213-3644

Website: www.frankcass.com

British Library Cataloguing in Publication Data

Griggs, Clive
    The TUC and education reform, 1926–1970
    1. Trades Union Congress 2. Labor unions and education–Great Britain–History–
    20th century 3. Educational change–Great Britain–History–20th century
    I. Title
    370.9′41′0904

ISBN 0-7130-0236-0 (cloth)
ISSN 1462-2076

Library of Congress Cataloging-in-Publication Data

Griggs, Clive
    The TUC and education reform, 1926–1970 / Clive Griggs.
        p. cm.
    Includes bibliographical references (p.) and index.
    ISBN 0-7130-0236-0 (cloth)
    1. Working class–Education–Great Britain–History–20th century. 2. Trades Union
Congress–History–20th century. 3. Labor unions and education–Great Britain–
History–20th century. 4. Educational equalization–Great Britain–History–20th century.
I. Title: Trades Union Congress and education reform, 1926–1970. II. Title.

LC5056.G7 T73 2002
331.88′3711′00941–dc21   2002024999

Typeset by FiSH Books, London WC1
Printed in Great Britain by MPG Books Ltd, Victoria Square, Bodmin, Cornwall

To
Sheila

CONTENTS

ABBREVIATIONS

AAM	Association of Assistant Mistresses
ACE	Advisory Centre for Education
AEU	Amalgamated Engineering Union
AHM	Association of Headmistresses (Est. 1874)
AMA	Assistant Masters' Association (Est. 1891)
AMMA	Assistant Masters' and Mistresses' Association
ARP	Air Raid Precautions
ASLEF	Associated Society of Locomotive Engineers and Firemen
ASTMS	Association of Scientific, Technical and Managerial Staffs
ATTI	Association of Teachers in Technical Institutions
BBC	British Broadcasting Corporation
BMA	British Medical Association
BOE	Board of Education (1900–1944)
CAC	Central Advisory Council (Est.1944; one for England, one for Scotland)
CASE	Confederation/Campaign for the Advancement of State Education (1960)
CATs	Colleges of Advanced Technology
CBI	Confederation of British Industries (formed 1965 from amalgamation of FBI, British Employers' Confederation & National Association of British Manufacturers)
CEA	Council for Educational Advance (Est. 1942)
CENTO	Central Treaty Organisation
CFEA	Council for Educational Advance (Est. 1962)
CNNA	Council for National Academic Awards (Est. 1964)

CSE	Certificate of Secondary Education
DES	Department for Education & Science (Est. 1964) see BOE and MOE.
EPA	Educational Priority Area
ETU	Electrical Trades Union
FBI	Federation of British Industries (Est. 1916)
FE	Further Education
GATT	General Agreement on Tariffs and Trade
GCE	General Certificate of Education (O = Ordinary, A = Advanced Level)
GDP	Gross Domestic Product
GMWU	General and Municipal Workers Union
HMC	Headmasters' Conference (Est.1869)
HMI	Her Majesty's Inspectors
HNC	Higher National Certificate
HND	Higher National Diploma
ICFTU	International Confederation of Free Trades Unions
IEA	Institute of Economic Affairs
IFTU	International Federation of Trades Unions
IMF	International Monetary Fund
IRSF	Inland Revenue Staff Federation
ILEA	Inner London Education Authority
IQ	Intelligence Quotient
ISIS	Independent Schools Information Service
LA	Local Authority
LEA	Local Education Authority
LCC	London County Council
LSB	London School Board
MOE	Ministry of Education (1944–1964)
NACTST	National Advisory Council on Training and Supply of Teachers
NAHT	National Association of Head Teachers (Est.1897)
NAS	National Association of Schoolmasters (Est. 1919)
NASUWT	National Association of Schoolmasters and Women Teachers (Union formed from merger of NAS and UWT in 1976)
NATO	North Atlantic Treaty Organisation
NCLC	National Council of Labour Colleges
NFEO	National Federation of Employers' Organisations
NFER	National Foundation for Educational Research
NHS	National Health Service
NUAW	National Union of Agricultural Workers

NUBO	National Union of Boot Operatives
NUGMW	National Union of General & Municipal Workers
NUM	National Union of Mineworkers
NUPE	National Union of Public Employees
NUS	National Union of Students (Est. 1922)
NUR	National Union of Railwaymen
NUT	National Union of Teachers (Est.1870) N.U. of Elementary Teachers until 1889
NUWT	National Union of Women Teachers
OFSTED	Office for Standards in Education
OU	Open University
PLEBS	The Plebs League
PLP	Parliamentary Labour Party
PRO	Public Record Office
RCA	Railway Clerks' Association
ROSLA	Raising of the School Leaving Age
RSG	Rate Support Grant
SEATO	South-East Asia Treaty Organisation
TC	Trades Council
TGWU	Transport & General Workers' Union
TUC	Trades Union Congress (Est. 1868)
TUCEC	Trades Union Congress Education Committee
TUCGC	Trades Union Congress General Council
UCCA	Universities Central Council on Admissions
UGC	University Grants Committee
URW	United Rubber Workers
USDAW	Union of Shop & Distributive Allied Workers
UWT	Union of Women Teachers (Est. 1965)
WEA	Workers' Education Association
WETUC	Workers' Educational Trade Union Committee
WFTU	World Federation of Trades Unions

ILLUSTRATIONS

1. Alec Firth, Assistant General Secretary and Education Secretary of the TUC 1923–31.
2. Trade Union School Ruskin College 1926. Middle front row: John V.C. Wray; second row from front, fifth from left consecutively: Alec Firth, Walter Citrine and John Price, Head of the Industrial Division of the ILO.
3. Poster advertising public meeting, chaired by Walter Citrine, with leading speakers on education campaigning against the 1936 Education Bill.
4. TUC pamphlet protesting against the provisions of the 1936 Education Bill.
5. The cover of a booklet setting out the comprehensive education policy of the TUC in 1937.
6. Sir Walter Citrine addressing 1941 Edinburgh Congress.
7. Poster by Dudley S. Cowes encouraging evacuation of school children in London during the Second World War.
8. Dame Anne Godwin speaking on Education at the 1955 Southport Congress. A suffragette at 15, she became Secretary of the Clerical Workers' Union and took a major interest in education.
9. Denis Winnard (front left), TUC Education Secretary 1957–76, at the TUC Summer School, York, in the 1960s.
10. (Left to right): Ray Buckton with Clive Jenkins and Roy Jackson, respectively, Chair and Secretary of the TUC Education Committee.

TABLES

ACKOWLEDGEMENTS

Anyone undertaking academic study knows how much they owe to other people who provide vital information and support in the pursuit of the necessary research upon which such work relies. The Leverhulme Trust granted me a two-year fellowship to undertake this study of the TUC and Education, and for that I am truly grateful. The staff at the TUC afforded me every possible help. My special thanks to my wife, Sheila, who helped with the research and wordprocessing. The staff at the Modern Records Centre of Warwick University where we spent several weeks working through the files concerning education deposited there by the TUC provided every possible assistance. So too did the librarians at the University of North London where other TUC archives are housed. Both sets of staff have generously continued to provide further information when asked to do so. Thanks are also due to the service provided by the Public Record Office staff who have been most helpful. Many individuals who are already fully occupied provided detailed replies to queries I sent giving credence to the old saying, 'If you want something done give it to the busiest person in the room.' Roy Jackson, past secretary of the TUCEC was most helpful in discussing ideas with me, Ann Morton at the Public Records Office identified key TUC documents among government files on education, Dr Dennis Dean read through part of the work and provided valuable advice whilst Len Stapleton also agreed to undertake the arduous task of reading the text. I would also like to thank the following for replying in detail to requests for information and suggesting sources to follow up other related issues further: Professor Richard Aldrich; Professor Philip Bagwell; Bill Bailey; Elizabeth Boardman; Alan

Clark; Christine Coates; Brigit Collins; Brian Cornish; Dr Keith Gildart; Professor Peter Gordon; Professor Peter Gosden; Alan Grant; Lawrie Harries; Halina Hassett; David Horsfield; David Kelso; Robin Limmer; Stuart Maclure; Janette Martin; Steve Mills; Dr Jane Palmer; Victoria Peters; Professor Brian Simon; Mike Smith; Richard Storey; Professor Ted Tapper; Richard Temple; Debbie Wall; Christine Woodland.

My thanks are also due to the staff at the University of Brighton Library who responded readily to requests for various books and journals when required. The staffs of the following libraries and organisations have also been most helpful: BBC Written Archives Centre; British Esperanto Association; British Library Newspaper Collection; British Library of Political and Economic Science; Campaign for State Education; City of Glasgow Civic Library; The Conservative Party; Department of Education and Employment Information and Library Network; Eastbourne Central Public Library; Eastbourne and District Hospital Institute of Nursing Library; Macmillan Publishers Ltd.; Moray House – University of Edinburgh; National Association of Teachers in Further and Higher Education; National Museum of Labour History, Railway, Maritime and Transport Union; Ruskin College, Scottish Labour Party; Trades Union Congress; University of Birmingham; University of Leeds; University of Leicester; University of Reading; University of Sussex.

I hope that this volume will go some way to satisfy the efforts of all those who provided help regardless of whether they agree with the opinions expressed.

Clive Griggs
Eastbourne
July 2002

I would like to thank the following for permission to include the illustrations: Modern Records Centre, University of Warwick, nos 3 and 4; TUC Publications Department, photographs nos 1, 2, 6, 8 and 10; TUC Collection, University of North London, no. 5; Public Records Office, no. 7; and Michael Frost, York, no. 9. All copies of photographs were kindly reproduced by TUC Publications Department.

INTRODUCTION

This study covers the years 1926 to 1970 – from the General Strike to Labour's electoral defeat in 1970 and, by following on from an earlier volume covering the years 1868–1925, completes just over a century of involvement by the Trades Union Congress (TUC) in education. To some extent writing the first volume was an easier enterprise, for the nearer one comes to the present so the amount of documentary material available increases dramatically. One result of this has been that whereas in the first volume it was possible to cover TUC campaigns regarding schooling for children and young people as well as education for trade unionists, with a few exceptions, it has not been possible to repeat the pattern this time. It was decided therefore at an early stage that education for trade unionists would be excluded and this decision was made easier by the fact that there were several books which already covered this area and there could be a question of repeating information already well established by such studies as A.J. Corfield's *Epoch in Workers' Education*; John Holford's *Union Education in Britain; A TUC Activity;* J.P.M. Millar's *The Labour College Movement* and Brian Simon's edited volume *The Search for Enlightenment*. This has also allowed certain aspects of other areas to be included such as further education, youth training and higher education. The study therefore concentrates upon the manner in which the Trades Union Congress, through its Education Committee, acted as a pressure group within the education system to campaign for improved educational opportunities for children and young people and the closely related welfare programmes which would make such provision effective.

A chronological approach has been adopted dividing the period into four sections which are reasonably convenient to deal with in this manner bearing in mind the danger of implying that history unravels in this way or that people experience life in such a sectional way. There is some logic to the divisions; a pre-war period, the war years, the immediate post-war years and the 1960s. The war did bring dramatic changes so the first two divisions are reasonably valid and the post-war period is fine, although the dividing line here is admittedly more arbitrary. Each section begins with a general overview and here there is a problem of deciding how much background information to provide. Yet as education clearly does not take place independently of economic, political and social developments some background information of the period is essential to any understanding of the changes which took place in the nation's education system. The danger here is in going into too much detail and ending up with potted histories of the period. How far this approach has been successful the reader will have to decide.

The TUC never confined itself to what might narrowly be called industrial questions and when the Labour Party in 1907 requested the deletion from their agenda 'of items dealing with such things as education, housing, land law, municipal trading, factory inspectors and nationalisation of national resources, (the) request was rejected in toto on the ground that none of these items was "outside the scope of (the TUC's) usual work".'[1] Their involvement in so many areas and the energy expended in carefully prepared policies pursued brought them increasing influence in many quarters. By the end of the Second World War there was probably no other major organisation with such extensive interests in so many aspects of British society.[2] The public saw them as an important body with growing status from the late 1930s onwards. They never affiliated to any other body and considered themselves the first among equals with the possible exception of the International Confederation of Free Trades Unions (ICFTU), but even here they saw themselves as the senior partner. They were in effect the parliament of the trade unions within the country and were able to speak on behalf of trade unionism. All governments, whether they agreed with TUC policy or not, were pleased to be able to deal with one central body on most issues rather than having to deal with numerous individual trade unions. For trade unions the TUC was a living example of strength through unity; a unity made possible by the fact that unlike some European countries there was no division within the British trade union movement on religious or political grounds. Religious disputes were avoided because in general delegates realised the divisive nature of such arguments. Political differences were inevitable and at times fiercely debated at Congress. Generally it was in matters of foreign policy that the TUCGC were likely to face criticism from delegates.

Congress was fed by resolutions from affiliated trade unions covering the widest possible range of issues affecting the lives of the majority of working people and their families. They were debated at Congress in September where resolutions were passed. The next month the Trades Union Congress Education Committee (TUCEC) met to respond to Congress resolutions dealing with education in order for the General Council (TUCGC) to take appropriate action. The TUCEC would refer back to previous policy statements and Congress reports. This practice ensured that they were always guided by 'where they started from' and to that extent never had a 'clean sheet'. For example, the important statements made by the TUC to the Malcolm Reports in 1926 and 1928 were still being used as guidelines in the 1950s and 1960s. Whilst most trade unionists lacked the lengthy formal education of government ministers and civil servants they did have one major advantage when entering into discussions about the public education system; namely that unlike many of the former they had experience of the system as pupils and often as parents. They knew the reality of plans devised and advocated by well-meaning politicians and civil servants who rarely chose to send their own children to local authority schools. A practice which showed little signs of change throughout the period of this study.

The response of the TUCGC might take the shape of a letter to a government department or large company or a deputation to a government minister. The relevant TUC department would provide the necessary information based upon official government documents, research articles and newspaper reports. These in turn were supplemented by material from their own information network, the numerous trade union branches and trades councils throughout the land which reported on their local scene providing case studies as further supportive evidence for TUC representatives meeting ministers or giving evidence to recognised appointed committees of experts. Sometimes it is possible to search back further along the line to a trade union conference resolution and find a trade unionist belonging to another interest group who put forward a policy on their behalf. This practice has been illustrated for education from the Edwardian period when members of small Socialist groups such as the Independent Labour Party or Social Democratic Federation successfully steered policies through their own trade unions and the TUC.[3] There was nothing necessarily underhanded about this activity for trade unionists would still need to be convinced in a debate as to the wisdom of the policy. However, the TUC was always wary about the danger of other organisations using them as a conduit to put forward policies of their own, as was the case sometimes with certain religious interests.

Education policy was therefore the product of the views of ordinary working people who had experienced the limited and limiting education system through which the vast majority of children passed and therefore were anxious that their own and other children should have better opportunities than had been afforded themselves. By the 1930s the TUCEC took a greater lead due to the need to respond more quickly to BOE initiatives such as the establishment of Committees to examine certain aspects of the educational system, e.g., The Hadow, Spens and Norwood Committees.

When faced by a government minister with rejection, possible compromise or a non-committal reply they might change their approach but still kept to the basic principles which underlay the policy. This was not born out of a failure to see an alternative view but a sound belief in objectives they were pursuing on the behalf of the interests of their members and their families. They exercised patience and worked within the system both by preparing papers based upon sound educational research and the intelligence they gained from the trade union network which kept them up to date with current developments. Apart from direct approaches to government departments they were willing to campaign through time-honoured practices such as the leaflet which could be spread widely through the trade union branch and trades council system and also by holding public meetings, often with like-minded organisations, to rally support in order to alert people to government plans and put forward alternative ideas.

The sheer volume of TUC detailed documentation is almost overwhelming and when one realises that the correspondence to so many organisations, production of reports and memorandum for TUC representatives, outline papers and summaries of reports from government-appointed committees of enquiry was undertaken by so few officers at TUC headquarters one is left wondering how the staff coped with such a work-load. The education department contained three members – the secretary to the Committee, a Director of Studies and an assistant who served both of them. As the TUC was based upon departments the education secretary set the agenda for meetings. It is remarkable that hardly any reference is made to these unsung heroes in histories of the labour movement. Even the secretaries of the TUC Education Committee during these years, A.S. Firth (1926–31), Jack Vernon Carl Wray (1932–49) and Denis Winnard (1950–74), each of whom was very able and expected to cover all aspects of education from schooling to higher education, as well as education for trade unionists, receives no mention in *Who's Who*, the *Dictionary of Labour Biography* or the obituary columns of *The Times*. Yet without their dedication the TUC could never have produced such well-argued policies in the field of education.

In the early years, TUC officers were called upon to serve more than one function. Firth, for example was Assistant General Secretary to Citrine as well as leading the education department. In the past, posts within trade union organisations had been filled by those who had worked in the trade and been active in their union. Their experience was invaluable for the work they undertook. The chairpersons of the TUCEC all came within this category, usually skilled workers with a minimum of formal schooling but well read, able and articulate. George Hicks provides a good example. He worked in the building trade as a bricklayer, was a member of the SDF and gained further education though the NCLC. He was a supporter of the Plebs League (PLEBS) – founded at Ruskin College in 1908 – and appropriately wrote a Foreword to the 1927 abridged edition of Robert Tressell's (Robert Noonan's) *The Ragged Trousered Philanthropists* dealing with the conditions in the building trade in 'Mugsborough' (Hastings).[4] He recognised the picture of the building trade described by Tressell only too well and readily grasped the political analysis woven into the story. Like many active trade unionists he constantly encouraged other trade unionists to read the book. In his Foreword he wrote, 'I know of no better book to give to the newcomer into our Movement, or for circulation amongst the unconverted...the lessons contained in this book should be learnt by heart by all toilers.'[5] This almost missionary encouragement of education to gain knowledge of the political and social system in order to change it was common among many trade unionists, especially those supportive of adult education provided for working people; Ruskin College, the Central Labour College, NCLC and WEA. Understandably some of these trade unionists were attracted to the TUCEC.

Citrine believed that it was also important to recruit graduates from higher education to some of the departments within the TUC to cope with changing circumstances facing the organisation. Hence applicants for some posts would increasingly come from those who had attended a traditional university, Ruskin College or as in the case of George Woodcock, both. In addition they had a record of considerable work experience. This policy applied equally to education. Alec Firth joined the TUC staff in 1921. He had attended Shelley elementary school, won a scholarship to Penistone Grammar School and then to Huddersfield Technical College where he studied economics. In 1915 he was awarded a Martin Fisher Travelling scholarship but could not take it up due to the outbreak of war. He studied for an external University of London B.Sc.(Econ) and was appointed assistant lecturer at Huddersfield Technical College. He joined the navy but was discharged shortly on medical grounds. He became deputy statistical officer in the Department of Wool Textile Production, then secretary of a large firm of wool brokers before taking a post in the Profiteering Act Department of the Board of Trade. Hence when he joined the TUC at nearly 30 years of age he was not only well qualified in economics and statistics but had also worked as a secretary at a senior level. He considered a political career, being asked to stand for Labour at Penistone in 1918, (an invitation he could not accept because he was a civil servant at the time), and he also stood for Labour in Cambridge in 1923 and 1924. However, he was probably best suited to the administrative career he chose having been described as having the 'temperament of a University lecturer and the training of a civil servant'. It was this combination of education and experience which enabled TUC officers to discuss relevant matters with their department counterparts in government.

Jack V.C. Wray took over the education role of Firth when the latter became Secretary of the WEA. He held the post for 18 years and was a member of the Crowther Committee between 1956 and 1959. Little is recorded about Wray's early years, but given his date of birth it is likely that he was in the First World War and from people who knew him at the TUC it has been suggested that he did not come from a manual worker's background. Denis Winnard won a scholarship to Rochdale Grammar School, matriculated as an Exhibitioner in history at Wadham College, Oxford, and graduated in modern history in 1937. He worked for the WEA as a tutor in Lancashire before joining the TUC in January 1950 as assistant in the education department, a post he took over on the retirement of Jack Wray. His successor, Roy Jackson, a graduate of Ruskin College and Oxford University, has spoken of Winnard's detailed knowledge of the public education system. Winnard served on the Newsom Committee from 1961–63. He retired in 1974. Hence two secretaries of the TUCEC spanned 42 years and this continuity, reinforced by other long-serving members of the Committee, brought not just stabilty but also the knowledge which comes from being so familiar with both past and present developments in an area, in this case education. Such long-serving Education Committee members included George Chester (1939–49), W.B. Beard (1948–67), R. Willis (1950–66) and

Dame Anne Godwin (1952–63). Anne Godwin was the first woman to become Secretary of a 'mixed' trade union, the Clerical and Administrative Workers' Union. Born in 1898 she had joined the suffragette movement upon leaving school at 15 but her major interest was to become education and she focussed upon this issue in her opening address as President of the TUC in 1962, only the third woman to have reached that position by then. Given the ability, years of experience and knowledge of the area it is no wonder that TUC deputations were well briefed and able to discuss matters on equal terms with government ministers and their department. They did not have the power to make the decisions but they often won the argument.

The expertise in education of the TUC was recognised by many organisations through invitations to the TUCGC to provide representatives to serve on their governing boards, a practice which increased as time passed (see Appendix 3). This was true also for the government who invited TUCGC representatives to serve on several Education Committees, although only one was appointed during the inter-war period, Ivor Gwynne to the Hadow Committee from 1924–26. Later there would be others, all of whom understandably came from the TUCEC: G. Chester (Fleming 1944), Miss A. Godwin and J.V.C. Wray (Crowther 1959), Roy Jackson who became TUCEC Secretary later (Albermarle 1960), Denis Winnard (Newsom 1963), and Dame Godwin (Newsom 1968 and Donnison 1979). There were also representatives from other sections of the labour movement on such committees at times: Dr R.H. Tawney and Dr. A. Mansbridge both of the WEA (Hadow 1926 and 1931), Dr A. Mansbridge and Lady Simon (Spens 1938) whilst Frederick Mander (McNair 1944) and Ronald Gould (Early Leaving 1954) were both in turn secretaries of the NUT, although at the time the union was not affiliated to the TUC. H.E. Clay of the Labour party also served with Gould. Some were chosen because of their knowledge of, and national prestige within, education; others brought their personal experiences of the system and great knowledge because of their deep interest and involvement, this was especially the case of the TUCEC secretaries. In contrast to the TUCGC representatives nearly all those chosen to chair committees examining various aspects of education within the country had been educated at fee-paying schools and Oxbridge (see Appendix 4). How far and often the pattern of attitudes towards education in terms of government policies and official education committees might have been influenced by the contrasting education experiences of different participants is but one of many themes which will be examined within this study.

NOTES AND REFERENCES

1. Martin, R.M. (1980) *TUC: The Growth of a Pressure Group 1868–1976*, p.14.
2. Ibid., p.328.
3. Griggs, C. (1985) 'Labour and Education' in Brown, K.D. (ed.) *The First Labour Party 1906–1914*.
4. Bellamy, J. and Saville, J. (eds) (2000) *Dictionary of Labour Biography* Vol. 10, entry on Robert Noonan, pp.156–62.
5. Tressell, R. (1927 edn) *The Ragged Trousered Philanthropists*, pp. vi–vii.

PART 1 – THE INTER-WAR YEARS
1926–1939

CHAPTER 1

PUTTING SECONDARY EDUCATION ON THE AGENDA

CITRINE BECOMES TUC GENERAL SECRETARY

Both at home and abroad the period 1926–39 was one of great turbulence by any standards: the General Strike of 1926, the Wall Street Crash of 1931, the rise of Fascism in Europe with the Nazis taking power in Germany in 1934, the outbreak of the Spanish Civil War in 1936, and the war between Britain and Germany in 1939. Throughout the years Conservative governments were in power whether under that name or that of a National government, with the exception of the ill-fated second minority Labour government of 1929, which in spite of economic difficulties contained members who did try to make progress in education matters. Throughout the period there were never less than 1 million people registered as unemployed with the numbers peaking at over 3 million in 1931; affiliated TUC membership reflected these figures although there was a time lag.

Table 1. TUC Figures for the Unemployed in 1931

	Insured Workers Unemployed	TUC Affiliated Membership[1]
1926	1,505,000	4,365,619
1932	2,829,000	3,613,273
1934	2,171,000	3,294,581
1939	1,408,000	4,669,186

Partly as a result of the General Strike, and owing to their ideology, many industrialists and Conservatives were hostile to organised labour at least until the second half of the 1930s and this needs to be borne in mind when making judgements about TUC policy and action. However, it also needs to be said that throughout the period there was hardly a significant official enquiry which did not include a TUC representative and there was an average of five TUC deputations per annum to government departments with only one year, 1931, when there is no record of such a meeting.

The TUC, with its long history going back to 1868, has often been depicted as an unwieldy organisation, criticised by various people for not being what they believed it ought to be; not radical enough is probably a common criticism. In fact, whilst such criticism can certainly be made, it is also possible to argue that they should at least be given considerable credit for surviving for a comparatively long time when some of the most powerful forces within the economy have been antagonistic to TUC activities. Whilst the leadership would have baulked in public at any association with the ideas of Karl Marx, nevertheless the German philosopher's writings may well provide an explanation for the tactics they learned to adopt: 'Men make their own history but they do not make it as they please; they do not make it under circumstances chosen by themselves, but under circumstances directly encountered, given and transmitted from the past.'[2]

As the opening paragraph of this section has illustrated the circumstances the TUC faced between 1926 and 1939 were extremely difficult. Pragmatism is probably the simplest description to apply to the TUC and those seeking signs of a clear ideology are likely to be frustrated. For example, to take at random two items from the Minutes of the General Council. In 1927, 'Letter sent to President Coolidge protesting over the condemnation to death of Sacco and Vanzetti' (the two Italian Anarchist immigrants) and the following year, 'Letter of sympathy sent on the news of the illness of King George V'.[3] It is not necessary to see support for anarchism or monarchy in these actions but rather a reflection of the wide range of views within the TUC and the lack of dogma as well as genuine concern for the lives of people in completely different circumstances.

The TUC regarded the General Strike as a tactical disaster and turned to gaining improvements in the lives of their members by working carefully to strengthen their organisation and by adapting methods which would gradually increase their influence as a pressure group through as many sections of society as possible, including that of the government. This approach was reinforced with the appointment of Walter Citrine as General Secretary in 1926. Citrine was born in Wallasey in 1886, attended elementary school leaving at the age of twelve and a half, having reached Standard VII.[4] He became an apprentice electrician, learned Gregg shorthand at evening classes and became full-time Assistant General Secretary of the Electrical Trades Union (ETU) in Manchester in 1920. He applied to become Assistant General Secretary of the TUC, a post which attracted over 200 applications from which five candidates were chosen for interview in January 1924. Citrine, aged only 37, was successful and joined Fred Bramley, the TUC Secretary at the time. Bramley was in poor health and asked Citrine to overhaul the filing system as he had done earlier at the ETU. Citrine was a brilliant organiser setting up the Committee and support structure as well as a new filing system. Every incoming letter was given a reference, date stamped and put on a file using the Library of Congress reference system. His attention to detail was well known, and Aneurin Bevan, who was at odds with Citrine in terms of both ideology and personality, referring to the card-index mind of Citrine said, 'poor fellow, he suffers from files'.[5] On Bramley's death Citrine took over as Secretary in 1926.

In fact Bevan's summary quip was less than just. Citrine was far more than a good organiser, important though that aspect of his abilities was to the TUC. He had joined the ILP in 1904 and was to write many years later in his autobiography that he 'never weakened in his socialist faith'. He stood up against the encroachment of Fascism in Europe during the 1930s, argued endlessly with the National government of Baldwin to supply armaments to the legitimate elected government of Spain. His pragmatism was born out of political experience and his doubts about the ability or preparation of the TUC and affiliated unions to sustain the 'General Strike' for a lengthy period of time. He was also uneasy about the tactics necessarily involved but not about the justice of the miners' cause nor the mean-spiritedness of those who were determined to make the working people bear the brunt of the country's economic problems, as he made clear in his diaries, when recording the meeting of the TUCGC at Downing Street on 12 May 1926:

> I looked at them with mixed feelings – bitterness – when I reflected one of them at least would have butchered our people without compunction on any pretext which offered. I thought to myself what an anomaly it is that there should be such a thing as a governing class. I comforted myself with the reflection that some day that would be altered.[6]

He was instrumental in encouraging opposition to the cuts proposed by the National government and in having MacDonald expelled from the

Labour party. All of these facts underline his commitment to strong support of the labour movement but his tactics were those of a negotiator carefully appraising each situation to determine what was possible in given circumstances.

In 1928, Citrine was made President of the International Federation of Trade Unions (IFTU), a post he was to hold until 1945. Within a year of his appointment the *Sunday Express* ran a story on its front page entitled 'Mussolini Whips Mr Citrine – TUC Chief fails to 'save' Italy. "Audacity".'[7] It claimed that Citrine and Mr J. Sassenbach, Secretary of the ITFU

> were severely whipped by Mussolini after they had bearded the lion in his den in Rome. These two Socialists secretly planned what they thought would be a dramatic coup – the persuading of Mussolini to allow Italy to join the IFTU . . . they were to go to Rome. . . and return in triumph hailed as saviours of the world trade union movement for apart from Russia, Italy is the only nation outside the Federation.
>
> Not even closest friends were told. Mr Citrine told his closest friend, Mr Ben Tillett that he was going away on holiday for three weeks.

The report related their meeting with Mussolini, the furnishings of the room in the palace and the clothing worn by 'The Duce'. Apparently Sassenach spoke for 40 minutes explaining how Italian workers would benefit from membership whilst Citrine spoke even more elequently for 45 minutes during which time the Duce remained strangely silent. He then gave his reply which took an hour and 40 minutes. He told them of his powerful role as prime minister and head of five government departments finally pointing to their 'audacity to come here and ask me to delegate the rule of my workpeople to a handful of political fanatics in Amsterdam. Your visit here today only emphasises the incompetence and lack of vision of the Socialist Party. I AM MUSSOLINI.' A bell then rang to signal the end of the audience 'and the two great Socialist leaders made a rather undignified exit'. It was further claimed that upon Citrine's return from holiday he 'was indiscreet and the affair leaked out, and now prominent labour leaders are making frantic efforts to place a cloak over the whole affair'.

The report implied that Citrine had been secretive and duplicitous, was alongside Sassenach browbeaten and made to look ridiculous by Mussolini and tried to hide a failed attempt to persuade the dictator for Italy to join the IFTU. The mocking tone towards Socialists came as no surprise given the political sympathies of the *Express* newspapers and the growing strength of Labour in the months prior to the spring General Election of 1929 may have been a factor in the prominent position the newspaper gave to the story. However in spite of the considerable power of the *Express* newspapers, Citrine sued for libel and in April of that same year the court was informed by Sir Henry Slesser acting for Citrine that he was 'a person of considerable public importance in the industrial world' referring to his prominent role 'in the Turner Nelchet proposals for conciliation and peace in industry'.[8]

The editor, James Douglas, and Express Newspapers Limited admitted that 'the whole story was a complete fabrication from beginning to end'. Citrine had never met Mussolini and the Italian Foreign Office confirmed that no such interview had ever taken place. The newspaper accepted 'the whole of the circumstances of the alleged interview are entirely without foundation'. They expressed 'their sincere regret that the article in question should have been published'. They agreed to pay substantial damages; £500 for 'very serious libel'– a sum approximately equivalent to twice the average annual wage in 1929. Citrine was satisfied and did not wish to take the matter any further. It was to be but one example of the hostility of so many newspapers to the labour movement during the inter-war period.

Under Citrine's new organisation, Education was one of eight departments serving the elected members of the TUCGC. At the time these mirrored government departments, making it convenient for direct communication with the appropriate source of government policy and administration. The Education Committee of about seven members met eight times during the year, commencing with the Annual Congress during the first week of September and thus coinciding with the academic year. Arthur Pugh, of the Iron and Steel Trades Federation, was in the Chair for most of this period. They dealt with masses of correspondence from individuals and organisations, provided briefing papers for the TUCGC on matters of government education policy and for TUC deputations to the President of the Board of Education (BOE) as well as providing written evidence on TUC education policy when requested to do so for committees such as Hadow and Spens. As a glance at TUC Education Committee (TUCEC) files will indicate, their representatives were provided with papers as detailed as those written by civil servants for government ministers.

The correspondence of the TUCEC indicates the range of issues they faced from those of national dimensions to those confronting individuals: a letter from a post-office worker in 1932 asking for advice regarding his son's career which received a detailed reply,[9] an invitation from the BBC to discuss 'talks for adults' with the TUCEC in 1929,[10] an invitation to visit the Rachel McMillan Nursery School in Deptford which resulted in a lengthy favourable report from the Committee in 1933,[11] and a recommendation from Ellen Wilkinson for a teacher of physical education to attend a TUC Summer School,[12] which was rejected. There was a belief in many quarters that the TUC had an educational fund which could be tapped into by individuals or organisations, a mistake possibly arising from their funding of trade union students at the Central Labour College and Ruskin College. This known support for adult education probably explains requests from a student at Coleg Harlech in 1932[13] as well as those from overseas, such as one in 1927 from a Mr Weimann of the Socialist People's College at Castle Tinz, Berlin, to provide a scholarship for a British trade unionist to attend there for five months[14] and another in 1931 from the Principal of the People's College Elsinore, to support two students from Britain to attend during the summer term.[15]

Yet it was not just adult institutions which sought TUC financial support. Mr W.M. Fletcher wrote from the Amalgamated Engineering Union (AEU), one affiliated to the TUC, that 'some of our members are under the impression that the TUC allot a certain portion of their income to a fund for the purpose of making grants to parents (whose children have been awarded scholarships)...' which brought the reply, 'I have to inform you that the TUC have no such fund as you describe...'[16] Mr M.L. Jacks, Headmaster of Mill Hill Public School wrote with a touch of condescension to the TUC informing them that,

> It has recently come to the knowledge of my Governors that the Headmaster's Conference has been considering the possibility of making Public Schools more accessible to boys of so-called working class parents; and although pressure on places is no way decreasing, we desire, if financially possible, to make an experiment along these lines. It is understood that funds are at the disposal of the Trades Unions which could be applied to educational purposes. The proposal would be that your Congress and the School should jointly found a scholarship to be held by such a boy. It costs about £180 per annum to keep a boy at this school... I should be glad to hear from you what proportion of this annual cost you would be prepared to find to forward this experiment.

A diplomatic reply pointed out that TUC education schemes were 'not yet sufficiently developed to allow of their giving serious consideration to the question of scholarships in public schools'.[17]

In fact TUC departments did have a small allocation to spend at their discretion and this was sometimes used as a contribution to an organisation which had asked for a TUC representative to join them on their Board, but it was always made clear that this should not be seen as an affiliation fee because the TUC never affiliated to any other organisation.

In terms of the gender issue the TUC in both membership and more in leadership, was predominantly male. Indeed Margaret Bondfield (1873–1953), of the General and Municipal Workers Union (GMWU) was almost the sole exception to the general rule of TUC leading figures being male during the first quarter of the twentieth century. She was the tenth of 11 children born in Chard, Somerset. Her father was a lace maker, strong non-conformist and held radical views. At 13 years of age she taught in her local school and at 15 moved to Brighton where she became a draper's assistant. It was here she was introduced to women's rights by a Liberal woman friend. In 1894 she joined the Shop Assistants' Union, became Assistant Secretary (1898–1908) and was the first woman delegate elected to the TUC in 1899. She subsequently served two spells on the TUCGC in the inter-war years (1918–24 and 1926–29). Such exceptions partly reflected the structure and values of society at the time but also arose from the fact that the most powerful unions at the TUC represented industries such as coal mining, railways, docks, heavy engineering and, increasingly, motor transport where the employees were overwhelmingly male. From this situation it would be misleading to assume that TUC education policy was framed in a way favourable to boys. Whilst it may be true that there were many parents in the country who regarded support for a boy to continue school as more important than support for a girl, there is no hint of such a view being expressed at the TUC in any debate upon education.

'Children' or 'juveniles' were words commonly used at the TUC and these clearly referred to boys and girls. An early TUCGC deputation to the BOE in 1925 provides just one example of the wide vocabulary used. Elementary schooling was listed among the proposals for discussion and 'children' mentioned later. It is true that Mr Hallas of the GMWU remarked that 'at present a boy left school at fourteen . . . ', but such phrases were usually understood to include girls. He could hardly have been more all embracing in his statement a little later when he referred to 'the problem of boys and girls, youths and maidens roving the streets'.[18] When it came to categories, TUC delegates wanted better schooling for their own children, boys and girls, and generally saw the barrier to post-elementary schooling in terms of fees and low parental income, matters more clearly related to social class than gender.

SECONDARY EDUCATION – THE MAIN FOCUS FOR ADVANCEMENT

There were three major concerns of the TUC concerning secondary schooling during the inter-war period: a growing demand for free secondary schooling for all, raising the school leaving age to 15 immediately and 16 as soon as possible; and the establishment of maintenance grants to enable parents to cope with the expense and loss of earnings involved by children staying at school for a further year or two. In addition there were other issues to which the TUC responded, e.g. the development of associated welfare programmes in the form of school meals, medical inspection and treatment; nursery education; facilities at school for physical education and the content of individual text books used in schools, which were considered unsuitable for children.

The TUC contributed evidence to three major reports on secondary schooling during the inter-war years, (Hadow 1926; Malcolm, two reports on Education and Industry – published 1926 and 1928; and Spens 1938). The terms of reference for the Consultative Committee (Hadow) had been worded in such a way as to escape the financial implications of the superior funding afforded to secondary schools, i.e. 'study suitable for children who will remain in full-time attendance at schools, other than Secondary Schools' but there is little doubt that the issue of post-primary schooling was becoming caught up in the growing demand of 'Secondary Education for All' even if this was interpreted in a variety of ways. In his edited study for the Labour party which bore this title and which was to become a rallying call for leading sections of the labour movement, R.H. Tawney had written, 'the phrase, "secondary education" is not free from ambiguity. No statutory definition of it, so far as we are aware, has ever been given.' He did however provide a definition based upon what he saw as the purpose of a secondary school:

> its main aim is not to impart the specialised technique of any particular trade or profession, but to develop the faculties which, because they are the attribute of man, are not peculiar to any particular class or profession of men, and to build up the interests, which, while they may become the basis of specialisation at a later stage, have a value extending beyond their utility for any particular vocation, because they are the condition of a rational and responsible life in society.[19]

This liberal approach and fear of an education tailored to a specific trade or industry permeated thought within the labour movement. If this seems like a contradiction from a movement which supported the apprenticeship system in fact this was not so. Specialisation and training were strongly favoured, providing they followed a general education.

The *Consultative Committee of the Board of Education of the Adolescent* (Hadow Report) set up by the Tory government in 1923, encouraged by Trevelyan when he was minister at the BOE in the first, short-lived minority Labour government of 1924, had framed a reference to investigate the different types of curricula suitable for children 11–15 years of age and the means by which they could be provided,[20] but the phrase 'other than secondary schools' prevented the intrusion of the 'Secondary Education for All' debate which had been stimulated by R.H. Tawney's paper of 1922. Apart from the wish to avoid increased expenditure on public education many did not believe that most children were capable of benefitting from secondary schooling. Both the high proportion of children failing the school certificate examination and the significant numbers leaving before the age of 16 gave some credence to this view but 'a comparison of fee-paying and free-place pupils reveals that the weaker were those paying fees, and the free-place or scholarship children not only tended to remain longer at school but were more successful in the School Certificate Examination'.[21] In 1927 for instance, 48.1 per cent of free-place but only 19.8 per cent of fee-payers gained the School Certificate, a tendency the BOE had noted three years earlier. Lord Eustace Percy, who had wished to reintroduce fees for elementary schools, argued that 'The attempts to bring all post-primary education on to one dead high school level, as it is, I am afraid, in the US, will do far more to prevent any real higher education in this country than anything else.'[22] He was to remain opposed to any compulsory raising of the school leaving age for many years.[23] Although considered reactionary by some he was believed to belong to the 'Socialist' or 'pink wing' of the Cabinet by the *Daily Mail*.[24] It says something about the political perspective of that newspaper when the views of Percy as given to a TUCGC Deputation are considered.

In May 1925 a meeting took place at the BOE between a 13-strong deputation from the TUCGC headed by George Hicks, MP., Arthur Pugh and Walter Citrine, and Lord Eustace Percy, Aubrey Symonds, E.H. Pelham and E.D. Marris.[25] The deputation presented a resolution on education asking that all future schools be built on the open-air plan, with playing fields, the school leaving age to be raised to 15 and maintenance grants provided, the gradual introduction of free secondary schooling and the provision of continuation schools to 18 years for youngsters as proposed in the 1918 Education Act. Percy listened to the trade unionists speaking in support of their programme then replied by saying, 'he did not think there was anything in what had been said which he could not agree with in principle. They were all agreed on the educational ideal for this country and the lines which they wanted to pursue.' He then went on to disagree with all the proposals before him! He did not think that public funds should be used for all educational developments, disagreed that some countries had a better secondary education than Britain, claimed it was impractical to suggest all future schools should be open-air or have playing fields, argued that there were insufficient male teachers to deal with a large rise in the school leaving age, and believed that all these proposals could not be pursued at an early date because of the impact they would have on increases in taxation and rates. In short there was no meeting of minds between the TUCGC and Percy. They were left with vague platitudes 'many of the things stated (by the trade unionists) represented exactly the lines on which he was working.' He suggested a few regional conferences to consider the issues of an extension in the school life of pupils and the problems of juvenile unemployment: 'If employers and organised labour would have regular meetings and consult with local authorities about the drawing up of these programmes, so they could be assured that for the next three or five years they would represent a consensus of opinion as to the best that could be done, it would be moving towards the aims they all had in mind.' If this was even true for some of the aims it was certainly not the prolonged time span the TUC had in mind.

Yet there was another statement by Percy which could be regarded as socialist in principle and seemed completely at variance with nearly all his other views. It was in an expression of his priorities for improving education in the country. Having listed the cost of getting rid of bad schools he said, 'There was one other fact which he thought was very bad where it happened, and that was the segregation of the fee-paying part of the population from the non fee-paying part of the population. The segregation of the population into two classes was, he thought, one of the worst things they could have in this country, and he was anxious to break it down.'[26] Even if one includes those paying fees in the county secondary schools this still seems like an expression of condemnation of the 'public schools' of the time. In this he must have been unique as an old Etonian Conservative Education Minister.

THE HADOW REPORT 1926

On 26 June 1925, George Hicks, MP, R. Richardson and W. Jenkins gave evidence to the Hadow Committee on behalf of the General Council of the

TUC. A summary of that evidence covered seven areas: raising the school leaving age and maintenance grants, organisation of post-elementary schooling, age of transference, curriculum, leaving examinations, transfer from central to secondary schools and Higher Tops. The evidence was prefaced by a statement pointing out that the TUC had interested itself in the question of education of children for many years, 'in particular the children of the working classes.'[27] It continued, 'No objection would arise from working-class parents about the legal age being raised to 15+ provided maintenance grants as approved in the 1918 Education Act were given... In some areas (it was pointed out) such powers had already been given – but it was believed that only a universal 15+ leaving age would be of real benefit.' It was not suggested that all children were suited to the kind of secondary schooling provided in secondary grammar schools but there were objections to the restructuring of elementary schooling being offered to most children and the accompanying inferior resourcing of this sector. 'Trade unions held the view that at least 75 per cent of the existing Elementary School pupils were fitted to be given some form of post-primary education for at least 4 years from the age of 11. They were anxious however that *all* children should be transferred to some form of secondary or central school administered under Secondary Regulations suitably modified. Reorganisation should make it possible to increase considerably the number of secondary school places... Additional central schools of the existing type were not the provision for post-primary education which (were) envisaged, but rather there should be considerable extension of the secondary school system as it was known... Trade schools should be ruled out. The proposed schools should be free. Parents should be allowed to choose the type of post-primary school their children should attend – the central school if there was one, the secondary school or the technical school.' Given the necessary finance and the time for a considerable building programme to be undertaken, parity of funding and resources could be achieved, although there would always be the issue of the status gained by institutions from past reputations. Yet experience would show that parental choice for different forms of post-primary schooling was destined to be a focus for continual controversy.

Eleven was agreed as the most suitable age for transfer, partly because it 'permitted of a continuous and homogenous four or five years course of secondary or advanced education up to the age of 15 or 16'. As for the curriculum, 'it would be necessary to organise a wide variety of educational courses. About 25 per cent of any age group might be expected to take the existing type of secondary course. The courses for other children should have a bias, e.g. scientific or mining, commercial, technical, agricultural, etc; whilst the possibility of transferring children at all ages from one course to another more suited to their abilities and needs, should be amply secured.' A vital corollary however, was the strongly expressed belief that parity of esteem should be given to all other forms of post-primary schooling. Hence the need for parity of funding. Within guidelines from the BOE, it should be the responsibility of the head teacher in consultation with 'responsible teachers' to design the curriculum. Furthermore, 'Any movement which would raise the status of handwork to that of bookwork, and relate instruction to local environment... would be welcomed,' although witnesses were opposed to any move 'to impose instruction of a narrowly vocational type or to confine the training of young people to preparation for employment in local factories'.

When Hadow published its 38 recommendations in 1926, the TUC gained some satisfaction in seeing that a considerable number of them were in common or closely related to the points they had made. A major agreement was a common division of schooling by age (excluding of course the private sector) – primary and secondary in name if not in curriculum or levels of funding; raising of the school leaving age to 15 by 1932; agreement that practical subjects should be given greater status and that there was need for teachers with an industrial, agricultural or commercial bias. Alongside such observations were statements such as 'courses of instruction, though not merely vocational or utilitarian, would aim at linking school work with interests arising from the social and industrial environment of the pupils'.[28]

NOTES AND REFERENCES

1. Cole, G.D.H. (1948) *A Short History of the British Working Class Movement 1789–1947*, Table 11, p.481 and *TUC Report 1970*, p.845.
2. Marx, K. (1852) 'The Eighteenth Brumaire of Louis Bonaparte' in *Marx and Engels Selected Work in One Volume*, p.18.
3. *TUCGC Mins.* 5.3.1927 and 28.11.1928.
4. Citrine, W. (1964) *Men and Work; An Autobiography*, pp.20–21.
5. Foot, M. (1975) *Aneurin Bevan Vol.1, 1897–1945*, p.180.
6. Citrine Papers 1/8, pp.336–9. Cited in Taylor, R. (2000) *The TUC: From General Strike to New Unionism*, p.36.
7. *Sunday Express*, 13.1.1929, pp.1 and 13.
8. *Daily Herald*, 24 April 1929, p.5.
9. Citrine to Post Office Worker, *TUCEC Mins.* 9.4.1932.

10. BBC to TUCEC, *TUCEC Mins.* 7.8.1929.
11. Report by TUC Visitors, *TUCEC Mins.* 28.10.1938.
12. Ellen Wilkinson to TUCEC, *TUCEC Mins.* Ibid.
13. Coleg Harlech to TUCEC, *TUCEC Mins.* 10.3.1932.
14. *TUC Report 1927*, p.181 and correspondence 21.7.1927; 27.12.1927 and 26.6.1928. *TUCEC Mins. 1927* and *1928*.
15. Principal, People's College, Elsinore to TUC, *TUCEC Mins.* 16.4.1931.
16. W.M. Fletcher to W. Citrine 28.8.1930; W. Citrine to W.M. Fletcher 8.9.1930, *TUCEC. Mins*, 1930.
17. M.L. Jacks to TUCEC 4.5.1925; TUCEC to M.L. Jacks 15.5.1925. *TUCEC Mins.*
18. TUCGC Deputation to President BOE 25.5.1925, *TUC Report 1925*, pp.89–90.
19. Tawney, R.H. (ed.) (1922) *Secondary Education for All: A Policy for Labour*, p.29.
20. For details concerning the origins of the Hadow Committee's terms of reference and the reception of its findings see Doherty, B. (1964) 'The Hadow Report 1926' *Durham Research Review*, No.15 and Simon, B.(1974) *The Politics of Educational Reform 1920–1940*, Ch.3.
21. Banks, O. (1955) *Parity and Prestige in English Secondary Education*, p.125. For a comparison of free-place pupils and fee-paying pupil examination results from 1926–1927 and 1938 see pp.127–128.
22. *Hansard* 8.4.1925, cited in Banks, O., ibid. p.122.
23. *Hansard 1114*, 6.11.1930.
24. Doherty, B. 'The Hadow Report 1926'.
25. *TUC Report 1925*, pp.88–94. The members of the TUCGC Deputation were: A.B. Swales (Chair – TUC), A.A.H. Findlay, A.A. Purcell, R.B. Walker, J. Bottomley MP, J. Beard, J. Turner, M.F. Titterington, H.H. Elvin and E. Hallas.
26. Ibid., p.93.
27. *PRO ED/10/147.*
28. *Report of the Consultative Committee on the Education of the Adolescent* (1926) p.88. Conclusions and recommendations of the Report are contained in Ch. XI.

CHAPTER 2

RESISTANCE TO SECONDARY EDUCATION FOR ALL

Early in April 1928 a joint Labour Party/TUC 90-page document was published covering the whole field of public education with a foreword by Ramsay MacDonald in which he stated:

> Labour approaches the problem from the experience of the elementary school and the workshop, the mine and the field. To it, the school is not a luxury that may be limited in a fit of economy, but a necessity that can be starved only at the national peril. The impetus that the short-lived Labour Government gave to everyone engaged in teaching was but a proof of what value it placed upon education and what enthusiasm it would spend to put it on a satisfactory footing.[1]

The joint document covered 19 points including areas associated with school welfare and challenged the constant question as to how far the government could afford to provide a good education for all young people. Ironically, within three years when Labour was returned to office, if not power, MacDonald was to support Snowden in finding economic reasons to thwart Trevelyan's best intentions to promote education.

The problematic and complex issues surrounding Trevelyan's Education Bills have been well documented:[2] the hostility of Snowden at the Treasury to increased expenditure on welfare; the failure of MacDonald to give Trevelyan support; the resistance to the Bills by the Roman Catholic Labour MPs from Glasgow and Liverpool under guidance from their bishops; and the fear that if means tests were applied to maintenance grants they would then be applied to unemployment benefits, which worried many trade unionists. When the customary antagonism of a Conservative House of Lords to measures which might lead to increased taxation was added this combination of vested interests proved too powerful for Trevelyan to overcome. The TUC carefully watched the passage of events and realised in the autumn of 1930 that there was a danger of their ambitions for raising the school leaving age to 15 with maintenance grants being postponed to an undetermined future date.

Citrine issued a TUC Circular in 1930 bringing to the attention of all affiliated unions the threat before them and urging them to bring pressure to bear upon MPs.[3] It was made clear that the TUCGC regarded the Bill as

> of very great importance both on educational grounds and industrial grounds...[it] would withhold from the Labour market a considerable number of juveniles and this must necessarily have an effect upon the unemployment problem. The TUCGC regret the necessity which has compelled HM Government to postpone the Bill, the date for the raising of the age for leaving school, but the Council feel that it is now all the more necessary in view of the opposition being engendered by Chambers of Trade and other such bodies, that affiliated unions should do everything possible to support the Education (School Attendance) Bill and to defeat the opposition to it being fostered by reactionary bodies who do not desire to see the raising of the school leaving age to 15 in September 1932.

There was also a call to make sure the reorganisation plans which had become associated in many minds with the Hadow Report were carried out so that the extra year at school would not be wasted.[4]

NATIONAL GOVERNMENT 1931

Within months the cause was lost, Trevelyan had resigned and MacDonald was leading a National government of whom four out of five MPs were Tory. The influence of the TUC declined in terms of discussions with government. A.J.P. Taylor has written that they were excluded from Downing Street from 1931 to 1938,[5] but if that is literally true in terms of Number 10 it is not true with regard to access to government ministers.[6] The TUC certainly did not give up the fight to promote their views. They attacked the Board of Education Circular 1421 containing new regulations for secondary schools raising fees and subjecting free places to a means test. They sent a resolution to the President of the Board of Education recording,

> their most emphatic protest against the proposal of the Government [for] if confirmed [they would] seriously increase the financial burden borne by working-class parents sending their children to secondary schools...in many cases [this] will result in the exclusion from these schools of children who, on account of their educational fitness, would otherwise attend them.[7]

SPENS COMMITTEE OF 1938

In the first half of 1934 the TUC were invited to submit evidence to the Spens Committee which had been set up in July 1933. Arthur Pugh, Morgan Jones MP and Wright Robinson gave oral evidence based upon the detailed memo they had submitted. They reminded the Committee of evidence they had provided 11 years earlier to Hadow and that their views 'were closely related to the views expressed in that year'. Referring to the Hadow Report they commented:

> We believe that, if the lines there laid down are to reach their full development and their logical conclusion, it is a corollary of the report that universal secondary education (in the wider sense of the term) should be provided. We think that the most urgent educational reform required to-day is that effect should be given to the report, but that much will be lost unless the far-reaching reorganisation proposed is carried out under the regulations of the Secondary Code. Indeed, in our view, the intended results cannot be achieved except under a single code of regulations applicable to all post-primary education.[8]

Again maintenance grants were suggested, the class distinctions resulting from the separation of public education into elementary and secondary highlighted, a belief in the need for all pupils to have some 'simple instruction in social and political science' to prepare them for citizenship. Much of this was well-established TUC Education Policy which they had been pursuing for many years. In terms of secondary reorganisation there was now carefully argued support for multilateral schooling. It was made clear that there was no wish for any stereotyped system of schooling for all pupils. 'We desire to see the greatest possible variety and elasticity within the system.' They were anxious to see neither narrow practical courses nor similar limitation for those pursuing a more classical curriculum. 'An education which produces a purely "bookish" man, with little understanding of his more practical-minded fellow, is as much at fault as the education which produces the man who knows nothing of "book learning" and despises it.'[9] This sentiment prepared the ground for the questioning of the Hadow Recommendations that there should be 'Grammar Schools and Modern Schools'.

Whilst not wishing for a common secondary course for all children there was a recognition that fundamental change was required to give them a fairer share of resources.

> The present division of education into elementary and secondary grade inevitably leads to class distinctions of a most undesirable kind [that] the great mass of children in the elementary school are condemned to remain there for the whole of their school life ... The elementary and the central schools of today are inferior species and are hampered by conditions of accommodation and equipment inferior to those of secondary schools ... the inferior provision extends to such items as floor-space, play-grounds and lavatories. We think it is vital to a state which wishes to maintain a full and free democracy that these artificial inequalities in the educational system should be abolished. And in effect that means there must be only [one] code for all post-primary schools.[10]

The President at the 1934 Congress devoted part of his introduction to education, repeating their policy aimed at raising the school leaving age, highlighting both the need for a four-year secondary school course and to rescue juveniles from the labour market, for as he pointed out, there were still more than 25,000 boys under 16 years of age in the coal mines alone. Using Tawney's famous quotation about 'the hereditary curse of English Education (being) its organisation on lines of social class' he expressed the strongly felt view of many of the delegates about schooling in the country:

> the demand of employers for cheap juvenile labour, the apparently mistaken conviction of the privileged classes that public education is a kind of charity, and feeling that the mass of the population are lucky to get any education at all, and finally, the belief that it is preposterous they should claim for their children the same educational advantages as are readily accorded to the children of their so called betters.[11]

The division of private preparatory and misnamed 'public' schools for some of the nation's children and the public elementary schools for the majority of working-class children was perceived as part of a plan:

'children who had to be taught a little because if wholly untaught they would be a danger to society, but who must not be taught more than a little since they were equally a danger if they were taught too much'.[12] Ideology concerning class divisions was not dealt with in such a frank manner when TUC Deputations met with the President of the Board of Education. Citrine, for example, in 1935 explained, 'the delegation urged the advisability of maintenance allowances as an economic necessity and not as a Socialist means of re-distributing the national income'.[13]

The National Federation of Employers' Organisations (NFEO) saw public education from a different perspective to the TUC. They argued that proposals for raising the school leaving age without exemptions were made

> ...often with little regard to its reaction on public expenditure, to its effects on industry, or even to the wishes of the parents...there are many classes of work for which juveniles are better adapted than adults... [it is] only by an early entry into industry that juveniles can acquire, by the time they reach adult age, that dexterity and skill which will enable them to develop into skilled workers.[14]

The views expressed by the TUC to the Spens Committee were largely endorsed in the same year by the publication through the Workers' Education Association (WEA) of R.H. Tawney's *The School Leaving Age and Juvenile Unemployment*. He too harked back to the Hadow Report's recommendations:

> The Educational case put forward by the Committee won general acceptance, and is still unanswered...there can be no question either of the desirability of the step on educational grounds or of its administrative practicability...The educational arguments remain what they were, and have been confirmed by experience of the impossibility of reaping the full benefits of Reorganisation as long as the majority of children leave school at the end of the term in which they become 14. It is not expedient to make educational policy dependent upon the state of the labour market at any given moment. Even if all children found work immediately on leaving school...it would still be the case, as the Hadow Committee pointed out, that the proper place for children of 14 is the school, not the factory.[15]

With juvenile unemployment increasing Tawney suggested that, 'The result has been to turn what was formerly a long overdue educational reform into a measure of immediate social urgency.'

RAISING THE SCHOOL LEAVING AGE AND MAINTENANCE GRANTS

Early in 1935 Prime Minister Ramsay MacDonald promised a TUC delegation that the question of the school leaving age would be reviewed and to that end on 14 April Lord Halifax headed a government team which met six representatives from the TUC including Citrine and Wray, the Secretary of the Education Committee. The Government's line that raising the school leaving age was both too complex and expensive to introduce at present and that maintenance grants were out of the question provided no common ground for discussion. The TUC's case was summarised in the last paragraph of the meeting's minutes:

> It seemed to be quite clear that the delegates were unanimously in favour of the flat raising of the school leaving age; that they regarded maintenance allowances as essential; and that they were deeply apprehensive of any attempt to base these maintenance allowances upon any inquisition into the parent's income.[16]

In July it was the turn of the NFEO to put their case to the new president of the BOE, as Oliver Stanley had taken over from Halifax following MacDonald's resignation in June to make way for Stanley Baldwin to become prime minister for the third time. The NFEO's notes for the meeting illustrate their concerns; which centred on the effects of raising the school leaving age upon the costs of employment and increases in taxation:

> It is, we think, generally accepted by its advocates that such a proposal would not be practical politics unless it were accompanied by Maintenance Allowances, and some idea of the cost of the proposals may be obtained from the fact that – even with a Maintenance Allowance of 5/- subject to a Needs Test, as envisaged in the Labour Government's Bills of 1929 and 1930 – the additional expenditure involved would be £8 million per annum, to the equivalent of nearly 2d on the Income Tax. In addition to that, there would also be the heavy wages cost to industry in the substituting of adult for juvenile labour... It is not generally appreciated that in a country dependent like our own upon its ability to compete in the world's markets... and that if the costs of Public Services are higher than those of other countries, they are bound to have some restrictive effect on our production.[17]

The NFEO saw no need for compulsory raising of the school leaving age as there were bye-laws which could be and were used in areas where parents wished their children to continue at school. It did not follow that employers would take on adult workers if juveniles were no longer available. Indeed it was more likely that increased mechanisation would be introduced leading to less employment. The idea of compulsory part-time continuation classes was also ruled out. In fact, a BOE memo prepared in June showed that the overwhelming number of responses to Halifax's consultations favoured the TUC's recommendations; compulsory raising of the school leaving age to 15 with maintenance allowances. Moreover, another memo prepared after the TUC Deputation to Halifax, dated April, specifically stated: 'In view of the TUC Delegation's attitude to the "Means Test" the Government would probably be well advised to accept a declaration by the parents; it is unlikely that this would lead to any serious fraud.'[18]

Throughout the summer, Halifax had also been sounding out the views of various religious groups, the Roman Catholics, Church of England and Nonconformists, in relation to building grants for the necessary expansion which would follow the increase in school population which an extra year would bring, and whilst it was made clear that he had taken no notes, a memo summarising his findings was produced. He expressed the feeling that there would be general sympathy for such a move. Similarly discussions with the LEAs and NUT suggested a favourable response, the latter 'are most unlikely to press any point to an extent which would endanger any raising of the school leaving age'. The general conclusion recorded at the BOE was that, 'there seems substantial ground for hoping that prompt and firm Government action on the lines proposed will generally create a feeling of relief that a tiresome problem has been disposed of'.[19] Tiresome it might have seemed, but the BOE was also aware of significant minority interests which they would have to face, apart from the financial implications involved. They knew that the reorganisation associated with Hadow was still incomplete after some eight years and in a comment deprecative of women teachers wrote: 'It must, however, be remembered that reorganisation will probably never be complete in several county areas and therefore in those districts the extra-age group will mark time in small all-age schools with women Head-Teachers.'[20] They went on to remark that rural areas were seen as a source of potential conflict with, 'probably very strong demand for exemption by farmers and possibly by parents' leading to 'the danger of agitation that the rural child is being fobbed off with inferior education than urban'.

EDUCATION BILL OF 1936

When Oliver Stanley did introduce the long-awaited Education Bill in February 1936 he suggested that to introduce compulsory raising of the school leaving age would create a demand for 2,500 extra teachers, provision of more school buildings and that it would take at least three years for voluntary religious schools to cope with the expansion. 'Therefore although the school leaving age would be raised to 15 this would not take effect until 1st September 1939 and there would be exemptions for children who entered "beneficial employment".'[21] Exemptions concerning raising the school leaving age or minimum age for children working had been a common practice in legislation well back into the nineteenth century and can be seen either as one way of giving in to the vested interests of some employers or a tactical pragmatic method of gradually extending protection for children at work and extending their education in the face of such opposition.[22]

Stanley claimed there would be all kinds of safeguards for children. It was 'not a general exemption for children in general and for employment in general. It is to be given to a particular child for a particular employment... after consultation with the Juvenile Unemployment Committee, and done of course by the education authority which has already in its possession the medical history and report upon the child and its capacity.' He also added 'I do not think that the term "beneficial employment" is difficult to define and understand.'[23] In this he would find himself in a minority of opinion.

Immediately the Bill's content was known the TUC moved into action. On 10 February they sent an eight-man deputation to Stanley, (who had already rejected requests to meet other bodies, including the County Councils Association),[24] which included Citrine, Arthur Pugh and George Hicks MP. They strongly condemned the policy of exemption and failure to provide maintenance allowances.

> It was pointed out to him that in 6 out of 10 areas which had already raised the school leaving age by bye-law, 90 per cent and more of the children were exempted before reaching the age of 15. In only one case was the rate of exemption less than 70 per cent; that was the area of Carnarvonshire, where maintenance allowances were paid and the rate of exemption was 37 per cent.

Perhaps thinking they had nothing to lose now as the government had clearly made up its mind, the TUC Delegation claimed:

The sole object of the exemption system is to save the small cost of maintenance allowances, and because of this meanness the Government forego the excellent opportunity which now presents itself to carry through an urgently needed educational reform, and to clear away some of the grosser inequalities which still exist in our public education system.[25]

The TUC kept up the pressure. Articles were sent to the Press, including one by Citrine to the *Daily Herald* which stated that 'if this Bill goes through as it now stands it will be class legislation'.[26] A few days later the *TUC Industrial News* published an article headed 'The Education Bill is unfair to the Poor' claiming, 'It is a topsy turvy state of affairs in industry which encourages the industrial exploitation of children who ought to be at school, and throws out of work youths and girls 2 or 3 years older.' Speakers' notes were produced for meetings and over 500,000 leaflets distributed putting the case against the Education Bill as constituted. Citrine sent a letter to the general secretaries of all affiliated unions enclosing a copy of their leaflet pointing out that the government proposed to proceed with the Education Bill at once, 'The Matter is therefore urgent'. The leaflet entitled 'School Bill Bungle' claimed, 'The Government's tactics are obvious, Public Opinion compels them to raise the school leaving age. Maintenance Allowances ought to be paid. But the Government sees a way to evade this responsibility. They will give exemption.' They also published TUC Circular 56 setting out the TUC objections to the Bill and again emphasising the need for maximum pressure to be put upon the Government. 'The General Council hope that both you and your executive and as many of your branches as possible will pass resolutions and forward them to the Prime Minister and to local MPs, protesting against the clauses of the Bill providing for exemption and demanding the provision of maintenance allowances.' At Central Hall Westminster on 29 February, one of many public demonstrations organised by the Association of Education Committees, the NUT, School Age Council and the WEA, was chaired by Citrine, and speakers included R.H. Tawney, Lady Simon and H.B. Lees-Smith, MP and former President of the BOE.

It was all to no avail. The Education Bill completed its stages in parliament by July without any major amendments thereby insuring a lengthy debate at Congress in September. J. Fletcher (Typographical Association) put forward a resolution urging the TUC to keep up the pressure arguing that when working-class children were able to follow up an opportunity for further, i.e. secondary, education they have to:

scrape and make sacrifices, not merely of pleasures, but of necessities. We do that in order that our children may have the advantages that other people take as a divine right... We want to get back to the good old principle that what is good enough for one is good enough for another, and we are not disposed to allow one law for the rich and another for the poor... [let us] press for equality of treatment as far as possible for the children of the working classes.[27]

The matter was debated at Congress again in the two following years with fears being expressed that some local authorities might be seeking to postpone the raising of the school leaving age by pleading that their plans were insufficient to deal with the necessary expansion.

EDUCATION AND DEMOCRACY 1937

In February 1937 the TUCEC prepared a draft paper which brought together the policies they had formulated from the evidence given to the BOE Consultative Committee in recent years. It was published a few months later as a 16-page pamphlet entitled *Education and Democracy*. It covered all aspects of TUC education policy, including a section dealing with the 1936 Education Act and a brief historical background going back to 1909, arguing:

> It is essential... to break down the last class barrier which assumes that children of working-class parents do not require the fuller education given as a matter of course, to those fortunate enough to be born in families substantially above the poverty line. Let it be remembered that many of the leading – and most expensively exclusive – educational institutions of today were founded for the benefit of poor scholars. They have wandered from their original aim; they must be brought back.
>
> There can be no relaxation in the struggle to establish the elementary rights outlined, as their establishment will be fought by the forces of privilege and reaction at every step.

Throughout January and February 1938 conferences concerning the Education Act with representatives from trades councils, trade union branches, Labour party groups, the Co-operative Movement, NCLC, NUT and WEA were mounted in Birmingham, Bristol, Cardiff, Leeds, Manchester, Newcastle, Nottingham and Southampton and 17,000 copies of the TUC memorandum on the Act circulated, especially throughout the labour movement.[28]

In June 1938 Kenneth Lindsay informed the House of Commons that the Education Act raising the school leaving age to 15 would come into effect on 1 September 1939. The 1938 TUC duly passed a resolution welcoming this assurance whilst reiterating its view that 'exemption for beneficial employment or for home duties constitute a serious weakness in the Act'. It called for a short amending Bill to remove the exemption clauses 'before the appointed day' and urged affiliated unions and 'all people interested in educational progress' to bring maximum pressure to bear upon the government to this end. This was followed up at the TUCEC by plans to arrange a conference on the administration of exemption clauses and a circular prepared and sent to all affiliated unions and trades councils.[29] The Committee had been receiving support from various organisations opposed to the idea of exemptions for some pupils. For example the Secretary had been invited to discuss the issue with the Chairperson of the London County Council (LCC) Committee[30] and a letter had been received from the London Teachers' Association (LTA) informing him of a resolution they had passed calling for the LCC to 'define its policy with regard to exemption... [and pledging]... itself to co-operate to the full with the LCC in endeavouring to secure the maximum benefit from the Act'.[31]

The TUCEC also considered the BOE plans outlined in Circular 1464 (14 October 1938) to limit expenditure on building secondary schools to compensate for the financial requirements needed in the reorganisation and development of elementary education. A letter of concern was sent to the Parliamentary Secretary to the BOE who met with the Committee the following year and confirmed that 'There is no intention of postponing beyond September next the Appointed Day for bringing into force the provisions of the Education Act 1936 for raising the school leaving age' and explaining that he was 'satisfied that secondary schools offered the least objectionable scope for some temporary easing of the burden on Local Education Authorities'.[32]

NOTES AND REFERENCES

1. Labour Party/TUC (1928) *Nursery Schools to University*.
2. Dean, D. (1969) 'The Difficulties of a Labour Educational Policy: The Failure of the Trevelyan Bill, 1929–1931' *British Journal of Educational Studies*, Vol.XVII, No.3. pp.286–300.
3. TUC Circular 31, 4.12.1930.
4. Ibid.

5. Taylor, A.J.P. (1965) *English History 1914–1945*, pp.412–13.
6. Whilst no TUC Deputations are recorded in 1931, in the following years down to 1938, 41 are listed in the Annual TUC Reports covering these years.
7. *TUC Report 1933*, pp.141–2.
8. TUCGC Evidence to the Board of Education Consultative Committee, 19.7.1934. *PRO ED/10.1151*.
9. Ibid.
10. Ibid.
11. *TUC Report 1934*, p.70.
12. Ibid., p.71.
13. PRO ED/24/1557, 18.4.1935.
14. Ibid., 25.7.1935.
15. Tawney, R.H. (1934) *The School Leaving Age and Juvenile Unemployment*, p.6.
16. PRO ED/24/1557, 16.4.1935.
17. Ibid., 25.7.1935.
18. Ibid., 29.4.1935.
19. Ibid., 21.6.1935.
20. Ibid.
21. *Hansard 1167–1169*, 13.2.1936.
22. See Barber, C. (1989) 'The Exemption System 1833–1944' *Journal of Educational Administration and History*, Vol.XII, pp.10–17.
23. *Hansard 1167–1169*, 13.2.1936.
24. Simon, B.(1974) *The Politics of Educational Reform 1920–1940*, p.219.
25. *TUC Report 1936*, p.158.
26. 'A School Reform Gone Wrong' *Daily Herald*, 7.2.1936.
27. *TUC Report 1936*, p.278.
28. *TUCEC Mins.* 4.3.1938.
29. *TUCEC Mins.* 17.10.1938.
30. *TUCEC Mins.* 7.1.1939.
31. London Teachers' Association to TUC, *TUC Mins.* 24.11.1938.
32. TUCEC Interview with Parliamentary Secretary to BOE, *TUCEC Mins.* 17.3.1939.

CHAPTER 3

MULTILATERAL AND TECHNICAL SCHOOLS

As early as 1925 support could be found for multilateral schools at a conference of the Assistant Masters Association (AMA); a view strongly supported by their journal, under the editorship of S.B. Lucas, a member of the Labour party's education committee.[1] Although the Labour party ignored the idea in its pamphlet *Labour and Education* published in 1933, focussing instead upon raising the school leaving age and the removal of fees in county secondary schools, when the party won control of the London County Council (LCC) for the first time in 1934, Barbara Drake, who alongside R.H. Tawney, was on the education committee of the Council, proposed the introduction of 'non-selective multiple bias' schools for London in the following year.[2] In evidence to the Spens Committee, a number of witnesses, especially those representing teacher organisations, such as AMA, the Association of Assistant Mistresses (AAM) and the Association of Headmistresses (AHM), supported the idea of multilateral schooling.[3]

When the Spens Report was finally published in the last month of 1938,[4] the TUC responded with a paper *Statement on the Spens Report* which came out clearly in favour of multilateral schools.[5] Each aspect of Spens was considered alongside the TUC's recommendations and the final outcome compared: '...there would be a single code, under which there would be established three types of school. In their evidence...the TUC asked that all secondary education should be under one code and under one roof. The first of our proposals has been met; the second rejected.'[6] As for equality between these different schools – or parity as it was termed – being achieved because there would be a single code...the TUC's response was, 'No doubt it should, but we gravely doubt that it will.'[7] Time was to prove their prophecy correct. In fact whilst the Spens Report did emphasise, 'with some reluctance we have come to the conclusion that we could not advocate the adoption of multilateralism as a general policy',[8] this was only after several attractions of multilateralism had been spelt out.

> We recognised the many benefits that would accrue when children of 11 were being educated together in the same set of buildings; how in such a school the transfer of pupils at various ages to courses of teaching most suitable for their abilities and interests would be facilitated, and how greater advantage there might be in the close association of children differing in background and objective.[9]

It is noticeable that these remarks appeared in chapter IX entitled 'Administrative Problems' and although there were arguments earlier in the Report as to the merits of a common school, such as the potential size of a sixth form given the staying on rates at school in the 1930s, the doubts expressed were based upon issues other than those directly related to pedagogy. These included the building in recent years of new secondary grammar and technical schools following upon the traditions of a socially divisive system of schooling so that 'the general adoption of the multilateral idea would be too subversive a change'.[10] Yet for all that the Report then added a sentence both vague and contradictory concerning the choice of separate grammar, technical and modern secondary schools. 'The multilateral idea, though it may not be expressed by means of the multilateral school, should permeate the system of secondary education as we perceive it.' Whether this suggestion was one of naivety, wishful thinking or an attempt to placate the growing multilateral lobby is impossible to know. In reality, the differences in status afforded the three kinds of secondary schooling perceived by the Report would ensure that the statement would be meaningless. Something the TUC had spotted straight away as has been shown above in their *Statement on the Spens Report*.

TECHNICAL AND POST-SCHOOL EDUCATION

There has been a long dispute on the relationship between education and industry in Britain, including suggestions that within prominent sections of society, including high-status areas of education, there was an anti-industry attitude.[11] Watson suggests the BOE was not really anti-industry but that there was confusion at times as a result of the Labour Exchanges Act of 1909 and the Education (Choice of Employment) Act of 1910 which gave the Board of Trade and the BOE similar powers to deal with juvenile employment.[12] One outcome of this, according to Chelmsford who headed a Cabinet Committee in 1921 to consider the disputes which had arisen from this process, was that 'the exchanges' juvenile advisory committees and the LEA's juvenile employment committees approached the matter from an exclusively industrial or an exclusively educational point of view when, in his opinion, neither interest was paramount, Watson suggests that the BOE was not anti-industry in 'any simple sense . . . in counter-opposing a liberal view of education to the needs of industry'. It was more the LEAs and the teaching profession who took this stance.

The area of contention between government departments dealing with juvenile employment on the one hand and LEAs, teachers and sections of the labour movement on the other, can be explained by their different approaches. The former were willing to support children entering industry and receiving the discipline in training required for much factory work in the form of punctuality, obedience and industriousness; characteristics emphasised in the elementary schools attended by the majority of children from working-class backgounds; practices which had been at their most mechanistic in the nineteenth century when pupils sat, picked up slates, commenced writing all to numbered commands called out by monitors in clear preparation for the discipline of factory life.[13] Many of those directly involved with children as teachers or parents, especially among those of the latter who had experienced harsh conditions in mines and factories hoped that success in formal schooling might enable their children to enter secondary school and thereby escape the destiny of most working-class children. Those with well above average incomes and wealth did not usually advocate a career in industry, at least not one needing direct participation in the manufacturing process, for their own children. In general they expected their offspring to attend fee-paying schools followed by entry into the armed forces, legal and financial services or for further study at a university. To that extent the message which came down from those with high status in society was that, with certain exceptions, such as those studying science or engineering at colleges and universities, industry was not regarded favourably as a career.

The TUC had always been concerned with technical education; indeed it was the sixth item of their first Congress in 1868.[14] By the inter-war years their policy was support for technical education on two conditions.

The first was that such teaching should only follow after a general basic education; the second that the curriculum would be based on general principles of a craft and not upon the specifics of a local industry. These views reflected those of Tawney in his definition of secondary education in the 1922 pamphlet *Secondary Education for All* and had been put before the Hadow Committee of 1926 and were part of their submission to the Spens Committee:

> We think it due to every child that he should receive a general education up to the age of 15+. Technical education may then follow, but it should not be given any place in the curriculum before that age. Technical education given before the school-leaving age necessarily involves some sacrifice of more general education, and whatever occupation may be in prospect, we do not think the child should be robbed of the wide cultural basis provided by a sound secondary education up to at least the age of 15+... We would emphasise that his need for it, both as a human being and as a citizen, is the same whether he undergoes technical instruction or not.[15]

Once pupils had passed the school leaving-age the TUC believed 'there is scarcely any job in which the worker, both from his own point of view and from that of industry, would not be better for suitable technical instruction'.[16] At the same time they were only too aware that some youngsters who had undergone further instruction, and who sought a job in a relevant industry, were disappointed by the lack of a suitable vacancy and forced to take a job which offered neither good prospects nor reasonable security; a view confirmed by some technical colleges which did not always find it possible to place their pupils in relevant jobs. This was partly the inevitable result of an unplanned economy, in spite of attempts at times to match up training programmes for youth with the requirements of industry and commerce as the Malcolm Committee tried to do.

On 5 December 1925 the TUCGC received a request from the joint secretaries to give evidence to the Government Committee on Education and Industry.[17] Mr A.S. Firth, Acting Secretary of the TUCEC, was the principal witness on 26 April 1926, accompanied by Ivor Gwynne, of the Iron and Steel Trades Confederation, and Alderman Hardaker. As might be expected many of the points made were a repetition of those given to the Hadow Committee only ten months earlier, especially the desire for the 'extension of the school leaving age to sixteen plus, with maintenance allowances where necessary'. Other areas dealt specifically with the training of juvenile workers, an area in which the TUC believed they had a key role to play not only in ensuring the provision of appropriate technical information but also, just as importantly, in the teaching of safety methods at work. To overcome the limited career patterns of many skilled workers the TUC suggested that technical institutions should be established of an intermediate grade to form a link between secondary technical schools and universities to which the best students would proceed. There was also emphasis on the need to regulate the juvenile labour market, provide modern equipment in technical schools and opposition 'to any attempt to impose instruction of a vocational type, or confine training of young people to preparation for employment in local factories'.[18]

When the First Report of the Education and Industry Committee was published in December 1926 it responded to TUC demands for raising the school leaving age to fifteen and later sixteen by agreeing: '[this] would remove the existing difficulties as regards unemployed juveniles of 14 and 15, [but] the change, if made, should be for educational and social rather than industrial reasons. The same applies to the establishment of compulsory continuation schools.'[19] However, money to make part-time education beyond the statutory schooling age compulsory was rejected. 'There could be a requirement for juveniles to attend unemployment centres or courses of instruction but whether agricultural workers or domestic servants should be included needed further consideration.'[20] Two years on the Second Report was to conclude 'that for boys and girls already in employment attendance at evening classes involves too great a strain...the only satisfactory method of arranging technical education is for employers to allow time off during working hours to attend day classes at the Technical School or College of Art'.[21] No serious criticism was found with public elementary schools but a recommendation was made for 'increased provision of handicraft and domestic subjects...[and] that Education authorities and Employers should consider the possibility of providing some form of initiation into employment for school leavers'. It was thought that secondary schools had 'little contact with industry, and probably the latter would benefit by a larger intake of secondary school pupils'.[22]

Many labour intensive industries such as mining, textiles and large areas of shipbuilding had traditions of workplace training which were still dominant during the 1930s.[23] Moreover the apprenticeship system, seen as the major source of skilled workers had serious weaknesses. As this was an area of juvenile employment it naturally came under the Ministry of Labour. An enquiry by this Ministry found a wide variation in quality between systems with a move towards company schemes which were opposed by trade unions. These views were reinforced by a series of reports from the International Labour Office which 'discovered that

Britain was unique among developed countries in its lack of restriction on the rights of employers to take on apprentices, regardless of the quality of the training provided, and the absence of generally agreed standards of curricula and examinations.'[24] This lack of standardised training and some form of control was a product of the *laissez-faire* attitude of many employers who were quick to argue that such matters came within the prerogative of management to manage all aspects of the work within their company. This meant that there were times when the apprenticeship system was used merely as a form of cheap labour.[25]

An alternative form of training including at least some of a junior's time spent at college whether on day release or evening classes was also bedevilled in some respects by similar problems in that there was no system of nationally recognised certificates related to technical education so that employers were sometimes uncertain as to the level of competence reached by those studying at a local college. In addition LEAs were never going to be able to provide the modern equipment found within leading companies and there were sometimes disputes as to who should pay for a course delivered by one LEA when some of the candidates might come from outside their area.

Parity of esteem between different forms of secondary schooling which was to become an area of contention in the years ahead was already apparent at this time. Trade unionists had in fact become only too conscious of the high status afforded to matriculation and the general school certificates awarded to successful candidates from secondary schools. Such qualifications were demanded by both employers and parents so that there was less demand for vocational qualifications.

> The West Riding Education Committee, in 1928, even went so far as to allege that pupils who, because they were following an alternative type of course had not obtained a matriculation certificate might be handicapped in obtaining a job even though the course they were following was in fact more suitable for the occupation they were hoping to enter.[26]

This general view expressed locally was sometimes echoed within the BOE. To take just one example from the Hadow file at the Public Record Office; a note from the Principal Assistant Secretary of the Technical Education Branch suggested,

> A Junior Technical School must be planned as a preparation for employment on completion of the course and not as a preparation for further full-time instruction end on to the Junior Technical School.

Previous attendance at a Secondary School is regarded as the normal desirable preparation for full-time attendance at a Senior Technical School.[27]

One qualification to this view about the lack of demand from employers for vocational education was that it would be more correct to say they wished for a traditional secondary education for the more secure and better-paid black-coated professions but when it came to work considered to be of lower status, such as technicians and supervisors, they were pleased to recruit the products of junior technical schools. Moreover, many parents with children showing an aptitude for technical work knew that the employment prospects from such schooling might not be so good as for those attending a secondary school but they were still superior to those of the majority who ended up in elementary schools.

Apart from the example given earlier in relation to the West Riding in 1928, another one arose at Exeter Junior College in 1935 where the principal complained that whilst the 'Post Office Engineering Department was impressed with the technical qualifications of his graduates, it was unwilling to employ them because they lacked the secondary school leaving certificate having a foreign language included in the curriculum'.[28] The inter-war period as far as technical education was concerned lacked any standardised system of apprenticeship or technical school certification.

It can be seen that the TUC's suggestions were closely linked to the society in which most of their members functioned. A rejection of training for specific local factory work which might limit the future prospects of young people but otherwise a belief in a much broader range of educational opportunities to meet the diverse aptitudes and interests of pupils, and an acceptance that the traditional secondary grammar school curriculum was unsuited to all children. Most trade unionists who had served a craft apprenticeship were proud of their skills and frustrated to find these were not given the status in society which they believed they deserved. To find later in their careers that those in managerial positions had often received a secondary school education, whether in fee-paying or local authority schools, in spite of having no practical experience or sound knowledge of the manufacturing processes for which they were responsible as managers could cause resentment and lack of respect on the factory floor. It also gave a message to some that they should encourage their own children to gain a traditional secondary school education rather than pursue technical education.

NOTES AND REFERENCES.

1. Simon, B. (1974) *The Politics of Educational Reform 1920–1940*, pp.141–2.
2. Barker, R. (1972) *Education and Politics 1900–1951: A Study of the Labour Party*, pp.70–1.
3. *PRO ED/101151.*
4. *Report of the Consultative Committee of the Board of Education on Secondary Education with Special Reference to Grammar Schools and Technical High Schools (The Spens Report)* (1938).
5. *PRO ED/12/479* and *TUC/HD6661/1939.*
6. There was considerable support for some form of multilateral schooling from a number of witnesses to the Spens Committee, especially from those representing teacher organisations, e.g. AMA, AAM and AHM. *PRO ED/10 1151.* See also Hyndman, M. (1976) 'Multilateralism and the Spens Report; Evidence from the Archives' *British Journal of Educational Studies*, Vol.XXIV, No.3.
7. Only a few years later the Norwood Committee was casting doubts upon the validity of the expression 'Parity of Esteem'. McCulloch, G. (1993) '"Spens *v.* Norwood"; contesting the educational state.' *History of Education*, Vol. 22, No.2.
8. *The Spens Report*, p.291 (Original statement in the Report in italics).
9. Ibid., p.291.
10. Ibid., p.292.
11. See Roderick, G. and Stephens, M. (eds) (1981) *Where Did We Go Wrong? Industry, Education and Economy of Victorian Britain.*
12. Watson, D. (1998) 'Relations between education and employment departments 1921–1945; an anti-industry culture versus industrial efficiency?' *History of Education*, Vol. 27, No. 3.
13. Lawson, J. and Silver, H. (1973) *A Social History of Education in England*, p.244.
14. Musson, A.E. (1968) *The Congress of 1868*, p.32.
15. *PRO ED/10.1151.*
16. Ibid.
17. The Committee on Education and Industry (England) was appointed in 1925 'To inquire into and advise upon the public system of education in England and Wales in relation to the requirements of trade and industry, with particular reference to adequacy of the arrangements for enabling young persons to enter into and retain suitable employment.' At the request of the President of the BOE and Minister of Labour, the second part of the terms of reference were

dealt with in the First Report published in 1926; the first part in the Second Report published in 1928.

18. *TUC Report 1927*, p.180.
19. *Ministry of Labour Gazette, (MLG)* December 1926, p.436.
20. Ibid.
21. *MLG*. July 1928, p.242.
22. Ibid.
23. Burgess, K. (1993) 'Education Policy in Relation to Employment in Britain 1935–1945; a Decade of "Missed Opportunities"?' *History of Education*, Vol. 22, No. 4.
24. Ibid., p.368.
25. Ibid., p.372.
26. Banks, O. (1955) *Parity and Prestige in English Secondary Education*, p.96.
27. *PRO ED/24/1557*, 18.4.1935.
28. Burgess, K. 'Education Policy in relation to employment in Britain 1935–1945', p.374.

CHAPTER 4

SCHOOL WELFARE AND NURSERY SCHOOL PROVISION

CHILD POVERTY

Numerous surveys during the inter-war period demonstrated that significant poverty remained although the situation had improved in the late 1930s compared with the early years after the First World War. There were also significant improvements between the inter-war years and those of the late Victorian and Edwardian periods as demonstrated by Seebohm Rowntree's detailed follow up at York in the late 1930s when compared to his earlier study in 1899. His first study had shown that poverty among the working class in that city was 43 per cent; it had fallen to 31 per cent in his second study. The causes however had hardly changed; low wages, illness, old age and unemployment. There was little change in the areas affected either; they tended to be found within the inner zones of the large cities such as London, Glasgow, Manchester and Liverpool, or else in areas of heavy industry, especially the coal-mining areas of South Wales and the North East. It was precisely because much of the poverty was confined to particular social groups, areas and industries that it was possible for many to believe that it no longer existed to any significant extent by the 1930s. The new light industries of the Midlands and South East tended to mask the situation of those not sharing in the new found prosperity of the late 1930s.

One of the most significant facts as far as schooling was concerned was that 'the proportion of children in poverty was much greater than the proportion of families in poverty'.[1] Tout's study of Bristol in the late 1930s and that of Rowntree in York demonstrated it to be the case that whereas about one third of working-class families were in poverty this included 50 per cent of working-class children.[2] Schools were therefore a good agent through which to work in terms of health and nutrition.

SCHOOL MEDICAL INSPECTION AND TREATMENT

The medical branch of the BOE, like the provision of meals and milk, was established by pressure from organisations with different motives. The perceived need by government was to improve the health in particular of young males following the exposure of the poor physique and health of so many when between 40 per cent and 65 per cent of potential recruits for the Boer War (1899–1902) had failed the medical test. (A generation later 35 per cent of recruits were still being rejected as physically unfit for military service in 1935.)[3] The 1904 Committee on Physical Deterioration had confirmed the unfitness of so many children of the poor largely as a result of insufficient diet and inadequate housing.[4] The labour movement were more concerned with the welfare of working-class children if only because these were their own children and in the past many trade unionists had suffered from poverty in their own childhood. The result of the findings concerning the physical condition of so many among the young was the framing of the Education (Administrative Provisions) Act of 1907 and the Local Education Authorities (Medical Treatment) Act of 1909 which led to the establishment of the School Medical Service.[5]

There were of course others in the community and within parliament who shared such concerns but there were always vested interests at work which influenced any plans to alleviate the suffering of the poorest members of the community. Hence medical inspection of children in elementary schools was first introduced with the suggestion that parents should take up any problems of ill health with their general practitioner and only later was treatment made available through school on an optional basis from 1918 onwards. This was because some doctors were reluctant to support these developments because they were concerned how far the offer of inspection or treatment might affect their livelihoods in the fee-paying system of medicine in which they worked. The London School Board had appointed a school medical officer as early as 1890; by 1905 85 LEAs had made such an appointment.[6] There is no need to trace these early beginnings in detail as they have been described fully elsewhere.[7] One theme worth mentioning because it recurs again and again, with reference to various aspects of welfare, including education, is the suggestion that if the State provided a service to parents for their children it would undermine the responsibility of parents. For some reason this view was never taken of wealthy parents who sent their children to boarding schools and thereby handed over the responsibility for much of their upbringing to school teachers and older boys in the school acting as prefects. The results in terms of harsh physical treatment for some of the boys in boarding schools have been well documented.[8] It is possible that expressed worries of some for the loss of parental responsibility were really just an argument to disguise the resentment of having to pay taxes to fund welfare programmes for those in the poorest circumstances.

By the mid 1920s, with the optional treatment of children now in place, progress was being made in the improved health of school children and a glance back to the statistics available for the Edwardian period confirmed this development. Gradually the resistance of general practitioners to the creation of school clinics declined and

> by 1928 there was rather a grudging acceptance that the clinics were usefully treating very minor ailments and doing preventive work not usually undertaken by the private doctors. The Annual Report of the Chief Medical Officer of the Board for that year suggested verminous heads, eyesight tests, and the removal of tonsils and adenoids, could be better dealt with collectively at a centre where there was always a nurse available, unlike the doctor's surgery. It would also help parents who could not afford the fees of a private doctor.[9]

In that same year the joint Labour party/TUC publication, *Nursery School to University*, called for an expansion in the service and for treatment to be made free: 'Authorities should be required to organise an efficient system of school clinics in their area. More especially there should be a large expansion of dental work. Parents' fees in respect of medical treatment should be abolished.'[10] The recognition that improvement in dental hygiene was crucial became highlighted by an examination in 1933 of elementary school children within the LCC. Among the 3,303,983 inspected, 2,263,135 required dental treatment; some 68.5 per cent of the children inspected.[11]

The great advantage of the School Medical Service was that for the nation it was comparatively cheap in obtaining results. Clinics examining large numbers of children were more cost effective than individual visits to private doctors; for the parents a real advantage was that the service was free. There is little doubt that without the clinics many parents would not have had their children examined. A good number lacked the money, some were apathetic and some did not recognise the symptoms which would have made a visit necessary. At the same time the School Medical Service provided detailed information on child health unavailable through any other system because medical inspection was compulsory, unlike the Child Welfare Service available to the under-fives.[12]

After initial improvements the expansion of the School Medical Service was hampered by the financial economies suffered by all the other social services forced upon them by government responses to the industrial depression of the early 1930s. Nevertheless, there were by now three times during a child's stay at school when they were medically inspected; 5 years as entrants, 8 years as intermediates and at 12 years as a leaver.[13] Yet illness remained the major reason for absence from school. It could be due to the illness of the school child or the requirement for a child, especially an older girl, to stay at home and look after a sick mother or sibling. Needless to say, frequent spells of absence were detrimental to the progress of a child, whether they were due to an illness contracted by the absent child or that of another member of the family.

SCHOOL MEALS AND MILK

The School Meals Service also owed its introduction to legislation introduced by the Liberal government, the Education (Provisions of Meals) Act of 1906; an Act which began its life as a Private Member's Bill introduced by the Labour MP for Lancashire South East, W.T. Wilson, and given support by Campbell-Bannerman's government as it progressed through Parliament.[14] Schemes run by voluntary bodies to feed necessitous children went back to at least the 1880s, including efforts by the Independent Labour party in Bradford which was the first local authority to provide school meals.[15] Bradford also went on to provide breakfasts with the result that their expenditure exceeded the halfpenny rate allowed so that the authority was surcharged by the auditor. Undeterred they continued to provide meals, financing the additional sums needed from the profits of the corporation gas company, an example of municipal socialism in action. By 1905 the LCC was providing food for their elementary school population.[16]

The 1906 Act led to the development of the School Meals Service and after the First World War 'the 1921 Education Act empowered LEAs to provide meals for children who "were unable by reason of lack of food to take full advantage of education provided for them"'.[17] It was this restriction on provision which was to lead to numerous disputes. This was especially the case during the nine days of the General Strike, 3–12 May 1926. The related lock-out of miners continued until the end of November.

> The day the strike began, the Ministry of Health issued a circular to the Poor Law Authorities, reminding them that although they had powers under the 1921 Education Act to provide meals, they were not meant to throw the burden of destitution upon the education rate. The Poor Law Authorities could use the school meal service but applicants would have to apply for relief the harder way through the Board of Guardians.[18]

Whilst both Boards of Guardians and Councils were generally Labour-controlled, the strict Ministry instructions made it difficult to provide meals as generously as they would have wished. In fact the communal kitchens established by the miners themselves were to reinforce the solidarity of a community under seige and some districts, such as the Rhondda, managed to provide meals for children in spite of Government restrictions:

> Rhondda's programme for the whole lock-out cost £57,708 with as many as 18,050 children being fed during the week ending 26 June. The Rhondda Schools' Medical Officer could boast with pride that 5,986,257 meals were provided from public funds from the beginning to the end of the lock-out. But Rhondda was not typical of the coalfield.[19]

Generally children qualified for meals according to the financial circumstances of their parents. In mining areas large numbers of families during the coal dispute had no income except through public relief. Destitute parents had to make applications for their children to receive free meals and they were examined by school teachers, school attendance officers and other local education officials; an invidious task for teachers living and working in the community. Initially they were generous in their support for the families who they knew from personal experience were suffering from the bitter industrial conflict. Inevitably there was an increase in the number of meals being served, fourfold of what it had been, reaching to about 400,000 in the academic year 1926/27 and stricter regulations were brought in to reduce the numbers qualifying. Most authorities provided a midday meal but some provided tea as well and a few who were particularly sympathetic to the miners included breakfast.[20] There can be little doubt that in some areas children suffered from the lack of nourishment in the mining communities and their parents' financial plight meant that many were poorly clothed as well. Restricting relief as far as possible to the mining communities was part of the pressure applied by Baldwin's Conservative government to end the dispute. It was one thing for miners to stand up against colliery owners determined to reduce their wages, and suffer the consequencies personally, but much harder to cope with the suffering inflicted upon their families.

In the Labour party's pamphlet 'Children First' it was accepted that local authorities had the power to supply meals but pointed out that they usually only did so in cases of acute distress. Where the family is in receipt of poor law relief, school dinners as a rule are refused. It was claimed that Labour 'would secure that every child should be properly fed and shod ... and organize a system of school dinners'. The reference to the need for footwear harked back to the clubs of the Victorian times which raised money for clothing and footwear to enable children to attend school. Whilst barefooted children could still be seen in photographs of the Edwardian period they were likely to be a rarity after the First World War, although there were still plenty of children whose footwear was inadequate, especially in inclement weather. Cardboard stuffed into shoes to cover a hole in the sole made a cheap makeshift repair in dry weather but was of little use if it rained or snowed. This practice declined but was still in evidence long after the Second World War.

By the late 1920s the value of milk for children lacking a balanced diet was recognised and the Milk in Schools Act of 1934 introduced subsidised milk. The studies of an earlier age showing disparities in height and weight between children of different social classes were repeated with similar results.[21] For example in Newcastle which had been severely hit by the industrial depression of 1931, a medical charity, The Newcastle-upon-Tyne Dispensary, published a report showing grave concern over the increase in poverty, sickness and malnutrition amongst the poorest classes in the city. The corporation instructed Dr J. Spence to undertake an independent inquiry into the health and nutrition of a selection of children in the city. It was published in 1933 and showed that 'at least 36 per cent of the children from the poor districts of the city which (sic) I have examined were unhealthy or physically unfit, and as a result of this appeared mall-nourished'.[22] Contrasting children from 'Professional Families Class' with those from poor families – 'City Children', he found that 'it appears that the children of the Professional classes have a decided advantage in height, as in weight, over the City children'.[23] They were also less likely to suffer from rickets, pneumonia, chronic or recurrent bronchitis. Moreover, it was demonstrated that there was 'a direct relationship between overcrowding and ill-health or nutrition'.[24]

In 1936 Chuter Ede echoed these findings during a debate on the BOE's Supplementary Estimates in which he drew attention to the comparison between children living in different areas. The examples he mentioned were from Spennymoor, Durham and Surrey where he lived. 'A Doctor was sent on behalf of the Board to investigate and he concluded that Spennymoor pupils were about one year behind Surrey pupils in physique and there was considerable difference in the nutritional state of the pupils.'[25] Attempts to define necessity were bound to create anomalies and seemed to reflect the fear that governments might possibly provide a nutritious meal to a child who was not actually hungry on the day. The TUC did not accept that necessity, let alone malnutrition, was the only need to feed children. They believed the activity of communal eating was a positive one in itself and in their pamphlet of 1937 claimed, 'The social advantage of common feeding, as of playing and learning, is equally as great as that of well-nourished bodies.'[26]

Although government officials tended to underplay the extent of poverty and hunger among some of the poorest children from working-class families the provision of subsidised milk was in itself an admission that there was a problem. Yet even then there was a reluctance to understand that families with insufficient income to provide a nutritious diet during term-time were unlikely to find the money somehow during the school holidays. This problem had long been recognised by those recording the weight of children and observing that some children recorded a loss in weight when they returned to school for the autumn term, which seemed to be related to the loss of school dinners during the summer holidays. As late as 1938 the Yorkshire Federation of Trades Councils wrote to the TUCEC informing them that a resolution had been referred to them by the Unemployed Association December Conference suggesting 'the time is overdue when all school children dependent upon unemployed persons should have a free and regular supply of milk – including holiday periods... irrespective of whether the School Medical Inspector prescribes it or not'.[27]

There were improvements during the inter-war period but it had to be pressed upon governments that a good standard of health for all children was in the long-term interests of the nation. In the end it was the higher incomes during the late 1930s which tended to bring better conditions for families rather than high-level government subsidies. These would become available only when there was a military threat to the country. Then once more the benefit of good welfare programmes for the young were readily accepted and financed. Not for the first time, war brought the substantial welfare changes to the nation's children which had been stubbornly resisted for so long in the previous 20 years.[28]

NURSERY EDUCATION

During the first quarter of the twentieth century progress in providing nursery schools had made little headway. This was partly a result of a report published in 1905 by five women inspectors who cast doubts on the quality and value of the education being offered to the very young attending public elementary schools.[29] By the 1930s a Report by the BOE showed there had been little increase in numbers since that time. There were only 55 nursery schools recognised by the Board in 1932, of which 25 were provided by voluntary bodies.[30] Those promoting nursery education might well have agreed with the assessment made by the women inspectors earlier, for they had in mind a completely different approach to schooling for the under fives. It was in effect more like an all round welfare programme for child development than the formal schooling offered to this age group in most elementary schools. Supporters of nursery education believed it to be of value both to the children concerned and for the country in the long run.

Government response took a predictable line; some support for the provision of improved conditions for young children, doubtless influenced by the results of medical inspection in 1908 of 5-year olds which found that 40 per cent of them needed medical attention.[31] Concern at the poor physique and health of so many male army recruits from the 1890s onwards had resulted in the introduction of school medical inspections in 1907 followed by duties for LEAs 'to offer treatment for defective vision, dental disease, enlarged tonsils and certain other ailments'.[32] In terms of potential army recruits, nursery provision was seen as a health issue rather than an educational one; a need to provide good physical conditions for young children, especially those living in the squalor experienced by so many families whose homes were located in some of the industrial and urban areas of the country. There was also a need during the 1914–18 War to provide child-care for the children of young mothers who were encouraged to work in munitions factories.[33]

With the war over, the military and economic reasoning for providing nursery schools faded and the 1918 Education Act failed to make statutory provision, merely providing 'local authorities with discretionary permission to provide or aid nursery schools for which grants might be available by the Board of Education...The circulars in 1921 and 1922 severely restricted expenditure and effectively prevented further action until they were withdrawn by the first (minority) Labour Government of 1924'.[34] The labour movement believed nursery education to be important. After all, Rachel and Margaret McMillan of the ILP were pioneer practitioners in this field, the latter being made President of the Nursery Schools Association when it was established in 1923. A joint policy statement by the Labour party and TUC three years later declared:

> Children under 7 may best be taught in open-air nursery schools, staffed by fully qualified nursery school teachers or in infant departments run on similar lines...It should be the duty of the authority to provide nursery schools over 2 and under 5 years where formal notice had been given that a certain number of children (say 30) were prepared to attend.[35]

Within a couple of years a pamphlet published by the Labour party, 'Children First', was setting out the party's educational policy including that for nursery schools. It pointed to the provisions of the 1918 Education Act enabling local authorities to establish such schools and classes but claimed that

> one Tory Government after another has deliberately discouraged them from doing so. There are today 2,000,000 little children between 2 and 5 years of age but in England and Wales only 27 nursery schools. Labour would compel authorities to provide open-air nursery schools for children over 2 – for at least one school to be available in every poor and crowded district.

There was not the same measure of support given to the idea of state provision of nursery education by the Conservative party during the inter-war period. To a much greater extent than in later years their views were still dominated by the wealthy and a diminished landed aristocracy, many of whom believed they were impoverished, although a significant proportion of them paid fees to send their children to private nursery schools or employed a nanny to look after them. A strong element within the party ranks argued that parents should be responsible for raising their own children and paying for services needed. Small wonder that Lord Eustace Percy, when at the BOE in Baldwin's Administration in 1926, reduced the grant for the under-fives in infant schools.

Nursery school provision could always be ignored when it was considered an inconvenient expense for governments constantly seeking cutbacks in public expenditure to keep taxation low. Moreover because schooling for the under-fives was outside the compulsory years of attendance it was regarded by many as of little importance. There was also a widespread view among the public, by no means confined to England and Wales, that the older the pupils the more important was their education and this was reflected in the salary scales of teachers from elementary schools through to universities. This in spite of the evidence that the earliest years were the most important of all in terms of physical and mental development as educational psychologists made clear to teachers in training. For example, by 5 years of age the brain of the average child reached 80 per cent of its maximum weight. Such evidence should have focused on the capacity for learning in the early years of childhood and the long-term benefits to both child and nation of a well-balanced programme of nursery education for all children.

In 1932 the TUCGC received an invitation from the Consultative Committee of the BOE to submit a memorandum and give oral evidence on ways in which existing infant schools and departments for children aged between 5 and 7 could be improved as well as for arrangements which might be made for appropriate training and education for young children below 5 years in nursery classes attached to existing infant schools, or in distinct nursery schools. Like so many of these major inter-war enquiries, evidence was taken from large numbers of organisations and individuals. In this case 19 representing LEAs, teachers' organisations and others with a direct interest in education, 15 individual witnesses including Cyril Burt and Susan Isaacs and a further 464 representing organisations and persons associated with education; schools, HMIs, academics both from Britain and overseas. At times those with similar interests contacted each other and obviously some liaison took place before views were presented. For example Citrine wrote to G.S.M. Ellis, Secretary of the Education Committee of the NUT informing him of their agreement to submit evidence and how they intended to protest against the false economy of inadequate educational funding.[36] The NUT had also been invited to submit a memo. Doubtless other organisations made similar contacts with like-minded groups.

On 2 November, Arthur Pugh as chairman of the TUCEC, together with Mrs Emmeline Lowe, leader of the Labour Group on the Education Committee of the LCC gave oral evidence on the basis of the memo submitted earlier:

> education below the age of 5 should be voluntary; modern opinion is inclined to the view that it is the third year of a child's life that certain developments take place, account of which should be taken by the education system of the country. Nurture and education must take equal place for youngest children. [At present] there was practically no provision ... made for under fives.[37]

They suggested that their concern for the lack of provision for the under-fives was supported by evidence from the annual reports on the Health of the School Child, but knowing that the Consultative Committee would be familiar with them, provided only one example given by Sir George Newman from the latest report available, that for 1930, in which he stated:

> The defects which commonly develop during the first five years of life are almost entirely preventable, and in theory there is no reason why the entrants to school should not consist, with few exceptions, of normal healthy children. The fact remains, however, that some 20 per cent of these entrants require treatment of some sort...a very considerable portion in addition...show some undesirable deviation from the norm.[38]

The TUC thought the humanitarian argument hardly needed stating, although they were perhaps being rather generous to sections of the population who were either ignorant of the living conditions experienced by so many people or thought that these were just an inevitable part of life in any society. Hence the accompanying reason given for improving the social conditions experienced by thousands of young children – that 'from a purely economic point of view it is vital and urgent that this wastage which occurs before the age of 5 years, and which brings with it costly consequences in later life should be stopped.'[39] The memo contained 20 detailed points, emphasising 'the need for nursery schools...in the most crowded areas...[in which the classes] should be equipped...with sleeping apparatus, small chairs and tables, hot water supply, indoor lavatory accommodation...and there should be easy access to the open air'. These provisions might be seen as the necessary social conditions to provide the environment for healthy development denied to children living in the crowded slums.

The second strand for nursery education was 'educational' in a different sense and here there was a call for 'a recognised type of curriculum...the aim of the nursery school should be to assist the child to grow physically and mentally, and to develop all its faculties harmoniously. Formal instruction should have no place, but by daily use and example the child should acquire good habits, powers of observation and of natural expression, and the art of living as a community.' In short – education for future citizenship.

It was recognised that there would be costs incurred in the establishment of nursery school provision on a national scale but there would be long-term economies on expenditure in later years on health services for those denied the healthier start in life which nursery schools could provide.

In the Report of the Board of Education for 1931 (p.58), we note with profound regret the statement in reference to nursery schools that: 'Prelimary proposals for several new schools have been submitted, but the need for economy may make it impracticable to proceed with these proposals in the immediate future.' We cannot imagine any 'economy' more false or more tragic than that of denying to those on whom the nation will depend 20, 30 and 40 years hence, the means they must have today if they are to be fitted to their task.[40]

In the event, the Report on Infant and Nursery Schools published in 1933 contained over 100 conclusions and recommendations concerning almost every conceivable aspect of schooling for the very young, including the curriculum, internal decoration of buildings (over which teachers' views would be sought!), the need to encourage nursery school superintendents to have three years college training and the practical need for adequate storage space for 'the amount of educational apparatus now required for training young children'.

According to the report, nursery and infant schooling, 'should reproduce the healthy conditions of a good nursery in a well-managed home', conditions which were probably far outside the experience of the majority of the population during the 1930s. The concern was to provide the best possible conditions for child development and this meant attention should be given to diet, the provision of welfare clinics, premises with emphasis on open-air buildings, playgrounds, gardens, indoor lavatories, arrangements for drying clothes and footwear, and an emphasis on hygiene – 'the thorough and frequent cleansing of the cloak-room and offices, and the floors, walls and furniture in the classroom is of particular importance'.[41] At times specific detailed recommendations are given, such as 'storage of overalls, brushes and other personal belongings may be provided in the cloakroom, the slippers being kept in racks below the coat rails. A space of 18 inches between each coat hook should be insisted upon, at least in new buildings.'[42] As well as buildings and equipment tailored to the needs of young children the approach to their learning needed to be different to the more formal methods experienced by older children. 'Training of nursery stage must be natural training, not an artificial one. Its aim is not so much to implant knowledge and the habits which civilised adults consider useful, as to aid and supplement the natural growth of the normal child.'[43] Social convention of the 1930s led to the assumption that nursery and infant teachers would be women.

The possession of a pleasant speaking voice is of the first importance. Child study should form the basis of her training and her studies in psychology should be directed with descriptions and observations of the actual behaviour of children. She should study the stages of development in children up to the age of 7 with due regard to every aspect of growth.[44]

The report came out against streaming children and whilst making a number of recommendations for curriculum content, nevertheless, concluded that freedom in planning and arranging her work was essential for the teacher if the ever present danger of a lapse into mechanical routine was to be avoided.

The TUC found that their arguments and approach were largely in tune with those of the Consultative Committee, especially in the view that the total environment of the child needed to be considered if the full benefit of nursery provision was to be gained. To take just one example; point seven of the TUC's submission stated:

Bad housing conditions and overcrowding, the lack of gardens and playgrounds, the lack of a quiet place to rest, the lack of bathing facilities, the lack of time, either as a result of domestic duties of the mother... all emphasised the need for public provision for the child.

The Report suggested:

The problem of the physical and mental welfare of children below the age of compulsory school attendance is essentially sociological. Any fundamental attempt to solve it must eventually take account of the provision of better housing conditions for large sections of the population and the consequent improvements in the child's early environment.[45]

The known interest of the TUC in nursery education was illustrated by the invitation received by the Education Committee to visit Rachel McMillan Nursery School in Deptford on 30 March 1933. A detailed report on the visit including the buildings, equipment, and the activities of the young children as witnessed by the visitors was produced praising the work undertaken and recognising the inspiration behind the McMillan sisters, 'from the success of which might be traced the development of the nursery school movement in Great Britain'.[46] As a mark of appreciation of the school's work it was agreed by the TUCEC to send a donation of £25 to the school from the Educational Facilities Fund; a substantial sum in 1933 at a time when trade union membership was falling.

There is little to suggest that the National governments of the 1930s took the recommendations of the Hadow's Report on Infant and Nursery

Schools to heart. Proposals for nursery school provision by local authorities were met by 'systematic obstruction' by the BOE until some measure of sympathy emerged from the BOE via Circular 1444, asking cautiously for surveys to ascertain nursery school needs and although there was some easing of the harsh attitude taken to public expenditure on education after 1935, nursery school provision was not considered an important priority by government.[47] The TUC was still supportive of the idea but by the late 1930s most of the focus of the labour movement was upon the need to extend secondary schooling for all pupils and to see an end to the elementary schools which denied anything other than a limited and limiting education to the vast majority of the nation's children.

Nursery expansion did come after 1939 but when it did it was not because government was about to act upon the findings of research into child development, but was, just like the short-lived 1914–1918 period of expansion, a policy emanating from the economics of war in which young mothers were in demand for paid employment. To enable mothers to work, funds were now found to provide the nursery schools which the TUC and other sections of the labour movement had called for throughout most of the inter-war years.

NOTES AND REFERENCES.

1. Stevenson, J. and Cook, C. (1994) *Britain in the Depression: Society and Politics 1929–1939*, p.44.
2. Ibid.
3. Mason, T. (1998) '"Hunger... is a Very Good thing": Britain in the 1930s' in Tiratsoo, N. (ed.) *From Blitz to Blair*, p.7.
4. *Report of the Interdepartmental Committee on Medical Inspection and Feeding of Children attending Public Elementary Schools 1905*, p.45.
5. Morton, A. (1997) *Education and the State from 1833; Public Record Office Readers' Guide No. 18*, p.107.
6. Forder, A. (ed.) (1953) *Penelope Hall's Social Services of England and Wales*, p.176.
7. Parker, D. (1998) '"A Convenient Dispensary"; Elementary Education and the Influence of the School Medical Service 1907–39', *History of Education*, Vol. 27, No. 1.
8. See Gathorne-Hardy, J. (1979) *The Public School Phenomenon*.
9. Leff, S. and Leff, V. (1959) *The School Health Service*, p.43.
10. Labour Party/TUC (1928) *Nursery School to University*, p.9.

11. M'Gonigle, G. and Kirby, J. (1936) *Poverty and Public Health*, p.58.
12. Ibid., pp.38–9.
13. Ibid., p.43.
14. Andrews, L. (1976) *The Education Act 1918*, p.70.
15. Griggs, C. (1983) *The Trades Union Congress and the Struggle for Education 1868–1925*, p.146; Horn, P. (1989) *The Victorian and Edwardian Schoolchild*, p.75.
16. Maclure, J.S. (1970) *100 Years of London Education 1870–1970*, p.151.
17. Morton, A., *Education and the State*, p.108.
18. Leff, S. and Leff, V., *The School Health Service*, p.77.
19. Francis, H. and Smith, D. (1980) *The FED; A History of the South Wales Miners in the Twentieth Century*, p.57.
20. Leff, S. and Leff, V., *The School Health Service*, p.78.
21. *Report of the Committee of the British Association*, see Griggs, C. (1983) *The Trades Union Congress*, pp.156–7.
22. M'Gonogle, G. and Kirby, J., *Poverty and Public Health*, p.131.
23. Ibid., p.134.
24. Ibid., p.138.
25. Leff, S. and Leff, V., *The School Health Service*, pp.88–9.
26. Labour Party/TUC *Nursery School to University*, p.9.
27. *TUCEC Mins.* 14.3.1938.
28. See Titmus, R.M., (ed.) (1963) *Essays on 'The Welfare State'*, pp.75–87.
29. Gordon, P., Aldrich, R. and Dean, D. (1991) *Education and Policy in England in the Twentieth Century*, p.158.
30. *Report of the Consultative Committee on Infant and Nursery Schools*, (1933) p.31.
31. Whitbread, N. (1972) *The Evolution of the Nursery/Infant School: A History of Infant and Nursery Education in Britain 1800–1970*, p.67.
32. Gosden, P.H.J.H. (1983) *The Education System since 1944*, p.127.
33. Whitbread, N., *The Evolution of the Nursery/Infant School*.
34. Ibid.
35. Labour Party/TUC *Nursery School to University*, p.5.
36. W. Citrine to G.S.M. Ellis, 26.10.1932.
37. *TUC Report 1933*, pp.142–4.
38. Ibid., p.143.
39. Ibid.
40. Ibid.
41. Ibid., p.194.
42. Ibid.

43. Ibid., p.182.
44. Ibid., p.191.
45. Ibid., p.186.
46. *TUCEC Mins*. 30.5.1933.
47. Simon, B.(1974) *The Politics of Educational Reform*, p.198

CHAPTER 5

POLITICS AND TEXTBOOKS

CHALLENGES TO SCHOOL TEXTBOOKS

In the early years of the inter-war period there were few comments about the curriculum of the elementary schools attended by most working-class pupils and none at all about secondary schools which were outside the experience of the vast majority of trade unionists. There was a general feeling that the standard of education offered had improved following the raising of the school leaving age for all to 14 as a result of the 1918 Education Act and this was expressed at the 1927 Congress. Trade unionists were aware that a different syllabus was on offer to those attending secondary schools and that success in these schools enhanced opportunities in respect of career, income and all the associated life chances such as better accommodation, nutrition and general health. This was the reason they pushed consistently at the door to secondary schools through the demand for more free places to be made available and later for all children to be given access to secondary schooling, not necessarily of the grammar school type.

Only a minority of trade unionists ever questioned material put before children in elementary schools although the issue had first been raised back in 1879 when objections had been voiced over a text book on Political Economy widely used in Church Schools; a matter which gained widespread coverage nationally at the time and did end with agreement by the National Society that the books were no longer suitable and reflected the feelings of an earlier age.[1] The main arguments at Congress concerning the curriculum had been in the rivalry between teaching at Ruskin and the Central Labour Colleges, and that between the Workers' Education Association and National Council of Labour Colleges.[2]

In 1927 a challenge was made to what seemed to some delegates to be a measure of complacency by the TUCGC in the synopsis of evidence submitted to the Committee on Education and Industry earlier in March and which was put now before Congress. It was felt that criticism of some subject matter had been overlooked. Miss Birch of the Workers' Union spoke out against the 'anti-working class education which is being dispensed from elementary schools to children of the working class'.[3] She claimed that, 'the type of education which is now handed down to the children of workers is that type which supports imperialism in all its fundamental aspects'. The conduit for such ideas were the text books used in schools, especially those for subjects such as geography and history; the latter in general presented 'as a long chronology of events with little or no relation to each other'. What was required according to Miss Birch was:

> a history of the development of society determined by the manner in which the means of production are owned and controlled, and the relation in which classes of society stand to the means of production available in any given period... the type of education we get is deliberately provided with a view to making the children turn out to be good citizens for capitalism, more efficient slaves of the machine, more technically equipped to become disciplined in the workshop in the interests of capitalism.[4]

Miss Birch was supported in her complaints at Congress by J.B. Figgins, a lay delegate from the NUR and from an examination of that union's annual conference reports it is clear that he was only speaking in a personal capacity rather than stating union policy. He believed history books were also the main source of distorted ideas: 'there must be eradicated from history books used in the schools at this moment all tendencies of an imperialist character... (the TUCGC should be asked) to examine history books and point out the bias – how they distribute imperialistic tendencies'.[5] He suggested that the TUCGC would do a service to the trade union movement if they would produce a pamphlet pointing out some of the problems.

There was an acceptance that Birch and Figgins were probably correct in their claims about some history texts, but J.W. Bowen of the TUCGC, who had been at school in the 1880s, believed things had improved. 'We entirely agree with those who have spoken in their condemnation of the kind of book many of us had to learn from in our youth. I was taught that one Englishman was worth five Frenchmen and a hundred Arabs. Those were the days when school books were of little value except to show the difference between one letter and another.' His belief that there had been improvements was partly based on the fact that the TUCGC had consulted 'men who are regarded by the labour movement as education experts.' In any case he argued that the General Council could not be expected to go before an impartial tribunal 'and urge upon them class warfare'. They were limited by the terms of reference and would not be taken seriously if they responded in that way.

One solution suggested was to bring the teachers' unions into the TUC for their members had experience of teaching working-class children and understood what kind of education should be provided. In fact, with the exception of the National Union of School Teachers led by the formidable Miss Walsh, an organisation for uncertificated teachers who were denied membership by other teacher unions, which was affiliated during the inter-war years, there was no evidence that the majority of teachers wished for their own unions to adopt this path. Indeed, initially they were to reject such overtures. The numerous teacher trade unions and associations reflected the social and academic divisions within the educational world. The largest, the NUT, founded in 1870 as the National Union of Elementary Teachers, comprised certificated teachers in the elementary schools. Arguments over equal pay between men and women teachers carrying out the same task led to conflicts within the union during the Edwardian era. The NUT tried to keep teachers united, giving support in principle to equality of pay but realising there was strong opposition both among some teachers as well as within parts of society.

The result was the establishment of breakaway unions; the National Union of Schoolmasters (NAS) establishing itself as a separate union in 1919 campaigning to retain higher salaries for male teachers and the National Union of Women Teachers a few years later campaigning for equal pay. To complicate matters further there was the National Union of School Teachers to cater for teachers who were unqualified in the sense that they had neither gained a certificate after working as a pupil teacher nor by attending a teacher training college course. These teachers complained with some justification that whilst receiving a lower rate of pay they were often given larger classes to teach and some of the most difficult children. Miss Walsh used the opportunity afforded by TUC affiliation to explain the situation faced by her members to Congress and speak with the authority classroom experience gave her.[6] There were also the Association of Assistant Mistresses (AAM) and the Assistant Masters Association (AMA), most of whose members were graduates teaching in secondary schools and receiving higher salaries than those in elementary schools. The different unions served the special interests of their members; the multiplicity of unions also encouraged divisiveness among teachers and enabled local authorities and governments at times to play one off against the other. Even more unions would form in the 1960s; the Union of Women Teachers and the Professional Teachers Association and there would be mergers too; AAM with AMA to form AMMA and the NAS with the UWT to become the NASUWT.

It is not possible to deal with the complex policies and tactics of these different unions and attempts to simplify some of their policies run the danger of distorting them. For example whilst the NAS for many years did campaign for higher salaries for men, part of the argument used was that in a profession which contained large numbers of women during the inter-war years the social convention of paying women less depressed the incomes of all teachers. They also argued that it was not good for boys to attend schools, and this was true for elementary and later primary schools, in which there were few male teachers to provide role models. Whilst these arguments did need to be addressed the idea of being paid more just because you were a man inevitably appealed to some male teachers so that self-interest was a useful recruiting agent when union representatives visited teacher training colleges. There was also the clear danger that if women were paid lower salaries some authorities might hire them in preference to men because they would be prove to be 'more economical'. In any case, none of these arguments could really stand up to the central principle that people with similar qualifications and training carrying out similar tasks deserved the same salary. Inter-union rivalry and different stands on education issues could lead to disputes within staffrooms but for much of the time teachers found the rivalry a source of irritation when they compared the system which had grown up of numerous teacher unions with other professional bodies which presented a united front, such as the British Medical Council or the Law Society. Eventually many of the unions did affiliate to the TUC; the Association of Teachers in Technical Institutions (ATTI) was the first in 1966, the NAS in 1968 and the NUT in 1970.

To return to Miss Birch's remarks at the 1927 Congress concerning teacher sympathy, they had in general been regarded as a conservative force, a view maintained due to neglected aspects of history until relatively recently. At local level teacher trade unionists were often members of trades councils in towns and considerable militancy at local branch level has been recorded from 1896 onwards. In that year the first successful teachers' strike took place at Portsmouth in response to attempts to persuade the school board to pay their teachers comparable salaries to those awarded to staff by school boards in other towns. Eleven years on, teachers went on strike in West Ham and after that there were numerous disputes through to the 1920s, ending with the Lowestoft strike when the town council voted by a majority of 23 to 16 to overturn the recommended 10 per cent cut in teachers' salaries by their own education committee.[7] It is also worth remembering that the longest strike in British history was that undertaken by school teachers at Burston School which lasted from 1914 to 1939. The resulting 'Strike School' built by public subscription, especially donations from the labour movement, still stands, now a museum and a monument to the principled stand taken by Mr and Mrs Tom Higdon.[8]

The Teachers' Labour League provides another example of teachers taking a radical approach to education. Formed at a conference in May 1923 it included well-known intellectuals such as Bertrand Russell, R.H. Tawney, Sidney Webb and H.G. Wells as well as professors J.J. Findlay and Frederick Soddy of Manchester and Oxford universities, respectively.[9] As an educational pressure group the League was active in supporting teachers and soon gained the attention of the Special Branch, whose reports on active members made their way from the Home Office to the President of the BOE.[10] The President of the League, H.S. Redgrove, claimed there was an anti-socialist bias within school textbooks and that a focus on citizenship in schools would help to counter this by explaining the principles of socialism to children.[11] By 1926 the League was successful in getting a resolution passed at the annual Labour party conference condemning 'the widespread reactionary imperialist teaching in the schools particularly with regard to Empire Day celebrations and the use of history and other text-books with an anti-working class bias...'.[12] The following year the League was disaffiliated from the Labour party.

There is evidence that the BOE was concerned about the content of some textbooks being used at the time. Two months before the 1927 TUC debate took place, the TUCGC received a letter from the Secretary of the Consultative Committee of the BOE asking for their views on the selection and provision of books for Public Elementary Schools together with recommendations for the improvement of their quality and supply. It can only be assumed that quality referred to content rather than product for the Education Committee agreed to consult with 'prominent educationists in the labour movement with a view to submitting a memorandum to the committee at the earliest possible date'.[13]

Three years later a book first published in 1916 entitled 'Elements of Military Education' by W.A. Brockington, Director of Education for Leicestershire and Adjutant of the 1st (Grammar Schools) Cadet Battalion of the Leicestershire Regiment, was brought to the attention of the TUCEC. Apparently it was still being used in some schools and particular parts were considered unsuited to the curriculum, especially chapter VII 'The School Curriculum in relation to other Military Subjects' in which section 8 dealt with bayonet practice. The book was in effect a manual on all aspects of soldiering in practice for war, from basic drill to firing a rifle and inevitably its aim was to produce a disciplined cadet who would know how to kill 'the enemy'. Written at the height of the First World War it doubtless provided sound advice for young cadets expecting to be sent to fight in the immediate future but by 1930 both the situation and the public mood had changed. The War Poets such as Siegfried Sasoon and Wilfred Owen had already cut through the jingoism of the war and now powerful books published the previous year added to the anti-war feelings of many people. Robert Graves' *Goodbye to All That* brought home the horrors of the trenches from the British soldiers' viewpoint; Erich Maria Remarque told of similar experiences from the German soldiers' side in *All Quiet on the Western Front*. Remarque's book was made into a powerful film in 1930 by Lewis Stone. It won two Oscars and in the genre of anti-war films, despite its age, has probably yet to be surpassed. With so much of the senseless slaughter of the war now exposed, instructions to school-boys on how best to use a bayonet no longer seemed appropriate. No further mention of the book appears in the TUCEC minutes and it can only be assumed that the use of this text in local authority schools ceased. Worry over militaristic material was also expressed by the Bradford ILP in a report on education criticising the 'social implications of an Officers' Training Corps' which encouraged playing at soldiers and resulted in "direct propaganda" for war'.[14] The next year the ILP asked Trevelyan, President of the BOE, to undertake a survey which would identify textbooks promoting a nationalistic and imperialistic outlook so that such material could be removed from schools.

One other book was picked out specifically for criticism. In June 1939 the TUC received a letter from the Secretary of the Scottish Labour Party stating that they had been collecting evidence of material from school textbooks making references to the Labour party and miners. No specific book was mentioned in the letter.[15] The TUC replied that several English local authorities with Labour party representatives had also been reviewing textbooks currently used in schools.[16] Within days the Scottish Labour Party had replied naming one of the books examined, *The Modern Book of English Literature; Book V* by E.J. Lay and published by Macmillan.[17] Apparently in the Preface Professor Hearnshaw of London University had stated that 'No pains had been spared to free them (i.e. the textbooks) from every suspicion of any sort of political or religious propaganda.' The Scots believed that the treatment of the Spanish Civil

War lacked objectivity. Support for the legitimate Republican Government of Spain was strong in the British labour movement and among delegates to the TUC. In 1937 for example, Ernest Bevin of the TGWU was president and had missed part of the discussion on Spain. He asked for the following resolution to be moved and seconded formally:

> This Congress places on record its high appreciation of the gallant struggle of our Spanish comrades, and those of the International Brigade, against Fascism which is the deadly enemy of Trade Unionism, and most heartily wishes them every success against the common enemy.[18]

By contrast, the National government led by Neville Chamberlain not only acquiesced in the intervention by Mussolini and Hitler on the side of General Franco but also on the attacks on British merchant shipping carrying goods to Republican Spain.

> Even the subtle vocabulary of Mr R.A. Butler, Parliamentary Under Secretary at the Foreign Office (with Lord Halifax in the Lords, he was chief spokesman on foreign affairs in the House of Commons – other than the Prime Minister), was taxed to explain why the government would not permit the export of anti-aircraft guns to Republican Spain, nor the merchant ships to carry their own arms.[19]

Thomas's long and detailed history of the Spanish Civil War brings out the interplay of forces between the political Left and Right in Europe during the 1930s and the view that much of the British Establishment sided with the political right if only because they feared the political left. School textbooks were likely to reflect this view.

The Scottish Labour Party believed the problem was twofold; that headmasters chose the books and some authors were ignorant of the events of which they wrote. They suggested the TUC make official representations to the publishers and discuss the matter at their annual Congress. This was the approach the Scottish Labour Party had taken and it had caused a 'great furore'.[20] The TUC agreed to pursue the matter further and agreed that one problem was that texts were chosen from an 'approved list'.[21]

There is little doubt that there were textbooks, especially in the subjects of geography, which echoed imperialistic views and were unlikely to be sympathetic to organised Labour. One obvious explanation is to suggest they were merely products of their time. A cursory glance at the media of the 1930s makes it clear that images of Empire were portrayed prominently through posters, comics, books, radio and films. This can be illustrated by reference to many of the popular films shown at the cinema, the most powerful 'new' media form of the time, often made from stories written in the period prior to the 1914–1918 War frequently displaying the values of another age. For example, *The Four Feathers* from the book by W.E. Mason (1865–1948) was filmed in 1929 (USA) and again in 1939 (GB), *Sanders of the River* in 1935 (GB) from a book written in 1911 by Edgar Wallace (1875–1932). Both portray the need for 'British values' to be upheld in foreign lands under their control against attempts by groups within those countries to challenge that power.[22] The books given out as school prizes were, like the two mentioned here, frequently the products of authors belonging to the previous century, such as *Coral Island* written in 1858 by R.M. Ballantyne (1825–94). There were of course others outside the category of imperial themes such as *Black Beauty* written in 1877 by Anna Sewell (1820–78) where cruelty to animals was highlighted. How far all this was a conscious effort as opposed to a mere reflection of the dominant ideas of the time is difficult to know.

To some extent dominant groups in society assume their views are the norm and ideas challenging them are somewhat deviant or even subversive. During the inter-war period there were Conservative Ministers and MPs worried about challenges to their ideology and practice from growing support for alternative socialist and collective philosophies. They might have learned to expect hostility from sections of the organised labour movement but were seriously concerned when they believed teachers, whom they had regarded as conservative in their behaviour and attitudes, and political views if they had any, were increasingly supporting and sometimes even joining the Labour party. The fear was that teachers would use their position in school to influence the political outlook of the next generation of voters. Hence Lord Percy in his role as President of the BOE warned the North of England Education Conference about 'a constant and conscious effort among a large section of our fellow-countrymen to conduct political propaganda, directly or indirectly among children'.[23]

Conservatives such as Colonel Sir Charles Yates who called for an oath of allegiance for teachers in 1926 and Colonel Vaughan Morgan MP who wrote to Percy about involvement of teachers in the General Strike illustrated the belief that support for Labour was considered incompatible with being a school teacher. The *Daily Mail*, *Morning Post* and *The Times* highlighted the activities of left-wing teachers, especially when they participated in public meetings, thereby drawing the attention to them of both their employers and members of the local community.

With the support of the NUT solicitors, Dan Griffiths, a Labour party candidate in Stroud, defended his position as a teacher in the face of a deputation of women who complained to Llanelly Education Committee and the Conservative MP, Major Boyd Carpenter, who ended up having to make a public apology for repeating the charges made by some parents. Similarly Miss Spurrell, a Labour party candidate for Totnes was attacked in a letter to the *Kingsbridge Gazette*, a writ was issued and high damages awarded against the local newspaper and correspondent. Less fortunate was Marjorie Pollitt who was dismissed by the LCC for activities in support of the General Strike and membership of the Communist party.

Right-wing organisations such as the National Citizens' Union, the British Womens' Patriotic League and the Imperial Fascisti spent much energy attacking socialist teachers, and some employers openly questioned candidates for teaching posts about their political views making it clear that acceptance of socialist ideology made them unsuitable for employment as a teacher in the area. This was especially true of areas with strong Conservative representation.[23] There are no records of criticism of teachers who openly supported the Conservative party. It was in effect a form of witch-hunting which doubtless deterred some teachers from expressing anti-Conservative views in public and threatening teachers who did with loss of employment.

The fact is that Conservative education policy between the two world wars seemed to be dominated by the idea of 'economies' including the imposition of a 5 per cent levy on teachers' superannuation, deterioration in staff:pupil ratios, threats of reduction in wages all resulting from the recommendations of the Geddes committee of 1922 and supported by campaign speeches of Baldwin the following year. Small wonder that many teachers perceived the Conservative party as hostile to public education in general and the teachers working in the public sector in particular.

NOTES AND REFERENCES

1. Griggs, C. (1981) 'The Trades Union Congress and the Controversy over the National Society's Standard V Reading Book' *British Journal of Educational Studies*, Vol.XXIX, No. 3.
2. See Craik, W.W. (1964) *The Central Labour College*; Griggs, C. (1983) *The Trades Union Congress and the Struggle for Education 1868–1925*, Ch.7; Millar, J.P.M. (1987) *The Labour College Movement*; Simon, B. (1965) *Education and the labour movement*

1870–1920, Ch. IX; Yorke, P. (1977) *Ruskin College 1899–1909*; Pollins, H. (1984) *The History of Ruskin College*, pp.17–25.

3. *TUC Report 1927*, p.333.

4. Ibid., pp.334, 335

5. For the activities of Miss Walsh see Griggs, C. (1983) *The Trades Union Congress*, pp.209–11.

6. Lawn, M. (1987) *Servants of the State: The Contested Control of Teaching 1900–1930* and Seifert, R.V. (1987) *Teacher Militancy: A History of Teacher Strikes 1896–1987*, Part 1.

7. Edwards, B. (1974) *The Burston School Strike*. For another example of the conflict between some Conservative dominated rural authorities and outspoken teachers see Betts, R. (2001) 'We've Got to Live Here After You've Gone' *Journal of Educational Administration and History*, Vol. 33, No. 1.

8. Simon, B. (1974) *The Politics of Educational Reform, 1920–1940*, p.72.

9. Lawn, M.(1987) *Servants of the State*, p.123.

10. Barker, R. (1972) *Education and Politics 1900–51: A Study of the Labour Party*, p.148.

11. Labour Party Annual Conference Report 1925, pp.265–6, cited in Barker, R. (1972) *Education and Politics*, p.149.

12. *TUCEC Mins*. 21.7.1927.

13. Barker, R. (1972) *Education and Politics*, p.144.

14. Secretary, Scottish Labour Party to TUC, 24.6.1939.

15. TUC to Secretary, Scottish Labour party, 26.6.1939.

16. Letters seeking a copy of the text have been sent to Macmillans and a number of university libraries with collections of school textbooks: Birmingham, Herriot Watt, Institute of Education of London University, Leeds, Leicester and Sussex. Unfortunately none of these institutions has been able to locate a copy. There is no correspondence of this episode in the archives of the Scottish Labour Party housed at Mitchell Library, Glasgow.

17. *TUC Report 1937*, p.280.

18. Thomas, H. (1965) *The Spanish Civil War*, p.680. See also pp.675–83 for the part played by the British Government in the Spanish Civil War as part of its policy of 'general appeasement'.

19. Secretary, Scottish Labour Party to TUC, 29.6.1939.

20. TUC to Secretary, Scottish Labour Party, 6.7.1939.

21. See Marsden, W.E. (1990) 'Rooting Racism into the Educational Experience of Childhood and Youth in the Nineteenth and Twentieth Centuries' *History of Education*, Vol. 19, No. 4; MacKenzie, J.M.

(1984) *Propaganda and Empire: The Manipulation of British Public Opinion 1880–1960* and Griggs, C. (1989) 'The Rise of Mass Schooling' in Cole, M. (ed.) *The Social Contexts of Schooling*, pp.48–50.
22. Barker, R., (1972) *Education and Politics*, p.150.
23. Lawn, M. (1987) *Servants of the State*, Ch.8.

PART 2 – THE WAR YEARS
1939–1945

CHAPTER 6

OUTBREAK OF WAR AND EVACUATION

WAR WITH NAZI GERMANY

With the outbreak of war against Nazi Germany in early September 1939, Britain braced itself for the expected onslaught. The inter-war National governments had been reluctant to introduce education reforms;[1] the reorganisation recommended by the Hadow Report of 1926 had never been fully implemented, especially was this true of the church schools. The raising of the school leaving age campaigned for steadily by the labour movement and many organisations associated with education, promised in 1936 was finally due to be introduced on 1 September 1939. These plans were now abandoned as all national effort and resources were needed for the task of waging war against Germany; a task which would be made all the more difficult when France withdrew from the conflict in June 1940.

Within days of the declaration of war, the TUC met at Bridlington and whilst the attention of delegates was inevitably concentrated upon the struggle to come, J. Hallsworth (Distribution and Allied Workers) in his Presidential address still believed it was important to 'emphasise the importance the General Council attaches to the fullest possible development of every form of educational and cultural service'.[2]

An Education Emergency Bill was introduced into parliament to postpone the raising of the school leaving age to 15 years. The TUC fully understood the new situation and in a letter to the Board of Education recognising the inevitability of this action the TUCEC expressed their regrets suggesting that in the future when the necessary legislation was

introduced it would be without the exemption clauses which so
undermined attempts to lengthen the school life of all children.[3] In his
reply, Earl De La Warr, President of the Board would give no such
assurances explaining 'that the revival of exemption clauses would be for
Parliament to decide when the higher school leaving age came into
operation'.[4] The TUCEC did not let this reply pass without comment and
made it clear that they expected children to receive special attention in
spite of the War; 'the serious curtailment of educational facilities now
being suffered by children ought to be compensated when normal school
life became possible again and as a contribution to this end the scheme for
the exemptions ought to be withdrawn'.[5] The tone of their communication
provides a hint of the approach they would take in the years ahead.

On the very day that De La Warr had written to the TUC, J.V.C. Wray,
Secretary of the TUCEC had a 45-minute discussion with Kenneth
Lindsay, parliamentary secretary to the Board of Education in which the
former told of the TUC worries that the Treasury would cut out all
expenditure not directly related to the war. Wray believed 'the Board
ought to dig its toes in and insist on the maintenance of educational
facilities'.[6] He expressed concern about the long-term prospects of
interruption arising from evacuation and on a specific point 'referred to
the action of the Isle of Ely Education Authority in releasing school
children of 12 years of age for harvest work'.[7] Lindsay was able to assure
Wray that on this occasion the LEA's illegal action had met with the
Board's censure but pressure to turn a blind eye to such activities would
be an ongoing issue in the years ahead.

EVACUATION

'At the time of Munich, over 80 per cent of London parents had said they
would want their children to be evacuated. Yet, in August 1939, whether
from added courage or greater apathy, only two-thirds were of the same
mind. In the event less than half of London's schoolchildren went.'[8]
Nevertheless, the numbers involved were still significant and in general
the operation went smoothly, without a single casualty, a remarkable
achievement given the scale of the operation. About 2 million made the
move on their own initiative from what were considered vulnerable areas
to rural parts of Scotland, Wales and the West Country.[9] Offers from
Australia, New Zealand, South Africa, Canada and the USA to take
children were received and a Children's Overseas Reception Board
established which received over 200,000 applications within a fortnight.

Children aged 10 to 16 were eligible and hundreds began to leave by sea until the sinking of the passenger ship *Arandora Star* on 3 July 1940 led to postponement of the scheme, which was abandoned after the *City of Benares* was sunk on 17 September with the loss of 73 of the children on board.[10]

Another million young children and women were evacuated through local authority schemes, usually with their school within a few days of the war to what were considered by the government as 'reception areas'.[11] By December, when the expected heavy aerial bombardment had not materialised, nearly 90 per cent of these mothers and children had returned home. In fact there was an ebb and flow of evacuees linked to the severity of bombing campaigns with two high points in terms of numbers; 1940–41 during the Battle of Britain and later again in 1944 when pilotless 'doodlebugs' followed by rockets, the V1 and V2 respectively, led to considerable loss of life and destruction largely in urban areas.

The government had hoped that nearly all children as far as possible would be evacuated from areas considered to be most vulnerable to air raids. Ideally the government and military wished to evacuate all these areas and compulsion was considered but rejected in the belief it might cause resentment.[12] The prime concern was the safety of the children but economic factors also played a part. School buildings were required for other purposes: for the use of the ARP, as possible casualty centres and in time many were in any case destroyed by bombing. There was the belief that parents would be less anxious if they knew their children were safe and mothers would be more free to work without the responsibility of looking after their children. Most schools in urban areas were therefore closed in the early months of the war.

One result of billeting children from some of the poorest inner city areas with higher income families in more leafy parts of the country was the clash of sub-cultures; the social customs and standards of hygiene of some evacuees struck some of their host families with surprise and horror. The shock brought by the revelation concerning the poor physique, diet and general health of many children was an indictment of the poverty suffered by many families during the inter-war period, which Neville Chamberlain as past Minister of Health 1924–29, was to describe as a matter of great regret. 'I never knew that such conditions existed, and I feel ashamed of having been so ignorant of my neighbours.'[13] This ignorance about the wide disparity in incomes and the social consequences in living conditions was shared by many in the country.

Numerous descriptions of the plight of both many of the children and their mothers from these poverty stricken areas have been produced,[14] and even allowing for some exaggeration at times, and the resentment some families felt at having to take in children from backgrounds with which they had little in common, the exercise did make some middle-class families aware of the plight of many less fortunate than themselves. Cultural shock was not all one way. The author was a child from a local authority estate built in the late 1930s in the suburbs of London. Here many parents returned home from working at the new factories along the Western Avenue, tired but relatively cleanly dressed. It was a surprise, and an education, to go with a young Welsh friend to meet his father from the local colliery and be faced by a crowd of miners blackened by coal dust with just the whites of their eyes peering into the daylight.

Half of London's children were not evacuated and large numbers returned home for a variety of reasons. For some the enhanced safety did not compensate for home sickness and at times the obvious resentment shown towards them by residents who outwardly seemed to have little in common with them. Whatever the reasons, the smaller take up of evacuation and the drift back towards the cities caused considerable problems for the government. For those remaining behind in the cities with their local schools utilised for other purposes and the need to shelter when air raids took place, there was the prospect that their education would suffer and that they would linger aimlessly for a year or two until they reached the age at which they might start work. Both issues exercised the TUC.

Whilst recognising the difficulties faced by the government in trying to finance education for children in both the town and area to which the children had been scheduled to move, the TUC was still active in seeking solutions to these problems. They concluded that,

> The risks to the children of keeping the schools closed appeared to be greater than the risks of bombing and representations were persistently made to the Board of Education until in the end they promised to restore the principle of compulsory attendance in the evacuation areas.[15]

The pressure for the re-establishment of compulsory attendance was allied to the knowledge that children would then also receive the benefits of the supervision of their health through the School Medical Services and the advantages of both milk and free or cheap midday meals.

At the outbreak of the war 120,000 'necessitous undernourished children' received free school meals; by July 1940 the number had fallen to 70,000. Part of this reduction was due to the closure of schools and canteens in areas of high risk. Given that many women were on shift work this was another factor in making it difficult to provide meals at home. The signs of recorded weight loss of some children spurred the government into action and increased grants were provided for the school meals service leading to an expansion. Between '1940–41 free and paid meals in elementary schools doubled to 280,000 a day and numbers taking milk rose to 3 million'.[16] In some areas tea was also provided for children who remained at school under supervision and within reach of air raid shelters giving parents time to return home from work.

Parents of children evacuated made a contribution to the maintenance costs met by the host family who in turn received payment from the government; ten shillings and sixpence for one child, eight shillings and sixpence for subsequent children. It came to the attention of the TUC that some host families were making requests for extra funding either directly to the parents of the children billeted with them or indirectly through a teacher. This created a difficult situation. It could be that children arrived with insufficient clothing and needed a new item and the host family were seeking the money for the expenditure incurred. On the other hand, parents of evacuees could be led to believe that if they did not provide extra money their children might suffer in some way. The TUC wrote to the Minister of Health about this matter, who replied that a circular had been issued dated 17 November 1939 sent to all authorities in evacuation and reception areas to the effect 'that any additional payment should be a matter for the individual parent to decide and that it was undesirable that any approach should be made to the parents'.[17]

One genuine need was for different clothing for those evacuated to more rural areas, especially in terms of footwear. For example children going from suburban areas of towns to the Welsh mining valleys where the streets running parallel along the valley sides were in places linked by unmade paths soon found that shoes were quickly worn through and that studded boots were needed. The TUC claimed that many parents would be unable to meet the extra cost of items of clothing and that whilst local authorities in Scotland were empowered to provide clothing for school children this was not the case in England and Wales.[18]

Employment of children was always an area to which the TUC could be expected to respond swiftly given the long battle they had fought over child labour from their very foundation in 1868. This now seemed to be on the increase in towns where there was a shortage of labour and in the early months of the war when some schools were closed, some older children and employers conspired to enable the former to work and earn money. Within the countryside there was a special need at harvest time for extra labour and given the need to grow as much food as possible whilst the threat to shipping by German submarines was so dangerous and effective it is understandable that there were special circumstances. The Board of Education duly published circular 1541 (20 February 1941) which stated that 'within limits permitted by law the fullest use should be made in agricultural employment of the assistance which could be given by older children, consistent with the maintenance of their health and the interests of their education'. Naturally harvest time fell within the period of the summer school holidays as the latter had been designed to correspond with the needs of a rural countryside, although there had always been some overlap at either end of the holidays when large numbers of children in rural schools were absent helping with the harvest. In addition significant numbers had been absent in earlier years helping with a variety of countryside pursuits from tending pigs to working as beaters for shoots. However it was now suggested that for secondary-school children 'for those periods when the need for seasonal agricultural labour was greatest, parties of pupils should be organised to visit local farms on certain days in term time in order to help with the work of planting and lifting potatoes'.[19]

The Women's National Advisory Committee of the TUC requested that the TUCEC should consider this circular further and it was agreed that a letter be sent to the president of the Board of Education about the proposals in circular 1541. They suggested there should be a number of restrictions applied including:

(a) only light agricultural work
(b) bye-laws to make certain that 12–14 year olds should not work more than four hours a day
(c) returns to be provided by LEAs providing details of the alterations to school holidays for this work and the number of days during term on which children are released for work on the land.

The Minister replied that he believed the circular already safeguarded conditions under which children might work but agreed to consult the National Union of Agricultural Workers (NUAW) to obtain further information as to how it was being implemented in practice. In fact the TUC were not kept informed about the regulations for employment of children and this was to lead to more letters of protest to the minister of agriculture, home secretary and president of the Board of Education.[20] The TUC was to keep up the pressure and two years later a deputation visited the Home Office in March 1944 to meet Mr Peake, the under secretary of state and Sir Robert Wood from the Board of Education with a view to seeking some revision in the law relating to the employment of school children. There were apparently difficulties over the definition of employment but it was hoped by then to clarify the situation by a new clause to be proposed in the Education Bill.[21] Apart from the traditional areas of child employment such as agriculture there were other areas which had been brought to the attention of the TUC by Equity urging the need for more stringent regulations of employment of children in film and theatre to prevent exploitation by 'schools' which also acted as employment agencies or which held children under contract to them.[22]

These matters which had been exercising the TUC had also been of concern within the WEA and the Co-operative Union. The result was a joint deputation which included A. Creech Jones, MP, R.H. Tawney, Barbara Drake and Lady Simon of the WEA, L.A. Hurt and Dr J. Thomas of the Co-operative Union and Miss F. Hancock (TGWU), G. Chester (NU Boot Operatives), George Woodcock and J.V.C. Wray from the TUC, which met with Herbald Ramsbotham, the president, and Sir Maurice Holmes, permanent secretary at the Board of Education. They pushed the president on all the issues which had been raised in terms of the provision of war-time education. He replied that 93.2 per cent of children were in full-time attendance in December 1940 with an average attendance of 76.8 per cent. On reflection, a meeting at the height of such an intense war to discuss these issues suggests a genuine openness on the part of the Board of Education as a realisation of the importance of organised labour to the war effort.

It was at this meeting in February 1941 that the joint deputation, having raised current education matters, proceeded to ask the president of his plans for after the war. They wanted his response to their demands for raising the school leaving age to 16, the abolition of exemption clauses and fees for secondary schooling combined with a single code for education. Ramsbotham agreed to the single code, the desirability of removing exemption clauses and assured the deputation that the Board was planning a new testament of education for the post-war period.[23] The TUCEC reported

> It is understood that the Board of Education have now put on paper some tentative ideas for post-war reconstruction. The President has been asked to supply copies of the document in question for consideration of the TUCGC, and has been assured of the Council's strong and active interest in this question.[24]

Acknowledgement of the existence of the 'Green Book' was now in the open and from now on Reconstruction would be the dominating theme of all groups with an interest in education. Increasingly the attention of the people would be turned towards post-war planning but unlike 1918, 'This time they were determined not to be cheated and therefore demanded the formulation of practical schemes while the war was on.'[25]

NOTES AND REFERENCES

1. This failure of the Conservative dominated governments was to be recognised in the findings of the First Interim Report of the Conservative Party Sub-Committee on Education in 1942. See Dean, D. (1970) 'Problems of the Conservative Sub-Committee on Education 1941-45', *Journal of Educational Administration and History*, Vol. 3, No. 1.
2. *TUC Report 1939*, p.75.
3. *TUCEC Mins.* 11.10.1939.
4. Ibid., 2.11.1939.
5. Ibid., 8.11.1939.
6. Ibid., 2.11.1939.
7. Ibid.
8. Calder, A. (1996) *The People's War: Britain 1939–45*, p.37.
9. There is a wealth of information on Evacuation in the Public Record Office. See Morton, A. (1997) *Education and the State from 1833: Public Record Office Readers' Guide*, p.33 'Education in Wartime'.
10. Gosden, P.H.J.H. (1976) *Education in the Second World War: A Study in Political Administration*, p.37.
11. Some areas changed status in terms of perceived safety. For example, Eastbourne received evacuees from London initially but within a year children were sent from the town alongside those from London to Gloucestershire. See Humphrey, G. (1989) *Wartime Eastbourne: The Story of the Most Raided Town in the South East*.
12. Gosden, P.H.J.H. (1976) *Education in the Second World War*, Ch.1.
13. Quoted in Addison, P. (1994 edn) *The Road to 1945: British Politics and the Second World War*, p.82.
14. Stevenson, J. (1984) *British Society 1914–1945*, pp.140–1; Hennessey, P. (1992) *Never Again: Britain 1945–51*, pp.12–15; Addison, P. *The Road to 1945*, pp.71–2 ; Calder, A., *The People's War*, pp.36–7.
15. *TUCEC Mins.* 6.2.1940.
16. Leff, S. and Leff, V., (1959) *The School Health Service*, p.98.
17. *TUCEC Mins.*, 9.1.1940.

18. *TUC Report 1940*, p.138 and *TUCEC Mins.*, 9.1.1940.
19. *TUCEC Mins.*, 26.3.1941.
20. Ibid., 12.5.1942.
21. TUC Deputation to the Home Office and correspondence concerning Education Bill, 4.4.1944, TUC 811/6.
22. Equity to TUC 28.3.1944 and 5.4.1944.
23. *TUC Report 1941*, p.123.
24. Ibid.
25. Taylor, A.J.P., (1965) *English History 1914–1945*, p.567.

CHAPTER 7

POST-WAR PLANNING

THE BOARD OF EDUCATION AND THE GREEN BOOK

The 'Green Book' as it became known, was submitted by branches of the Board of Education to the Educational Reconstruction Committee which discussed, amended and edited them into chapters for the final memorandum. The practical experience of the participants in terms of their schooling as pupils, and in the case of a few who had been teachers, was confined to the public schools. Moreover they were all products of either Oxford or Cambridge universities. (See Appendix 6.) Although the official view was that it was an informal discussion document it 'indicated clearly the attitude of some of the most influential members of the educational hierarchy'.[1] Even the Committee responsible for the Memo was claimed to be an informal group of people discussing the possible paths for educational change which might lie ahead. The members included the five principal assistant secretaries; N. Bosworth-Smith, W.C. Cleary, H.B. Wallis, G.G. Williams and S.H. Wood, the three chief inspectors, R. Charles, F. Duckworth and W. Elliot, and the senior woman inspector, Miss Hammond. It was clear to everyone that the change in political climate during the war meant that the reforms grudgingly introduced in the late 1930s would be insufficient to meet the higher expectations stimulated by the experiences gained both among the personnel of the armed services and those at home.

The question which has attracted the considerable attention of historians of the war period when looking at the way these demands for change were met is whether it is believed in general that the Board's proposals were sympathetic to these aims and provided a system to satisfy them or whether calculated moves were taken to satisfy some of these popular demands whilst at the same time preserving the privileges in the education system enjoyed by higher income groups, especially the matter of the public schools.[2] Whichever of these two broad interpretations, with the benefit of hindsight seems to offer the most accurate analysis of the evidence, another fact which has to be considered is the political reality of the time. Powerful pressure groups were at work throughout the period and these, combined with the views of a Conservative-dominated parliament together with the political ideology of R.A. Butler in particular, as well as Churchill as prime minister, need to be weighed in the balance of what was possible at the time. Butler's role whilst crucial was not as straightforward as sometimes portrayed. He was certainly not the architect of the 1944 Education Act:

> The evidence now available shows quite clearly that Butler exerted little influence on the educational aspects of the Act. It is not his Act in the sense that it embodies his policies or was designed by him. His contributions to its success were great, but they were not concerned with the future shape of schooling in Britain. He was, rather, the protector of other men's plans. Indeed the main decisions about secondary education were taken before Butler was asked by Churchill in 1941 to become President of the Board of Education.[3]

As has been shown it was Ramsbotham, Butler's predecessor, who was involved at this stage. Indeed it was the former who 'declared publicly that the Green Book offered a suitable basis for action at the end of the war', and it was this public advocacy which was 'the main cause behind Ramsbotham's removal from the Board and his elevation to the peerage in 1941'.[4] It was not a move he had sought.[5]

That some people in all manner of groups and institutions plot to protect and promote their perceived interests cannot be in doubt. That those who are in positions of power can be more effective is also generally true, although of course there are times when due to unforeseen circumstances the outcome of such scheming is not that which was originally intended.[6] The problem for historians is finding sound evidence of such activities; private conversations are not recorded although they may be the occasion when key ideas are discussed and conclusions reached. Even so, there is enough evidence within official records and previous studies to show the way in which officials at the Board of Education sought to control the development of post-war schooling in order to fashion it as closely as possible to their educational philosophy.

It is generally accepted that among the key civil servants at the Board of Education G.G. Williams was the dominant character. He was a traditionalist holding elitist views who believed that secondary grammar schools had been too generous in their intake during the 1930s; a view he supported by reference to the significant number of pupils who did not stay the full course or performed poorly in external examinations. He was a product of Westminster and Oxford University, and a teacher at Wellington and Lancing public schools. These associations with fee-paying schools were reinforced by frequent attendance at meetings of the Headmasters' Conference. A hard-working bachelor, his social and educational connections had enabled him to build up a considerable power base:

> he did much of the drafting for the Spens Committee, was Secretary to the Secondary Schools Examination Council, an intimate colleague of Cyril Norwood, helped to promote the Norwood committee, was involved with Norwood in selecting the Committee's membership and drafted much of its work.[7]

It would be tempting to suggest that given his background it was inevitable that his views would be conservative in education if only because the privileged system in which he had been a participant had served him so well. However, it is difficult to find any of the civil servants in senior positions within the Board of Education, let alone ministers, who did not have similar restricted experiences of the education system, with the exception of teaching experience in public schools as well. This was not considered unusual for even outside of government in such areas as the law, the Church, the armed forces (with the exception of the RAF) top positions were dominated by ex-public schoolboys, whilst 'over 70 per cent of the Conservative MPs elected in 1935 had been educated at major public schools'.[8] Educational views within the Board of Education at times may have been more closely related to the areas with which civil servants were involved, at least in the case of R. Charles (Chief Inspector Elementary Schools), W.C. Cleary (Principal Assistant Secretary Elementary Schools) and R.S. Wood (Principal Secretary Technical Branch).[9] Crude deterministic explanations cannot be sustained in this respect; more pertinent is the fact that those who exercised the most influence, had similar views, held the most power and were able to have their way in the long run. Various views would be expressed but they would not receive equal support when the key papers were written upon which decisions would be made.

Charles, Cleary and Wood all gave qualified support to the idea of multilateral schools. They were not alone in recognising the tide of opinion beginning to turn against the resistance to changes in education during the inter-war years. The begrudging concessions of the 1936 Education Act would no longer be acceptable to a country where the demands on the population of a massive war were challenging the social structure of so many institutions which had perpetuated the social divisions in place only a few years earlier. Education was among these and it became clear to the conservative-minded in positions of authority and power that if limited concessions were not granted by them greater changes would be forced upon them. As Taylor pointed out, 'The governing classes were on their best behaviour, from conviction as well as calculation.'[10] Cleary in a note to the Educational Reconstruction Committee in June 1941 warned, 'schools will be expected to conform and contribute, and indeed they may be its chief help as they could be its greatest obstacle if the types of post-primary education were to remain as sharply distinct as they are a present';[11] a view endorsed by R.S. Wood when he wrote that the war, 'is moving us more and more in the direction of Labour's ideas and ideals'.[12] Further evidence of the pressure for change outside the Board of Education had come when a deputation from the WEA had visited Arthur Greenwood who had been made responsible for post-war reconstruction, and invited him to submit his ideas for education after the war. Holmes was annoyed at the thought that representation on education matters had been made to any Department other than Education and equally displeased at Greenwood's response which could prejudice the Board's planning 'at the outset if Greenwood and Chrystal (a permanent secretary working with the minister), who naturally know nothing of the public system of education, give ear to everybody who has some grievance to air'.[13] In fact Greenwood had more personal experience of the public education system than Holmes as he had attended Cockburn High School before going to Leeds University.

By March 1941, Ramsbotham was informing the NUT Conference that the unofficial ideas within the Board would soon be available for consultation with interested parties. Upon publication of the Green Book in June, actually entitled *Education After the War*, the president attracted immediate criticism by designating it a 'strictly confidential' document; a decision which was as impractical as it was unnecessary once the extent of the circulation became apparent – all local education authorities, teachers' organisations and churches but not political parties or the inspectorate. Citrine's request on 3 July for copies was met the next day when six arrived, so that when the Co-operative Union wrote to the TUC about the existence of the publication it became 'a little embarrassing in view of the fact that we have officially received copies of the Board's memo, whereas (they) have not'. The TUC played along with the farce of secrecy whilst enabling the Co-operative Union to copy the section on adult education with which they were concerned, and carried on the charade several months later when asking for two more copies due to the size of their Education Committee, writing to the Minister, 'I may say that in passing on the memo to members of the Education Committee I am stressing the strictly confidential nature of it.'[14]

The document in question was a lengthy booklet of some 70 pages.[15] It covered full-time and day continuation schools, the youth service, further education, university entrance, child health, teacher recruitment and training, local education administration, the dual system and the financing of education including teachers' salaries.[16] In effect there was nothing that was revolutionary; rather many of the proposals were seen as moving only a little further than reforms already accepted. Hence the raising of the school leaving age to 15 was suggested now without the exemptions which had attracted such strong criticism a few years earlier. The division of schooling based upon chronological age into primary, secondary and further education rather than the social criteria partly based upon the ability of parents to pay fees or hope that their child might pass a 'scholarship' examination, still faced them with the expenses associated with secondary schools and the sacrifice of potential future earnings. Secondary schooling would be available but divided by selective processes into separate modern, grammar and technical schools. The suggestions for day continuation schools were an attempt to resurrect an idea from the 1918 Education Act whilst ideas concerning the dual system, whatever they might have been, were unlikely to meet the demands of all the contending religious sects.

TUC MEMORANDUM ON EDUCTION AFTER THE WAR

The TUC did not respond to the Board's memo until the following year. The reason for the delay was because very early on they had decided to produce a report of their own. As George Chester, a member of the General Council who had joined the TUCEC in 1939, explained to the 1942 TUC Conference:

> The TUC Education Committee were invited to furnish the Board with whatever observation the General Council desired to make. The Education

committee had therefore before them two responsibilities: one, to prepare their own scheme of educational reconstruction, and the other to furnish the Board of Education with the General Council's view on the private document before them. The Committee felt that they could very well take the two things together, and in replying to the Board enclose their own proposals for educational reform.[17]

The Labour party central committee on reconstruction, chaired by Emmanuel Shinwell with Harold Laski as secretary, had met in July 1941 and set up ten sub-committees to take on domestic concerns including education.[18] The TUC had also been working out its ideas on educational reform for some time. As early as April 1941, R.H. Tawney was writing to Wray to thank him for his offer to send an advanced proof for him to read through. Instead Tawney suggested it would be as well to wait until the report was published and it could then be sent to him care of the British Embassy, Washington, to wait his arrival in early October following his lecture tour of the USA. He also asked for any TUC material on 'social and economic matters' to keep him in touch with events. He wrote:

> I am very sorry to be absent when the Board's proposals are under discussion. Some of them are good, some bad; but I think the whole attitude is 'pre-war' and if adequate then, is quite below the level needed and expected by the public now. I hope the TUC will press in particular for:
> (1) Raising the school leaving age to 16, not 15.
> (2) Establishment of half-time continued education 16–18 years.
> (3) The abolition of fees in all secondary schools, including those receiving direct grant.
> (4) The withdrawal of the proposed 'block grant', and the retention of the percentage grant system.

Tawney's letter indicates clearly that already in 1941 his analysis of the Board's proposals believed they were already out of date and it is interesting to see how far his own suggested minimum programme would find a place in what would be considered the widespread reforms of the 1944 Education Act.

Lady Simon had been involved in discussions with J.V.C. Wray, Secretary of the TUCEC and her contribution was acknowledged by the Secretary when he wrote, 'I greatly valued the help and advice you gave me.'[19] In turn she thanked him for the copy of the Memo enclosed stating, 'It is certainly a splendid document to take to America... I assume there will be no opposition to this report or if there is not on important points.'[20] In general her confidence was justified but ghosts in the form of religious disputes from the nineteenth century would return to plague all those trying to provide an improved educational system of schooling for the second half of the twentieth century; the TUC no less than government ministers.

In his opening presidential address to the 1942 Congress Frank Wolstencraft (Woodworkers' Union) drew delegates' attention to the *TUC Memorandum on Education After the War*, reinforcing the main points which he argued were fundamental to a democratic educational system but also to the building of a democratic state. Although he recognised that the reforms they advocated could not be implemented until after the war he emphasised that,

> plans and legislation must be made ready for them now, and certainly before the war ends. If we wait until then before attempting new legislation, it will never reach the statute book, because we shall be beset with other pressing questions and educational reform will be crowded out. I should like to see a Bill introduced before Christmas.[21]

George Chester referred to the education system familiar to many of them as pupils and parents for many of them would have received their own schooling before the passing of the 1918 Education Act:

> Force of circumstances had forced them to witness the development of an educational system which left the majority of our people in a condition of mental starvation. Within that system a wide range of inequalities had been permitted, and insufficiencies and anomalies had been allowed to appear. We had permitted a colossal waste of cultural and human possibility, and had left undeveloped the potential resources of many millions of our people...It was those and other considerations which constituted the background to the discussions of the meetings of the TUC Education Committee, which ultimately resulted in the memo.[22]

Chester was part of that generation of trade unionists who were so aware of the formal education to which they had been denied access by being confined to elementary schooling; angry too that those in power who had received such an education, which they took for granted for both themselves and their children, should resist the changes which would have offered some measure of that to the children of the working class. Writing of Chester a few years later, Arthur Allen, also of the National

Union of Boot and Shoe Operatives, noted, 'He was much too conscious of the handicaps of his youth . . . We have heard him apologize for his want of education when there was not the slightest need to have done so.'[23] It took considerable self-confidence for working-class leaders, let alone ordinary rank-and-file trade unionists, to discuss issues on even terms when confronted by those who had received an expensive public school education and the luxury of three further years full-time study at a university. This helps to explain the strong motive and desire behind consistent efforts of the TUCEC to open up the education system more widely.

The key demands of the TUC Memo were summarised by Chester to TUC delegates as equal opportunities for every child, a 'common school' system in which social distinction and privileges no longer played any part, a change towards the principle of service to the community in place of the competitive motive as the main factor in school life, lifelong education and an education system adequate to the task of creating a real social democracy.[24] The Memo was well received and would have gained unanimous approval but for the opposition by several Roman Catholics to section 9 dealing with the dual system. Initially this appeared like a re-run of Congress education debates during the period 1896–1912, when a small Catholic opposition, led by James Sexton of the Liverpool dockers, had opposed the introduction of secular schooling, a policy partly born out of the frustration of so many aroused by the squabbling between different religious sects. There had never been any chance of their winning the debate and by the 1940s their opposition received even less support.[25]

This time there was a desire to avoid the inevitable disagreements which always emanated from discussions over the role of religious organisations and education but also the recognition that in terms of facilities and equipment the Church schools were most likely to be among the worst in the country. Whether this was due to their education policies or lack of financial funding or commitment was largely academic for most TUC delegates. The TUC spelt out the nature of the problem of the dual system; covering the economic, denominational and position of teachers. To begin with:

> the local authority for elementary education has complete control of the provided schools, the non-provided elementary schools are in the hands of the managers, including the appointment of teachers . . . control of the education authority is limited. The denominations have been unable to finance the building improvements required . . . Of the schools on the Board's black list of schools with defective premises, two-thirds are non-provided schools . . .

[with]... the Hadow scheme for reorganisation, the church schools have again lagged behind.[26]

Given the plans for expansion with the future raising of the school leaving age the Church schools would fall even further behind and to avoid the pupils being disadvantaged the State would have to step in again and bail them out. The reality was that whatever the contribution of religious bodies might have been to schooling in the past, the ever-increasing demands of a modern society were beyond the resources now of voluntary societies. Moreover, and this was to show a measure of insight concerning a problem which would arise at a much later date, unless denominational schools could be fully self-financing they should be taken over by the State, otherwise 'there would seem to be no reason why any and every kind of non-State school should not expect the same kind of aid from public funds which church schools now enjoy'.[27]

The more thorny problem of religious teaching was not side-stepped. 'In the view of the TUC denominational instruction of any kind should not be allowed in State schools... let that rather be done in the home, the Sunday school and the church.' An agreed syllabus was essential and if this took place at the beginning or end of the school day parents could have a choice as to whether their children should participate in denominational teaching. As for the teachers, they were sometimes in a precarious position, for those honestly devoted to a religion could at times receive preference 'which judged on educational standards alone, they would not enjoy'.[28] There were enough anecdotal tales to suggest that this had been the case and suspicions that it continued to be so in certain schools.

Speaking in support of the Memo before Congress Chester only touched briefly on the Dual System although what he had to say was frank enough:

> the dual system during the last quarter of a century had been one of the main handicaps to educational progress. If the system was to be unified, if the objectives the movement sought to foster were to become realities, there could be no place for sectarianism, divided responsibilities and interests. The ethics of social responsibility must take the place of religious dogma. This was not to deny the ethics of Christianity... but that the public moneys subscribed for educational purposes should be wholly spent on the purpose for which it was subscribed.[29]

Not one affiliated trade union spoke against the TUC proposals for the dual system but a number of Catholic delegates speaking in a personal capacity did so. J. Donovan (TGWU) quoted his experience of leaving school at twelve-and-a-half years of age:

> all the education he had received was obtained in an ordinary elementary Catholic school. The building was a poor structure, but at least the standard of education in the school compared with that in any other... He knew the report would go through, but from that moment onwards hundreds of thousands of Catholic trade unionists to Church of England trade unionists in this country... would be critical of Congress and its leadership.[30]

H.E. Mathews from the same union claimed 'Education divorced from moral tyranny was not education at all. It was merely very highly skilled instruction... the effect of State-aided education or instruction was to put into a person to an extraordinary degree the ability to commit the sin of avarice.'[31] M. Walsh (Dyers, Bleachers and Textile Workers) told Congress, 'Catholics would not surrender their schools... [one could] have the finest buildings in the world, with the best educated teachers in the world, but unless permeating through that school was the love of God and the love of one's neighbour, they would not get what they wanted in the final result.'[32] These speeches opposing TUC education policy were weak in fact but strong in rhetoric. In the few areas of Britain where schools were provided for different religious sects, such as Northern Ireland, parts of Scotland and Lancashire there was not too much evidence of neighbourly love between the communities. Indeed in Northern Ireland many of the working class were divided in terms of religious affiliation rather than social class and separate schools played a part in maintaining the separation of communities along such lines in a manner which was foreign to most of the rest of Britain.

The wish for sectarian schooling within the trade union movement was only ever supported by a minority of members. Most believed the key purpose of the school was to provide the information which would allow children to make progress beyond that which had been possible for their parents. Harold Clay (TGWU) pointed out that , 'The majority must rule, though the minority had a right to be heard. But the minority must also accept that view, and not think they were in a position to determine on this and other matters the way the majority should go.'[33] Most delegates wished to concentrate upon the overall policy for progress in education and not get sidetracked into a religious dispute although there were exceptions. F.J. Burrows (NUR) was not so enamoured with Church schools.

> He could speak with some knowledge as a church man, coming from a rural area which had been cursed with the dual system of control... There were

> classes of 50 or 60 pupils, with probably a headmistress who had graduated 30 years before through a training college, and an assistant whose only qualification was that she must be over 18 and vaccinated . . . Non-provided schools furnished neither amenities nor education and cried aloud to heaven as an abomination to be abolished . . . there would be no dissent among the parents . . . What should be got rid of was the interference of the parson.[34]

Chester knew that discussions of religious conviction were futile. 'Many people had been doing that for thirty years, and everyone knew how deeply rooted that conviction was.' Attempts by a few to get Congress to refer the policy document back were overwhelmingly defeated and it was accepted as TUC education policy.

The TUC's pamphlet was generally well received. The NUT wrote to thank them for the copy which had been sent to them and in return sent a copy of their own memorandum on the subject. Frederick Mander wrote, 'I think not more than a cursory examination will be necessary to show you how wide is the area of agreement between our two bodies. The fact that it is so is personally very pleasing to me.'[35] The Chairman of the Conservative party sub-committee on education having seen the Memo asked for a copy and commented in reply,

> May I congratulate you on the admirable good temper and good sense of the Memorandum? In doing so, I must of course not be understood to imply that I agree with everything contained within it, but it does appear to me that over a very large measure of the whole field the views in the Memo may expect to command fairly general agreement.[36]

He went on to explain that his Committee had also produced a pamphlet on 'Educational aims' concerned with general principles rather than details and enclosed a copy, not expecting the TUC in return to agree with all the points made, 'But I hope that the main doctrine of our report will be read sympathetically outside the ranks of our own party.'

Chuter Ede asked the TUC for more copies explaining he had given his to 'an ecclesiastic who came here saying that Congress had decided in favour of the exclusion of religious teaching in schools'. He continued, 'May I be allowed to say that I think the document was an exceedingly statesmanlike one and that while on details I may be at variance with it I believe it to be most helpful in its general trend.'[37] R.A. Butler had a personal message conveyed to Mr F. Wolstencraft, President of the Congress, to the effect that he looked forward with great interest to having the valuable report of the TUC.[38]

The TUC memo was widely circulated to libraries, the WEA, teachers' organisations, Working Men's Club and Institute Union, the NCLC, International Friendship League, numerous individuals and overseas to widely different organisations such as the American Youth for Democracy and the New South Wales Government. Some of these in return sent copies of their own plans for future post-war education. Many wrote in praise of the TUC Memo's contents; for example, trades councils at Blaydon, Chelmsford, Sheffield, Slough and Wallasey, the Radio Officers' Union and the Co-operative Union. The few replies of a critical nature came from Roman Catholic groups; the Birmingham Catholic Teachers' Association 'disapproves of all references to voluntary schools', the Liverpool Board for Catholic Action who 'deplored the Church section of an otherwise excellent memorandum', the Bolton Catholics who 'regret all references to dual control' and Fife Catholic Trade Unionists.[39] The TUC responded by issuing Circular No. 7 to all trades councils and affiliated unions clarifying the TUC position,

> urging that the misinterpretation of the TUC Programme should be corrected whenever the need might arise. They explained their key proposals pointing out there was nothing anti-religious in the TUC proposals and that the only motive regarding church schools was to promote equality of opportunity for all children, something they believed could not be achieved under a dual plan.[40]

There would be no solution to the religious dispute in education which would accommodate all parties.

As a generalisation it would be true to say that the minority of trade unionists who were supporters of sectarian schools at Congress came from Catholic areas in Lancashire. They continued to try to change TUC Education Policy. G. Gardner (Preston Weavers Association) for example spoke out in support of such schools at some length until Anne Loughlin (Tailors and Garment Workers) in the chair intervened to refer him to paragraph 80 of the General Council's Report pointing out that both sides of the argument had been put and that Congress had overwhelmingly approved the TUC Memorandum. Therefore, 'It was impossible at that Congress to re-argue something which had been decided last year, and there was no resolution on the agenda upon which to make the point.'[41]

When the debate upon the Government's White Paper took place T. Yates (Card and Blowing Room Operatives, SE Lancashire) was quick to return to the religious issue claiming that the aims were to squeeze out the Denominational Schools; 'it was unreasonable to expect...in a period of four or five years to find the money to recast and reorganise the whole system'. The reality was that the record of the denominational schools for Hadow reorganisation from 1926 onwards was a poor one; a point G. Cole (ETU) was to make in reply. He represented the thinking of so many when he stated, 'Congress is not against religion as such but against the system that permitted differences to stand in the path of the child's future...Congress policy should be public money, public control.'[42]

NOTES AND REFERENCES

1. Gosden, P.H.J.H. (1976) *Education in the Second World War: A Study in Political Administration*, p.329.
2. Gosden, P.H.J.H., *Education in the Second World War*, Pt. III, and (1995) 'Putting the Act Together' *History of Education*, Vol. 24, No.3; Jeffereys, K. (1984) 'R.A. Butler, the Board of Education and the 1944 Education Act' *History*, Vol. 69; Middleton, N. (1972) 'Lord Butler and the Education Act of 1944, *British Journal of Educational Studies*, Vol. XX, No. 2; Simon, B. (1986) 'The 1944 Education Act; A Conservative Measure?' *History of Education*, Vol. 15, No. 1; Wallace, R.C. (1981) 'The Origins and Authorship of the 1944 Education Act', *History of Education*, Vol. 10, No. 4.
3. Wallace, R.G. 'The Origins', p.283.
4. Jeffereys, K., 'R.A. Butler', p.417.
5. Gosden, P.H.J.H., *Education in the Second World War*, p.196.
6. Simon, B. (1985) 'Can Education Change Society?' in Simon, B. (ed.) *Does Education Matter?*
7. Wallace R.G. (1981) 'The Origins', pp.284–285.
8. Middleton, N. and Weitzman, S. (1976) *A Place For Everyone*, p.267.
9. Gosden, P.H.J.H., *Education in the Second World War*, pp.243–6.
10. Taylor, A.J.P., *English History 1914–1945*, p.567
11. Wallace, R.G. (1980) 'Labour, The Board of Education and the Preparation of the 1944 Act' Ph.D. (London) p.47.
12. Gosden, P.H.J.H., *Education in the Second World War*, p.248.
13. M. Holmes to H. Ramsbotham 29.1.1941, quoted in Gosden P.H.J.H. *Education in the Second World War*, p.251. Gosden's study provides details of the views contributed by those involved in the BOE's Reconstruction Committee drafting of the Green Book, pp.237–67.
14. W. Citrine to R.A. Butler 25.9.1941, TUC 810.25 (1).
15. It is reprinted in full in an appendix in Middleton N. and Weitzman, S. *A Place for Everyone*, pp.389–462.

16. The memorandum is examined in detail in Middleton N. and Weitzman, S. *A Place for Everyone*, Pt. 2, Ch. VII.
17. *TUC Report 1942*, p.212
18. Clegg, H. (1994) *A History of British Trade Unions Since 1889 Vol III 1934–1951*, pp.270–1
19. J.V.C. Wray to Lady Simon, 25.8.1942, TUC 810.25 (1).
20. Lady Simon to J.V.C. Wray 27.8.1942, TUC 810.25(1).
21. *TUC Report 1942*, pp.12–13.
22. Ibid., p.212
23. Fox, A. (1958) *A History of the National Union of Boot and Shoe Operatives 1874–1957*, p.641.
24. *TUC Report 1942*, p.213.
25. Griggs, C. (1983) *The Trades Union Congress and the Struggle for Education 1868–1925*, Ch. 3.
26. *TUC Memorandum on Education After the War*, p.22.
27. Ibid., p.23.
28. Ibid., p.24.
29. *TUC Report 1942*, p.214.
30. Ibid., p.218.
31. Ibid., p.219.
32. Ibid., p.221.
33. Ibid., p.220.
34. Ibid., p.219.
35. F. Mander to W. Citrine 28.8.1942, TUC 810.25 (1).
36. G. Faber to W. Citrine 9.9.1942, TUC 810.25 (1).
37. J.C. Ede to W. Citrine 15.10.1942. TUC 810.25 (1).
38. *TUCEC Mins.*, 11.9.1942.
39. Ibid., 16.3.1943.
40. *TUC Report 1943*, pp.62–3.
41. Ibid., p.178.
42. Ibid., p.186.

CHAPTER 8

NORWOOOD AND RECONSTRUCTION

THE NORWOOD REPORT

Given that the Spens Report of 1938 had reported on examinations it is not easy to understand why the Board of Education should have set up a committee to examine this area again, among other aspects of secondary education. Furthermore, it was not the independent Consultative Committee of the Board of Education which had produced the major inter-war reports such as the two Hadow Reports of 1926 and 1931, or Spens, but the Secondary Schools Examination Council, whose chairperson, Cyril Norwood was asked to set up a small committee 'to consider suggested changes in the secondary school curriculum and the question of school examinations in relation thereto'. Norwood was another traditionalist; Merchant Taylors School and Oxford, Classics teacher at Leeds Grammar School, head teacher at Bristol Grammar School, followed by teaching at Marlborough and a headship at Harrow, during which time he was initiated into the Freemason lodge of the school.[1] He believed, '...it was the duty of the working class to know their place and to obey those in positions of authority...girls should be educated quite differently from boys. "The majority will eventually marry. At school they are taught exactly as if they were going to university".'[2] By now he was President at St John's College, Oxford University. He had written in favour of the elementary school system provided for the majority of children: 'Incomplete as it is, elementary education has become a steadily civilising agency. It has, I think, been the main influence which has prevented Bolshevism, Communism, and theories of revolt and destruction from obtaining any real hold upon the people of this country.'[3]

Simon has described the setting up of the Committee as devious because its existence was kept secret for ten months before Butler informed parliament, its report went straight to Butler instead of the Secondary School Examination Council of which it was a sub-committee, and when objections were raised they were ignored.[4] When one considers the motives of some of those involved within the Board of Education to retain at all costs selective grammar schools and the public schools by conceding other areas which the conservative-minded had resisted for so many years it is difficult not to see the Norwood Committee as a part of that thinking. G.G. Williams and F.R.G. Duckworth alongside W.F. Williams were appointed assessors. The Secretary was R.H. Barrow, Inspector of Classics, nominated by G.G. Williams and Duckworth for the post and well known to Norwood as both were based at Oxford, which provided the former with considerable influence, especially given his friendship with Norwood.[5] The 12 members of the Committee included representatives of two secondary school teachers' associations, Miss. O.M. Hastings of the Association of Assistant Mistresses and A.W.S. Hutchings of the Association of Assistant Masters, but nobody from the larger NUT; two head teachers, Miss M.G. Clarke of Manchester High School for Girls and Dr Terry Thomas of Leeds Grammar; and representatives of the Examining Boards. When Butler raised the matter of representatives from outside the selective school system G.G. Williams' response was that Duckworth, who had been chief inspector of secondary schools and was now senior chief inspector, could be relied upon to make sure the views of elementary and technical school branches were considered.[6]

It is quite clear that Norwood wished to widen the brief of the Committee and gained Butler's approval for so doing. They were aware that they ran the risk of being seen to go into the territory regarded by Will Spens as his area of interest and of contradicting a report by the Board's own consultative committee, a question which would be raised by the TUC with Butler, and to some extent this is what happened. As McCulloch has shown, past views which implied that Spens and Norwood could be seen as following largely a pattern of progressive linear development in the field of secondary schooling, are not really valid. The uncertainty expressed by Spens was to a large extent absent from the Norwood Report which strongly favoured traditional secondary schooling.[7]

Initially there was some tension between the Norwood Committee and the TUCEC due to the method adopted by the former. The Committee adopted a procedure of seeking evidence from a considerable number of associations and individuals. To ascertain preliminary thinking they devised a questionnaire but instead of distributing this to all parties chose to send certain questions to some and different questions to others. This was considered unacceptable to the TUCEC and on 26 February 1942 J.V.C. Wray wrote to the Committee protesting about this behaviour. Barrow, the Secretary, wrote from Oxford:

> I should explain that the Committee proposes to take evidence from a large number of Associations and individuals representing many different interests. For this purpose a long list of questions was drawn up, some relating to highly specialised matters and capable of answer only by persons with special experience, others relating to broad issues. To none of the Associations or individuals consulted has the full list of questions been sent, and it appears to have been generally understood that the selected questions were those on which the Committee felt it would like to have the views of the body consulted. I am to assure you therefore that the omitted questions are by no means necessary, or indeed closely related to the questions sent to the Trades Union Congress; and, since the complete list has not been sent to any body or individual, it cannot now be sent to the Trades Union Congress.[8]

The dispute now moved up a gear. Instead of Wray writing again Citrine took up the matter and wrote directly to Butler. A substantial part of this letter is worth quoting because it covers both the matter of the questionnaire, and just as important, questions the manner in which the Norwood Committee's terms of reference were being notably exceeded:

> I really must draw your attention to the way in which your Committee on Curriculum and Examinations is proceeding, and I must lodge a protest. The Committee has written to us asking if we will help it in its work by furnishing replies to a Questionnaire. The questionnaire sent to us contained questions ranging from number 1 to number 15, but questions 2 to 5 and question 9 were omitted. It was, moreover, obvious that there might be more questions than 15 in the complete document. Not caring for this selective method of obtaining the views of interested witnesses, we wrote to the Secretary of the Committee and asked for a complete copy...I thought it was our job to judge what questions we would answer, – not the Committee's. I have this morning had a letter from the Secretary to the Committee, a copy of which I enclose. I do not for a moment accept the argument contained in it. Let me give one instance only of the manner in

which the Committee's method of selection has been applied. In questions 7 and 8 we are asked whether we consider that enough scholarship assistance is already available to enable all pupils who can derive full benefit from University education to receive it, and whether the present system affords equal opportunity as between one area and another. The next question (Number 9), reads as follows:

Do you suggest changes in the methods by which such assistance is now made available?

This question is omitted from our copy of the questionnaire. Why, if we are judged competent to answer questions 7 and 8, are we not allowed to express a view on question 9? I have seen other questions omitted from our copy of the questionnaire in which my Education Committee will certainly be interested, and on which they will wish to express a view. But even now I know that I have not seen all the questions contained in a complete copy of this Committee's questionnaire.

If your Committee is to proceed on the basis of a questionnaire formulated by itself, I think we have the right to see the whole questionnaire, and to make our own selection of those questions on which we wish to express an opinion...

As to the terms of reference of the Committee, I am much disturbed to see that in their letter inviting replies to their questionnaire they say that 'while the reference put before the Committee is of a limited nature, the Committee find it impossible to review the subject of the Curriculum and Examinations of Secondary Schools without first considering the lay-out and organisation of Secondary Education in general, and it is with this in view that questions of a broad scope are included in the questionnaire'. In effect this means that the Committee is re-opening the whole territory of the Spens Report. The Spens Report was drawn up by a Committee which had, in the course of its work, made a complete review of the public education system; a Committee which had on it not only those directly concerned in the operation of the education system such as teachers and administrators, but also educationists of very wide interest and outlook, and commanding the confidence of the non-professional interests concerned in educational planning.

I must submit very strongly that the Committee on Curriculum and Examinations is not a Committee which we should approve for the purpose of re-opening the Spens Report. If the terms of reference given to the Curriculum and Examinations Committee are to be interpreted and extended, as has been done, by that Committee, then I do not see why the reference itself was not given to your Consultative Committee. It certainly seems to me no less a body is entitled to review the Spens and related Reports.

I appreciate the difficulty the Curriculum and Examinations Committee will have in dealing with their terms of reference, unless they are clearly told what kind of secondary schools they are to contemplate in framing their proposals. But the point is that the Committee should be told this, and should not be left to make up its own mind what the secondary school system of the future ought to be. Judging from the questionnaire – so far as I have seen it – the Committee is clearly indulging in this kind of speculation, which, as I have suggested above, is the rightful ground of the Consultative Committee. You yourself know our wide and real interest in educational questions. The Committee on Curriculum and Examinations seems to take a very narrow view of our interests, and is to   that extent misinformed. I shall not communicate further with the Committee until I hear from you, but I think when next I write, I might send the Secretary a copy of our Statement on the Spens Report as indicating the nature of our educational interests. In the meantime I enclose a copy for your own information.[9]

Within days Butler had replied to Citrine informing him that he had written to Sir Cyril Norwood and 'he has replied that he will have the full questionnaire sent to you, so that your Congress may give the Committee the benefit of its views on all or any of the questions'. This issue raised by the TUC was therefore easily resolved but as to the central political question of the future secondary school system Butler sought to assure Citrine:

But you need have no fear that this Committee is going to re-plough the whole field covered by the Consultative Committee. The idea rather is that they should preface their report with a preliminary section describing the background against which their conclusions have to be viewed. Most of this section will consist of material on which there already is a wide measure of agreement, but there may be some points on which the Committee can usefully contribute towards the framing of policy as seen from the particular angle of curriculum and examinations.[10]

Citrine thanked Butler for intervening to provide a complete copy of the Questionnaire to the TUCEC but still expressed reservations about the Committee's work.

I welcome your assurance that the Committee on Curriculum and Examinations is not to re-plough the whole field covered by the Consultative Committee. For the reasons I have explained...we should take a strong line against any such policy. I am still not easy in my mind on this point, and sincerely hope that the Committee will not be found to have wandered too far afield when it presents its report.[11]

That the TUC had been correct in guessing that the questionnaire exceeded 15 questions was made clear when the full document was received by the TUCEC; there were 35 questions, those beyond 15 dealing with the aims of a secondary school, the curriculum, external examinations and other forms of assessment, homework and the training of teachers. The questionnaire incident illustrates the high-handed approach of the Norwood Committee, and their perception of the value of the contribution trade unionists could make to proposed reform in secondary education. Butler's intervention also shows the change in attitude towards trade unionists which the war had brought about: it was no longer possible to ignore the views of working people who were so fully involved in the defence of the country. At least not in such a public manner.

It is difficult to believe that the Norwood Committee were unaware of TUC Education Policy, not least because G.G. Williams had been closely involved with the Spens Committee which had sought responses from Congress during its deliberations. The copies of the TUC statement on Spens sent to Butler and Norwood would act as a reminder of their understanding of the public system of education through which they had all passed. How far the reading of this Statement would influence the thinking of the Committee was another matter. It is likely that the dominant members of the Norwood Committee, namely Norwood and G.G. Williams, had largely decided the outcome they desired and were reluctant to entertain views contrary to their own. Barrow doubted the wisdom of 'further consultations with various interested parties, he wondered where the process of seeking advice would end',[12] whilst Norwood never entertained any doubts as to the validity of his own ideas.[13]

There were questions from Norwood on which the TUC did not venture an opinion: the extent to which pupils in secondary schools might be subjected to serious injury; whether secondary schools 'stand too much upon the ancient ways'; the place of external examinations in art, music, handicraft and domestic subjects; the suitability of certain university courses for potential secondary school teachers. Some questions received a simple reply. Secondary education should begin at 11+ but the age of transfer should be 13. This reflects thinking quite prevalent at the time that all pupils should receive a common two-year course whatever the type of secondary school they attended and only then should the suggestion of different courses be contemplated. It was no surprise for the Norwood Committee to read that the TUC did not believe there were enough state scholarships for university places, they were opposed to fees for secondary schooling and that they believed there was inequality of opportunity for children between different areas. They disagreed that the main purpose of the secondary grammar school was to prepare pupils for university, professional and business careers; rather it was to prepare pupils for life. Why should pupils from other schools not aspire to such careers? The implication that the jobs, life styles and destinies of adults should be decided by the educational paths they were assigned to as children permeated several of the questions of the Norwood Committee:

> Q.14:   In what ways can education in secondary schools in rural areas help to solve the problem of retaining sufficient numbers of men and women on the land engaged in agricultural and related work?
>
> TUC Reply: We do not think it should be any part of the aim of rural secondary schools 'to solve the problem of retaining sufficient numbers of men and women on the land'. The solution of the problem depends on very much more than the nature of secondary school education in rural areas, and for our part we should strongly oppose any system of predestination such as is suggested in this question.[14]

TUC Policy on multilateral schools was quite clear. 'We strongly support the idea of the multilateral school and hope that extensive experiments will be made.'[15]

The Norwood Report was published in July 1943 but unlike most previous reports no comment was made upon it in the Annual Report of the TUC's Conference in September at Southport. In fact at a meeting of the TUCEC the following month, having resumed their consideration of the Norwood Report and welcomed at least the proposals for reform of the examination system in secondary schools, they decided 'It was not necessary to publish any statement on this Report.'[16] It could be that this was because attention now needed to be focussed upon what was considered to be more important; the Government's White Paper on Education Reconstruction which had just been published and directly pointed to the thinking behind a new Education Act.

In reality neither Spens nor Norwood could be termed radical reports. The idea of secondary schooling for all had long been conceded; as had the raising of the school leaving age. The real question was what form these would take. Multilateral schools had been considered by both and, whilst not dismissed out of hand, the fact was they could not really run alongside a selective system of secondary schooling and it was support for the selective grammar school in particular which was favoured overwhelmingly by the Board of Education. Hence multilateral schooling did not receive the support it might otherwise have gained at the time.

By contrast, proposals for changes to the examination system were in many respects progressive and Barrow believed they were resisted by 'the very people who are conservative and over-cautious who need to be jolted violently out of their rut;'[17] yet he could not seem to grasp that in terms of the secondary school proposals a similar charge could just as easily have been made concerning his views and those of the Committee.

The tripartite secondary school system suggested by the Norwood Committee, which argued that there were three types of children who could be fitted into three types of secondary school, was based upon an attempt to categorise the aptitude and 'innate' intelligence of children in a way which seemed to owe something to Plato's men of Gold, Silver and iron and bronze, perhaps a reflection of many of the Committee members' studies of the Classics. Even more it could be related to the 1868 Taunton Report's division of secondary education according to the social situation of a pupil's parents which would determine the length of time a boy (no mention is made of girls) would remain at school; first grade for those staying at school until 18 years of age and contemplating further education, second grade for those leaving at 16 and third for those leaving at 14. A different curriculum is recommended for each category which will obviously lead them to the appropriate occupations associated with their parents' position in society.

Norwood's categories would also prove to be self-fulfilling; 'the pupil who is interested in learning for its own sake, who can grasp an argument or follow a piece of connected reasoning, who is interested in causes... [and]... the pupil whose interests and abilities lie markedly in the field of applied science or applied art'.[18] These two categories were in crude terms considered the academic and technical but that still left the majority of children unaccounted for so they were considered en masse as a third general category: 'the pupil in this group deals more easily with concrete things than with ideas...he finds little attraction in the past...His mind must turn its knowledge or its curiosity to immediate test; and his test is essentially practical.' The more one reads of the descriptions of the pupils placed into these three categories the more surprising it is that such unsubstantiated generalisations could be the product of a report by what were considered well-educated people. There was not a shred of substantial evidence from either the fields of psychology or educational research to provide any foundation for such statements. Masquerading as a carefully considered report based upon a broad range of evidence submitted from a wide range of organisations, including those representing the educational world, the statements about children provided a recipe for a system of secondary educational and social apartheid.

WHITE PAPER ON EDUCATIONAL RECONSTRUCTION

The White Paper on Educational Reconstruction was published on 16 July 1943, several days before the appearance of the Norwood Report. As Butler and the civil servants at the Board of Education had been involved with both there were no real surprises. The shape of future secondary schooling was to be that outlined by the Norwood Report although the language used was softer and the divisiveness made less explicit. 'After 11, secondary education, of diversified types but equal standing, will be provided for all children.'[19]

It is possible to place the proposals into a series of categories: those finally granted at the end of the inter-war period, such as raising of the school leaving age to 15; those which arose out of the pressures of a nation in which almost everyone was needed in some way for war-time production, such as the promise of nursery schools provided by local authorities; items which owed their introduction to the demands of organised labour, especially secondary education for all; and those which could be seen as the result of pressures by traditional forces, especially the defence of the grammar schools. Finally, there were those areas of privileged education removed from discussion altogether, the public schools, except the suggestion that they be registered and inspected.

Citrine wrote to Butler inviting the Board of Education to attend the September 1943 TUC Conference at which the White Paper was to be discussed.[20] The invitation was accepted and G.W. Buckle, divisional inspector, arranged to attend the educational debate.[21] The TUC's response to the White Paper was favourable as far as the total contents were concerned: 'The General Council welcome the forward march in educational affairs proposed in the Government's White Paper...The Government plans accept in principle many of the major reforms for which all progressive educationists have been fighting for so long.'[22] They listed these items: raising of the school leaving age to 15, and subsequently 16; secondary education under a single code for all children; the abolition of the special place examinations and fees in maintained secondary schools; introduction of day continuation schools; obligations for LEAs to provide nursery schools; and throughout the age considered – from 5 to 18 – free medical inspection and treatment to be provided. It would be difficult to assess the contents as anything other than progressive, even if they were the culmination of so much struggle in the past by the TUC and those who might be considered allies in educational policies, in face of sustained resistance by the forces of conservatism.

This positive reception to the proposals was not uncritical. 'Unfortunately, the welcome given to these proposals, though genuine cannot be unqualified. Some important criticisms of the White Paper must be made, but the General Council are anxious that it should be understood that their criticism is offered in the hope of improving the Government's proposals and not with the intention of obstructing such educational advance as is outlined in the White Paper.'[23] A series of critical points were made commencing with the belief that, 'The Government have adopted a far too leisurely approach to the whole question of reform. This ill fits the necessities and temper of the times, and lags a long way behind the large body of public opinion which is eager that the opportunity for reconstructing our educational system should be grasped now.'[24] The TUC were anxious that at least a start should be made to implementing the proposals before the War ended as they had become aware that the raising of the school leaving age to 15 would not take place for 18 months and no fixed date had been given to an extension to 16. Not only would this leave children aged 14 to 15 on the labour market but 'Until there is a common leaving age there can be no equality between the different types of secondary school, nor indeed will any adequate secondary education be possible.'[25] These would be the educational measures which would effect the largest number of children.

Similarly, delays to plans for continuation schools were noted, as was the silence on the issue of direct grant grammar schools. It was recognised that the question of dual control remained contentious. There was no wish 'that this ancient controversy should be allowed to wreck or to retard the promise of educational advance on a wide front'. The TUC's view was clear: if denominational bodies wish to have their own schools they should pay all the costs involved and that in an area where a denominational school was the only one this was a most unsatisfactory situation. However, whilst maintaining this philosophy they were willing to support a compromise which would provide adequate LEA control of educational provision in an area '... and would not propose to press their view to the point of defeating a Bill, the other provisions of which were sufficiently attractive and sufficiently specific'.[26]

The debate at Congress on the White Paper reflected the TUC's original response to the document with G.W. Thomson of the General Council and chairperson of the TUCEC introducing the Report repeating the organisation's general support whilst drawing attention to 'certain grave defects in that document' and emphasising their concern. 'A good reform was never half so good as it might be if it was given tardily and too late, and that was one of the complaints about the proposals.'[27] He pointed to the ability of the State to act quickly in undertaking difficult tasks of organisation, like provision of equipment and training of personnel in preparation for the battles of North Africa and Sicily, and suggested similar efforts could be made to build a new system of education. H.E. Clay (TGWU) enlarged on some aspects of the White Paper, focusing upon fears arising from the results of earlier legislation.

> We had some experience of the Hadow reorganisation. Some authorities had done very well, some had done less well, and some had done nothing at all. Those people who had wished to press for reorganisation had been told there were no buildings, no teachers and no equipment. That was precisely what would happen in regard to the White Paper if the Movement was not careful.[28]

Both Thomson and Clay told delegates they believed Butler was interested in education and wished for the proposals in the White Paper to be implemented, but Clay gave a warning. '... behind Mr Butler there was a body of opinion that rendered lip service to democracy and freedom during the war but paid little regard to it when the country was not at war. That was an element which the Trade Union Movement had got to watch.'[29]

NOTES AND REFERENCES

1. Rich P.J. (1989) *Elixir of Empire: English Public Schools, Ritualism, Freemasonry and Imperialism*, p.84.
2. See McCulloch, G. (1991) *Philosophers and Kings: Education for Leadership in Modern England*, pp.46–7.
3. 'The English Tradition of Education' (1929) quoted in Gordon P., Aldrich, R. and Dean D. (1991) *Education and Policy in England in the Twentieth Century*, p.181.
4. Simon, B. (1991) *Education and the Social Order*, pp.60–4.
5. Wallace, R.G. (1981) 'The Origins and Authorship of the 1944 Education Act', *History of Education*, Vol. 10, No. 4, p.112.
6. Ibid., p.114.
7. McCulloch, G. (1993) '"Spens v. Norwood": Contesting the Educational State?', *History of Education*, Vol. 22, No. 2.

8. R.H. Barrow to J.V.C. Wray, 2.3.1942, *PRO ED/12/478*.
9. W. Citrine to R.A. Butler, 2.3.1942, *PRO ED/12/478*.
10. R.A. Butler to W. Citrine, 6.3.1942, *PRO ED/12/478*.
11. W. Citrine to R.A. Butler, 9.3.1942, *PRO ED/12/478*.
12. Gosden, P.H.J.H. (1976) *Education in the Second World War*, p.385
13. Ibid., p.386.
14. Norwood Committee Questionnaire, p.3. *PRO ED 12/479*.
15. Ibid.
16. *TUCEC Mins.*, 20.10.1943.
17. Gosden, P.H.J.H. (1976) *Education in the Second World War*, p.385
18. *Norwood Report 1943*, Ch.1., pp.1–15.
19. *White Paper on Reconstruction 1943*, para. 15
20. W. Citrine to R.A. Butler, 30.7.1943, *PRO ED 136/421*.
21. R.A. Butler to W. Citrine, 3.8.1943; Buckle to Miss Goodfellow, 8.9.1943. *PRO ED 136/421*.
22. *TUC Report 1943*, p.64 and *PRO ED/136/421*.
23. *TUC Report 1943*.
24. Ibid.
25. Ibid., p.65.
26. Ibid., p.66.
27. Ibid., p.181.
28. Ibid., pp.183–4.
29. Ibid., p.184.

CHAPTER 9

PRESSURE GROUPS AND THE 1944 EDUCATION ACT

COUNCIL FOR EDUCATIONAL ADVANCE

It is necessary to go back to 1942 in order to deal with an educational pressure group in which the TUC played an important role. The Council for Educational Advance (CEA) was formed in November of that year. It came about as the result of an approach by the WEA to the TUC, Co-operative Union and NUT to form a pressure group to campaign on educational issues, because there was general agreement between these bodies as had been demonstrated by their joint deputation to the Board of Education in the previous February.[1] Its progressive programme was inevitable given the CEA executive which included R.H. Tawney, Arthur Creech Jones (Labour MP for Shipley), Harold Clay (TUC), Lady Simon (Labour Party's Advisory Committee on Education) and Richard Crossman, a journalist with the *New Statesman*. Butler's address to the 1942 NUT Conference prompted the WEA to convene a meeting which duly took place in July attended by 300 delegates, most of whom came from the four organisations, although there were later protests from or on behalf of organisations not invited, such as the Assistant Masters' Association and the National Council of Women.[2] The similarity of the educational policies of the four bodies involved made agreement between them easy so that there was no real wish to include members who might disagree with fundamental aspects of their policy. The joint four provided the finance for the CEA and circulars were sent out in January 1943 by the TUC to affiliated trade unions and trades councils inviting co-operation with it and encouraging such organisations to campaign locally.

A joint deputation visited Butler on 22 January 1943 and by the autumn about 200 meetings and conferences had been held throughout the country. The NUT offered space in its headquarters for the CEA and use of its publishing and distribution facilities, 'which at the height of the educational campaign meant publishing and circulating some quarter of a million leaflets'.[3]

The leading figures were in influential positions. Tawney was leader writer on educational matters for the *Manchester Guardian*, Creech Jones private secretary to Ernest Bevin, one of the most powerful members of the Cabinet, and Harold Dent was editor of the *Times Educational Supplement*. Its contacts with prominent public figures from Citrine to Temple, Archbishop of Canterbury, gave it national recognition and status. The 12-point programme adopted at its second meeting in September 1942 was identical to TUC education policy; such as raising of the school leaving age to 15 without exemptions, and to 16 not more than three years later. Letters to the press, including an article by Tawney in the *Manchester Guardian*, requested an early Education Bill for fear that if left much later education reform would be pushed aside in the face of numerous other demands upon resources once the war ended; a view which would be repeated by many people over the next year or so. Indeed, Butler told a deputation from the CEA that 'the extent of what could be achieved directly after the war would have to be related to other measures of reform'.[4] The CEA continued with their activities, producing two leaflets in 1943, 'The New Britain and the Children' and 'The School Leaving Age and Educational Opportunity'; the latter in response to a speech made by Butler in May 1943 which ignored the question of raising the school leaving age and referred to part-time continuation from 14 to 18. It is difficult to see this as an oversight on the minister's part, more like an attempt to placate some of the more traditionally minded of the Conservative MPs of the time. Creech Jones' contacts with Bevin proved useful here and a quote from the Minister of Labour was reproduced in the second pamphlet, arguing that if the school leaving age had been raised 20 years earlier 'he would not have had the skilled labour problem of this war...[and]...he had made up his mind to see that in future children should have a fair chance'.[5]

Butler sent invitations to R.H. Tawney, Ronald Gould, the General Secretary of the NUT and Harold Clay of the TUCGC to attend parliament for the debate on the White Paper, much of the content of which led to enthusiastic if not uncritical support from Tawney for 'a plan not a mere collection of belated instalments of long overdue reforms...which would give the nation what it never possessed, an education system'.[6] At the next meeting of the CEA, Wray, the TUCEC Secretary voiced several reservations; the timetable, the proposed settlement with the voluntary schools, and the failure to deal with either fees for direct grant grammar schools or indeed the whole issue of fee-paying schools.

The co-operation between the four organisations which comprised the CEA was not welcomed by all trade unionists. At the autumn TUC Conference of 1943, E. Colham of the Durham Miners, speaking in his personal capacity, condemned the involvement of Congress with the National Union of Teachers: 'the most reactionary organisation in the country. They came to the TUC for assistance in order to gain educational advance, but they would not pay a penny piece to make any effort to affiliate to the TUC, though there was nothing that barred them from affiliation such as barred the Civil Servants and the rest.' The NUT Colham claimed was using the TUC, and 'tomorrow would seek the co-operation of the Conservative or any other party which would give them what they desired'.[7] E. Jennison (AEU) criticised the method by which the TUC had worked to form the CEA which had resulted in the exclusion of the National Council for Labour Colleges (NCLC), considered by many to be the major organisation for the provision of working class education. The relationship between the TUC and NCLC had never been an easy one and there was a history of rivalry and conflicting political ideology between several organisations offering education to trade unionists and adult members of the working class.[8] G.W. Thomson, replying for the TUCGC, stated that the NUT did not ask for any assistance from the TUC whilst the NCLC was left out 'because there was no evidence from the public pronouncements of that body that they were particularly interested in the general education questions necessarily envisaged in an Education Bill, which was a measure of machinery for the general education of the children of the country'.[9] Apparently when a deputation from the NCLC had visited the TUC and been asked if they would accept an invitation if it was offered to join the CEA, Thomson who had chaired that meeting claimed that he was told 'that they could not or would not answer that question'. J.P.M. Millar was to suggest later that this statement was 'seriously misleading'.[10] Even when at the request of the NCLC in Scotland a conference was held with representatives from the Scottish TUC, Labour Party and Labour Colleges, resulting in an invitation for the NCLC to join the Scottish branch of the CEA, the NCLC declined 'in view of the belatedness of the invitation'. No doubt the fact that the chairperson and secretary of the Scottish CEA, respectively, held similar offices in the WEA was also a factor. The reality was that the four organisations within the CEA had programmes so similar in education that joint deputations to the Board of Education were a practical proposition, as were the contents of pamphlets on education matters. By contrast the NCLC disagreed fundamentally with the philosophy and approach of the WEA, which it saw as too closely aligned to and influenced by middle-class academics, knowledgeable in their specialised subjects but not in the life-styles or political needs of the working class.

The CEA were able to gain considerable attention for their education programme between 1942 and 1944. They arranged some 400 meetings in various parts of the country reaching a climax on 12 February 1944 with a meeting in Kingsway Hall, London, at which the Archbishop of Canterbury, H.N. Penlington (NUT treasurer), L.A. Hunt of the Co-operative Union Education Committee and R.H. Tawney of the WEA were on the platform with Citrine in the chair. A resolution was passed giving approval to the Education Bill but wishing it to be strengthened by firm dates being given for raising the school leaving age to 15, then 16.[11] A sub-committee of the CEA met in December to draw up a list of amendments to 'improve' the Bill, most of them similar to TUC concerns over precise dates for action over the school leaving age, abolition of fees in schools supported by public funding, continuation classes at colleges for two days a week and the abolition of all paid child employment.

For all the activity and the publication of a further pamphlet entitled *A New Start in Education*, Butler largely ignored their proposals. Indeed he even decided to postpone the raising of the school leaving age to 15 years. The CEA had by now just about run its course. There would be a protest to the minister when the Fleming Committee Report was published but as a pressure group within education its effectiveness gradually declined.

CONSERVATIVE SUB-COMMITTEE ON EDUCATION 1941–1945

At least some members of the Conservative party realised that they were seen as closely associated with the pre-war conditions of unemployment, means-tested benefits and an obsession with keeping public expenditure on social services to a minimum in order to maintain low levels of taxation. As a crude generalisation this could be seen as favouring the wealthier members of society and showing little concern for the socially disadvantaged. Removing this perception was a key task of the Central Committee on Post-War Problems established in October 1941 under R.A. Butler. A series of sub-committees were devoted to different areas of home policy: agriculture, housing, local government and education. The last mentioned can be seen as a pressure group acting from a right-wing point of view in contrast to the CEA.[12] Butler persuaded the publisher Geoffrey Faber, who had only recently joined the Conservative party, to become chairperson. Butler's aim was 'to secure people to run these committees who are of the Conservative faith but are yet outside the party machine. Those who would be most valuable to help would be controversalists who are known and can break lances with the leading knights of the left.'[13] This was a recognition that since the 1930s, as a result of the economic slump, the rise of Fascism and in particular the Spanish Civil War, so many intellectuals were sympathetic to the political left, providing strength to many of the arguments opposing the forces of Conservatism in society. The success of Victor Gollancz's *Left Book Club* provides a good example of success in the information battle which had no conservative equivalent, and which went some way towards combatting the general Conservative views of most national daily newspapers, especially the *Daily Mail*, *Daily Express*, *Daily Sketch*, *Daily Telegraph* and *The Times*. Things did not proceed smoothly for Faber's sub-committee. An early draft of the first interim report of the sub-committee by Faber entitled *Looking Ahead* was criticised within the group as 'interesting but not acceptable'. It was critical of previous party education policy, the Spens Report and the move towards child-centred learning. Instead it proposed a national education which would encourage pupils to gain 'an ardent understanding of the State needs, and to render him capable of serving those needs'.[14] Favour was shown to religious schools; France, Germany and the USSR were all believed to have suffered from ignoring Christianity, although how this could have been applied to France with its large Roman Catholic population and higher church attendances than in the UK it is not easy to understand. Preference was given to part-time education rather than raising the school leaving age beyond 14 for all. It went on to declare that children 'must be taught to be proud of their ancestors and their inheritance, and to accept the consequent responsibilities of a colonising and missionary world power'.[15]

The second report also published in September 1942, this one largely written by W. Oakeshott, headteacher at St Pauls, entitled *A Plan for Youth*, called for the entry of all 14–18 year olds into organisations designed to give service to the State. This report was also harshly criticised for seeming to advocate the kind of approach to youth training more in keeping with Fascist ideology than that of the schools and youth movements in Britain, such as the Boy Scouts and Girl Guides. It was the compulsory element which brought condemnation from people of a wide spectrum of political beliefs, incensed by the fact that the country was fighting those societies which had developed youth movements which encouraged uncritical support among the young, such as the Hitler Youth Movement in Germany. The most charitable interpretation of Oakeshott's ideas might be that he believed a more organised form of patriotism was necessary to reinforce national opposition to the dictatorships of Germany and Italy which seemed to be so well entrenched. Moreover, it needs to be remembered that whilst voluntary, many of the organised youth movements in the UK, such as the Boys' and Girls' Brigades, at the start, were linked to ideas of militarism in the form of uniforms, ranks and parades. Even the Scouts, the least militaristic by the 1940s, had originally organised the young at times in supportive military roles. Baden-Powell's use of boys as runners in the defence of Mafeking at the turn of the century and his advocacy of the role boys could play in war after the Scout movement was officially launched in 1907 point to an earlier time of imperialism when efforts were made to provide organised youth movements which would encourage support for British military actions.[16] It could be argued that the experiences of the First World War had completely changed such perceptions so that Oakeshott's ideas now seemed to belong to another age.

The two earlier reports of the sub-committee have been seen as a reflection of the back benches of the Conservative party of the time which contained, 'a large number of old die-hard Tories, sure that as soon as the war was finished they would return to a world of privilege ... Their draft was so reactionary that it was not circulated to the public. Finally, after considerable modification had been agreed on Butler's suggestion, a third report was issued in January 1944 under the title *Looking Ahead – The Statutory Education System.*'[17] It was no surprise that the Education Sub-Committee gave strong support to the public school system; of the 365 Tory MPs, most of whom had been elected in 1935, 263 had been to public schools, 29 to grammar schools, whilst not one admitted to attending elementary school.[18] On this evidence not one had any personal experience of the schools attended by the vast bulk of the population. In fact they did not issue a report on these schools for fear of drawing the attention of the labour movement towards them which might lead to searching questions instead of awaiting the report of the Fleming Committee.

The comparative lack of success of the Conservative Sub-Committee on Education was largely due to the fact that the policies advocated were now out of tune with the country's expectations; there was by now little support for a pre-war leaving age of 14, especially as this had already been conceded in 1939. Nor was exemption defensible any longer.

Religious schools were not seen any more as preferable to local authority schools whilst the public schools were beyond the experience of most people. Although there would be attempts a generation later, when the reality of the schooling provided for most children was a distant memory, to regard such schooling as a golden age of education, the contemporary evidence told a different story; in the early years of the war 'mobilization had shown how inadequate and shallow was the service given in the schools. The armed services were handicapped in their training by the virtual illiteracy of some quarter of their recruits',[19] a point which would be confirmed by Bevin with regard to the training of skilled workers on the home front. There is, however, one idea of the sub-committee which would find favour with the Board of Education; namely their concern that the problem for the future was not so much the provision of education for the mass of the population but 'how to make the best of our best material', in other words selection for different types of secondary school. This view would be behind the policy adopted for secondary schooling which would be an area of growing controversy in the years ahead.

R.A. BUTLER AND THE CHURCHES

Those practising a religious faith in Britain during the 1940s were in a minority. Most people saw themselves as nominally Christian but played no part in the activities of the churches as regular worshippers and apart from the ceremonies of marriage, christening and funeral, rarely stepped inside a church. In everyday life Britain was largely a secular society. Religious disputes between different sects were of little concern to most of the population. There were a few areas where there was some conflict between people of different religious beliefs, such as Liverpool and Glasgow – and there was always Northern Ireland where for so many religious bigotry seemed to be endemic. However in general these attitudes were foreign to most of the population where tolerance or indifference to religious doctrines and past squabbles was the norm.

The Roman Catholic Church was smaller in numbers than the other Christian sects but unlike them experiencing steady growth. Whilst Church of England schools dominated rural areas, a reflection of the Victorian age when more people had lived in the countryside and the parish church had been of major influence, Catholic schools were more likely to be in urban areas serving a considerable number of low-income families. The Church of England and Nonconformists had been witnessing a slow decline in their congregations for many years although the Church of England retained an influence out of proportion to its active members. As the Established Church this was to be expected and past power was still reflected in many areas of life: seats in the House of Lords, influence in many of the public schools which were often Anglican, and Church teacher training colleges established during the nineteenth century. A general Christian influence also permeated other organisations such as the armed forces, youth movements and BBC broadcasting.

At the TUC there had been little support for religious schools except where they were willing to provide their own financial support. Enough, however, to witness emotional pleas from some delegates for special consideration; a foretaste of the pressures Butler would face from competing groups wishing to be seen as 'special cases'. Solving this problem to the satisfaction of all would be impossible. The question which awaited an answer was how Butler would deal with the different and often conflicting secular and religious interests.

In terms of buildings and resources the schools of religious societies were in a poorer state of repair than council schools. The division between religious and council schools was wasteful and educationally unsound. Many Church schools were too small to be economically efficient and lacked the number of staff necessary to provide the range of teaching required. The movement of population from rural to urban areas had been continuing throughout the inter-war period so that many were serving a declining school population. Yet they were reluctant to allow older pupils to move to larger council secondary schools in the nearby towns. In rural areas, frequently the only school available was one managed by the Church of England which provided a Hobson's choice for parents who were not members of this faith but hesitated to exercise their right to withdraw their children from religious assembly due to the social pressure which might accompany such action in a small village. Teachers' organisations disliked the power held by clerics and their supporting school managers because religious tests put teachers who were not of the school's faith at a disadvantage when seeking employment, or in some cases encouraged a measure of dishonesty.

As for the Roman Catholics their approach was that religion and education could not be separated and therefore the two went together. They wished for financial support from the State but wished to retain complete control over their schools and the appointment of staff. Their uncompromising stance was bound to make negotiations in planning the future education system extremely difficult and was a main source of bitter remarks in debates over the religious issue. They sent copies of their pamphlets arguing their case to the TUCEC, among which was one reprinted from *The Tablet* (16 October 1943) entitled 'Catholics and the White Paper on Educational Reconstruction' and another called 'The Catholic Claim for Justice'. Most organisations within the labour movement were reluctant to be drawn into sectarian disputes which they saw as divisive, unhelpful and likely to detract from the main educational aims they were pursuing. One exception to this approach was the response of the National Association of Labour Teachers. In their 'Bulletin' of December 1943, with reference to Roman Catholic opposition to the Education Bill they launched into an attack upon the Church drawing attention to

> its international scope – its world wide political power – the inner meaning of the Catholic agitation over their schools during the past few months to enlist world Catholicism on their side. It is not an exaggeration to say that their deliberate and calculated lying statements about the NUT, and even Mr Butler were designed with an eye upon world catholicism more than with the simple demand for justice at home.[20]

The Labour MPs Stokes (Ipswich) and Tinker tried to dominate the education debate at every opportunity pressing to move amendments to increase State aid to Catholic schools: '[they] had more to say in Committee than most other Labour MPs, including the party's front-bench spokesmen'.[21] In fact the Labour Education Sub-Committee had favoured a unified State system with common standards of education and culture since at least 1942 and whilst they were in favour of religious instruction of an 'ethical nature' it needed to be put into the context of personal, 'social, economic and international relations'.[22] Alec Walkden, Labour MP for Bristol South, who had represented the Railway Clerks Association at the TUC where he had been on the GC from 1921–35, wrote to Citrine,

> We had decided to support the Minister but he had a bad time for the first two hours. Eleven speakers tried, on behalf of the Roman Catholics to 'get him down'. Three were Labour men; one (Joe Tinker) spoke from conviction and two (Brown and Beaumont) from 'sheer political expediency', which being interpreted to honest men, means fear of losing Catholic votes.[23]

Citrine assured Walkden that he did indeed represent the TUC approach to the issue[24] but a letter in the Catholic *Universe* (10 March 1944) criticised Walkden for an anti-Catholic speech in which he 'opposed Catholic amendments to the Bill'.

The dual system originating from nineteenth-century developments in education stood in the way of educational progress because religious organisations could not provide the resources necessary for modern schooling requirements and sometimes resulted in the best-qualified teacher being denied a position because of the system by which preference was given to another candidate who was of the required religious faith.

More than 80 per cent of all religious schools belonged to the Church of England. Given the number of schools they managed they were the major organisation which had to be convinced of any new proposals for schooling in the country. The Church of England was no longer the force for conservatism in social and political affairs it once had been. The change in attitudes of the Established Church and the Free Churches since the turn of the century was that in general the Church of England's major stance was that Christian teaching should still be taught in all schools whereas among the Free Churches although there was some sympathy for this view, many would rather see the schools secular than sectarian.[25]

Memories of the bitterness resulting from the Conservative government's 1902 Education Act which favoured the Established Church and swept away the democratically elected school boards still lingered in some minds, including that of Winston Churchill, one of the reasons he was apprehensive of early plans for a new Education Bill. There was genuine concern that the religious issue would again dominate discussions even though it was far from the major wishes of most people for improved opportunities in education. This was one of the dilemmas facing Butler. There is no doubt as to his political skills in dealing with this complex and controversial issue although it needs to be born in mind that he was a practising member of the Church of England which needed convincing of any government proposals. Given his relationship to the Established Church it was unlikely he would approve of plans which might be damaging to them in the long run. Indeed he would use all his connections – religious, political and social – in his negotiations over the Education Bill.

William Temple, who had been appointed Archbishop of Canterbury, had a genuine interest in education as his chairpersonship of the WEA made clear. In fact this had meant that, 'There had been some doubt about his preferment in Conservative circles where his political tendencies were suspect.'[26] Temple was dismayed by the dilapidated condition of many Church Schools when he was provided with the details in which Butler 'took the opportunity of reading out some very "damaging statistics" concerning Church schools'; a meeting which Butler later described as attended by 'the Dean of St Albans and the Bishop of Oxford, two zealots indeed, and Mr Hussey, Secretary of the National Society'.[27]

Butler's approach was to discuss many of the issues privately, a tactic he was able to adopt due to the connections he had which have already been mentioned:

> Another very important figure in the whole negotiations was Sir Robert Martin, the prominent layman in the Church Assembly and the National Society. Taking advantage of a visit to Leicester, I had gone to stay a night with Martin in the early part of the year and had sat with him at 'The Brand' until a late hour. He had told me he thought if I could grant the Church up to 75 per cent of their expenses, they would be very satisfied. I was obliged to point out to him that I would not be able to go as high as this and, having heard what I had to say about the plan, he very gallantly gave it the National Society's backing in speeches at the Church Assembly.[28]

Those within the Church who were opposed to change could not make much impact when confronted by the statistics. 'Of the 10,553 voluntary schools, 9,683 were over 40 years old. On the Black List were 543 voluntary schools out of a total of 731.'[29] They knew that the scale of programme necessary for refurbishment of their schools would take years to complete and was beyond their means to accomplish. After considerable discussion within the Church, including the National Society, Temple, on behalf of all sections, accepted the amended White Paper Butler had put forward. The Roman Catholic Educational Council were also made aware of their poor situation financially when they met in February 1941 which meant they would also be unable to bring many of their schools up to the standard recommended by Hadow. They continued to seek maximum financial assistance with the minimum loss of control, with Archbishop Amigo of Southwark seeking 100 per cent State financial assistance.[30] Their lack of compromise throughout the period 1941–44 only served to isolate them and thereby reduce their influence which was already limited due to their numerical inferiority.

R.A. BUTLER AS POLITICIAN

It is necessary to say something about the background of Butler because his ideas, like those of anyone else, were partly shaped by the experiences of his childhood and family circumstances. Apart from his autobiography *The Art of the Possible*, there are numerous sources of information concerning Butler. Much of the detail about his life in this chapter has been taken from two biographies, Gerald Sparrow's *'R.A.B.': Study of a Statesman* and Anthony Howard's *RAB: the Life of R.A. Butler*. The former was a contemporary of Butler at Cambridge. Howard's book written 20 years later with access to his private papers probably provides a more detailed, objective yet sympathetic account. Mainly only those aspects of his life which it is believed are relevant to his approach to education are included although inevitably some of his political activities need to be considered where they are believed to play a part in the career moves which led to his appointment as minister at the Board of Education. He came from a prosperous family; one which can readily be described as part of 'the establishment' in terms of education, occupation, religion and political outlook, in a word, Tory. So many of his ancestors went to Cambridge University and taught in public schools. His great grandfather George Butler went on to become head teacher at Harrow and then Dean of Peterborough, and his sons in turn were similarly educated – George became a public school teacher then Canon of Winchester, Spencer Percival after Cambridge went into Law, Arthur Gray went to Oxford and became head teacher at Haileybury whilst Henry Montagu became head teacher of Harrow at 26 years of age.

In turn, Spencer Percival married Mary Kendal when she was 17 years of age and they had 13 children of whom 11 survived. Nine were sons; two went to Harrow where their uncle was head teacher, two to Rugby, three to Haileybury, one to Clifton and the other to the Royal Naval College at Dartmouth.[31] There is no mention of the education of the daughters. Montagu was the third son and Butler's father. From Haileybury he went to Pembroke College, Cambridge, and was made a Fellow at 22 years of age. He came top in the Indian Civil Service examination and went on to become Governor of the Central Provinces. He married Ann Smith, the daughter of a Scottish Presbyterian family. Later he became master of Pembroke.

R.A. Butler was born in India into the life of the British Raj, 'based not so much on force – though that existed – as on an absolute assumption of British superiority, collectively and individually. It is a trait that was to come out in RAB discreetly from time to time.'[32] As to the extent of force, other methods, such as financial bribery of important princes, were used but when all else failed force was used extensively and ruthlessly whenever there was any serious challenge to its rule.[33] Butler was sent back to England for his schooling; the Wich Prep School at Brighton, and following his failure to win a scholarship to Eton, to Marlborough before continuing almost a family tradition, to Cambridge University. Here he became president of the union, met and married Sydney Courtauld, the daughter of the owner of the textile company of that name. Sydney and RAB went on a grand tour in 1926 and entered the social life of his father, now knighted and governor of the Central Provinces. He took part in the hunting and killing of wild animals, a panther and tiger, then considered a form of sport by the leading families of the Raj. More important, he met the man who was to become Lord Halifax with whom he was to serve later at the Foreign Office.

His entry into parliament was aided by his family connections. A cousin of Sydney's, who knew Foot Mitchell the Tory MP for Saffron Walden, had approached him with news of his failing health and advice on how RAB could be considered as a serious candidate by buying a house in the constituency and spending money, 'about £1,000 a year in the way of subscriptions, charities, etc.'.[34] Contact also came from his uncle, Sir Geoffrey Butler, MP for Cambridge who had also spoken to Foot about the same issue. Having acted upon the advice given, RAB was duly selected as candidate and entered the House of Commons in 1929 at 26 years of age. Moreover, 'Through the intervention of his uncle, who was already conducting a losing battle with ill-health, RAB was invited by Sir Samuel Hoare early in 1929 to become his unpaid Private Secretary.[35] Within three years he had a ministerial role at the India Office but his political advancement came at a cost; he became closely associated with Halifax, Hoare and Neville Chamberlain and supported the policy of appeasement towards Hitler. Indeed when Eden and Cranbourne, the under secretary for Foreign Affairs resigned, Butler was happy to take his place, partly as another move forward in his political career but also because he was favourably inclined to Germany. On a visit to their London embassy in February 1938 he spoke of how he had '"learned to know and appreciate Germany" from his travels ... (and) "desired a close and lasting co-operation" with Germany'.[36] It would seem that his association with appeasement had not been abandoned altogether by the day France surrendered to Germany in 1940, according to an incident concerning remarks attributed to Butler in a conversation with a Swedish diplomat which infuriated Churchill and generated considerable internal correspondence.[37]

Yet Churchill gave him a ministerial post as president of the Board of Education. Several explanations have been offered for this action by the prime minister: he did not bear grudges and recognised Butler's talents, it was a 'home front' position which on the face of it would not provide a base for much influence, he was not particularly interested in the area of education. Apparently when Churchill sent for Butler and offered him the job his parting remark was, 'you will be in the war. You will move poor children from here to here – this will be very difficult.'[38] It is possible that Churchill did not expect Butler to do any more than keep a system of schooling functioning within the restraints imposed by the war. He certainly did not contemplate or want any serious moves towards a new Education Bill. At the time Butler's new post seemed to offer little room for political advancement, partly because the Board of Education lacked status as far as many Conservative MPs were concerned given the record of the inter-war years: 'in the ten years since the foundation of the National government in 1931 to Butler taking up the appointment in July 1941 there had been six ministers in the office averaging a stay of 18 months and the running of the department had fallen into the control of the permanent officials'.[39] More evidence as to the opportunity civil servants had enjoyed in producing the influential Green Book.

There is no doubt that Butler was highly intelligent and was to become a skilful politician. By the same token he had every possible advantage in life that money, cultural capital, social, economic and political connections could provide. As has been illustrated more than a touch of nepotism aided his early political career. His connection with the Church of England would allow him to negotiate with the Established Church over the contentious issue of dual control. His position in the numerically dominant party in parliament and his ministerial role gave him the power to shape the way the education system would develop. Yet not for the first time the minister responsible for the education system of the vast majority of pupils in the land had no personal knowledge of it as pupil, parent or teacher. This ignorance was exposed when he asked at a meeting with senior officials in August 1941, '"what is an elementary school?" not having grasped the difference between an elementary and a secondary school'.[40]

Butler's school experiences, like those of all his family, were of the public schools and that is where his sympathies were to be found. He defended them and protected them from being exposed to serious parliamentary scrutiny. When in 1943 he had been invited by Churchill to spend the night at Chequers, after dinner he was given the section on education of a draft speech the prime minister had prepared which contained 'some very pungent remarks about the old school tie (the time for which, he said, was past)'.[41] Working in the small hours Butler 'substituted for the rather rude remarks about the old school tie a statement about the need for every type of school and every type of tie'.[42] This was just one example of Butler's sensitivity to the privileged education he had received and desired to protect. He also watered down Churchill's 'definite assertion that the school leaving age must be raised to 16' to the non-specific 'must be progressively prolonged'.[43]

CHUTER EDE – PARLIAMENTARY SECRETARY AT THE BOARD OF EDUCATION

Chuter Ede was born in 1882. His background in almost every respect was a complete contrast to that of Butler. His father was a shopkeeper and his schooling commenced at an elementary school in Epsom, followed by Dorking High School on a Surrey Technical Instruction Committee Scholarship before attending Amies Street Pupil Teachers' Centre at 17 years of age where he trained as a pupil teacher for the London School Board. He gained a King's scholarship to Christ's College, Cambridge at the Day Training College but gave up after two years without taking his degree. He taught in elementary schools in Ewell and Toleworth before taking a post at the latter where he taught until 1913.[44] Attendance at Cambridge was the one thing he had in common with Butler.

He was an active member of the NUT in Surrey and soon on the County's Education Committee. Initially he was a member of the Liberal party but changed to Labour whilst serving in the Royal Engineers during the First World War. He was a County Councillor in Surrey from 1918 to 1949; and a Labour MP for Mitchum in 1923, and South Shields for 1929–31 and 1935–64. The time he gave to education at both local and national level provides an incredible example of dedication and it was his encyclopaedic knowledge of education which made him such a valuable deputy to Butler, who willingly inherited him from Ramsbotham as secretary of the Board of Education, a post to which he had been appointed in May 1940. As a Nonconformist, member of the NUT, with access to the Labour leader, Attlee, and ministers in the Coalition, it would seem that Butler and Ede made a good partnership as they had personal contacts with nearly all the parties with an interest in education. In fact it does not seem as if his contacts with the leaders of either the NUT or Free Churches were as strong as has been suggested, at least he expressed some disappointment as to the measure of support they gave him.[45] Butler was aware of the value of Ede's greater experience and supported him when he declined Churchill's suggestion to move to Transport. He also asked him to lead the debate in November 1941 on the complex religious instruction question. Ede's speech received plaudits in the House of Commons and in the Press, as well as an evening telephone call from a grateful president of the Board.[46] Ede helped to keep up pressure for a major Education Bill at times when Butler had doubts as to the feasibility of such a measure due to the difficulties posed by religious issues. For example in June 1943 Ede wrote to Butler opposing any further concessions to the Church of England and the Lord President's Committee, faced with organised pressure from the Roman Catholic lobby, decided 'no further financial concession could be made'.[47]

Within the Cabinet Butler received strong support from Bevin. 'According to Chuter Ede, Bevin contributed more to it than anyone else outside the department...Ede found him ready to talk over the detailed provisions and give advice at any time; he was full of suggestions of his own and when the Bill came up for discussion in the Cabinet gave powerful support, without which, Ede believed, it was unlikely to have been passed during the war.'[48]

THE 1944 EDUCATION ACT

The details of the 1944 Education Act and events leading up to it have been discussed in numerous articles and books.[49] Suffice to say, as has been shown so far, the sticking points were the religious issue, especially the terms of financial support for sectarian schools, and the abolition of the smaller Part 3 Authorities which had only been responsible for elementary schools. The establishment of the tripartite system of secondary schooling was generally accepted at the time. Its significance was not fully understood for there was the belief, or at least a hope, that there would be 'parity of esteem' between the different types of secondary schools to be established. The direct grant grammar schools and public schools had also been removed from the agenda with assurances that they were being dealt with by the Fleming Committee – which indeed they were.

It has been argued that one of the reasons Butler was able to introduce a major Bill on education containing measures which had been resisted by his own party for so long was because many Conservatives believed it to be less revolutionary and expensive than the proposals made by the Beveridge Report for major reform in social welfare. In this matter Butler displayed his political skills.

> I was very careful at all stages to say...that their full implementation would take at least a generation. This was naturally a great comfort to Sir Kingsley Wood and Sir John Anderson, the two chancellors with whom I had success- fully to deal, and they and their treasury officials were therefore reasonable and helpful over finance. I was also encouraged by the Whips' Office, then under the direction of James Stuart for whom the beauty of the Bill was that it would keep the parliamentary troops thoroughly occupied; providing endless opportunity for debate, without any fear of breaking the government.[50]

The Bill was a long one containing 122 clauses but the contents were known to be generally acceptable to the majority of MPs. Over 1,000 amendments were tabled, 340 of which were debated and 113 accepted.[51]

The TUCGC welcomed the Bill as a whole but pressed their point of view on certain important issues. Most important for them was the raising of the school leaving age to 15 years, a matter which had been the cause of so much effort during the inter-war years, granted finally in 1939 only to be lost by the outbreak of war. The Bill proposed what would in fact be a restoration of that gain on 1 April 1945 but with power given to the president to delay the start for up to two years whilst the wording for further advance to 16, when the minister is 'satisfied that it has become practicable', was vague enough to contain no firm promise. The TUCGC pleaded for the immediate rise to 15 because 'great numbers of the present school population have suffered material loss of educational opportunities as the result of the war,[52] and this was the least that could be offered to go some way towards making good the deficit. They were willing to accept a delay to 16 providing it was no more than three years later. This provoked a response from Sir Herbert Williams, Conservative MP for Croydon South who wrote to Citrine: 'I think it is perfectly stupid to suggest fixing a date for raising the school leaving age to 16. You know perfectly well it cannot happen for years. We have neither the buildings, nor the teachers, nor the assent of the parents.'[53]

The TUC were aware of the difficulties but their retort to such protests was that 'the achievements in many directions during war-time suggest that, given the determined spirit, these problems can be solved'.[54] They were disturbed at the complete absence of any mention in class size in the Bill and wished to see a programme which would work within a set period to establish 30 pupils as the maximum number for a class.

DEFEAT FOR THE GOVERNMENT

The Education Bill could claim at least one first during the period of coalition war-time government; namely the only significant defeat for the government. It was not over the contentious religious issue but over equality of pay. Mrs Thelma Cazalet-Keir was an advocate of multilateral schools and a member of the Tory Reform Committee, a group of about 40 MPs in the party, the most prominent of whom were Lady Astor and Quintin Hogg (later Lord Hailsham). At their weekly dinners, at which Thelma Cazalet-Keir was not in fact a regular participant, 'the first business was to discuss the agenda in Parliament for the next week'.[55] She had taken part in the committee stage of the Bill and been narrowly defeated over the demand for a date to be given for raising the school leaving age to 16. She now decided to put forward an amendment calling for equality of pay for women teachers. On 28 March 1944 the government was defeated by 117 to 116 votes, a result which would have been avoided if Sir John Anderson had arrived a little earlier from his Whitehall Office. Butler argued that if the measure had been passed it would have affected the whole of the civil service. He saw the result as one of irresponsibility by a small group which had raised a contentious issue – the principle of equal pay – at least contentious among many of the Tory backbenchers.

He believed:

> It arose because of the clear resolve of the Tory Reform Group, led by Quintin Hogg to whom I had fruitlessly appealed for a modicum of uncharacteristic restraint, to vote with the Labour rebels against the government. Owing to their jubilant and overweening attitude, I did not feel right to adopt an appeasing line, particularly as they had for some time been creating difficulties for my other colleagues in the government. After the event I am sorry to have shown a measure of irritation.[56]

Hailsham regarded the matter in a different light. He claimed that Thelma Cazalet-Keir, a Christian Scientist, supported, 'equal pay for equal work. We agreed with her, and even now I find it difficult to see how any sane man or woman with an eye to the future, let alone the politically sensitive R.A. Butler, could have disagreed with Thelma or with us. I can only suppose that secretly, he did agree...I never counted candour amongst his virtues. Even by his standards, however he excelled himself in his book.'[57] Butler's autobiography had been published three years before that of Quintin Hogg, by then Lord Hailsham.

Butler's annoyance, admitted in his autobiography, was recorded at the time; 'he slammed his documents into his despatch case, banged its lid and walked out'.[58] In reality the defeat was a single issue matter and not intended to bring down the government. Even if accepted equal pay would not have been introduced until the war was over. Churchill, however, was furious. He insisted on a vote of confidence. Harold Nicolson, the National Labour MP, told him that it had been excessive to make the rebels swallow their votes. 'Could not some other method be devised to humble them? "No, Not at all," Churchill replied. "I am not going to tumble round my cage like a wounded canary. You knocked me off my perch. You have got to put me back on my perch. Otherwise I won't sing."'[59]

Whilst the Government announced their intention of putting down a confidence motion it was to be a further 24 hours before a vote could be taken, during which time widespread support for Butler was expressed, including a threat of resignation from Bevin and the full backing of Chuter Ede. The result was a 425 to 23 victory for the government. Equal pay for women teachers was adopted by the NUT Conference in 1951 and the Labour Party in 1953 but not granted until 1955. Even then the National Association of Schoolmasters continued their policy of opposition to equal pay for many more years whilst the National Union of Women Teachers complained about the phasing in over a period of six years.[60] The NAS and the NUWT had each broken away from the NUT over the issue of equal pay; the NAS in 1922 because of their opposition to the idea, the NUWT in 1932 because they did not believe the NUT commitment in 1919 to equal pay was sincere. The continued fragmentation of teachers' organisations frequently prevented a united approach from the profession to the frustration of many teachers; a situation which has continued in both schools and higher education. Cazalet-Keir's political career did not suffer; she was to be made parliamentary secretary to the Minister of Education by Winston Churchill in the caretaker government of 1945. He clearly bore her no grudge, a trait displayed earlier in his appointment of Butler in 1941.

As to the thorny issue of dual control it was the view of the TUCGC that 'the proposals embodied in the Bill constitute an exceptionally generous offer to the church schools and represent the very limit of compromise which can be expected'.[61] There was also unease about the position of single school areas which they believed should be 'provided schools'. Hence whilst not to their liking they were willing to accept the situation to ensure the Bill as a whole could proceed.

The TUC worked through the CEA formulating amendments to those aspects of the Bill which they believed could be improved but were later to report to Congress that 'it is regretted that on the major points at issue as between TUC policy and the Government's Bill, the government did not yield'.[62] The Bill became law on 3 August 1944 but that did not mean the TUC would let the matter closest to their heart, raising the school leaving age, fade from their attention. When Butler issued a circular on 15 August announcing the postponement to a date not later than 1 April 1946 Citrine wrote to him, 'the council of course appreciate that further disorganisation has been caused by the flying bomb attacks...these attacks had for a long time been anticipated by the Government, certainly before the debates took place'.[63]

In his reply Butler pointed out that in his second reading speech he had warned how the war had a bearing upon the recruitment of teachers, the supply of building labour and materials and whilst accepting that the flying bomb attacks had indeed been anticipated they had not been able to assess the damage to school accommodation which would result:

> I need hardly say that I personally deeply regret the necessity for postponing the raising of the school leaving age...No Minister, having got a measure of educational reconstruction on the Statute Book could view with anything but the profoundest distaste the almost immediate postponement of one of the first advances for which that measure provides...I could not have allowed any consideration of personal prestige to lead me to impose upon parents and children by requiring a measure of educational advance an extended life during which I could offer many of them a most inadequate measure of education.[64]

Then in personal handwriting at the end of his letter Butler had written, 'I am taking an early opportunity of making a public statement of the above effect. You cannot if I may say so personally exaggerate my personal concern on this matter.'

The WEA were also dismayed at the delay. They believed 'the problem could be overcome by early release of teachers from the forces and allocation of all necessary priorities for school buildings'.[65] An unlikely prospect given the desperate need for housing following the bombing Britain had suffered for the last few years. Lady Simon wrote a 32-page pamphlet for the Fabian Society entitled *The Education Act: How to make the Best of It* and many trades councils wrote to the TUC informing them of critical resolutions which they had passed; for example that of the Exeter and District TC (2 September 1944) 'That as War-time schoolchildren had already suffered much dislocation of their education as a result of the War, we protest at the Government's decision to postpone the raising of the school leaving age.' Similar resolutions were received from trades councils at Aylesbury and District, Birmingham, Nottingham and District, Southall and St Pancras and letters of protest were sent to the Minister with copies to the TUC from the Union of Post Office Workers, NU Blastfurnacemen and the Amalgamated Union of Building Trade Workers, to which the TUC replied thanking them for their action.

The interest raised by the Act led to local meetings all over the country. Plymouth TC organised meetings at different schools over a period of four evenings in October 1945 culminating in a large central meeting at the Girls' High School with the lord mayor in the chair. Other meetings took place in parish church halls, such as one at Dunstable where representatives from the NUT, WEA and Trades Council together with

H.A. Turner from the TUC met to discuss educational plans. The distances and complicated journeys by public transport undertaken by speakers from the TUC and other organisations were formidable. H.A. Turner wrote to Dunstable to explain, 'I shall not be able to leave London much before 12 noon and I have been advised to go by bus from Luton to Dunstable. My train gets to Luton at 1.15 pm. I do not know how long it will take to get there to Dunstable...I might be on the late side.'[66]

By autumn 1945 the TUC was taking stock of the main aspects of the Act. Their disappointment at Butler's delay in raising the school leaving age to 15 from 1 April 1945 was made clear, even if the language used was moderate. 'It was, to say the least, unfortunate that in the first Circular issued under the auspices of the new Ministry of Education, the Minister should have announced his intention to exercise his power under Section 108 of the Act to defer the operation of the higher leaving age...[and]...that he would defer the raising of the age at least until April 1946.'[67] The practical response of Congress was to continue the campaign of public meetings through their association with the CEA using the network of trades councils to disseminate relevant material, including 'a Memorandum of the Council for Educational Advance indicating the various points on which it was necessary to arouse public opinion in connection with the new Act'.[68]

A caretaker government led by Winston Churchill for three months had come and gone, swept away by the general election of 1945. During that brief period Butler had been moved to the Ministry of Labour and National Service and Richard Law, the son of Bonar Law, had taken his place in Education, a position considered by Churchill as no longer warranting a place in the Cabinet. Ellen Wilkinson was now the Minister of Education, an MP with a radical past as the representative and champion of Jarrow in the 1930s who had been fully involved with the marches of which she was to write a book entitled T*he Town that was Murdered*. The workings and interpretations of the Act, and past hopes of the labour movement concerning the country's educational system now became her responsibility.

NOTES AND REFERENCES

1. For a detailed account of the activities of the CEA see Brooks, J.R. (1977) 'The Council for Educational Advance during the Chairmanship of R.H. Tawney 1942–49' *Journal of Educational Administration and History*, Vol. IX, No. 2.

2. Ibid., p.48.

3. Ibid., p.42.

4. Ibid., p.44.

5. Ibid., pp.44–5.

6. Ibid., p.45.

7. *TUC Report 1943*, p.179.

8. For accounts of the arguments between these competing educational organisations and the part played by the TUC see Craik, W.W. (1964) *The Central Labour College*; Griggs, C. (1983) *The Trades Union Congress and the Struggle for Education 1868–1925*, Ch. 7; Millar, J.P.M. (1987) *The Labour College Movement*, Chs. 1-4; Pollins, H. (1984) *The History of Ruskin College*, pp.9–21; Simon, B. (1965) *Education and the labour movement 1870–1920*, Ch. 9.

9. *TUC Report 1943*, pp.179–80.

10. Millar, J.P.M., *The Labour College Movement*, p.129. Millar (1893–1989) was General Secretary of the NCLC for almost the whole of its existence, 1921–64. Arising out of the Ruskin College Strike of 1909 and the publication of the Plebs magazine, Labour colleges developed to provide working-class education financed solely by the labour movement. The NCLC was a federation of colleges with Millar as Secretary and his wife, Christine, as organiser for the correspondence courses. With his agreement, it was finally taken over by the TUC. See Millar, J.P.M. 'How the Labour Colleges were Destroyed' *The Times*, 2 May 1975 and obituary of Millar by Brian Simon in the *Independent*, 11 December 1989.

11. *TUC Report 1944*, p.76.

12. See Dean, D. (1970) for an analysis of the work of this sub-committee, 'Problems of the Conservative Sub-Committee on Education 1945–1951', *Journal of Educational Administration and History*, Vol. III, No. 1.

13. R.A. Butler to G. Faber 2.6.1941, quoted in Dean, D., 'Problems of the Conservative Sub-Committee on Education 1945–1951', p.26.

14. Dean, D., 'Problems', p.28.

15. Simon, B. (1974) *The Politics of Educational Reform, 1920–1945*, footnote 99, p.84.

16. MacKenzie, J.M., (1984) *Propaganda and Empire: the Manipulation of British Public Opinion 1880–1960*, p.22 and p.75.

17. Middleton, N. (1972) 'Lord Butler and the Education Act of 1944', *British Journal of Educational Studies*, Vol. 20, No. 2, pp.187–8.

18. Middleton, N. and Weitzman, S. (1976) *A Place for Everyone: A History of State Education from the End of the 18th Century to the 1970s*, p.247.

19. Middleton, N. (1972) 'Lord Butler', p.184.

20. TUC 810.26(1) 1943–44.

21. Wallace, R.G. (1981) 'The Origins and Authorship of the 1944 Education Act', *History of Education*, Vol. 10, No. 4, p.33.

22. Confidential Paper – Labour Party Sub-Committee on Education – RDR 82/Mar.1942, TUC 810.25(1).

23. A. Walkden to W. Citrine, 2.3.1944, TUC 810.26(1) 1943–44.

24. W. Citrine to A. Walkden, 3.3.1944, TUC 810. 26(1) 1943–44.

25. See Cruickshank, M. (1963) *Church and State in English Education*, Ch. 7 for detailed information on the religious issue and the 1944 Education Act.

26. Butler, R.A. (1971) *The Art of the Possible*, p.102

27. Cruickshank, M. (1963) *Church and State*, pp.151–2; Butler, R.A. (1971) *The Art of the Possible*, p.102.

28. Butler, R.A., *The Art of the Possible*, p.103.

29. Ibid.

30. Barber, M. (1994) *The Making of the 1944 Education Act*, pp.39–42; Gosden, P.H.J.H. (1976) *Education in the Second World War*, pp.290–2.

31. Howard, A. (1987) *RAB: The Life of R.A. Butler*, pp.1–6.

32. Sparrow, G. (1965) *'R.A.B.': Study of a Statesman*, p.13.

33. See James, L. (1998) *RAJ: The Making and unmaking of British India*, Chs. 2 and 3.

34. For details of the relevant correspondence behind this scheming see Howard, A. (1987) *RAB: The Life of R.A. Butler*, pp.33–5.

35. Ibid., pp.37–8.

36. Gilbert, M. and Gott, R. (2000) *The Appeasers*, pp.77–8.

37. Ibid., pp.96–100.

38. Butler, R.A. *The Art of the Possible*, p.90.

39. Middleton, N. and Weitzman, S. *A Place for Everyone*, p.240.

40. Bailey, B. (1995) 'James Chuter Ede and the 1944 Education Act', *History of Education*, Vol. 24, No. 3, p.212.

41. Butler, R.A. *The Art of the Possible*, p.112.

42. Ibid., p.114.

43. Ibid.

44. Most of this information is based upon studies by Bill Bailey, in particular 'James Chuter Ede', *History of Education*, Vol. 24, No. 3.

45. Bailey, B., 'James Chuter Ede', p.215.

46. Ibid., p.214.

47. Gosden, P.H.J.H., *Education in the Second World War*, p.288 and pp.314–15.

48. Bullock, A. (1967) *The Life and Times of Ernest Bevin, Vol. 2, 1940–1945*, p.237.
49. Most of the relevant studies have been mentioned in this chapter: Bailey, B., 'James Chuter Ede'; Gosden, P.H.J.H., *Education in the Second World War*; '*Putting the Act Together*', Jeffereys, K., 'R.A. Butler'; McCulloch, G., '"Spens v. Norwood"'; *Educational Reconstruction*; Middleton, N., 'Lord Butler and the Education Act'; Middleton, N. and Weitzman, S., *A Place for Everyone*; Simon, B., *Education and the Special Order 1940–1990*; Wallace, R.G. 'Labour, the Board of Education and Preparation of the 1944 Act' and 'The Origins and Authority of the 1944 Education Act'.
50. Butler, R.A. (1971) 'The Art of the Possible', p.117.
51. See Middleton, N. (1972) 'Lord Butler and the Education Act', p.187. A contemporary guide to the provisions of the Act can be found in Dent, H.C. (1944) *The Education Act 1944*.
52. *TUC Report 1944*, p.74.
53. Sir Herbert G. Williams to Sir Walter Citrine, 21.3.1944, TUC 810.26(1) 1943–44.
54. *TUC Report 1944*, p.74.
55. Howard, A. (1987) *RAB: The Life of R.A. Butler*, p.136.
56. Butler, R.A. (1971) *The Art of the Possible*, p.120.
57. Hailsham, Lord. (1990) *A Sparrow's Flight*, pp.217–19.
58. *Daily Telegraph* 29 March 1944, quoted in Howard, A. (1987) *RAB: The Life of R.A. Butler*, p.137.
59. Gilbert, M. (1992) *Churchill – A Life*, pp.770–1.
60. Seifert, R.V. (1987) *Teacher Militancy: A History of Teacher Strikes 1896–1987*, p.61.
61. *TUC Report 1944*, p.75.
62. Ibid., p.76.
63. W. Citrine to R.A. Butler, 28.8.1944, TUC 810.26(1) 1944–59.
64. R.A. Butler to W. Citrine, 30.8.1944, TUC 810.26(1) 1944–59.
65. W.E.A. to TUC, 12.9.1944, TUC 810.26(1) 1944–59.
66. H.A. Turner to Dunstable T.C., 11.4.1947, TUC 810.26(1) 1944–59.
67. *TUC Report 1945*, p.93.
68. Ibid.

CHAPTER 10

THE PUBLIC SCHOOLS:
A Case of Special Treatment?

THE PUBLIC SCHOOLS – EDUCATION FOR A MINORITY

The term public school is used here because it was the name given to much of the private sector of schooling during the period under discussion. Hence although in the minds of most people the kind of school usually covered by the term would be one which was a member of the Headmasters' Conference it was not always a distinction made when discussions about 'public schools' arose. It was also the term used by the Fleming Committee which reported in 1944.[1] Most people in the country had no direct experience of public schools and knew little of direct grant grammar schools or how the latter differed from county grammar schools. As the majority of the population had received only elementary education, 88 per cent of 5 to 14 year olds in 1938, it was access to 'secondary education' through county grammar schools that was held out as a difficult but attractive prize offering the prospect of social mobility through improved employment opportunities. Even here a considerable number of places had been taken by pupils who had parents able to pay the fees required although the number of free places had been steadily increasing throughout the inter-war period.

Within the broad labour movement of the Labour party, Co-operative Society, the TUC and affiliated trades unions, as a generalisation, the first named was the only section in which there was any significant number of ex-public schoolboys. Of the trade unionists who were active at the TUC from 1868 to the 1940s for whom it has been possible to trace their schooling not one attended a public school. Indeed, up until the General

Strike, using the same criteria, only one had attended a secondary school. By the 1930s some were beginning to get scholarships to secondary grammar schools but they were a small minority. The Labour party by contrast, at least among some of its leading members, did contain a sprinkling of ex-public schoolboys; Clement Attlee (Haileybury and Oxford), Stafford Cripps (Winchester and London) and Hugh Dalton (Eton and Cambridge) are among the better known but as many Labour MPs had come up through their trade union, there were few on the back benches who had experienced more than an elementary schooling. Attlee's views probably represented that of many who had attended public schools but realised that the system as it stood was unfair in social and educational terms:

> My idea is that like most of our institutions, they should not be killed but adapted ... Some of them which are essentially local could be absorbed into county secondary schools. Others which are national should be brought under control without killing their individuality. They should of course have a large proportion of scholars from elementary schools.[2]

Attlee had been educated at home, like his sisters but unlike his brothers, until he was nine. His governess, Miss Hutchinson, had been employed in the same position for Winston Churchill. At 13 he followed his older brother Tom to Haileybury and whilst Tom hated the experience 'Clem' enjoyed his time there. Although a strong supporter of state education he sent his children to fee-paying schools, the girls to St Hilda's in Bushey, his son to Belmont and then Millfield. He congratulated Tom on learning that his eldest son was to go to a public school. When a school friend of his daughter Felicity asked why he had sent her to a fee-paying school when he supported state education he replied, '"The man who lives in the world as though the world is the way he hopes it is going to be is a crank."'[3]

Bevin and Bevan were more typical in their early educational experiences than Attlee or Dalton. This could be one reason why the TUC were more forthright in their attitude towards the public schools. They had already expressed surprise that 'There appears to be no reference ... to the problem of the private schools' in an early response to the government's memorandum *Education After the War*, declaring 'consideration of private schools can scarcely be omitted from any discussion of educational advance and reform'.[4] The TUC could not see how public schools had been or were likely to be of benefit to the majority of children. Indeed, what they understood from their experience as working people was that those who often confronted them from government and the civil service had received a privileged form of education which was largely a product of the better financial circumstances of their parents. At its simplest, whilst most trade unionists had been working from 14 years of age onwards those in senior government positions and the professions had been able to ignore the need to go daily to the factory, mines, mills, docks and railways, undertaking work at unsocial hours and often in an unpleasant environment, and instead enjoy the comparative luxury of seven more years full-time education. It was not that many trade unionists denied serious study was also hard work but that this opportunity had not been available to them too. It needed a strong personality and considerable self-confidence not to feel a sense of an inferiority complex when trade unionists were in discussion with those who had received a lengthy formal education. This was one of the reasons they were so incensed when people who had received such educational benefits and assumed that their own children should follow this path, were in a position to deny even an extra year of schooling to the majority of children in the country.

The Labour party's reluctance to tackle the public school system may be explained by other factors. It is true that there were ex-public schoolboys in the party who had sympathy for the system of private schooling, and Attlee was one, but this by itself does not provide a very convincing explanation as one can just as easily point to critics of the system, such as R.H. Tawney, who attended Rugby and Balliol College, Oxford. However, it should not be dismissed altogether. It is more likely that as a prospective future government the leadership of the party believed that the public school lobby with its connections throughout the Establishment was so powerful that they did not think they could push through any major reform which would lead to radical changes within the fee-paying sector, especially if at the time, meritocracy was to replace the ability to pay fees as a criterion for entry to county secondary grammar schools. With so many vested interests posing a hostile threat to any future Labour government could they afford to take on another? In 1944 almost all sections of the labour movement saw the main prize to be won as the end to the separate elementary and secondary school system and the raising of the school leaving age. They were willing to compromise in other areas rather than risk losing these elements of the Education Bill.

The situation of the public schools had changed during the inter-war years as the economic depression had reduced the ability of some to pay fees, and whilst the well-known schools were unlikely to have major problems in filling their places dozens of less well-known, often quite small in size and to be found in leafy suburban or seaside towns faced closure as the parents of their potential customers fell upon hard times. To take but one example, in Eastbourne during the Edwardian era, F.G. Chambers, in his book *Eastbourne – Memories of the Victorian Period 1845–1912*, wrote, on public schools in the area, 'I know not the present number; but as far back as 1894 they had grown to more than 200.' Admittedly some of these were no more than large houses taking from a dozen to 20 pupils for the summer season providing limited schooling for the children of middle-class visitors, but others were substantial in terms of buildings and numbers, e.g. New College – now the centre for the Dental Estimates Board. This was but one of many colleges closed in the inter-war period as well as Granville, Queenwood, St Cyrians (attended and detested by George Orwell who wrote about it in *Such, Such were the Joys*) and Clovelly and Kepplestone, two schools for girls merged in 1910 and closed in 1935.

Miss Goodfellow at the Board of Education had prepared a 'strictly confidential' memo for the president on the financial problems of public schools and attempted to categorise their prospects; **A** for a future almost certainly assured, **B** for those who have suffered a decline but are still believed to be healthy, **C** for future doubtful with **D** in danger of extinction. **A** included Eton, Westminster, Winchester and Marlborough; **B** Charterhouse, Rugby, Shrewsbury, and Stowe; **C** Harrow, Cranleigh, Eastbourne College and Bryanston whilst **D** included Dover, Imperial Service College, Brighton College and Canford. Eastbourne College was one of many schools which had accumulated vast debts for capital projects, in their case £100,000, which became all the more difficult to fund during the years of economic depression.[5]

As with many private organisations, praising the virtue of independence from the State, when faced with financial problems, at least some of the public schools considered seeking government help. It is here that the social network of ex-public schoolboys, with an Oxbridge education and common London club membership provide some evidence of joint efforts to support the public schools. Bearing in mind that these schools were outside the regulations, responsibilities or interests of the Board of Education, it is perhaps surprising that permanent officials should spend time discussing ways of providing for their future. G.G. Williams and Holmes had close contacts with public schools, discussed problems unofficially with some public school heads whilst denying this had taken place.[6] Canon Spencer Leeson, Head of Winchester, who had served at the Board of Education 1919–24, outlined the problem of the schools in a confidential memorandum sent to a few other heads, a copy of which was sent to Holmes. He wanted a policy, 'which would enable the public schools to continue without government or statutory control but with some guidance and possibly help from the Board'.[7] These views were shared by Holmes, Norwood and Spens. Norwood wrote to Holmes of the pressures on some headmasters 'literally spending half their time in commercial travelling and touting on preparatory school doorsteps'.[8] A Royal Commission was considered but rejected by the Headmasters' Conference.

To keep control and make certain that any liaison with the State sector was on their terms, the most practical approach from the schools was for them to offer some places to pupils from elementary schools, part of the fees to be met from local authority funds. It would not be the only time that public schools would make such an offer for this system brought them a double benefit; the funding from the LEA provided a subsidy for the school and by selecting pupils they would be able to choose the potentially brightest children who would in turn enhance the reputation of the school, albeit at the expense of the academic results of local authority schools.

Norwood supported such a scheme in which the boarding schools would provide free tuition whilst the boys would be chosen by interview and examination with the local authority paying a reduced fee per pupil. A meeting to discuss an agreed plan between the Incorporated Association of Headmasters and Headmistresses was held at the Guildhall and Norwood wrote a letter to G.G. Williams describing the result of the debate.

> The scheme fell absolutely flat, save that I got a certain amount of abuse from Blimps and Die-hards as being a concealed 'Red'. I think myself it was the last chance. I do not see how as a system they are to survive this war. They have had their hundred years and have rendered very great service with certain limitations. But the order of society to which they belong is at an end, or near it, however we may regret the fact.[9]

Both Holmes and G.G. Williams had shown more interest in supporting the public schools of which they were both a product than of establishing secondary schools for the vast majority of children condemned to crowded elementary schools. Finally, in 1942, a Departmental Committee was established in response to a request made to the president of the Board of Education jointly by the Governing Bodies Association and the Headmasters' Conference the terms of which were 'To consider means whereby the association between the Public Schools and the general educational system of the country could be developed and extended' and to see how far the measures designed for boys would be suitable for girls.[10]

The Committee, chosen by Lord Fleming, the Scottish Law Lord and Senator of the College of Justice in Scotland, included Dr Geoffrey Fisher the Bishop of London and ex-Head of Repton, Robert Birley, Head of Charterhouse, M.L. Jacks, Director of the Education Department at Oxford and ex-Head of Mill Hill, Miss E. Tanner Head of Roedean, as well as G.D.H. Cole, lecturer on Economics and chairperson of the Fabian Society, H.N. Penlington, NUT Treasurer, and Harold Clay of the TGWU and TUC. The assessors were G.G. Williams, F. Duckworth and W.F. Williams, all serving with the Board of Education and past contributors to the Green Book. Whilst much discussion would take place in the Committee about the desire of the public schools to 'be of service to a wider range of pupils' whose parents could not afford the fees, and at least a wish to lessen the social divisions their schools were perceived to reinforce, the reality was somewhat different:

> The Fleming Committee came about not so much in an endeavour to 'democratize' the public schools – even although that appeared to be its purpose – but rather out of an attempt to find a politically acceptable way of bringing State-supported pupils, and therefore public money to the salvation of the financially unstable and threatened public schools.[11]

Of the 54 organisations submitting evidence to the Committee, eight represented sections of the public schools and the majority of the remainder were connected with education, including the teachers' unions, the NCLC, WEA, and Education Service of the Co-operative Union. The FBI and TUC provided documentary and oral evidence. Those listed as giving evidence totalled 158, although some of these included people speaking on behalf of organisations which had already submitted written evidence. In addition many of the Heads of public schools, direct grant and county grammar schools gave evidence and G.G. Williams submitted evidence even though he was an assessor for the Committee.

TUC EVIDENCE TO THE FLEMING COMMITTEE

The initial response of the TUC was to refer the Fleming Committee to their pamphlet *Education After the War* drawing attention to paragraphs 12 to 24 which dealt specifically with the Direct Grant Grammar Schools and Private Schools. Direct grant grammar schools were a product of the 1926 Hadow Report in which grant-aided schools were given a choice of the means by which they were funded: fully maintained by the LEA; aided by the LEA; or on condition they reserved a minimum of 25 per cent of their places as free places chosen by the LEA – a direct grant from the Board of Education. A minority, 235 schools, chose the last named method and became known as Direct Grant Grammar Schools. The TUC had sought to examine what were the features of these schools which qualified them for special treatment and had concluded that the direct grant system of funding, which was higher than that provided for local secondary schools, could only be justified if the schools were non-local, drawing many pupils from outside their area. Using the criteria that any school with 25 per cent or more of its pupils as boarders could be considered non-local they found that only 42 of the schools came within this category whilst 186 did not. Their conclusion was that the 186,

> local schools ought to be handed over to the appropriate LEAs and to take their place in the public education system, where they should be treated in all respects as other secondary schools. Fees should be abolished, and pupils admitted on exactly the same terms prevailing in respect of secondary schools already provided by LEAs.[12]

The remaining schools with a considerable boarding element 'should be fully subject to all the conditions on which grant is given to any other school'. Again, fees should be abolished, and places allocated to children in circumstances where boarding was required. Their views were shared by the WEA and the Labour party. (The Labour party had already urged the abolition of fees to direct grant grammar schools in a deputation to the minister of education in February 1943.)[13] The Association of local authorities and their officers also supported this approach but for rather different reasons in their case: that if they were to be given the duty of providing secondary schools in an area they should have control of all the schools in that area. The TUC had every right to believe that their view on the abolition of fees would prevail because 'It is now supported by a majority of the Fleming Committee in the course of a special report on the Abolition of Fees in Grant-Aided Secondary Schools.'[14] Evidence that some skilled workers did manage to pay the lower fees for county secondary school places is provided by an isolated letter to the TUCEC in 1943 'received from the National Union of Vehicle Builders transmitting a proposal received from the Swindon Branch that payments made on account of school fees should be allowed in income tax relief'. They were advised to put down a resolution either for the TUC or Labour Party Conference 'as wide implications were involved'.[15]

As for the private schools, some exception was made where they were experimental or run and fully financed by religious organisations. Otherwise they could not be permitted to continue:

There would appear to be no reason for the continued existence of private schools. The great majority of these schools are based on class distinctions, and in so far as that is their only claim to existence, they should be abolished. On the other hand, there are a number of private schools with very high educational claims. Such schools may well be brought within the State system, and it is to be hoped that they will be free to preserve and develop any special characteristics which they may possess. So far as entry of pupils is concerned, however, they would be placed on the same footing as all other schools.[16]

All schools, it was believed, should be subject to official inspection which would cover premises, which were poor in some of the lesser known private schools, and facilities. All teachers should be qualified as they were required to be in LEA schools and the children should be brought within the school medical services system. Earlier the TUC had brought it to the attention of the Board of Education that, 'At the present time anybody, whatever his or her qualifications, may start an independent school in any building, and unless the use of the building constitutes a nuisance under the Public Health Act, its improvement or closure cannot be obtained.' They referred to an inter-war Departmental Committee for 1931–32 which reported on 'a number which were so defective, both structurally and educationally, as to be harmful to the mental and physical welfare of their pupils'. It was believed that only regular inspections could change these deplorable examples in the private sector.[17]

To amplify the points made in *Education After the War* the TUC submitted a memorandum to the Fleming Committee repeating the central core of the TUC position; that with the exception of a few experimental schools, the public schools 'should be absorbed altogether within the national system...whether...the schools are to come under the direct control of the Board of Education or be placed under the control of the appropriate Local Education Authorities, largely depends on the use to which each school is to be put'.[18] It seemed clear to the TUC that various alternative suggestions being proposed in discussion might lessen some of the abuses of privilege associated with the Public Schools but that whilst the system remained more or less in tact, with the schools controlling entry and setting the scale of fees, they would remain socially exclusive and merely invite a comparatively small number of high-achieving pupils to join the privileged whilst doing nothing to help the vast majority of children in the country. The wording of the TUC memorandum was direct and concise on the key elements associated with public schools: the advantages of pupils boarding; the standards achieved by some of the schools; and their wish to maintain control whilst receiving government funding through proposals for what would be in effect 'State scholarships'.

The value of long-term boarding seemed doubtful. 'In our view the proper residential environment for the normal child from the normal home is the home itself and we should prefer that children spent by far the greater part of their school life at a school within daily reach of their homes.' They favoured a residential experience for a short period, of perhaps a term, to be provided for all children, especially those in their early teens, and believed the boarding facilities of the public schools could provide one source of accommodation but also favoured camping because 'young persons should be learning to stand on their own two feet and...without ceasing to regard the family as the focal point of their social existence...steadily acquiring the capacity to lead an independent and separate existence'.[19] They favoured an end to the public school system because of the way it favoured a comparatively small group in society at the expense of the majority of people.

> We consider it a major criticism of the present public school system that its advantages are necessarily restricted to a very small class. It becomes a system of privilege, the privilege itself depending upon the strict limitation of the number of persons who enjoy it. Its worst feature is that the whole system rests on private wealth and is open, in the main, only to those who can afford to pay.[20]

As for the oft quoted belief that the public schools provided leaders, the TUC could accept that many positions were held by ex-public schoolboys but believed this was because through economic and social privilege the products of the public schools have an altogether unfair chance when selection of such people is being made.

> The argument that public schools are necessary to produce leaders rests on the assumption that the community consists of two pre-determined groups of leaders and led...As we do not believe in pre-destination we do not think that selection can be made at the age of 11 or thereabouts of the group from which is to be drawn a substantial proportion of those who control the political and economic destinies of the country. The result of practising this system in the past is that our rulers have been drawn from a class apart from the general community, and have for that very reason been less well-fitted to occupy their positions than they might have been. It should be the aim of the state to abolish this caste system.[21]

This view was not only held on the political left. In 1939 Boothby had written to Lloyd George,

> It is inconceivable that our present hereditary system, or our 'caste' system of education can survive without drastic modification. In the case of Churchill any diminution of power of the governing class will involve a clash between his natural instincts and his imagination. But is there anyone in the present day set up who possesses sufficient imagination even to see the issues involved?[22]

As for claims about teaching leadership A.L. Rowse had a letter published in *The Times* (27 February 1942) which acknowledged the contribution of the public schools in the nineteenth century to national life but believed that now,

> there are all too evident signs around us that their standards are not wholly adapted to the conditions of the contemporary world. For example the disproportionate importance they attach to character rather than intelligence; a wrong emphasis for which we are now paying the price in every field of national life in the conduct of the war, in politics, in administration in the services and in the Empire.

The questions put to the TUC by the Fleming Committee were familiar enough to those involved in the ongoing controversy over public schools. Would abolition lead to removal of governing bodies and appropriation of property and endowments? Thomson of the TUC agreed that it would but argued, 'Most of the endowments have been founded for the benefit of poor children.'[23] How far this was true of 'most schools' was debatable but it was certainly so for some and three years earlier Chuter Ede had stated in Parliament that when Labour formed a government, 'one of the things we shall have to do is to see that the ancient endowments of education are returned to the people for whom they were left'.[24] If the claims were less true for the later nineteenth-century foundations the Board of Education was aware of the validity behind the statement concerning some of the more famous schools as a paper had been prepared by G.G. Williams examining this very issue:

> In dealing with this point we may ignore Eton, Winchester and Westminster which were never, (except for a small minority) local schools for the poorer classes... As reference to the original Charters and Statutes of some schools [shows] there is no doubt that the original intentions have been

largely departed from...It may be freely admitted that many of the older schools were founded with the intention of benefitting the poor.[25]

He then went on to list a series of well-known schools to illustrate the point:

Harrow –   A competent number of scholars as well as poor to be taught freely.

Charterhouse – A free school for the instructing, teaching, maintenance and education of poor children and scholars

St Pauls –   For 153 children as day scholars who are to have free instruction etc.

The way in which funds from the charities established for the schools were diverted from their original purposes to the benefit of masters and the tactics used to exclude poor local children in order to attract higher income families who would pay fees during the nineteenth century has been well documented.[26] It is unlikely that TUC representatives were aware of such details, although the minister and government officials must have known the truth of the situation if only through the paper prepared by Williams. When it was suggested to Thomson that compulsory abolition of most private schooling was an invasion of the liberty of the subject he replied, 'the history of liberty was the encroachment on private rights in the interests of the freedom of the community'.[27] By contrast there was no mention by the committee that the removal of poor local children to make way for fee-paying pupils from outside the area might also be an encroachment of the rights of the local inhabitants.

P. Wilson, who was joint secretary with R.N. Heaton to the Fleming Committee, commented on the TUC memorandum to Mr Sharam at the Board that the:

Committee were not required by their terms of reference to suggest means of abolishing the public school system or eradicating social or economic privilege from society at large. Their task was limited to suggesting means of associating the public schools with the general education system and this they had done.[28]

It was indeed the specific point which limited the scope of the committee's enquiry and thereby prevented any radical changes being made. When an earlier report of the Fleming Committee proposed the abolition of fees in direct grant grammar schools by a majority of 11 to 7, Butler rejected the decision. Wilson explained the situation again by referring to the limiting terms of the committee:

> The abolition of tuition fees was not strictly the Committee's purview and the Special Report issued on this subject last year was undertaken only at the express invitation of the Minister before he completed plans for reorganization of the educational system. By the time the report was signed the decision had already been taken by the Minister not to require the abolition of tuition fees in Direct Grant Grammar Schools.[29]

Butler's behaviour in this matter had been duplicitous. Whenever questions had arisen over fees in discussions on the 1943 White Paper he had replied that this matter was being dealt with by the Fleming Committee and that no decision had been reached. Given his agenda these tactics were successful: 'contemporary parliamentary debates are replete with references to the effect that no action was possible on the public schools until the Fleming Committee had reported'.[30] He had wavered in late 1942 when Ede had suggested, as the TUC had done, that a distinction should be made between those direct grant schools largely of local as opposed to national character before obviously deciding against the idea.[31] Saran has shown the significance of the timetable of events:

> The interim report on fees was commissioned in November 1942. This report was signed on 2nd April 1943, but was not published until August, by which time Parliament had risen. Thus the White Paper on Educational Reconstruction, published and debated in July, was considered by MPs who were still in ignorance of the contents of the report.[32]

Butler opposed the removal of fees in the private as opposed to the public sector of secondary schooling and when the Fleming Committee came to a contrary conclusion he merely overrode it. In the vote over fees in the House of Commons the Government supported their retention and were supported by 183 to 95 votes, 'although it has been claimed that on a free vote the decision would have been reversed'.[33]

FLEMING COMMITTEE PROPOSALS

There were two schemes recommended by the Fleming Committee; A and B. The former dealt with the direct grant grammar schools suggesting that local authorities should be able to reserve a significant number of day or boarding places and that all places should be open according to 'the capacity of the pupil to profit by education in the school'. The LEAs participating in such a scheme would also have the right to appoint governors to the school. Scheme B dealt with public schools with the intention of providing up to 25 per cent of their places by bursaries to primary school children whose parents would contribute according to their income. There was an extension of the direct grant list but with the exception of a few local arrangements little came out of Scheme B. The reality was that the Fleming Committee looked more and more like a political guise than a serious study which would make any real move towards bringing the private and public sectors of education nearer together, except on terms favourable to the former.

Wilson wrote a paper for the Board of Education on the responses of the TUC memorandum to Fleming. With reference to Schemes A and B, he wrote: 'It is true as the TUC Memorandum recognises, success of Scheme A will depend on the extent and whole-heartedness of the response of the schools' whilst for the latter Scheme B 'If the TUC do not believe in the preservation of the public schools there is no ground even for discussion.'[34] As for the doubts the TUC had over selection through Scheme B Wilson could only suggest that whilst it was 'open to any sceptical person to believe that the process of selection will not be free from prejudice and favour... the most experienced judges were induced to feel hopeful... about the possibilities of making a fair and discriminating selection of pupils'.[35]

Several handwritten comments were added at the end as the paper circulated within the Board of Education. One dated 13 September suggested there was 'no need for action except a letter indicating that the Minister will consider the Memorandum with representations made by other bodies before reaching a decision regarding the recommendations of the Fleming Report'. Another, two days later, a comment clearly addressed to Butler stated, 'You will wish to read this report before you see W. Clay,' of the TUC. Butler's note confirms his whole approach to the matter. With regard to the TUC he wrote: 'They are of course too late. The Public Schools are saved and must now be made to do their bit. All this is whining.'[36] This document went to five other people within the department, one suggesting Williams should see this, another hardly thought he should be troubled to read it all.

The senior figures involved with educational reconstruction were well aware of developments in detail through both internal meetings and those at the London clubs which so many of them frequented. The nature of the comment made by Butler on this internal document was to be confirmed later in his autobiography when he boasted that with regard to the public schools, 'though Labour members breathed a certain amount of ritual fire and fury about social exclusiveness and privilege, the appointment of the Fleming Committee had temporarily removed the fire. Or, in railway metaphor, the first class carriage had been shunted on to an immense siding.'[37] Here his intention to remove the public schools from the general debate about the reconstruction of the educational system for the post-war period had been achieved and he was pleased to recognise his achievement.

At the TUC regret was expressed at the wide discrepancy between the proposals which had been put to the Fleming Committee on behalf of the TUC and the final recommendations of that Committee.[38] The 1944 September Congress in Blackpool was informed of the proposals of the Fleming Committee. It was realised that the proposals

> do not incur any risk that the Public Schools will be called upon to merge their identity with those of the national system...Recurrently in the course of their Report the Committee refer to the principle of equal accessibility – but, if their recommendations are accepted, the Public School system will remain. It was the system which the TUC opposed...The Public Schools represent a system which is inevitably accompanied by social and economic privilege. The TUC do not merely wish to transfer this privilege from one group in the community to another. They wish to abolish it.[39]

There were 14 points made by the TUC in respect of the Fleming Report, including the regret 'that the majority view of the Fleming Committee in favour of the abolition of fees was not allowed to prevail when the Scheme was formulated'.[40] The contrast between the success of the 1944 Education Act compared with the inability of the Fleming Committee to democratise 'the privileged sphere of education' was highlighted. To some extent it could be argued that the euphoria surrounding the Education Act helped to screen from public debate the special treatment afforded the public schools; an illustration of the power, influence and social network of the public school system which had enabled it to survive virtually in tact until they were ready to introduce internal reforms which would reinforce their position in the education market inevitably resulting from fee-paying.

Butler received a deputation from the TUC in December to discuss direct grant grammar schools, because it had come to the attention of the TUC that a number of these schools in the north and south west of

England had made independent approaches to the Minister of Education seeking to secure terms for their continued existence which would widen the gap between them and publicly controlled secondary schools. If representatives of such schools should be seen 'so should the Education Committee of the TUC have an opportunity to amplify their views on Fleming'.[41] Butler's agreement to the meeting seems to have been largely a move to imply fairness for the matter had already been settled as far as he was concerned.

Butler was accompanied by Chuter Ede, Holmes and G.G. Williams, all implacable supporters of the public school system, except Ede, who was not however opposed unreservedly to the fee-paying principle. From the TUCEC were H. Bullock, J.V.C. Wray and Miss F. Hancock.[42] They explained that whilst disagreeing with certain proposals of the Fleming Committee they did recognise they were the recommendations of a Departmental Committee and would like to consider them as a basis for discussion. Their main concern was that the principal proposal by the Fleming Committee that all places in direct grant schools should be equally accessible to all pupils could only be guaranteed if the schools were free from fees with a single method of entry. As Butler had personally intervened to prevent this from happening there was no chance that he would reconsider this issue. He excused the retention of fees by stressing their removal in all aided and maintained secondary schools. 'The schools on the Direct Grant list numbered only 232, and thus the field was small.' This was true, but he knew fully well that, just like the major public schools, they were better resourced and gave pupils who attended them higher status, whether deserved by their academic performance or not, for in England where a person attended school has at times been considered by some as important as their academic achievement. The deputation were unhappy about access to the schools being either by pupils selected by the LEA or the governors of the school. They believed that the second method could be unfair and Butler assured them that he was reconsidering this matter so that the prime factor for all candidates would be the ability to pass an entrance test so that 'the pupils were selected in accordance with their educational fitness and on no other ground'.

When the regulations were published in the spring of 1945 the TUC examined those specifically dealing with direct grant grammar schools and wrote to Butler expressing their fears over the principle of equal accessibility being achieved in practice, suggesting this would best be achieved by a joint committee of schools and LEAs concerned. Butler's response on the 19 April was to give an assurance that it was his desire and intention to ensure fairness in accessibility but he would not consider altering the regulations drafted. The TUC could only repeat their desire that all fees for secondary schools should be abolished.[43]

THE FLEMING REPORT – A DIVERSIONARY TACTIC?

If the public schools had been included as a topic for discussion within the general discussions for the reconstruction of the school system after the war there is little doubt that they would have attracted more criticism and less favourable treatment. At the very least many of the direct grant grammar schools would have become incorporated within the local education authority system. The fear of the major public schools then, and since, was that the loss of any part of the private sector would lead to a more searching examination of the whole private sector, from the bottom end of the market, where small schools run by unqualified staff provided poor resources and an education of doubtful quality, to the top end of the market where social exclusivity would be even more clearly exposed.

Any proposal to offer a substantial minority of places to children in the local community was unlikely to be accepted by all the parties involved. Where the boarding facilities were seen of value to some local authorities, the pupils the London County Council for example had in mind for such facilities were, 'orphans, convalescents, delicate, defective, unstable or neglected children', a group which coincided with those considered most suitable by the Ministry of Education.[44] By contrast the public schools had in mind pupils who would be academically successful and enhance the reputation of the public school. Local authorities were apprehensive about both the cost and the morality. Long before the Fleming Committee had reported Bournemouth had rejected the idea of providing bursaries at Winchester School in the knowledge that the money needed to support ten pupils at this particular school could provide accommodation for 30 or 40 scholars if boarding was provided at a local secondary school.[45] Even a few years later there was a general lack of parental interests in the Fleming Report's Schemes. 'In Middlesex, for example, applicants for places actually decreased between 1947 and 1952,' a trend found to be in evidence in other areas too.[46]

However much some of the staff of public schools were genuinely interested in helping pupils from the maintained sector there was no denying that the source of their income for many years had been reliant upon the wealthier parents within the country. Any radical move to take in large numbers of pupils from outside the traditional social groups, especially significant numbers of children from socially disadvantaged families, would have adversely affected their traditional clientele, for whom part of the rationale of the public school was that their children would meet in the main children from similar social backgrounds. There was no major move to take in large numbers of children whose parents could not afford the fees. A few local authorities provided scholarships to public schools, as they had done long before the Fleming Report was published. The recommendations of Fleming gradually faded, although a successful stage play, *The Guinea Pig*, by Waren Strode, adapted for the cinema in 1948, did bring out some of the issues considered at the time, which might arise from such a scheme.[47]

The fact was that not only had Butler skilfully removed the public schools from the agenda of the debate on a post-war system of education but the eyes of most people were in any case fixed upon the goal which would be of most value to their children: secondary education for all. The granting of this reform, which would affect all children in the future, and the general euphoria which accompanied the passing of the 1944 Education Act, captured the attention of the population thereby obscuring the deliberations of the Fleming Committee which seemed to be only significant for a minority of the population – a view which with hindsight would prove to be considerably mistaken.

At local level, pressure from trade unionists could help in retaining a local school for the community when it might have sought private status. For example correspondence between the Lincoln Trades Council and the TUCEC showed how Lincoln School and Lincoln Girls' High School had sought voluntary aided status then direct grant status but the latter did not materialise. The TUC congratulated Lincoln TC on the part they had played in retaining the schools for the local community.[48] When Biggleswade and District TC wrote to the TUC pointing out that the Hampden Trust of Bedford School and Bedford High School for Girls had applied to the Ministry of Education to become independent 'thus depriving working class people's children of the full benefits of the [1944 Education] Act', the TUCEC advised them to rally local people in the same successful manner as Lincoln TC.[49]

Making an assessment of the success of developments on war-time planning and negotiations concerning the future path of the education system has to take account of the political realities of the time. Those involved were limited by the power and influence of conflicting interests: rival sections of education and religious sects; political philosophies; and social classes – to say nothing of the need to fight a ferocious war for survival. Radical reform of the public schools, from the abolition of fees to an intake of large numbers of LEA pupils, let alone moves to take over the schools even in some form of partnership with local education authorities, would not have stood any chance of being accepted by the Conservative-dominated parliament. The social network of the public schools throughout all branches of government, the judiciary, senior ranks of the armed forces, the Church of England, financial services – in a word what has been referred to as the Establishment – was too powerful for forces opposed to the schools, patronised by many of the former, to have any serious hope of curbing their privileged position. The key ministers, Butler and Ede, were complex figures. Butler, later seen as a reforming Conservative, appears so largely because so many of the Tory MPs who had been elected in 1935 were so reactionary by comparison. He was a career politician and skilful negotiator; progressive in his views on India but one of the major appeasers in the pre-war period. A practising member of the Church of England, he was a strong supporter of public schools and ignorant of the schools attended by the majority of children. He genuinely wished to see better provision in the form of secondary schooling and improved career opportunities for the children who would attend the new free secondary schools but at the same time wished to protect the privileged sector of the public schools of which he was a product. He could not see any conflict of interest in such a position. Even the claim of his devotion to the cause of education must be tempered by his later activities as Chancellor of the Exchequer when he ruthlessly forced cut-backs on educational expenditure.[50] Jeffereys makes clear how hard Butler worked after his appointment and how skilful he was as a negotiator.[51] That was his major contribution to the 1944 Education Act. However without taking away the credit due to him his role has to be put into perspective. As has been shown, the origin and writing of the Green Book had already been undertaken by his predecessor and civil servants before he moved to the Board of Education. This pamphlet would provide the basis for the Act. Butler would play a key part in the years following but the conclusion of Wallace seems to provide an accurate assessment of his part: 'Butler, generally considered to have been the father of the 1944 Education Act, had not been present at its conception. His role was rather that of the midwife, and his triumph was to deliver the infant safely after a prolonged and difficult labour.'[52]

The Fleming Report proved to be a good predictor of the future for the public schools. 'The picture of the future, as we see it, is one of consolidation of the ground already won, combined with a steady and general advance to new gains.' In that respect they would be proven correct. 'If success is attained, the benefits for future generations will be incalculable.'[53] For the minority who would attend these schools this would also prove true. However it would be difficult to find how the Fleming Report's proposals were ever of any benefit to the majority of children in the country.

The 1944 Education Act was considered a landmark in the development of education and was seen by nearly all pressure groups in this light because each group could look at the Act and identify an important change which they favoured. At the same time there was compromise by all parties: conservative forces gave some ground in the realisation that if they did not they risked losing even more of their long-established privileges and progressive forces accepted the settlement because it granted them significant parts of the policies for which they had campaigned for over 20 years. It would only be years afterwards when the role of some of the key participants became clearer that a re-assessment of the benefits of the 1944 Education Act would suggest it had not been as radical as had first been considered at the time. It would then be possible to argue that changes in the school system considered bold enough in the 1920s were by war-time standards the minimum acceptable for the majority of children whose parents had been called upon to make such sacrifices during the war. In many ways this had been true also in relation to the 1918 Education Act, parts of which had been abandoned during the inter-war depression.

It is also probably true to say that in focussing upon the granting of secondary education for all without fees the contradiction of parity of esteem in a system where there would be different types of secondary school had only really been grasped by a few. The TUC had been among the few, having foreseen the problem very early on, seeking to draw attention to what they saw as the seeds of another hierarchical system of secondary schooling for children. Questions have been raised as to why Chuter Ede did not play a bigger part in obtaining a programme nearer to the desires of the labour movement – like Attlee he had wished for the public schools to be considered alongside the majority of schools in the country and not dealt with by a separate committee. He was able to demonstrate to the Labour party conference in 1943 that the main parts of the party's education policy were covered by the Government's White Paper and produced a paper to show the match.[54] At times he did feel there was a failure on the part of some of the Labour politicians and teachers to appreciate the complexities of government and partly for that reason was a firm advocate of party discipline.[55] In the final analysis he was the junior minister in a Tory-dominated coalition government and parliament.

To that extent it could be argued that Butler's political skills enabled him to achieve what was possible. It just so happens that for most of the time it coincided with what he and most members of the Board of Education together with the majority of Tory MPs wanted too. Given the opposing views of the labour movement, their weakness in parliamentary numbers, the pressures of the war and powerful pressure groups lined up against them, they only gained in areas in which opposing forces were willing to give ground. The TUC had the most cogently argued case and the most radical education policy, they therefore gained the least. They had in fact already seen well beyond 1944 into the problems of the post-war years. If their policies had been adopted in 1944 some of the bitterly fought battles of the next decade could have been avoided.

NOTES AND REFERENCES

1. Rae, J. (1981) *The Public School Revolution*, pp.15–16, provides an explanation for changing the name 'public school' to the less exclusive sounding 'independent school' in the post-war period.
2. Beckett, F. (1997) *Clem Attlee: A Biography*, p.191.
3. Ibid., pp.9–11, 111.
4. TUC Memorandum to the BOE, 14.4.1942, *PRO ED 136/250* and TUC 811/2/5.
5. Memorandum, 4.10.1941, *PRO ED/12/510*.
6. Wallace, R.G. (1980), 'Labour, the Board of Education and Preparation of the 1944 Act', p.150.
7. Ibid., p.151.
8. C. Norwood to M. Holmes, 19.10.1938, quoted in Simon, B. (1974) *The Politics of Educational Reform 1920–1940*, p.275. For the discussion, correspondence and proposals with civil servants at the BOE with public school headmasters as to how the schools might be helped see Simon, B. ibid., pp.275–8.
9. C. Norwood to G.G. Williams, 13.12.1939, *PRO ED 12/518*
10. *Report of the Committee on Public Schools Appointed by the President of the Board of Education (The Fleming Committee)*, p.2
11. Gosden, P.H.J.H (1976) *Education in the Second World War*, pp.332–3.
12. TUC memorandum (1942) *Education After the War*, p.5.
13. Barker, R. (1972) *Education and Politics 1900–51*, p.114.
14. Supplement to TUC General Council's Report 1943, para. 83, TUC 810.26(1) 1943–1944. See also *TUCEC Mins*, 20.10.1943, TUC 811/6.
15. *TUCEC Mins.* 12.5.1943.

16. TUC memo *Education After the War*, p.6.
17. TUC correspondence concerning 1944 Education Act – July 1943, TUC 810.26(1).
18. TUC memo to Fleming Committee, Paper No. 18, *PRO ED 12/518*, Published in *TUC Report 1943*, p.67.
19. *TUC Report 1943*, p.69.
20. Ibid., p.68.
21. Ibid.
22. Quoted in Addison P. (1985) *Now the War is Over*, p.72.
23. Summary of evidence given by representatives of the TUC on 20 April 1943, p.1, *PRO ED 12/518*.
24. House of Commons 5.3.1940, quoted in Barker, R. (1972) *Education and Politics 1900–51*, footnote 1, p.112.
25. The Place of Boarding Schools in a Federal System of Secondary Education – memorandum by G.G. Williams, (n.d.) *PRO ED 12/510*.
26. See Bamford T.W. (1967) *The Rise of the Public Schools*, Ch. 8.
27. *PRO ED 12/510*.
28. P. Wilson to Mr Sharan, 13.9.1944, p.1. *PRO ED 12/518*.
29. Ibid.
30. Tapper, T. (1997) *Fee Paying Schools and Educational Change in Britain*, p.100.
31. Wallace, R.G. (1980) *Labour, the Board of Education and the Preparation of the 1944 Act*, pp.168–9.
32. Saran, R. (1973) *Policy Making in Secondary Education – A Study*, p.36.
33. Ibid., p.39.
34. Wilson, P., Response to TUC Memorandum on Fleming Committee Report, 10.9.1944, *PRO ED 12/518*.
35. Ibid., p.2.
36. Ibid., p.3.
37. Butler, R.A. (1971) *The Art of the Possible*, p.120.
38. *TUCEC Mins.*, 10.8.1944, TUC 811/6.
39. *TUC Report 1944*, p.90.
40. Ibid., p.91.
41. *TUCEC Mins.*, 5.12.1944, TUC 811/6.
42. TUCEC Deputation to Ministry of Education, 9.12.1944, *PRO ED 12/518*.
43. *TUC Report 1945*, p.94.
44. Banks, O. (1955) *Parity and Prestige in English Secondary School Education*, p.236.
45. Ibid., p.235.

46. Ibid., p.237.
47. The film, *The Guinea Pig* was directed by Robert Boulting, and starred Richard Attenborough (at 25 playing the part of a 13-year-old), Robert Flemyng, Cecil Trouncer, Sheila Sims and Bernard Miles. It was entitled *The Outsider* in the USA.
48. Lincoln TC to TUCEC 8.6.1945; TUCEC to Lincoln TC 12.6.1945, TUC 810.26(1).
49. Biggleswade and District TC to TUCEC 16.6.1945; TUCEC to Biggleswade and District TC 25.6.1945, ibid.
50. Winstone, R. (ed.) (1995) *Tony Benn – Years of Hope; Diaries 1940–1962*, p.160; Hattersley, R. (1997) *Fifty Years On*, p.67; Middleton, N. (1972) 'Lord Butler and the Education Act of 1944', p.185; Simon, B. (1974) *The Politics of Educational Reform, 1920–1940*, p.163.
51. Jeffereys, K. (1984) 'R.A. Butler, the Board of Education and the 1944 Education Act'.
52. Wallace, R.G. (1981) 'The Origins and Authorship of the 1944 Education Act', p.290.
53. *The Fleming Report* (1944) p.69.
54. Bailey, B. (1995) 'James Chuter Ede and the 1944 Education Act', p.216.
55. Wallace, R.G. (1980) 'Labour, the Board of Education and the Preparation of the 1944 Act', pp.30–31.

PART 3 – THE IMMEDIATE POST-WAR YEARS 1945–1959

CHAPTER 11

LABOUR GOVERNMENTS AND THE IMPLEMENTATION OF THE 1944 EDUCATION ACT

LABOUR IN POWER 1945–51

The Second World War ended in Europe on the 7 May, in the Far East on 14 August, 1945. The cost of the war was almost incalculable in terms of loss and injury to life and the destruction of large parts of the infrastructure of so many countries. The depths of inhumanity inflicted by advanced technological societies, in particular Nazi Germany and Japan upon prisoners of war and civilians in the countries they occupied almost defies description or understanding.

> As many as 15 million soldiers, sailors and airmen had been killed in action. At least 10 million civilians had been murdered in deliberate killings – 6 million of them Jews. Between 4 and 5 million civilians had been killed in air raids. Four million prisoners of war had been killed or allowed to die in situations of extreme cruelty after capture – 3.5 million of them Soviet soldiers in German captivity. Millions more soldiers and civilians alike had been physically maimed and mentally scarred.[1]

British deaths of military and merchant navy personnel numbered about 380,000, of civilians around 60,000. In Britain half a million homes were destroyed; half that number again severely damaged. In the first two years of the War out of approximately 23,000 schools about 1,100 were seriously damaged whilst another 3,500 received minor damage.[2] Further destruction took place when V1 and V2 bombs landed in 1944. The disruption to the education of children was caused by many factors:

evacuation whereby children experienced different schools within a short period of time; absence for a variety of reasons from the closure of schools in towns during the early years of the war to time off when a parent came home on leave; part-time schooling where there was a shortage of teachers when some pupils from the area had been evacuated whilst others stayed behind; and time spent in school air-raid shelters. Gosden provides evidence to show the pupil hours spent by children in shelters in 1940. In general, areas in the south east such as Canterbury (51 per cent), Rochester (34.3 per cent) and Maidstone (31.7 per cent) were the worst affected.[3] The author remembers spending time in such shelters where, owing to the limitations of light and confined space, planned lessons were inevitably abandoned and the teacher read a story whilst the raid lasted, to be continued on the next occasion. The rule was that when an air-raid siren sounded pupils were to run to school or home, whichever was nearest. Not surprisingly there were times when although within easy distance of the school gates and despite the call of the teacher on duty, they turned round and ran the longer distance home.

Much industrial plant was wrecked; transport and fuel supplies had also suffered, although in comparison with other European countries involved in the war, with the exception of neutral Sweden and Switzerland, Britain suffered the least.[4] The USA had lost about 235,000 military personnel but their industrial and commercial base had grown as it provided much-needed equipment for large-scale war, and 'peace time' products continued to be produced. Hence while Britain's economy had suffered through being devoted to the needs of war, by contrast, the American economy had prospered. While the two countries had been allies in the war since December 1941 they were also economic rivals and it was the latter relationship which soon became prominent as the war ended.

Six days after the war against Japan came to an end, Harry Truman, on the advice of Lee Crowley, Director of the Foreign Economic Administration in Washington, without warning or discussion, ended 'Lend Lease' which had been Britain's life-line during the war. Even goods in transit were to be paid for immediately. The consequences were potentially devastating and Maynard Keynes went to Washington to try to negotiate a loan from a position of economic weakness: one third of the country's gold reserves had been disposed of and a similar proportion of overseas assets sold. Britain faced war debts of £3.5 billion.[5] A loan was negotiated with the USA of £3.75 billion over 50 years with interest of 2 per cent but there were harsh conditions attached. Britain had to agree to enter the General Agreement on Tariffs and Trade (GATT) which would liberalise trade. This would limit the ability of the Government's scope to plan and control foreign trade.[6] The American aim was to gain access to markets previously dominated by Britain through the system of Imperial Preference established by the Ottawa Conference of 1932 which gave a measure of protection to British and Commonwealth goods. (It could be argued that the USA was following the policy which Britain had forced on so much of the world years before.) The second condition which brought problems was the insistence that sterling was made convertible within a year. The danger here was that those holding sterling would convert to the much coveted dollars which would thereby lead to a rapid decline in the value of sterling. There were a few protests within the country at the conditions attached but there was really no alternative for the country's economy. It is difficult for debtors to act with complete independence of their creditors and there were to be examples of the Labour government having to bow to American pressure to accept policies with which they disagreed such as German rearmament in their last weeks of power in 1951 and within only six years of the war ending in Europe; a bitter pill for many to swallow.

Within the USA there were strong feelings in many quarters of hostility in principle to Britain's Empire, which was on a scale out of all proportion to her post-war power, and tension arose when Americans criticised aspects of British rule.[7] (American journalists in India who were critical of some of the actions of the British within that country during the War were kept under surveillance and their mail secretly intercepted.) Others wished to 'colonise' some of these areas themselves by economic penetration. There was also a feeling in some quarters that the USA should not be subsidising a Socialist government in introducing a welfare programme the extent of which was neither available nor wanted by significant groups in their own country. Sir Isaiah Berlin in the British Embassy in Washington thought that the American government might be trying to 'jerk the rug' from under the new Labour government to cripple it from the start.[8]

In fact, the Labour government began to make progress. There was a setback to morale when there was a fuel shortage in 1946/47 in what turned out to be the coldest winter in the country since the turn of the century, and a problem of devaluation in 1949 when the rate for sterling changed from just over $4 to under $3 to the pound. Nevertheless the economy began to pick up as the change from production for war to peace-time got underway before other war-torn countries such as Germany could become serious economic competitors. Post-war reconstruction progressed, even if many much-wanted goods produced were made 'for export only' as the country struggled to regain markets abroad and pay back the debts accumulated by the war. By 1948 a large part of the legislative programme of the government had been approved by parliament and was being put into practice: in 1946 the repeal of the Trades Disputes Act of 1927, the National Health Service Act, the National Insurance Act, the nationalisation of coal and civil aviation, with gas, electricity and transport to follow in 1948.[9] Moreover, the balance of payments was now in surplus and one result of devaluation a year later was to strengthen exports further. This was a remarkable achievement when the conditions of immediate post-war Britain are considered. It really seemed as if the government which had done so much to improve the living conditions of the majority of the population in such a short time through the expansion of the welfare state, would be able to continue this progress at an increasing rate thereby fulfilling the high expectations of the majority of the electorate.

That this recovery did not continue at the same pace was primarily because the government chose to divert a disproportionate amount of investment to a programme of armaments. In response to the decision of the American government to end collaboration on atomic weapons with the UK and Canada, Attlee decided the UK would produce its own nuclear bomb. The Cabinet was not consulted and the £100 million cost was hidden in the supply estimates.[10] In 1950 Britain became involved in the Korean War, 'The painfully achieved economic recovery was halted in its tracks.'[11]

Defence expenditure was increased in 1950 to £3,400 million over the next three years, an increase of over £1,000 million on previous plans and another £1,200 million was added by the beginning of 1951. Hence defence spending would double within two years. Attlee stated the obvious: 'we shall all have to make sacrifices in the face of rising prices and shortages of consumer goods'.[12] Part of the sacrifice came from Gaitskell's plans as Chancellor 'to freeze NHS expenditure at £393 million...by cutting spending on hospitals and saving £20 million by charging for false teeth and spectacles...although the saving on the NHS was less than half of one per cent of the total rearmament package'.[13] A further sacrifice would be in the school building programme as materials were diverted from such capital projects. One of the reasons for the policy, apart from pressure from the USA, was because many members of the government, and particularly Ernest Bevin, seemed to believe that it was possible to restore Britain to its strong pre-war position, failing to grasp that the world had changed radically and many people wished to be independent however paternalistic the power was that had occupied them. The Netherlands and France also deluded themselves in this respect and fought bitter, and in the long run, futile wars in Indonesia, Indo-China and Algeria. (Portugal fought a 16-year war before leaving Angola and Mozambique!) Britain intervened in the post-war conflict in Greece and in 1948 became embroiled in a guerrilla war in Malaya.

> There were circumstances in which Britain was willing to forgo an orderly retreat from Empire and dig their heels in but this was exceptional. Britain was engaged in the Cold War, and no colony could be allowed to pass under Communist control after independence. So while committed to future Malayan self determination, Britain was prepared in 1948 to fight an extended campaign (euphemistically called 'an 'emergency' to avoid charges of colonial oppression) against local Communist Guerrillas.[14]

Fortunately Attlee was able to ensure that the Indian sub-continent gained independence and thereby avoided a protracted and costly armed conflict. A different outcome might have followed if Churchill had won the 1945 election. There were 'Cold War' elements to all of these struggles even if only because some people interpreted almost any independence movement in this light. As for the Korean War, this was a direct product of the 'Cold War' for democracy was not at stake here as both of the regimes were corrupt and dictatorial both before and after the conflict and therefore no different in this respect. Bevin's determination to have British garrisons guarding the sea-route from Britain to India via the Mediterranean and Middle East was condemned by Attlee as an outmoded strategy and one far too costly but opposition from Bevin, the General Staff and the threat of resignation by Montgomery forced him to give way.[15] It was hardly the foreign policy that many expected of a Labour government – more like something out of the nineteenth century.[16]

COLD WAR

There is no wish to become side-tracked here into a detailed account of the effects of the Cold War upon the TUC and trade unionists in Britain. It lasted decades, blighting the lives of people throughout the world as a sterile campaign of fierce propaganda from all the combatants raged, each trying to promote themselves as wedded to the pursuit of freedom and democracy whilst engaged in tactics which denied these qualities, usually with the excuse that the means justified the ends. Among trade unionists, Arthur Deakin of the TGWU frequently denounced communists and pronounced upon the need for democracy yet was dictatorial within his own union which has been described as an oligarchy during his reign. Both the TUC and Labour party produced a number of anti-communist pamphlets including Vic Feather's *Defend Democracy* in the late 1940s and Denis Healey's *Cards on the Table* (1947). As late as 1961 the TUCGC refused to accept an invitaton to attend the British Trade Fare in Moscow even though Reginald Maudling went as government minister as well as hundreds of British businessmen to help boost British exports.[17] With hindsight the wisdom of the approach sometimes taken has been questioned. Taylor has suggested 'More controversially, it is arguable that the TUC, for much of the post-war period, made too sure its own foreign policy kept too closely in line with the views of the mandarins of the Foreign Office.'[18] The TGWU banned communists from holding office but this kind of overall condemnation by official leaders failed to make the distinction which many rank-and-file trade unionists did, between the practices of countries within the Soviet sphere of influence and individual communists who were often regarded at the workplace as trustworthy representatives able and willing to speak on their behalf to employers. In addition, it was not lost on many trade unionists that there were regimes which received considerable support, if not complete approval, from the governments of the UK and USA, which denied freedom and democracy to their own citizens, e.g. Saudi Arabia and South Africa. Moreover British trade unionists were well aware of the treatment afforded negroes in the southern states of the USA for many years after the war and this helped to undermine the credibility of that country's rhetoric about freedom and democracy.

There was never the scale of hysteria, blacklisting and denouncement in Britain as that which permeated the USA. The House Committee on Un-American Activities was formed in 1938 but it was not until the witch-hunting activities of Senator Joseph McCarthy during the 1950s got underway that it had a traumatic impact upon the country.[19] At the height of the Cold War there were organisations in the UK such as the Economic League, established back in 1919, actively involved in listing those considered to be hostile to aspects of capitalism and there is little doubt that the careers of some talented people were damaged as a result of their left-wing ideology. In general, a greater tolerance prevailed although speeches in 1950 by Lord Vansittart in the House of Lords and the Tory MP Tufton Beamish in the House of Commons attacked teachers and lecturers who were communists or left-wing.[20]

Debates arising from the Cold War within the TUC mirrored those of the Labour party, which was not surprising considering that there was an overlap of membership. As a rule most members of the General Council supported government policy. Yet substantial numbers of delegates objected to the diversion of precious resources to the manufacture of armaments when so much needed to be done at home. Speakers also questioned the loss of British lives in conflicts thousands of miles away which posed no realistic threat to the UK. In 1950 Victor Tewson told the TUC: 'We have no bomb, but we have our atomic development plants and our atomic products are flowing to different parts of the earth for the assistance of human suffering in illness, and also to the aid of peace-time industry.'[21]

The kindest interpretation of his words is that his naivety was based upon complete ignorance of the fact that plans had been underway since December 1945 by the Attlee government to develop atomic weapons, an early result of which was the first British atomic bomb being exploded on the Monte Bello islands off Australia in 1952. The atomic weapons programme was driven on by Bevin in the mistaken belief that the possession of nuclear weapons by the UK would persuade the USA that Britain was also a superpower.[22] Only later was it seen as a small contribution to the 'balance of power'. Moreover much of the 'information' which fuelled the Cold War conflict was misleading on both sides as Healey was to write later when referring to 1958: 'It was now clear that the picture which the West had painted of the Soviet Union in the early post-war years needed drastic revision.'[23]

Heated debates took place at Congress when Britain was drawn into the Korean War in 1950. Mr L. McGee (Amalgamated Society of Woodworkers) spoke out strongly against US intervention: 'We cannot permit our boys to die in Korea to replace Syngman Rhee in control', a sentiment endorsed by Mr R. Bond (Association of Cinematographic Technicians). However, the TUCGC produced a 12-point programme supporting the United Nations, USA and UK governments in the Korean War. At the height of the Cold War, Alfred Roberts, in his presidential address to the International Congress of Free Trade Unions (ICFTU) stated that:

> The cost of our own programme of national defence is colossal. It involves expenditure of £4,700 million... it means, unhappily, a continuation, for some time at least, of domestic shortages and still rising prices of goods... It is the burden we have to carry because we have accepted the obligation to maintain the defences of the free world against aggression.[24]

The contradiction inherent in the declared policies of the TUC at this time was that the TUCEC were asking for resources to expand educational provision with the approval of Congress whilst at the same time the TUCGC was supporting government policies which diverted these same resources for long-desired social reforms to other purposes. These joint aims were incompatible. It is possible to argue whether Britain was morally right to get involved in some or all of these conflicts but there is little doubt that in both the short and long term the diversion of so much of the nation's wealth into the accompanying arms programme held back the much-needed reconstruction of the infrastructure of the nation, especially in industries such as the railways. Constant cutbacks to meet the increased burdens of the defence budget were also the prime reason for programmes proposed for the development of the National Health Service and education being slowed down or abandoned, nursery schooling being a good example of the latter. Moreover, with a Labour government having set the precedence for military involvement overseas it was to be of little surprise to find successive Conservative administrations following suit, committing British troops to Kenya in 1952 and Cyprus in 1955. Some sectors of the labour movement were reluctant to criticise the foreign policies of their first majority government even when they could see the effect on their plans for economic and social reform.

The TUCEC was caught up in this dilemma. Their policy document on *Education After the War* was an ambitious one aimed at extending educational provision for all children. Once more they would find themselves in the familiar position of having to persuade the minister for education of the logic of their programme and the need to finance it. The former always proved easier than the latter. Like most people they had great expectations of the new Labour government, although in education cautious optimism would probably be a more accurate description for, as their comments on the war-time negotiations in education had shown, they had serious reservations about the way some of the legislation would work out in practice.

ELLEN WILKINSON AT THE MINISTRY OF EDUCATION 1945–47

Labour's overwhelming victory in the polls meant that the short spell of Richard Law as minister of education was at an end. The obvious choice to succeed him was Chuter Ede, whose experience has already been described. His knowledge of the educational world at both local and national level was probably unmatched by any other Labour MP. It seemed as if his recent experience working in partnership with Butler to gain the approval of several competing pressure groups for the 1944

Education Act would ensure his continuation at the ministry, and now in the key position. This was expected by most people and what he wished himself:

> Ede came down to London from his constituency for the meeting at Beaver Hall on Saturday 28th July after the results [of the election] came out on the Thursday. Before the meeting began Will Whiteley told him Attlee would speak to him the following Wednesday. Ede said there was one job he wanted – Education. Whiteley, who was to be the Chief Whip, said that wasn't 'big enough' for him and that Bevin said he should be Minister of Labour. Ede protested. Attlee told him he would see him Wednesday morning.[25]

Ede was in fact sent to the Home Office and Ellen Wilkinson became minister of education. There was little to suggest at the time that this was an area of great interest to her; even less that it was an area in which she showed much knowledge. A lack of expertise in an area then was no more a barrier to a Cabinet post than it had been previously, or has been since. She had a reputation as being on the Left within the Party during the 1930s, especially from her indictment of working conditions and treatment of workers, specifically the miners and shipbuilders. She had given strong support to the Jarrow marchers and the Spanish Republican government in the Civil War.[26] She was a member of the Plebs League. However by the time she entered government she had moved politically to the right, to some extent under the influence of Churchill, but even more so as a result of her close relationship with Herbert Morrison, the Deputy Leader.[27]

Wilkinson came from a working-class background and won a scholarship to Stretford Road Secondary School and graduated from Manchester University. Her success against the odds led her to believe, like some other members of the Labour party with a similar experience, that if certain barriers to education for working-class children could be removed, such as the abolition of secondary school fees and the raising of the school leaving age, large numbers of working-class children would gain social mobility by their intellectual ability. It can only be a matter for speculation how far the Labour government's education policy would have differed had Ede been appointed, but it is at least probable that he might have given local authorities greater freedom to redesign their secondary school system because of his strong associations with local education authorities and that he would have allowed the development of comprehensive schooling in London and Middlesex. He had shown conditional support for multilateral schools in 1941 and 1944; on the latter occasion in his expressed disapproval of the Ministry of Education's dismissal of multilateral schools as one possible form of secondary education for the future.[28] He had also pointed out that the 1944 Education Act did not propose the establishment of a tripartite system of schooling;[29] this step had followed an assumption that the proposals of the 1943 Norwood Report should be carried out.

Wilkinson saw her main task as ensuring that the 1944 Education Act was implemented in the face of great demands upon the education service. Whilst secondary school organisation would gradually grow as a central issue of debate in the immediate aftermath of the war there were other matters which required attention:

> The accommodation of an extra year of pupils from 1 April 1947...the provision of some form of distinctive post-primary education for all children; and the making good of the severe inroads caused by the war – all these involved the provision of class-room space, teachers, and teacher training on a scale unparalleled before or since.[30]

Initially the prospect of selection to a secondary grammar school by what was believed to be an accurate measure of a pupil's intelligence, regardless of any ability by parents to pay fees, was seen as a great step forward. To think that just as access to such schooling had been won it would in effect be removed by a system which ended grammar schools seemed to significant numbers in the labour movement and among ambitious parents within the working class like snatching away at the last moment a prize they had just won. It would take some time before it became obvious that, as with all competitive systems, there are a minority of 'winners' and a majority of 'losers'. The idea that it was possible to measure accurately the intelligence of a pupil at eleven, that the measured intelligence of a person never changed and that such tests were equally fair to children from different social backgrounds, physical development or sex would take a little longer to become widely doubted. All of these issues would lead to long and bitter arguments within the world of education and among the general public.

In December 1945 the ministry issued a circular entitled *The Organisation of Secondary Schools*, which largely accepted the earlier Conservative government pamphlet *The Nations' Schools*, suggesting a tripartite system of secondary grammar, technical and modern schools as advocated in the 1943 Norwood Report. Wilkinson was aware of the danger of secondary modern schools, to which the majority of children would be sent, continuing as elementary schools under a new name and believed that in the absence of external examinations these schools would be free to develop a range of exciting new approaches to schooling. Yet it is difficult to understand how she could have failed to grasp that even with similar resources, they would not be considered as having parity of esteem given the long-established status of the grammar schools, the higher academic qualifications of the staff, with selected pupils who stayed at school longer and took examinations which provided them with better career prospects, either directly upon leaving school or by the opportunity to continue with their studies into the sixth form or in higher education. It can be argued that there is evidence to justify her support for the tripartite system, (which in reality soon became a bipartite system as technical schools were never built on the scale originally envisaged), because it reflected the views held at local authority level: 'Despite the fact that by 1946 Labour controlled ten counties apart from London and fifty-two county boroughs, a mere handful of local education authorities proposed organising their secondary education on the basis of the common school.'[31] This obscures the fact that London, the biggest education authority of all, had begun planning for a system of common schooling in 1935 and published proposals for its implementation in 1947 but did not gain ministerial approval until 1950.[32]

The reluctance of Wilkinson to consider seriously experiments with a common school system has been partly explained by the view among some that the prize of grammar school entry without fees had just been won. However, another reason why local authorities were apprehensive about planning for a form of multilateral secondary schooling was that the message emanating from the Ministry of Education made it clear that secondary school reorganisation should be carried out by the establishment of different schooling with entry based upon a competitive system of selection; a by-product of which was an increase in the indirect control of the curriculum by central government.[33] The minister faced strong criticism for her inflexible approach to secondary schooling at the Labour Party Conference of 1946 where she was asked to withdraw the circular The Organisation of Secondary Education whilst her constant and harshest critic, W.G. Cove, Labour MP and active member of the NUT, (he had been president of the union back in 1922), put forward an unsuccessful amendment in parliament in 1946 to have her salary reduced.[34] Her one significant achievement was to carry through the raising of the school leaving age to 15 years of age, promised by the 1944 Education Act, postponed by Butler and facing problems in 1947.

In January some doubts were expressed as to the feasibility of raising the school leaving age to 15 years in April with suggestions that it might be best to delay this move until September. This was because of competing demands for rebuilding other sectors of the economy, factories and in particular housing, not only to replace homes destroyed by the war but also to replace so much of the poor inner-city housing which lacked basic facilities such as an indoor toilet, bathroom or hot water system. Raising the school leaving age, however, had been such a fundamental demand from all sections of the labour movement for so long, in a way that other aspects of education policy of the movement were not, that any attempt at postponement when there was already no firm commitment to a date for the next stage to 16, would have been seen as a complete betrayal of thousands of children. Even on this issue she was in one particular out of step with some sections of the labour movement as she believed priority to increase educational opportunities for youngsters should be through new county colleges as outlined in the 1944 Education Act in preference to extending school life.[35] In Cabinet Wilkinson made a strong plea pointing out that the children affected would be precisely those who had suffered most from disruption to their schooling during the years of war. Whilst Cripps and Morrison were opposed and Dalton initially expressed doubts before acquiescing, Bevan, Bevin and Ede supported her, as did Attlee.[36] She had the satisfaction of knowing that at least in this area of education which she regarded as most important of all, she had been successful. She died a month later from an overdose.

GEORGE TOMLINSON TAKES OVER 1947–51 – BUSINESS AS USUAL

Unlike Wilkinson, Tomlinson did have a record of considerable interest in education. In December 1937 the Labour party had established an Education Advisory Committee, alongside others concerned with issues such as housing and health, to prepare for a possible general election in 1940. W.G. Cove, Morgan Jones, Chuter Ede, H.B. Lees-Smith, Michael Stewart, R.H. Tawney and George Tomlinson were some of those appointed to the committee. Others were Barbara Drake, two well-known teachers and NUT members, W.H. Spikes and Elsie Parker. Brian Simon as a member of the University Labour Federation was also a member acting as assistant secretary to Barbara Drake.[37] One subject of agreement by the Committee was an emphasis on what was then termed multilateral schooling, a view shared at the time by Tomlinson.[38]

When Tomlinson took over from Wilkinson at the Ministry of Education in 1947 there was no pronounced change in policy. Like her, he also came from a working-class background and, as with so many of his generation, his formal education had been limited to that provided by an elementary school. It was generally agreed that he was far more amenable and easier to deal with than his predecessor, yet by the time he took office his views were very much in line with those she had pursued and increasingly, in time, this would put him on the defensive at Labour party conferences and in parliament, especially as initial enchantment with the selective system of secondary schooling began to fade. If he was a product of the elementary school that was certainly not true of his permanent secretary John Maud, who was an old Etonian. Tomlinson in any case was not a radical thinker. He 'had great respect for established British institutions whether it was the monarchy, the public schools or the university, and was anxious that his party should not go out of its way to antagonise influential sections of opinion'.[39]

Tomlinson faced certain administrative problems which would have confronted and taxed any education minister. There was the problem of a shortage of school accommodation, partly as a result of schools destroyed or damaged by bombing during the war, and now the need to provide extra buildings to cope with an increased school population since the raising of the school leaving age by a further year to 15 years. In addition, there would be further increases in demand within a couple of years to allow for the increase in the number of babies born during 1946–48, an extra 500,000, which would have a dramatic impact on demands for nursery and infant school places with later pressures upon junior and secondary schools as the 'baby boomers' passed through the system.[40] Within the next ten years, allowing for the raised school leaving age in 1947, the school population would increase by an extra 2 million. This at a time when there was strong competition for building materials for new factories and homes. Priority within the school building programme was given to schools constructed on new housing estates being built in the suburbs and new towns built to provide housing for those moving out of inner city areas of Victorian flats and terraced houses lacking in basic amenities. For the next 15 years or so the issue of large class sizes in local authority schools would be a problem and teachers might be forgiven for wondering as the years passed, why, at times, governments seemed to fail to grasp that the 'baby bulge' in the primary schools would occur in secondary schools later. One 'temporary' solution was the provision of mobile huts which became a feature of most local authority schools; many of which were still in use at the end of the century. Allied to a lack of sufficient classrooms were teacher shortages, which plagued the schools for many years to come for a variety of reasons ranging from what were considered comparably low salaries to the short career of many women teachers who left within a few years of qualifying at college to raise families.

The government could have reduced the number of women teachers leaving for this reason had they continued to provide and expand the nursery school system developed during the War, instead of allowing it to contract. Military conscription introduced by the government in 1947 for an 18-month period, later extended to two years, added to delayed entrance to colleges and universities by those male 18-year-olds proposing to enter teaching but selected for a period of military service.

It is possible to plead extenuating circumstances to some extent for Tomlinson as to why he did not pursue an education policy more in line with that of the Labour Party Conference, for as it has been seen many of the problems with which he was faced were inherited. Even allowing for these difficult circumstances the fact was that he did not approve of Labour Party Conference policy in education. He supported the idea of selective secondary schooling, believing grammar schools offered 'clever' working-class children a fairer chance of advancing in society and whatever Conference might have thought was best in educational terms he believed that in electoral terms, multilateral schools would be unpopular.[41] 'Tomlinson resisted strongly any moves in education which threatened to lose votes.'[42] In the late 1940s, given the strength of the grammar school lobby, his political judgement may have been correct nationally as far as England was concerned but there were areas within the country where this was less so. When comprehensive schools were introduced in the late 1940s in certain rural areas such as the Isles of Anglesey and Man, as well as Westmoreland, it was for pragmatic purposes, for the small school population in these areas made the Norwood proposals of three types of secondary schools irrational regardless of educational considerations. The real test was Middlesex which had submitted plans for a comprehensive system only to find them rejected by Tomlinson in 1948. London, with its many years of planning for an end to selective secondary schooling, was given permission with various conditions attached in 1950.

Even if both Wilkinson and Tomlinson publicly supported the claim that the tripartite system would be one in which there was parity of esteem between the different types of secondary schools, they must have been fully aware of the manner in which the plans for the reorganisation of external examinations resulted in – and it seems were designed to – undermining the prestige and status of secondary modern schools. With the raising of the school leaving age to 15 in April 1947 some secondary modern schools were planning to enter a small number of pupils who could be persuaded to stay on for one further year to take the School Certificate Examination. A lack of confidence in the infallibilty of the 11-plus examinations as early as May 1946 is suggested by a circular *Examinations in Secondary Schools* issued by the Ministry of Education preventing schools other than grammar schools from entering pupils under the age of 17 for any external public examination. Originally Wilkinson had argued that the examination system dominated, and in some instances dictated, the secondary school curriculum. If secondary modern schools were removed from these pressures the curriculum could be moved away from the traditional grammar school approach and thereby made more relevant to the majority of children. The TUC were sympathetic to this approach in 1946.[43] This was naive given the circumstances of the time for if it was to be applied only to secondary modern schools these would now become seen as the non-examination schools whose pupils would be excluded from careers requiring public examination success for entry; a situation for some reason the TUC failed to grasp one year on.[44] In May 1947 the newly reconstituted Secondary School Examinations Council, whose membership had been confined to those from the examination boards, teachers and LEAs, now had appointees from the ministry included, among whom were Maurice Holmes and R.H. Barrow, (the latter secretary to the Norwood Committee), whose allegiances to selective secondary schooling were well known. The Council now proposed that 16 years be the minimum age for the new General Certificate of Education (GCE) that was being planned but that the pass level should be raised to that needed to obtain a credit in the School Certificate Examination.[45] The results were not as they might have predicted; a significant number of grammar school pupils were to fail the GCE and an increasing number of secondary modern schools were to establish GCE streams from which pupils passed the examination. These developments helped to undermine the belief in the accuracy of the tests upon which children's future abilities were predicted at 11 years of age, when children deemed to be incapable of successfully pursuing an 'academic course' proved otherwise. The examination failures of some grammar school children also suggested that proof of academic ability as measured by a test at 11 years of age might not be the most significant element in academic success at school in later years.

Even allowing for the scale of problems facing any government immediately after the most destructive war in lives and infrastructure the world had ever witnessed, the record of the Labour government in education was less successful than that in other comparable areas of the welfare state, such as health. Morgan concludes that, 'education was an area where the Labour government failed to provide any new ideas or inspiration'.[46] This would probably have needed a new Education Act to amend parts of the 1944 Education Act of the Tory-dominated war-time coalition government, in which Butler had skilfully thwarted radical reforms, especially attempts to change the nature of the privileged position of the public schools. Gordon's conclusion similarly finds the Labour government's education policy confused and uninspiring:

> The Labour Party's attitude on the comprehensive issue was neither enthusiastic nor clear...The six years which spanned the Labour government's record in office after the war produced no national policy which altered the basis of selection. The initiative in this matter was taken at local level, especially in Labour-controlled areas.[47]

Caroline Benn and Brian Simon concluded that part of the reason for lack of progress was due to,

> a characteristic of British political life, that what may be called 'official' policy, frequently survives changes in political administration...In 1945 the Labour Party came to power...[it] was specifically committed to the common secondary school, by a series of conference resolutions dating from the early 1940s, so that a mandate for development on these lines had been given. But when this government left office in 1951, after six years, there were only a dozen comprehensive schools in being, with some others 'approved'. In other words, official Ministry policy had prevailed to the exclusion of a reorganization of secondary education.[48]

The tide of opinion was now against Tomlinson throughout the labour movement. In 1950 the Labour Party Conference passed a resolution supporting the implementation of the party's policy on comprehensive education; it became Labour party education policy for the 1951 general election, with acknowledgement that local education authorities should be the final arbiters in planning their own secondary school system. This was to mark a new phase in the fierce arguments which lay ahead concerning selective secondary schooling.

THE TUC AND THE LABOUR GOVERNMENTS

The war had seen an increase in trade union membership and growth of the shop steward movement. The post-war period saw that membership increase continue, reflecting an economic structure of pre-war times for at least another ten years before changes began to take place which would impinge upon the TUC. In 1945, the majority of trade unionists were male manual workers and almost half of union members affiliated to the TUC belonged to one of the big six unions; Transport and General Workers Union (TGWU), National Union of General and Municipal Workers (NUGMW), Amalgamated Engineering Union (AEU), National Union of Mineworkers (NUM), National Union of Railwaymen (NUR) and the Union of Shop and Distributive Allied Workers (USDAW). Women accounted for approximately 20 per cent of TUC affiliated union membership. Amalgamations had been taking place steadily throughout the century in response to changes at the workplace as some jobs declined and others became more in demand. In 1939, 217 affiliated societies had represented 4,669,186 workers, by 1945 the number of societies had decreased to 191 but membership had increased to 6,575,654, and this pattern would continue so that by 1951 there were 186 societies with 7,827,945 members and by 1960, 184 societies with 8,128,251 members. Full employment and a government favourably disposed to trade unionists encouraged increases in membership. The latter feature was a logical outcome for a government formed by a political party which was created with the help of the TUC, had many trade unionists who were now MPs and was supported financially, especially at general election time, by major trade unions. Given these circumstances, liaison between government and the TUC was inevitable although other interest groups like the CBI were also involved in discussions with government departments over issues which affected their members and in which they took an interest, including education.

The TUCEC therefore continued to press the education policy of Congress through channels previously established: delegations to the Ministry of Education; written and oral submissions to committees dealing with education; and participation by TUCEC members on committees of a wide range of organisations from those with which they had been associated for many years, such as Ruskin College, to those with which their involvement was more recent, such as the National Association of Boys' Clubs and the National Co-operating Body of Education. The number of organisations requesting members of the TUCEC to serve on their managing committees continued to increase, as did applications for grants which were sometimes linked with such requests. (See Appendix 3.) All pointed to a growing recognition of the importance of the TUC within society and the value of the contribution they could make in providing help to institutions in terms of experienced personnel and, on a more limited scale, financial support.

The 1945 Labour government started with a fund of good will from the TUC. It was after all 'their government' in the sense that it was seen to represent so many of the working people who were members of trade unions affiliated to the TUC and its programme was clearly designed to introduce reforms which would drastically improve the conditions of the majority of the population: a health service free at the point of delivery; a system of national insurance to provide income if people were unemployed and adequate state pensions; a programme of nationalisation aimed at running major industries for the benefit of the nation instead of in the interests of shareholders; full employment; and free secondary education for all children. By contrast the Conservative party, in spite of being led by Winston Churchill who had been such an inspiring national leader during the war, was seen as representing pre-war governments which had seemed so indifferent to the hardships faced by ordinary people who remembered with bitterness the experiences of communities blighted by unemployment, families faced with means-tested dole payments, difficulties in being able to afford medical fees for much-needed treatment, the restricted educational opportunities provided by the elementary schools attended by most working-class children and the need to leave school at the early age of 14 in order to supplement meagre family incomes. When Attlee promised the 1945 TUC Conference a continuation of consultation with the TUC in peace just as there had been during war-time his appeal met with enthusiastic response.[49]

For the most part the 1945–51 Labour governments did carry through their main pledges.

> No other British government has come to power with so far-reaching, elaborate and precise a programme as the Labour government that took office in July 1945. If any government has come anywhere near the achievement of Attlee and his colleagues in that respect, they have not fulfilled their promises as meticulously as the government of 1945–51.[50]

Yet there were tensions at times between the government and the TUC, if only because their interests whilst similar were not identical. For example in a government publicity campaign aimed at promoting exports the Board of Trade sought the co-operation of the TUC, only to be told that whilst sympathetic they did not think it wise for them to be identified too closely with a government department, in case 'indiscriminate support... might hamper... the pursuit of such objectives of trade union policy as... reduced working hours'.[51] The TUC were not willing to be taken for granted by or get too close to any government however much they might identify with its aims and ambitions.

The government did feel empathy with the TUC, who they regarded as 'natural allies', but at the same time they in turn did not offer preferential treatment to them compared with other pressure groups. Indeed, there were times when the TUC felt they had been treated unfavourably and were under-represented on various government appointed bodies. They believed that the government, especially in its first year of office, 'was guilty of gross imbalances in the representation it allowed them on administrative bodies'.[52] They were given only two of the representatives out of the 12 on Agriculture, there were only nine trade unionists among the 46 full-time members of divisional coal boards, one out of five on the Transport Commission and one out of seven on the Railway Executive Committee. By 1951 only 44 out of 350 members of the central regional boards of all nationalised industries had 'some previous connection with the Trade Union Movement'.[53]

Appointments to such bodies were not without their difficulties. On the one hand there was the feeling that trade unionists would be able to represent the views of ordinary working union members and this was certainly the hope initially. There was also the danger that the new life-style which went with such duties ran the danger of them becoming distanced from the everyday experiences and conditions on the 'shop floor' they were appointed to represent. Accepting knighthoods could add to this perception; Walter Citrine, A.G. Walkden of the Railway Clerks Association (a union which rarely worked in liaison with the NUR and ASLEF in times of rail disputes), Charles Dukes of the NUGMW, William Lawther of the NUM and Vincent Tewson of the TUC all received titles, although Arthur Deakin refused. Certainly some trade union leaders showed little regard for the views of their members or the democratic process within their own organisation.[54] The quality of trade union appointments varied. Few were likely to be up to the ability of the efficient and versatile Walter Citrine who became chairman of the Electricity Authority in 1947, but because TUC appointments were usually based on long service, at the other extreme there were some who were not of a sufficiently high calibre showing little interest in the work they were expected to do, leading George Woodcock, who became TUC Secretary in 1960, to state later, 'there was no reporting back. We never knew what they were doing. In fact, they did damn all.'[55] This harsh comment which may well have applied to some trade unionists, was doubtless equally applicable to some non-trade unionists on the various boards of appointees. All of this was a far cry from the hopes of those trade unionists who would have liked to see trade union representatives within the place of work participating in the organisation and production process in order to give working people a feeling of greater affinity to and responsibility for the success of the enterprise in which they worked. Such moves based upon co-operative principles might have led more people to see nationalised industries as really belonging to them instead of just another form of impersonal organisation, even if conditions of work were so much better within industries such as coal mining and the railways than they had been under pre-war private ownership.

Most trade union leaders gave their support to the government and as a generalisation, just as within the Labour party, were more likely to find themselves in dispute with significant parts of their membership at annual conferences over matters of foreign rather than home affairs. Again, as with the government, there was an uneasy feeling when it was realised that social reforms desired and campaigned for by trade unionists sometimes back to pre-war times when they were contested by Conservative forces, were placed at risk by resources being diverted to foreign affairs which seemed to be of no direct concern to ordinary trade unionists. On these occasions the arguments from the platform were not always convincing and as can happen in any large organisation, the policies promoted by the leadership did not always reflect the views, wishes and sometimes long-term interests of the members. Arthur Deakin of the TGWU was not alone in being seen as a dominant union leader out of touch with considerable numbers within his union.[56] If this dichotomy in support for welfare reform, including education, as opposed to costly military involvement overseas, is mentioned here it is only to point to the difficulties faced by those such as the TUCEC in trying to convince government to support their calls for improvements in the education system.

RAISING OF THE SCHOOL LEAVING AGE TO 15

The high expectations of trade unionists for significant progress in education were tempered by a realistic acknowledgement of the economic situation of the country in the immediate post-war years. The implementation of the 1944 Education Act was seen as the way forward in achieving the goal of secondary education for all and the raising of the school leaving age. The latter was and had been a priority for the TUC for so many years and by 1946 they had been denied this goal twice just when it was in sight; on the first occasion by the outbreak of war in 1939 and on the second occasion by Butler's decision to defer its implementation. Therefore Ellen Wilkinson's assurance to the General Council of the TUC that the school leaving age would be raised to 15 in April 1947 was welcomed as a sign of the importance she attached to this issue. It also explains why, having given her word, she fought so hard in Cabinet months later when there were suggestions that it should be delayed once more, even for a matter of five months.

No sooner did the TUCGC have her affirmation for this first step than they sent her a note, which was followed up by a deputation on 5 June 1946, to urge upon her the need to consider the second stage promised in the Act, even if no specific date had been given, to raise the leaving age by a further year to 16. They put forward two main grounds in support of their proposals:

1. ...on the recognition of educationists that it was impossible to provide a child with a secondary education in any full sense of the word unless he or she stayed at school until 16...
2. ...that unless a common minimum school leaving age was established for all three types of secondary school envisaged in the publications of the Ministry of Education, equality of opportunity would not exist...[57]

Whilst wishing to see county colleges introduced, their priority was for an extra year in school. They believed the latter would be of more educational value than one day per week in a county college; a point they had elaborated on to the Central Advisory Council for Education in England. This was not a view shared altogether by the minister although she did give them some grounds for optimism, explaining that she would be raising the age again 'at the earliest possible moment' while pointing out that the same problem would determine the pace of this move as had influenced the rise to 15 years; the shortage of both adequate school accommodation and teaching staff. She believed completing secondary school reorganisation and reducing class size would need to come first before an extra year of schooling could be introduced. The optimistic note was her statement to the TUC deputation that 'she had asked Local Education Authorities, when submitting their development plans, to make provision for this additional age group'.[58]

The TUCEC met on 1 April 1947, the very date the school leaving age was raised. To mark the occasion the Committee passed a resolution which was sent to the minister of education, George Tomlinson, who had taken over from Wilkinson in February:

Meeting this first day of April, 1947, the Education Committee of the Trades Union Congress welcome the advent of the new school-leaving age of 15 plus. The Committee most heartily and most sincerely congratulate the Government and the Minister of Education on their determination, despite many difficulties, to carry through this vital educational reform. The Committee believe that this act of faith will bring forth an abundant reward in human, social and economic betterment and that the future may be contemplated with greater confidence because of this day's good work.[59]

THE 1944 EDUCATION ACT – A WORKING BASE FOR REFORM

The 1944 Education Act established the Central Advisory Council (CAC) to the Ministry of Education and early in 1946 they invited the TUCGC to submit their views as to how well education prepared boys and girls for their transition from school to life in the community. The terms of reference were wide, aimed at covering 'an appreciation and criticism of existing education as a preparation for a useful and satisfying life', whilst education was to include from nursery to secondary school. To respond adequately to such a wide-ranging area the TUCGC included a copy of their war-time memorandum *Education After the War* which reviewed the education system as it had been in 1942 with their proposals for future educational advance. It was pointed out that by now the well-known TUC memo still represented 'the broad educational policy of Congress' adding it was not their concern 'at this juncture to pursue the points of difference which exist between the TUC Memo and the provisions of the Education Act, 1944'.[60] Their support had always been of a pragmatic nature and, unlike some groups, the TUC did not see the Act as the culmination of educational reform but as the best that could be obtained in the circumstances of a Conservative-dominated war-time coalition government trying to cope with competing vested interests. Two years on this view was reiterated:

For the present purpose we are prepared to assume the new Act is to be taken as the working base for reforms which are to be sought in the immediate future ... Our present concern is to assist, as far as possible, in the translation of the new provisions into living realities in the field of education provision.[61]

Trade unionists were only too aware of the sudden change which had confronted most working-class children of 14 years of age when their elementary schooling had come to an abrupt end and they had been required to enter full-time work because this had been the experience of nearly every one of them.

It needs no big effort of the imagination to understand what a disturbance this sudden and drastic change must make in the life of the young person. We hear constantly of misplacement of young people in industry, of boys and girls in blind alley occupations and in jobs which are calculated to destroy any lively interest and initiative with which the young worker may be endowed.[62]

Hope was expressed in the reforms expected by the 1944 Education Act especially as they were by now aware that the school leaving age was set to rise the next year with indications that a further year would be added relatively soon. Furthermore, there was the additional 'provision of the County Colleges [which were] to become a duty of local education authorities in 1950'. This proposal of the 1944 Education Act was never realised. The TUC suggested the public education system should provide equally (but not identically) for all children as was promised in the 1944 Education Act. Until a common leaving age was established and given that in grammar schools pupils stayed at least until 16:

equality and status between these schools and the new secondary modern schools cannot be established until 16 becomes the minimum leaving age in all secondary schools. [This is] important also because until equality of status and equality of regard have been established between the various types of secondary school the right allocation of children between the various types will not be achieved. It is inevitable and proper that the parents' wishes should play a large part in determining the course of education which their children are to follow. Until equality of regard is established there will inevitably be an undue seeking after admission to the grammar school. Children who, if equality of status between schools were in fact established and recognised, would go the modern school or the technical high school, will be found misplaced in the grammar school. The children and the community as a whole will suffer accordingly. The grammar school has a long start. If the new secondary schools are to achieve their rightful standing in the educational scheme it must be made abundantly clear that they are not less generous in their provision than the grammar schools.[63]

This statement by the TUCGC illustrates that at the time, although they favoured a common school, they were still willing to consider a system of selective secondary schooling providing all schools received similar treatment and their submission made clear just what they believed the conditions should be for that to be fulfilled. It would not be long before their analysis of the way in which selective secondary education was to develop in practice would persuade them to return to their earlier thinking as outlined in their evidence to the 1943 Norwood Report – that given the higher social status of the grammar schools compared to other forms of secondary schooling, in practice, 'parity of esteem' would not be realised. In 1946 however the TUC were still doing their best to make the 1944 Education Act work.

COUNTY COLLEGES, CITIZENSHIP AND LEISURE

The 1918 Education Act outlined a scheme for continuation schools although Rugby was the only authority ever to implement the plan. So too the county colleges proposed by the 1944 Education Act suffered a similar fate, at least in the form envisaged, and for the same reason. In spite of the statement, 'not later than 3 years after the date of this Act, it shall be the duty of every local education authority to establish and maintain county colleges', they never materialised.[64] No government was willing to provide the expenditure necessary. Later Colleges of Further Education would develop from a variety of educational institutions offering access to a much wider range of courses than proposed for the original county colleges, whilst also catering for many of the 16–18-year-olds.

Ellen Wilkinson's approval of the county colleges has been mentioned; even her preference for them over raising the school leaving age to 16. By contrast, the TUC were in good company with R.H. Tawney in taking the opposite view, which he expressed when leading a deputation from the CEA, (which included TUC representatives), to the minister of education in 1945.[65] The truth was that the TUC did not see it as a matter of either one or the other; they wanted both the raising of the school leaving age to 16 and the introduction of county colleges to provide part-time education for the 16–18-year-old age group, even if it was initially only for one day per week as suggested. So whilst priority was given to the former they had firm proposals ready as to the curriculum which should be pursued in the county colleges 'so long as the period of education at the Colleges is limited to one day per week, that period should be devoted to continuing general education of the young people in attendance'.

There was the belief that it was important to 'imbue young people with the spirit of intellectual adventure' which would serve as a link between school and adult life in order to prepare people for participation in a democratic society. 'The County Colleges should afford a very special opportunity for extensive experiment in education for citizenship'; a view echoed at the Labour Party Conference in the same year.[66] Three years earlier Congress had passed a resolution proposing that 'For the benefit of the future nation this Congress recommends that citizenship, including parentcraft be taught to senior boys and girls in all schools.' This was in anticipation of extra time being available when the school leaving age was to be raised after the war. The Standing Joint Committee of Working Women's Organisations had prepared a memorandum on *Instruction in Parentcraft* at the invitation of the Minister of Health's Advisory Committee on Mothers and Young children. It included areas such as cleanliness and personal hygiene, principles of nutrition, biology, physiology and psychology. These subjects it was suggested should be linked up with the teaching of citizenship. This was approved by the TUCEC who went on to produce a memorandum entitled *Education for Citizenship*.[67] The aim was to encourage the future generation to participate in the mechanism of local and national government, and it was believed this could be achieved by direct teaching in civics, indirectly in some subjects such as contemporary history but above all by the creation of a 'general atmosphere of the right kind' by teachers and parents, the home background being seen as the most important of all in this respect. Hence learning to co-operate within the family group and the observance of people participating in local community affairs would provide good role models for the children to follow. The memo was forwarded to the President of the Board of Education who informed the TUCEC that their suggestions 'would be taken into account' by his department.

Obviously related to this thinking was the submission to Congress by several trades councils of suggestions which found approval with the TUCGC, outlining moves to support closer contacts between parents and teachers 'to arrive at a better understanding of the other and encouraging their co-operation for the welfare of the child'. Representations to the minister of education met with a sympathetic response. The importance of co-operation was recognised and reference made to many parents' associations with a qualifying note that 'parents and teachers should be allowed a wide measure of discretion regarding the form of organisation adopted.'[68] An attitude familiar throughout government departments: whenever possible rely upon voluntary efforts rather than introduce legislation to establish a structured system.

The emphasis on general education which had always been a central theme of TUC education thinking was based upon the view that technical education tends 'to separate men, it is from general education that men derive those interests which all may share ... It acts as a corrective to over-specialisation in technical interests and by bringing together the maximum number of citizens on the maximum common ground can add to the stability of the community.'[69] It was further argued that it was the most suitable education from an industrial point of view because 'In coming years it will be more than ever necessary that our people should be adaptable and should be able to meet new needs with a readiness and an ability to acquire new skills and new methods.'[70] It would also be valuable if 'as confidently expected' more leisure time becomes available in future years. The memo illustrates how forward-looking the TUCEC was in envisaging widespread changes in industry and working practices long before they were introduced into the economy. Increased leisure was increasingly realised by the introduction of the 40 hour working week. Further ahead some of the changes hinted at in the TUCEC memo would be introduced in a manner which would bring enforced leisure in the form of widespread unemployment, part-time and short contract work. At the time of the memo it was assumed changes would be planned so that all would benefit, thinking influenced by the efficiency of war-time planning and bitter memories of the pre-Keynsian economic policies of the inter-war years which many thought, or at least hoped, had gone forever.

The 1943 Southport Congress had passed a resolution asking the TUCGC to enquire into the 'problem of the right utilisation of leisure'.[71] After consultations with several organisations such as the Men's Club and Institute Union, the Workers' Film Institute and the British Workers' Sports Association a memo was produced which provides one more example of how the TUC was willing to undertake investigations dealing with complex social issues, pick out those aspects they felt competent to study and produce concise analyses and recommendations relevant to trade unionists and their families. They avoided any attempt to discuss in a comprehensive manner the various ways of employing leisure time realising this was impracticable. Instead they confined their remarks to establishing certain principles which they believed should underlie their approach to leisure time proposals. They pointed to two forms of leisure in recent times; 'relatively unrestricted enjoyment of leisure [as] a privilege of a limited social group and at the same time, through unemployment, enforced leisure upon others under circumstances which made enjoyment an impossibility'.[72] The former would continue to be the case whilst the latter would disappear for a generation before returning with a vengeance. The nature of much 'work in modern industry and commerce is dull, monotonous and even frustrating for the individual... not so much from the nature of the job to be done, but from the fact that the worker is frequently divorced from any interest in the task in hand';[73] a process Marx had recognised half a century before.[74]

These memoranda on citizenship, parentcraft and leisure illustrate the way in which the TUC saw the whole pattern of social life inter-related and how education underpinned moves to improve the conditions in which people lived and their ability to participate in the organisation and running of society. General education to provide a sound background of knowledge, citizenship to make them aware of the power structure in society and how to take an active part in the way society functioned, information at school through parentcraft to help future parents understand matters affecting the health of their family and how to provide a good home. Then leisure because:

> The function of trade unionism does not end with securing the worker improvements as regards his conditions of work and employment. Beyond any day to day question it is concerned with seeing that the worker has the widest opportunity for a full life, and if there are respects in which the facilities available to him for the use and enjoyment of his leisure can be improved, in pursuing such improvement... [in addition] In so far as it relies for its strength on a conscious community of interest and aspiration, it is concerned that the mass of the population shall not be entirely passive recipients of provided entertainments and past times. Mental inertia is the greatest enemy of trade unionism, as of democracy generally. We are therefore concerned that people should be alive and critical in their appreciation of and participation in social activities of all kinds... to take some part in an organisation with a definite social purpose, such as a trade union or political party... is essential to such a life.[75]

EMPLOYMENT OF CHILDREN

During the war the TUC had acquiesced to the employment of schoolchildren in agriculture providing that certain safeguards in terms of hours worked were upheld. With the war over they returned to a critical stance against child labour arguing that it was indefensible: it took children at times away from their studies during school-time and was therefore detrimental to their education, it was used by some landowners and farmers as a form of cheap labour and it had the danger in such circumstances of discouraging some farmers from employing adults at decent rates of pay. The National Union of Agricultural Workers wrote to the TUC in September 1948 highlighting regulations which still permitted exemption of children from school attendance to undertake 'urgent seasonal work' and gave an account of how trade unionists were trying to gain an end to these regulations.[76]

In the following January the TUC sent a deputation to the Ministry of Education. No progress was made at this meeting. They were told that precise numbers were not known but that around 100,000 children were working part-time to harvest potatoes. The minister informed the representatives that labour was needed for two reasons, the decline in the number of agricultural workers and the loss of prisoners of war who had previously undertaken this work! He did say that parental consent was necessary but there were clearly pressures upon rural parents especially those in tied cottages. There was a tradition of rural child labour which many of the parents would have experienced themselves when young and given the low wages paid by farmers, the extra money, however small, earned by children, helped to supplement the family income. Allowing their children to work on the farm also might help to safeguard their own jobs. The only satisfaction the minister provided for the TUC representatives was a vague promise to continue to monitor the system.

The situation for children participating as actors in film, theatrical work or the ballet was less straightforward. A Departmental Committee of Inquiry appointed by the home secretary in 1948 presented its report in August 1950. The TUCGC submitted 20 observations to the secretary of state which in general felt the report made some useful suggestions but was far too lenient with the film and theatre industry. They accepted the findings that:

> Safeguards adequate for the education, health and welfare of the children *must* be devised; whether the effect of these safeguards will be to curtail, or in certain contingencies prevent altogether the use of children in entertainments, we have regarded as a secondary consideration only, though it has not been entirely discounted.

The criticisms of the TUCEC were that whilst they did not wish to exclude children from employment in entertainments they did not believe the report offered enough safeguards to children. The recommendation to end the employment of children 'on tour' with the exception of children acting an individual part was welcomed but there should be a rise in the age of these children from 12 to 13, and licensing for employment in entertainments from 15 to 16. They preferred the Advisory Committee to oversee child labour to be under the Ministry of Education rather than the Home Office. However the main points of disagreement arose over the length of time a child could be employed in any one year. It was suggested that with the engagement of a private tutor a child could be employed for

100 days; a period they were 'far from convinced is necessary... to enable a child to take even a "star" part in a film'.[77] A substantial reduction was needed in this area. In any case the employment of a private tutor would not compensate for the loss of 'intangible but no less real, educative forces which are generated by the corporate life of the school'.[78]

As for the statement in the report that 'it is important that every care should be taken not to create a class of "child actors" set apart from other children' and 'that... children who are employed as film actors shall grow up like other children' this seemed to contradict the 100 days children could be involved in the entertainments industry. The TUCEC referred to the 1944 Education Act which provided for the education of all children of school age: 'if this were to be lightly waived in favour of every sectional interest claiming a concession in respect of a few children it would be difficult to draw any line'. It was clear that the length of time a child could be working would interfere with normal school attendance; if the 100 days were consecutive at least a term's study would be lost whilst if it was spread throughout the year breaking into two or three terms 'the educational results can easily be foreseen'.[79]

The system of matrons appointed to overlook the welfare of the children being an employee of the film company was also considered unsatisfactory to the TUCEC:

> It does to our mind place in a most invidious position a matron who is herself an employee of the producing company if she is expected to assume responsibility for ensuring the welfare of children, if necessary in resistance to demands upon their services by the management by whom she is employed. No action by licensing authorities in these circumstances could eliminate the danger of a subtle black-listing of 'un-co-operative' matrons ... in this connection... the Committee have not sufficiently considered the practical implications of their proposals.[80]

There followed a whole series of counter proposals for conditions of work: children aged 13–16 not to work beyond 7.30 pm, attendance for no more than 6 hours in any one day and all children to have a complete week-end break. The TUCEC document was forwarded to the Home Office in November 1950.[81] A few months later a letter was received from the Variety Artistes' Federation enclosing a memo of their views of children employed on the stage. Support was given to better conditions of employment but they were 'opposed to any thought of banning children on the stage',[82] something the TUCEC had never suggested.

COMMITTEE ON EDUCATION AND COMMERCE

In June 1946 a Special Committee was appointed by the Minister of Education 'To consider the provision which should be made for education for commerce and for the professions relating to it.' The TUCGC were invited to submit evidence and accordingly presented a memorandum. It explained that they had a threefold interest in the area: as representatives of a number of workers in commercial occupations; a general interest in the opportunities available to children of workers who wished to follow a career of their choosing in this area and obtain satisfactory training; and finally because they had an interest in the efficiency of the service in which some of their members worked. The memo from the TUCEC found commercial education lacked co-ordination and any generally accepted standards, comparing it unfavourably with technical education. Pursuing a familiar theme of the TUC and other sections of the labour movement, they claimed:

> We do most emphatically believe that the purpose of primary and secondary education must be to prepare the young person for adult life as a citizen and human being. This conception of the education of children by no means overlooks the fact that the good citizen must earn his keep in the community. But this is not to say that it is the job of the secondary schools to train clerks or typists.[83]

Acknowledging that there were courses covering typing, shorthand, bookkeeping and other commercial subjects in some secondary schools and accepting that they provided a good education the TUC still believed that 'the proper place for such teaching, where it is necessary for a trade or profession, is in a special period of training after the normal school leaving age, conducted as part of the young person's introduction to the occupation of his or her choice'.[84] Even then a sound general education should be provided. This response underlies the consistency of TUC education policy which wished to see the general standard of education raised for all children to enable them to understand more than the techniques of becoming an efficient worker. Subjects such as economic history, geography, languages and mathematics, with economics for older pupils were fine because while they were regarded as a valuable preparation for the study of commerce they did not unduly restrict opportunities for pupils to follow other courses. It was for professions 'to provide such initial training in practical instruction in essential skills combined with general preparation for entry'. The TUC were opposed to special commercial secondary schools concentrating upon a comparatively narrow syllabus. Their preferred system of schooling was made clear. 'In principle we favour the "multi-lateral" or "comprehensive" secondary school.'[85]

The Special Committee on Education for Commerce presented its report in October 1949. The TUCEC were pleased to observe that many of the points they had made had been 'satisfactorily met'. Their central point of schools providing a sound general education with teaching of commerce held back until a later age was agreed, as was their suggestion that such teaching should preferably be full-time so that it was not at the expense of leisure time. As for the lack of co-ordination from teaching to certification, again the report was in line with TUC thinking to rationalise the system: 'Schemes for Ordinary and Higher National Certificates in commerce should be introduced as a generally recognised award of an advanced standard, equivalent to a university degree.' One difficulty facing the TUCEC's concern with commercial education in secondary schools was that they were aware that many parents and employers approved of the teaching of typing and shorthand because it was seen to provide good career prospects for many girls. The danger as far as the TUCEC was concerned was how far the teaching of these subjects was carried out at the expense of other subjects.

The one serious disagreement was over the location of commercial teaching. The Special Committee reasoned that as children in secondary modern schools left at 15 years of age they would not have the time to pursue such studies, which prompted the TUCEC to respond:

> We cannot accept the implication which appears to arise from the Committee's proposal that certain occupations should in effect be barred to pupils of secondary modern schools. The placing of a boy or girl at the age of 11 plus in a given type of secondary school must not be allowed to determine his or her whole future career.[86]

It was this categorisation of people the TUCEC objected to in the report under the subheading 'A Classification of Needs' which stated: 'As we see it, there should be educational facilities for three distinct groups of persons engaged in commerce in order to reach all requirements.' These were:

1. persons engaged in minor routine operations;
2. persons aspiring to more responsible positions;
3. those whose ultimate requirements are for professional training or for advanced education in the special techniques and processes of commerce.

To these three groups the different education requirements provided were in some respects reminiscent of the 1943 Norwood Report. The TUCEC claimed this implied that the 'distinct groups' were seen as groups of 'human beings in relatively static terms' instead of putting the emphasis upon the different grades of employment required. The latter would provide for opportunities for individual movement with the scheme outlined, the Committee's classifications suggested people would be perceived as fitted for a particular grade only with no prospects of advancement.[87] The criticisms in the report of a lack of adequate funding for staffing, buildings and equipment were noted: 'Not one of the eight specialised colleges and departments is wholly satisfactory...not one...has a building satisfactory in its planning, layout, equipment or accommodation, while all lack any semblance of dignity.' Not surprisingly, the TUCEC regretted the lack of any adequate recommendation for participation by trade unions in bodies concerned with education for commerce, or the inclusion in the commercial curriculum of 'the function and methods of trade unions'.[88]

NOTES AND REFERENCES

1. Gilbert, M. (1998) *A History of the Twentieth Century, Vol. Two; 1933–1951*, p.275.
2. Gosden, P.H.J.H. (1976) *Education in the Second World War*, Table 3.2 'War Damage to Schools, 30.9.1942', p.62.

Type of School	Number Recognised	Serious Damage	Minor Damage
Public Elementary	20,916	962	3,053
Secondary/ Prep.	2,164	132	334
Special Schools	597	55	121

3. Ibid., p.48.
4. Hennessey, P. (1992) *Never Again: Britain 1945–1951*, pp.98–110.
5. Ibid., p.99.
6. Clegg, H.A. (1994) *A History of British Trade Unions since 1889, Vol. III 1934–1951*, pp.323–4

7. James, L. (1998) *RAJ – The Making and Unmaking of British India*, pp.558–9.
8. Nicholas, H.G. (ed.) 'Washington Despatches 1941–45', p.609, quoted in Morgan, K. O. (1985) *Labour in Power 1945–1951*, p.145.
9. For a concise summary of the Labour Government's Legislation and some of the issues they faced, see Coxall, B. and Robins, L. (1998) *British Politics Since the War*, pp.17–22.
10. Eatwell, R. (1979) *The 1945–1951 Labour Governments*, p.90; Hennessey, P. (1992) *Never Again*, pp.265–72; Hattersley, R. (1997) *Fifty Years On: A Prejudiced History of Britain Since the War*, p.37.
11. Clarke, P. (1996) *Hope and Glory; Britain 1900–1990*, p.238. Also: Barker, E. (1983) *The British Between the Superpowers 1945–1950*, p.215.

    Bevin and Gaitskell, in a joint paper to the Cabinet, summed up the impact of the Korean war and the resulting rearmament plans on the British economy. By the middle of 1950, they said "the British economy was doing better than could have been hoped...3 years earlier...We had full employment but suffered from neither inflation nor deflation. There was steady and rapid increase in production and productivity...We were, provided the current trends continued, within sight of the objective which, we had set ourselves at the beginning of the European Recovery Programme – independent of external assistance." But then came the Korean war. Rearmament, Bevin and Gaitskell said, would compete with exports for production, and the rapidly rising price of imported raw materials was already worsening terms of trade, so threatening a deficit in the balance of payments..." it will be still more difficult to obtain the surplus which our external commitments require if we are not to run into debt." All this meant was that if Britain was to rearm it would have to give up the target of "independence of external assistance".

12. Hansard, Col. 588, 29.1.1953, Quoted in Carr, F. (1993) 'Cold War' in Fyrth, J. (ed.) *Labour's High Noon*, p.145.
13. Thorpe, A. (1997) *A History of the British Labour Party*, p.133. Thorpe points out that within Cabinet some colleagues in supporting Gaitskell's plans 'put personal distaste for Bevan before political realities'. Aneuran Bevan, Harold Wilson and John Freeman all resigned over the issue.
14. James, L. (1995) *The Rise and Fall of the British Empire*, pp.542–3.
15. Carr, F. (1993) in Fyrth, J., *Labour's High Noon*, p.140; Barker, E. (1983) *The British Between the Superpowers 1945–1950*, p.49.
16. Morgan, K.O. (1984) *Labour in Power 1945–1951*, Ch. 6 provides a detailed account of Bevin's Foreign Policy and some of it's inherent contradictions.

17. *TUC Report 1961*, pp.447–8.
18. Taylor, R. (2000) *The TUC: From the General Strike to New Unionism*, p.15.
19. See Mitford, N. (1978) *A Fine Old Conflict* and Duberman, M.B. (1989) *Paul Robeson*, Chs. 19–21.
20. Simon, B. (1991) *Education and the Social Order 1940–1990*, pp.122–5.
21. *TUC Report 1950*, p.407.
22. Hennessey, P. (1992) *Never Again: Britain 1945–1951*, p.268.
23. Healey, D. (1990) *The Time of My Life*, p.184; Alexander, A. (2002) 'The Soviet Threat was Bogus', *The Spectator*, 20 April.
24. *TUC Report 1951*, p.76.
25. I am very grateful to Bill Bailey for this information. He went on to state:
   That's all there is in the diary (kept by Ede) – that day's entry is the last of all. I have never been able to find any evidence of or any comment on Attlee's thinking on Cabinet-making with reference to Ede. Obituaries in 1965 usually referred to the expectation that he would be Minister of Education – and that it was a big disappointment to him that he was not.
   (Letter from Bill Bailey, 18 June 1998).
   Beckett agrees Ede was expected to go to the Ministry of Education: 'But Clem wanted Ede for the Home Office, and Education went to Ellen Wilkinson, partly because Clem wanted a woman in the Cabinet.' Beckett, F. (2000) *Clem Attlee: A Biography*, p.205.
26. Wilkinson, E. (1939) *The Town That Was Murdered*.
27. Dean, D. (1986) 'Planning for a Post-War Generation: Ellen Wilkinson and George Tomlinson at the Ministry of Education, 1945–51', *History of Education*, Vol. 15, No. 2, p.97.
28. A measure of conditional support for multilateral schools by Ede is given in an interview he had with Harold Laski in 1941. Bailey, B. (1995) 'James Chuter Ede', pp.216–17. See also Simon, B. (1991) *Education and the Social Order 1940–1990*, footnote 44, p.145.
29. Rubinstein, D. and Simon, B. (1969) *The Evolution of the Comprehensive School 1926–1966*, p.31.
30. Barker, R. (1972) *Education and Politics 1900–51*, p.85.
31. Ibid., p.84.
32. Simon, B. (1991) *Education and the Social Order 1940–1990*, p.131.
33. Chitty, C. (1988) 'Central control of the school curriculum, 1944–87', *History of Education*,Vol. 17, No. 4, p.323.
34. Wann, P. (1971) 'The Collapse of Parliamentary Bipartisanship in Education, 1945–1952' *Journal of Educational Administration and History*, Vol. 111, No. 2, p.26.

35. Dean, D. (1986) 'Planning for a Post-War Generation', p.108.
36. Hennessey, P. (1992) *Never Again: Britain 1945–1951*, pp.175–6; For a more detailed account of the issue see Simon, B. (1991) *Education and the Social Order 1940–1990*, pp.97–100.
37. Simon, B. (1998) *A Life in Education*, pp.29–32.
38. Ibid., p.32.
39. Dean, D. (1986) 'Planning for a Post-War Generation', p.110.
40. Clarke, P. (1996) *Hope and Glory: Britain 1900–1990*, pp.220–21. As Clarke explains, this partly echoed the increase in 1920 following the 1914–1918 war. It was not that mothers were having more children but rather that a higher percentage of women were getting married: 'in 1911 less than a quarter of women aged 20–24 were married; in 1951 half were, and by 1971 sixty per cent'.
41. 'Gradually the phrase "common school" or "comprehensive school" was used to differentiate the more thorough-going experiment in which no attempt was made to stream the children into grammar, technical or modern sides. From 1948 the Labour party dropped the use of the term multilateral and pressed instead claims of the true comprehensive school.' Banks, O. (1955) *Party and Prestige*, p.134.
42. Dean, D. (1986) 'Planning for a Post-War Generation', p.101.
43. *TUC Report 1946*, p.122.
44. *TUC Report 1948*, p.163.
45. Simon, B. (1991) *Education and the Social Order 1940–1990*, pp.111–15 for a detailed examination of these events.
46. Morgan, K.O. (1985) *Labour in Power 1945–1951*, p.177.
47. Gordon, P. (1980) *Selection for Secondary Education*, p.230.
48. Benn, C. and Simon, B. (1972 edn) *Half Way There: Report on the British Comprehensive School Reform*, p.43.
49. *TUC Report 1945*, p.316.
50. Clegg, H. (1994) *A History of British Trade Unions since 1889 Vol. III 1934–1951*, p.320.
51. Martin, R. (1980) *TUC: The Growth of a Pressure Group 1868–1976*, p.287.
52. Ibid., p.290.
53. Ibid.
54. Coates, K. (1982) 'The Vagaries of Participation 1945–60' in Pimlot, B. and Cook, C. (eds) *Trade Unions in British Politics*.
55. Jones, J. (1986) *Union Man*, pp.122–3; Hyman, R. (1993) 'Praetorians and Proletarians; Unions and Industrial Relations' in Fyrth, R. (ed.) *Labour's High Noon*, p.184.
56. Coates, K. (1982) 'The Vagaries of Participation 1945–60', p.181.

57. *TUC Report 1946*, p.121.
58. Ibid.
59. *TUC Report 1947*, p.154.
60. *TUC Report 1946*, p.116.
61. Ibid.
62. Ibid.
63. Ibid., p.117.
64. See Morrish, I. (1970) *Education Since 1800*, pp.156–7.
65. Dean, D. (1986) 'Planning for a Post-War Generation', p.108.
66. Barker, R. (1972) *Education and Politics 1900–1951*, p.141 and p.154.
67. *TUC Report 1944*, pp.81–3.
68. Ibid., pp.84–5.
69. *TUC Report 1946*, pp.118–19.
70. Ibid.
71. Ibid., pp.124–5.
72. Ibid., p.125.
73. Ibid.
74. Marx, K. (1891) 'Wage Labour and Capital' pp.91-92, in Marx, K. and Engels, F. (1968) *Selected Works in One Volume*.
75. *TUC Report 1946*, p.125.
76. *TUCEC Mins.* 14.9.1948, TUC 811/9.
77. *TUCEC Mins.* 10.10.1950, TUC 811/9. See also *TUC Report 1951*, p.178.
78. Ibid., p.179.
79. Ibid.
80. Ibid.
81. *TUCEC Mins.* 14.11.1950, TUC 811/9.
82. *TUC Mins.* 8.5.1951, ibid.
83. *TUC Report 1947*, p.159.
84. Ibid.
85. Ibid.
86. Ibid. p.160.
87. Ibid. p.161.
88. Ibid. p.159.

CHAPTER 12

THE CONSERVATIVES BACK IN POWER, 1951: CONTRACTION AND EXPANSION

SOCIAL CHANGES IN THE 1950S

The post-war Labour governments had faced the worst of the time when so much needed to be done with such limited resources. It may be interesting to speculate how they might have fared had they won a further term of office in 1951 in what would become easier economic circumstances – but it would not be a very productive exercise. In reality it was the Conservatives who were able to benefit from some of the groundwork laid by Attlee's administrations. People would inevitably compare the austerity of the Labour years with the increasing availability of goods during the 1950s which had previously and necessarily been labelled 'For Export Only', even if it was principally the middle classes who would initially benefit the most. Motor cars were one obvious example as British automobile manufacturers prospered, unfettered by foreign competitors who were busy restoring war-ravaged economies. Other events, difficult to measure in terms of the 'feel good' factor of the electorate played some part in the popularity of Conservative governments of the 1950s, however irrational they might seem on reflection: the conquest of Everest by a British-led team; the coronation of Elizabeth II in 1953; and even the breaking of the four-minute mile by Roger Bannister the following year. The Cold War engendered hostility to the political Left and this did not help the Labour party's public image any more than the perceived rift over nuclear weapons.

At the workplace Britain's class structure had changed little from the pre-war years. Manual workers made up about 65 per cent of the occupied population and social divisions persisted at work. Compared to their middle-class contemporaries in white collar jobs their conditions were inferior in most respects. They lacked occupational pensions and received fewer holidays (indeed until about 1948 many received no holiday pay and had to rely on savings clubs to cover resulting loss of income). They were paid on an hourly rate instead of a monthly salary and when absent due to illness received no pay from their employer. They started work an hour or more earlier than white collar workers and ate their meals in factory canteens in sections sometimes separated from staff dining rooms. These are necessarily generalisations but they would be recognised as the experiences of large numbers who worked in the factories in which thousands were employed as well as many other areas of manual work – coalmines, the docks, agriculture and transport. The main difference between the 1950s and the pre-war period was that there was a shortage of labour so that unemployment, at least among those starting their working lives in this period, was no longer the threat hanging over them as it had been for many working people in the past. Indeed the shortage of labour was so acute that employers went to the West Indies to persuade people to emigrate to Britain to gain employment. The first arrivals, mainly from Jamaica, came in 1948 and after the arrival of people from the Caribbean Islands new Commonwealth immigrants came in increasing numbers from the Indian sub-continent. They took on employment which many of the native inhabitants rejected because of the unsocial hours or low paid work often lacking in status. They often filled vital roles in the public sector. Many were employed in local transport systems, hospitals and routine manual work. Jobs were available but accommodation was not and there was no government plan to help immigrants settle into a country very different from their homeland in almost every respect – culture, climate, clothing, diet and for some, language and religion. Immigration was hardly a new phenomenon for Britain but the fact that the new arrivals became concentrated in inner cities where work and accommodation at prices they could afford could be found, as well as the fact that initially many were refused accommodation in certain areas, led to considerable changes in the country, not least in schools.

Full employment gave the expanding trade union movement increased bargaining power which they were able to use to win gains long fought over many years. The 40-hour week became agreed for most factory workers in the 1940s ending the need to work half day Saturdays thereby giving them a full week-end free, and rest days as compensation for working on Sunday became widespread in the transport industry. Frequently these gains were undermined by workers choosing to work extra hours of overtime paid at enhanced rates and work the rest day due to them. The engineering industry was one sector of manufacturing in particular where overtime was so common that it was expected of employees. These practices suited both employers and initially employees, the former gained by keeping down the expenses which would have been incurred in national insurance payments and general administration if they had been forced to employ the requisite number of workers and the latter, mesmerised at times by their gross earnings, failed to act in order to raise the comparatively low basic rates of pay which were widespread in many areas of the economy. These practices were storing up problems for the future. Employers had little incentive to invest in new machinery when labour was so cheap and the productivity of British workers remained low because they worked long hours and frequently used outdated equipment. The resistance to change in working practices also contributed to this problem. For the meantime full employment and wage packets together with more consumer goods kept the majority of the electorate contented enough to sustain Conservative governments for another 13 years after Churchill's election in 1951.

Changes could be seen in the occupational structure as traditional labour-intensive industries came under threat from overseas competition. The writing was on the wall for those who were able to look ahead. Past and future economic rivals were rebuilding their economies from scratch and taking a different approach, employing modern machinery, providing better technical training for their employees and better conditions, especially in the removal of the divisive conditions between people of different skills and grades, thereby increasing rates of productivity. For much of the 1950s most people could see their standard of living rising especially those who were rehoused from inadequate inner-city Victorian tenements and terraced houses and the growing number of people buying their own homes. Consumer goods such as refrigerators, television sets and radiograms were becoming increasingly available. The former reduced the need to shop so frequently and practices such as placing milk in a bucket of cold water in a shady spot to prevent it going sour would become folk tales within a few years. The main beneficiaries of enhanced prosperity were those employed in white collar salaried jobs and skilled blue collar work. Many of the former wished to distance themselves from the working classes and adopted values which they saw as contrary to support for the Labour party. Skilled blue collar workers were usually willing enough to identify with the working class and maintain their links with various aspects of the culture, but at the same time that would not prevent many of them from voting Conservative at election time.

CHURCHILL'S POST-WAR GOVERNMENTS 1951–1955

The February 1950 General Election had been won by Labour but the 2.9 per cent swing against them left the new administration with only a five seat majority in the House of Commons whilst the hereditary House of Lords remained overwhelmingly filled with members whose allegiance remained loyally Conservative. The result illustrated how much ground the Conservatives had made up since the end of the war. It also showed how impatient many people were who expected the economy to be transformed rapidly from war-time restrictions to peace-time prosperity. It might be also observed how short the memories seemed to be of many of the electorate. Rationing of most items had gradually been abolished but even here not quickly enough for some and this provided the Conservative party with useful electoral ammunition. In spite of the early progress made by the Labour government the economic implications of the Korean War had blighted the promising advances of the Welfare State. There was great pressure on the government many of whose leading members, such as Bevin and Cripps, were seriously ill. The internal divisions over Gaitskell's cutbacks to meet the massive rearmament programme led to the resignations of Aneurin Bevan, Harold Wilson and John Freeman. There were further problems when the new Iranian government decided to nationalise the installations of the Anglo-Iranian Oil Company in Abadan and by September 1951 there was a balance of payments crisis. Attlee decided to go for an election the following month although he would probably have done better to delay the date for at least another six months. Apparently he had decided against what might have been a more favourable date because King George VI was scheduled to visit Africa in 1952, a tour which he never made as he died on 6 February.[1]

At the election Labour gained a higher percentage of votes than they had in 1950 yet lost seats. They polled more votes than the Conservatives; 13.9 million to 13.7 million but without any form of proportional representation the electoral system awarded them only 295 seats to the Tories 321 in the House of Commons. This was the highest number of votes ever recorded by a political party in a general election. However Labour lost important marginal seats in Lancashire and the Home Counties; many of those who had voted Liberal in 1950 gave their support now to the Conservatives rather than Labour by a ratio of 2:1. Working-class support remained solid but many middle-class voters deserted them for the Tories. The constant drip of anti-Labour articles in the newspapers, most of which were overwhelmingly Conservative in terms of both proprietorship and political sympathies, especially the *Daily Express*,

Daily Graphic, *Daily Mail* and *Daily Telegraph* also played a part in undermining support for Labour. 'Margach, a lobby correspondent from the Forties to the Seventies, says: "I have never known the press so consistently and irresponsibly political, slanted and prejudiced" as during the years of Clem's government.'[2] The 77-year-old Winston Churchill became prime minister once more but the new Conservative administration did not set out to reverse all the changes of the post-war Labour governments.

Most of the welfare measures were continued and it has since been suggested, to some extent at least, that for a considerable time there was a period of consensus politics even if those involved at the time did not see it that way. Consensus between the major political parties was only ever partial and at times even tactical. Bevan's struggle to establish a National Health Service (NHS) free at the point of delivery was fiercely resisted by the British Medical Association, especially the president, Guy Davis, and secretary, Charles Hill. The former secretary Dr Alfred Cox claimed it would be a large step towards national socialism as had been practised in Germany whilst Dr Roland Cockshut claimed doctors would become 'West Indian Slaves'. The *Daily Graphic* described Bevan's plans as 'Hitlerian coercion'.[3] The Conservative Party opposed the NHS at every step and forced a division in the House of Commons in the third reading of the Bill.[4] David Eccles claimed it was a 'concerted attack upon the middle class'. In spite of resistance from these traditionally minded forces and vested interests, Bevan's Bill was passed in November 1946. Just as the public who welcomed free medical treatment rapidly forgot Conservative party resistance to the NHS, so too this party reinvented their immediate past and would soon be claiming they had been in favour all along.

Some of the younger Tory MPs realised that given the party's pre-war record in government, in 1951 they were very much 'on probation'. They realised the Welfare State was popular and so was the commitment to full employment. As for education the policy which had been followed was largely one they would have chosen anyway: selective secondary schooling for the majority; indifference to the decline in nursery schooling; and the public schools which most of them had attended untouched by any government reforms.

The main political consensus was in foreign policy because the reasoning of the leadership in both major parties in this sphere was similar. They believed Britain was still one of the major powers in the world as implied by membership of the Security Council of the United Nations and confirmed by the possession of nuclear weapons. Hence Churchill carried on with Attlee's nuclear weapons programme and the explosion of the atomic bomb in 1952 was followed by the even more destructive hydrogen bomb on Christmas Island in 1957. The Conservatives benefitted financially from 'the ending of the Korean War in 1954 and the terms of trade moving back in Britain's favour'.[5] It could be argued that Britain really did have a world role but this was primarily due to American support which came at a price:

> the fact that the British were active and willing members of all the military alliances the Americans set up – NATO, SEATO, and CENTO; that they were prepared to rearm and to maintain armed forces in Germany and a network of bases around the world; that they fully accepted the new economic and financial institutions, in particular the IMF and GATT... In return the Americans were prepared to underwrite aspects of the British world role...[6]

There was continuity in most other aspects of foreign policy acted out, with British troops being sent to intervene in various areas culminating in the Anglo-French attack on Egypt with the collusion of the Israelis over Nasser's nationalisation of the Suez Canal which had so frustrated Eden even though he had been assured that Egyptian action was legal. With Selwyn Lloyd (foreign secretary) and Harold Macmillan (chancellor) supporting military intervention Eden completely miscalculated the situation, the General Assembly of the United Nations condemned the military invasion by 69 to 5 votes. The United States Government made plain its disapproval and there was a large fall in the value of sterling.[7] Eden had to back down and shortly went off to the West Indies to recuperate. In January 1957 he resigned and Macmillan, who had been just as hawkish over military intervention was chosen as leader of the Conservative party in preference to R.A. Butler. He would remain so until 1963.

There were fewer substantial changes in domestic policy than might have been expected from a new administration. Rather there were changes in emphasis to past policies. Housing probably provides the best example. Even allowing for the fact that the worst of the shortages in building materials which the Labour government had experienced were now past, the house-building of Macmillan (housing minister 1951–54) was impressive, an increase from 260,000 dwellings in 1952 to 318,750 in 1953. What was different was the change in ratio of private to public housing construction. Whereas only one in four houses built in the early 1950s was private, by the early 1960s this had changed to one in two.[8] Owner-occupiers were increasingly favoured, tax subsidies were provided for those with mortgages in 1963 and private sales were free of capital gains tax. Local authority tenants received a measure of subsidy in terms of rent but those renting privately were faced with the full costs which rose with the passing of the 1957 Rent Act. It cannot have escaped the minds of leading Conservative politicians that, in general, owner-occupiers were more sympathetic to Tory ideas than those living in local authority accommodation. This change in emphasis of building private houses was summed up in the slogan 'Property owning democracy' which the Conservatives used to their advantage in gaining electoral support.

Another phrase which would become well known was 'Stop–Go' which became associated with government economic practice. R.A. Butler was not the only chancellor to be associated with the policy but serves as a useful example. In 1952 he imposed limits on the amount of money tourists could take abroad, raised bank rates and restricted hire purchase to reduce demand. As the economy improved, taxes were reduced to allow expansion to take place once more. Tax cuts seemed to become closely linked to forthcoming general elections whilst the cut-backs followed not too long afterwards. This was seen in the budget of April 1955.

> Faced with a budgetary surplus of £242 million, he decided to give away £134 million in the standard rate of income tax. After a brief mood of political and stock-exchange euphoria (which spanned the Tories' election victory of May) this led by the Summer of 1955 to acute inflationary pressures and a calamitous slump in the British balance of payments.[9]

By September the chancellor was desperately seeking to reduce consumption again and three months later his position at the Treasury had been taken over by Macmillan. It could be suggested that Butler had put the fortunes of his Party above those of the long-term interests of the national economy.[10] These economic policies which encouraged expansion only to be followed by contraction affected all aspects of the public services which often felt the brunt of the instability created and demands for plans to be put on hold or cancelled. Education was frequently among the areas under pressure, especially during the period of Churchill's government. Full employment was accepted as a prime aim by the main political parties and the post-war economic conditions of labour shortages meant that this was not difficult to achieve. Education would be affected by these shortages too, especially in the areas of teacher supply, building materials for new schools and the finance to support necessary programmes of reform and expansion.

FLORENCE HORSBURGH – MINISTER OF EDUCATION 1951

When Florence Horsbrugh became minister of education on 2 November 1951 she was affected by the diversion of resources to the Korean War. Just as Churchill had excluded Richard Law from the Cabinet in 1945 so he continued this policy with Horsburgh until September 1953; a comment on the status of education as perceived by the prime minister. This is partly explained by his own experiences as a schoolboy at Harrow. (Churchill liked to maintain a belief that he was a poor scholar at school.) It is true that he failed his officer entrance examinations twice before attendance at a 'crammer' led to success on the third occasion. However, several letters from his teachers contained praise of his studies in chemistry, English, history and mathematics.[11] The controversy which raged over the introduction of the 1902 Education Act by a Conservative government, which he witnessed as an MP, adversely influenced his undertaking widespread reform in this area of government administration.

R.A. Butler was now chancellor of the exchequer with no more qualifications in economics than he had possessed in education. For all his war-time association with the Board of Education he showed no special sympathy to this area, consistently demanding cuts to their expenditure.[12] In spite of the expectations aroused by the Conservative electoral slogan 'Set the People Free' directly they were returned to power their initial regime was one of tight economic control, as Tony Benn as 'baby of the House' recorded in his diary: 'Butler's debut as Chancellor was the occasion for some Labour glee. The policy of austerity he announced was a complete vindication of Labour's policy and sounded the death knell of most Tory pledges. There were many glum faces behind him as he spoke.'[13] Almost all means of reducing expenditure were seriously contemplated: reducing the school leaving age back to 14 years; raising the school entry age to six; introducing fees in all maintained schools, at least for those staying on past the statutory leaving age. This stimulated a letter of protest from the TUCEC to the prime minister.[14] In the event none of these measures was introduced although it was not until January that assurances were given by the prime minister that statutory ages for school entry and leaving would not be changed.

Whilst Horsburgh protested within government she defended all manner of proposals in public thereby giving the impression that she was unwilling to champion education. This meant that the TUC were to find themselves in conflict with the minister as they sought to defend the advances made in schooling and have them expanded further. The conflict began with the issuing of Circular 242 in December 1951. The Circular, calling upon local education authorities to make economies came out on the day parliament was adjourned for a prolonged break at Christmas. The TUC were worried that some LEAs would undertake these cutbacks before any discussion could take place. A TUCEC meeting a few days after the Circular's publication expressed concern that,

> It is nowhere clearly stated in the Circular that the economies urged upon the LEAs are contemplated as being of a temporary or emergency character... It can only be assumed therefore, that this Circular indicates an intention on the part of the present Government to halt the process of development and expansion of the education service.[15]

At first a joint meeting of representatives from the NUT, Co-operative Union and WEA was considered but the NUT expressed doubts as to whether their political neutrality would be compromised by such action. Instead each organisation agreed to issue statements on the economies proposed.

In the event the TUC responded with a statement referring first to the earlier Circular 210:

> Circular 210 has already brought about substantial economies in school building by reducing the standards of new schools, postponing new building for the school meal service in existing schools, by restricting additions to schools to such work as will provide new school places to limiting building work for further education... to maintenance.[16]

Other reductions included economies reducing staff required for administration and inspection, recreation and social training, school uniforms, school transport whilst increasing the price of school meals and fees at evening institutes by 10 per cent. 'A not unimpressive contribution by the educational services to the need for national economy.' Now came Circular 242 in which the minister in one breath stated that she 'does not expect reductions which would impair the essential fabric of the service' yet went on to say that she 'must ask authorities... to review the whole field of their expenditure with a view to making immediate and continuous savings' amounting overall to 5 per cent of their 1952/53 estimates. Horsburgh did not wish to specify where all the cuts should be made but was willing to make suggestions: 'administration... capital expenditure, school transport, fees in Further Education colleges... and to make recreational classes financially self supporting'.

The TUC saw Circular 242 as a second bite of the Circular 210 cherry and argued that 'The Minister's demand for a further cut of five per cent in the educational estimates of local authorities cannot be met without "impairing the essential fabric of the service".' The 5 per cent amounted to £14 million and would be at a time when prices were rising. Moreover this would not be the end as she had made it clear that 'further measures may be required'. Proposals by LEAs to cut the number of teachers, close nursery schools and curtail school dental services led the TUC to declare, 'Thus the rot has in fact started . . . [and] . . . unless this process is stopped the already much modified hopes of the 1944 Education Act will be dashed.'[17] In the interest of the national welfare they proclaimed, 'there shall be no retreat in education'.

Using the trades councils network, the TUC sought information from the regions concerning proposed cutbacks and received more than 100 replies including trades councils from Derby, Lancaster, Leeds, Leicester, Wolverhampton and London Districts. The most common problems reported were overcrowding in primary school classes and infants accommodated in rented properties which were often unsatisfactory.[18] The report compiled by the TUC provided a useful source of information which they were able to use when pressing the government and a number of educational bodies asked for copies. It was described by *The Times* (28 February 1953) as covering 23 county boroughs and parts of 36 counties.

CHURCHILL'S SUPPORT FOR ADULT EDUCATION

One suggested economy in education which was criticised by the TUC brought a response from Churchill the sincere passion of which took them by surprise. On 12 February 1953 the TUC had protested to the minister of education about the proposed reduction in grants for certain adult classes.[19] She gave a guarded non-committal reply suggesting that they should refer to the answers she had given in the House of Commons on 12 and 13 February and told them 'we are still in the middle of discussions with the educational bodies concerned'. In fact in her reply on 12 February she had stated, 'In my view it is reasonable in the present situation to propose a small reduction. The savings in a full year will be about £34,000.'[20] A Leader in the *Manchester Guardian* (21 February 1953) claimed, 'The truth is that the Minister has not been happily inspired in her choice of economies. She will earn the public gratitude if . . . she thinks again.' The *Observer* (8 February 1953) and *Daily Herald* (11 March 1953) were also critical of her approach.

Sir Vincent Tewson wrote directly on 27 February to Winston Churchill enclosing a copy of a resolution passed by the TUC critical of grant cuts to adult education. Churchill's reply began with a defence of his minister's policy. 'The Minister of Education put forward proposals for a minor reduction in the grants paid by her Department with the object of preventing waste ... The Minister does not intend to do anything that will have an adverse effect on this branch of our educational system, but only seeks, as is her duty, to get good value for the money spent.' This first part of his letter was the kind of formal reply which the TUC expected but then Churchill continued in his letter in a vein which clearly illustrated his strong views concerning adult education:

> When you speak of 'this most reactionary decision' I can assure you that nothing has been settled either by the Department concerned or by the Cabinet. There is perhaps no branch of our vast educational system which should more attract within its particular sphere the aid and encouragement of the state than adult education. How many must there be in Britain, after the disturbances of two destructive wars, who thirst in later life to learn about the humanities, the history of their country, the philosophies of the human race, and the arts and letters which sustain and are borne forward by the ever-conquering English language?
>
> This ranks in my opinion far above science and technical instruction, which are well sustained and not without their rewards in our present system. The mental and moral outlook of free men studying the past with free minds in order to discern the future demands the highest measure which our hard pressed finances can sustain. I have no doubt myself that a man or woman earnestly seeking in grown-up life to be guided to wide and suggestive knowledge in its largest and most uplifted sphere will make the best of all pupils in this age of clatter and buzz, of gape and gloat. The appetite of adults to be shown the foundations and processes of thought will never be denied by a British Administration, cherishing the continuity of our island life.
>
> Yours sincerely,
> Winston Churchill[21]

The TUC were delighted with his letter and, with his permission, the letter and their reply were printed in the *Daily Herald* (11 April 1953). 'We eagerly welcome your own estimation of the purpose and importance of adult education and this estimate encourages us to hope that nothing will, in fact, be done which will curtail this valuable service.' Lady Simon wrote to J.V.C. Wray, secretary of the TUCEC, 'I must congratulate you and the TUC in drawing Mr Churchill – and such a draw! I feel quite sorry for

Florrie [Florence Horsburgh]. But I wonder how you got to the PM? In any case its a wonderful result and his testimonial to adult education will be widely read.' Wray's delight was conveyed in his reply to Lady Simon:

> Yes, isn't it great fun to have got the letter out of Churchill? It was, as a matter of fact, pure good luck – when we sent [the resolution] to the PM, expecting no more than that he would receive it 'for information' and that we should have a formal acknowledgement. Instead we got the beautiful testimonial, obviously from the Old Man's own hand. As you say, we shall all of us quote this handsome testimonial to adult education for the rest of our lives.

Other newspapers weighed in criticising the minister, including the *News Chronicle* (14 March 1953) and the *Schoolmaster* (1 May 1953) A cartoon showing the minister as Lady Macbeth about to murder 'Adult Education' summed up the interpretation given by many to her approach to this area of education. There can be little doubt that the prime minister's expression of support for adult education made her harsh stance difficult to maintain and she was forced to back down from her proposed 10 per cent cut to adult education. For the rest of her term at the ministry she was constantly faced by a barrage of sustained criticism from the TUC for the cutbacks she sought to impose on education.

The outcome of all this was to be seen when the Ashby Committee established by the minister of education, to which the TUC had submitted evidence, published its report in August 1954. The TUC issued a statement welcoming the report: 'The report emphatically endorses the major claims made in the TUC's own statement in evidence to the Committee. First and foremost the value of adult education, not only to the individual but to society as a whole is recognised.'[22] Unable to resist a dig at Florence Horsburgh, who had been somewhat humiliated by the findings they concluded by saying, 'It is hoped that, braced by the recommendations of the Ashby Committee, the Minister will clear the decks of her past hesitation and will give the word for "full steam ahead".'[23] Within two months in fact she had been asked to 'clear her desk' and by the time the matter was reported to Congress they were able to quote the supporting words of a new minister. 'This is the most valuable Report and I am able to agree to almost all its recommendations.'

In January Florence Horsburgh was assuring the TUC that 'in the light of national resources and all the urgent claims upon them a fair share was being devoted to education.'[24] As for complaints about the rise in the price of school meals 'most experience showed increases in prices led to decreases in the number of meals – but then numbers recovered'. In any case there was now a 'greater quantity of food in the shops'. In direct discussions her replies were not so curt and there were hints that she was trying to get more money for education. When a TUC deputation had met her in January she told them, 'she was continuously pressing for the allocation to education of the greatest possible proportion of the available resources...a greater amount of school building was being done than ever before'.[25] Total live births had peaked in 1947 and were working their way through the schools. By 1953 the boom had entered infant schools. Primary schools already had 48 per cent of their classes with more than 40 pupils and future years would see the situation in secondary schools worsen before it improved.

Whatever the reality behind the scenes Florence Horsburgh came across to trade unionists as unsympathetic and patronising. At the 1954 Congress Mr C.T.H. Plant (Inland Revenue Staff Federation) moved a resolution expressing concern at the 'serious setback to the implementation of the Education Act of 1944 resulting from the present financial and other restrictions'. In his supporting speech he stated, 'A fortnight ago I would have said that there should be a Minister in the Cabinet responsible for education. It is probably a tragedy that the most reactionary Minister of Education we have had for many years has been promoted to Cabinet rank. Her vicious cuts in relation to education are something we will remember.'[26] Later in the debate Mr H. Eastwood (United Rubber Workers) in his final Congress appearance also commented upon the education minister, He was 'incensed at the sheer cruelty which inspires these education cuts'. He went on to tell Congress of the minister's remarks to working-class women in Scotland. As Conservative MP she said, 'I am afraid that the average housewife has not yet learned the full advantage of the stock pot. A thrifty housewife can make a ham bone last the whole week with care.'[27] The next time she passed down a working class street in the town 'the people hung ham bones out of every window'.

Neither were her insensitive marks confined to an isolated incident. On a further occasion she said, 'The nutritional advantage of carrots in hot water has been greatly neglected by the average housewife.' Such remarks had contributed to the fact that she was no longer the MP for Dundee. When Florence Horsburgh left the Ministry of Education in 1954 she had gained a reputation as one who had achieved little for the education system. It is true that her stewardship had taken place during years of economic cutbacks in social services due to the high level of expenditure on armaments due to the Korean War and that R.A. Butler had pressed her relentlessly to this end. Both Labour and Tory governments were learning the lesson that wars were a drain on the economy. It seems incredible with hindsight that having survived the Second World War, successive governments became involved in one military conflict after another so that the economic infrastructure frequently lacked the necessary scale of investment required to renovate industry to enable it to compete with the fast-growing economies of Germany and Japan, both understandably forbidden to spend large amounts of money on military materials. By 1953/54 the rearmament budget in the UK was seven times that of the estimated budgetary expenditure on education.[28]

SIR DAVID ECCLES – IMPROVED RELATIONSHIPS WITH THE TUC

By the time Sir David Eccles took over at the Ministry of Education in October 1954 the Korean War was over and it had become imperative to push ahead with the school building programme to replace some of the worst of the Victorian school buildings. In addition a general election was only six months away! The government was conscious in particular of the poor facilities available for education in many rural areas often dominated by Church schools which lacked financial resources. These areas traditionally voted Conservative. In addition the economy was beginning to pick up and this would be reflected in the significant increases in educational expenditure from approximately just over £500 million in 1953/54 to about £1,330 million ten years later; in effect an increase in expenditure from 3 per cent to 4.3 per cent of gross domestic product. Impressive though these figures are at first glance the reality was that nearly all the extra money was absorbed in catering for the increase in the school population, firstly in sheer numbers as more children entered the primary school and then later by the greater expenditure per pupil as these extra pupils moved on to secondary schools where the costs for pupils were higher. To that extent pupils individually experienced little improvement in resources.

In introducing the education report to Congress in 1955, Mr W.B. Beard, the chairman of the TUCEC, gave his personal impression of the new Minister after their first meeting

> Along with my colleagues I met Florence Horsburgh when she was Minister of Education, and I have to say that on meeting the present Minister of Education we formed the impression that there is a distinct difference and that possibly some progress would be made. The reason for

1. Alec Firth, Assistant General Secretary and Education Secretary of the TUC 1923–31.

2. Trade Union School Ruskin College 1926. Middle front row: John V.C. Wray; second row from front, fifth from left consecutively: Alec Firth, Walter Citrine and John Price, Head of the Industrial Division of the ILO.

THE EDUCATION BILL

A Public Demonstration

ORGANISED BY THE

Association of Education Committees, National Union of Teachers, School Age Council,
and the Workers' Educational Association

WILL BE HELD IN THE

CENTRAL HALL, WESTMINSTER

ON

Saturday, February 29, 1936

at 3 p.m.

Chairman :
Sir WALTER CITRINE, K.B.E.
General Secretary, Trades Union Congress

Speakers :
Rt. Hon. H. B. LEES SMITH, M.P.
Formerly President of the Board of Education

Dr. R. H. TAWNEY
President, W.E.A.

Councillor J. W. CATLOW
Chairman, Association of Education Committees

Mr. FRED MANDER, M.A., B.Sc.
General Secretary, National Union of Teachers

Sir PERCY HARRIS, M.P.

Lady (ERNEST) SIMON

Supported by Dr. J. J. MALLON, J.P., Secretary of School Age Council, A. CREECH
JONES, M.P., HAROLD CLAY, ERNEST GREEN, J.P., and others.

A Resolution will be moved urging that the exemptions clauses in the Bill will defeat its object and that maintenance
allowances provide the only alternative policy.
The meeting is open to the public and all who are interested in securing a fair deal for the children are invited to attend.

To : H. C. Shearman, Education Officer,
The W.E.A., 38a St. George's Road,
Victoria, S.W.1.

Please let me have............................reserved tickets for the Demonstration on February 29, 1936.

Name.. Organisation (if any)....................................

Address ....

London Caledonian Press Ltd., 74 Swinton Street, W.C.1.—59229

3. Poster advertising public meeting, chaired by Walter Citrine, with leading speakers on education campaigning against the 1936 Education Bill.

SCHOOL BILL BUNGLE

THE Government's *Education Bill* has now been published.

For years the whole Trade Union and Labour Movement has pressed for the raising of the school-leaving age.

The Labour Government tried to do it, but was defeated by the House of Lords.

Supporters of the higher school age are to be found in all parties.

Local Education Authorities, teachers, and all progressive interests want it.

The "National" Government, facing an election, dared not resist this demand.

They promised action. They have introduced their Bill. AND WHAT A BILL!

The school-leaving age is to be raised to 15 in **1939. FOUR YEARS HENCE!**

AND THEN

EXEMPTIONS are to be allowed

(a) for "beneficial" employment

(b) for home duties where "exceptional hardship" would be caused if no exemption were given.

AND

there are to be NO MAINTENANCE ALLOWANCES

The Government's tactics are obvious. Public opinion compels them to raise the school age. Maintenance allowances ought to be paid. But the Government see a way to evade this responsibility. They will give exemptions.

What does this mean? We already know. In nine out of ten of the areas where the school age has been raised by bye-laws the proportion of children exempted ranges **from 79 to 96 per cent.**

The exemption system inevitably means that the poorest children must be found jobs, for their parents cannot afford to keep them at school.

It is bound to be a money test—not an educational test.

These children are not wanted for industry. The unemployment situation would be eased by their retention at school.

Exemptions from school attendance were first introduced in 1870. They were only abolished in 1918.

WE MUST NOT TURN BACK

The Local Education Authorities, who do the job of educating the mass of the children, know what they want. Public opinion supports them. The Labour Movement has led the way.

THE SCHOOL AGE MUST BE RAISED TO 15 With Maintenance Allowances and

WITHOUT EXEMPTIONS.

Send a resolution to the Prime Minister and to your own Member of Parliament.

ACT QUICKLY

Printed by THE VICTORIA HOUSE PRINTING CO. LTD. (T.U.), all Depts.), Tudor St., London, E.C.4, and published by the Trades Union Congress General Council, Transport House, Smith Sq., London, S.W.1 Ref. P.E. 2/10

4. TUC pamphlet protesting against the provisions of the 1936 Education Bill.

5. The cover of a booklet setting out the comprehensive education policy
of the TUC in 1937.

6. Sir Walter Citrine addressing 1941 Edinburgh Congress.

7. Poster by Dudley S. Cowes encouraging evacuation of school children in London during the Second World War.

8. Dame Anne Godwin speaking on Education at the 1955 Southport Congress. A suffragette at 15, she became Secretary of the Clerical Workers' Union and took a major interest in education.

9. Denis Winnard (front left), TUC Education Secretary 1957–76, at the TUC Summer School, York, in the 1960s.

10. (Left to right): Ray Buckton with Clive Jenkins and Roy Jackson, respectively, Chair and Secretary of the TUC Education Committee.

that might well be that he has been able to talk to Mr Butler ... and open the Treasury doors a little wider. But he certainly gave the impression that he was prepared to do more than has been done in the past to help educational progress.[29]

In spite of the improved personal relationship between Sir David Eccles and the TUC they kept up the pressure on the minister, especially when a fresh circular was published aimed at restricting some aspects of educational development. Butler continued to push for economies as the school population continued to grow but Eccles was either more willing or more capable than his predecessor in resisting the chancellor's pressures.

In December 1954 Circular 283 had been published restricting building for primary schools to those designed to serve new housing schemes whilst the bulk of building was to be focussed upon secondary schools which were facing an increase in numbers of almost 750,000 during the next few years. The rate at which the remaining all-age rural schools were being replaced should be increased and limits to minor building works increased from £7,000 to £10,000. New buildings for Further Education, especially where devoted to technical education related to industry were to be promoted and the past contentious Circular 242 was withdrawn. There could be no doubting the poor state of some rural primary schools, many of them built during the nineteenth century. One of many notes within the Ministry of Education concerning a school in Lancashire provides an example of a situation which had become all too common.

A Church of England School, junior and infants (voluntary aided) near Wigan: 'Some 500 children in a very old and dilapidated building which suffers from wet and dry rot. No alternative accommodation is available. The divisional medical officer considered the premises a danger to the children's health.[30]

The 1954 TUC had passed a resolution deploring cuts which had resulted from Circular 245, issued in February 1952, demanding a slow-down in the school building programme. Consequently a deputation from the TUC arranged to meet the minister of education in February 1955. However, by the time the meeting took place, Circular 283 had been issued which signalled a relaxation of the previous policy of cutbacks pursued by Butler. A briefing note to the Minister in preparation for the meeting suggested, 'in view of the TUC's preoccupation with unsatisfactory school buildings in urban areas it would be helpful if something could be added to show how Urban Authorities are reacting to the minor works ceiling...[now raised]...to £10,000 per job.'[31] When the deputation from the TUC led by Mr Beard and including Dame Florence Hancock, Miss B.A. Godwin, J.V.C. Wray, D. Houghton MP and Denis Winnard met they welcomed the main contents of Circular 283 but as predicted pointed to the state of many urban schools. Sir David Eccles agreed with their desire for more rebuilding to make his main attack 'on all-age schools in rural areas for the first advance'.[32] He suggested further building could take place now that the minor works limitation had been raised and it was now for LEAs to take advantage of the new conditions. His whole approach was one of conciliation and accordingly the TUC responded later by urging 'Trades Councils and Federations to take action to ensure that Education Authorities in their areas should implement the provisions of Circular 283'.[33] There were grounds for general agreement on the progress underway and this is apparent from an internal note dealing with a letter from Mr Beard following the deputation's meeting with the minister. 'Any reply called for, or is the ball dead?'[34]

Better relations between the minister and the TUC are also suggested from an internal memo with reference to their recent visit. 'Mr Beard is a good type of trade union leader and will do his best to help. I know him personally, and if the minister would like me to pursue the question further, I could do so unofficially.'[35] Just what the precise question was is not made clear but obviously the minister approved of Mr Bray's initiative because on 4 March he wrote a note to Mr Beard; 'I should like to have a chat with you in the near future on one or two educational matters. Could you spare the time to have lunch with me at the Authors Club...on say 10th or 14th March?' In fact Mr Beard was 'bedfast with a nasty chill' but wrote his thanks for the 'kind invitation'. Apart from a note of sympathy from Mr Bray to Mr Beard over his illness there is no further correspondence to indicate whether the meeting took place. Inevitably one is left wondering what it was Mr Bray wished to discuss unofficially away from the presence of other members of the TUCEC or at the Ministry or even whether Mr Beard's illness was an excuse not to get involved. It is more likely that such meetings were not uncommon when it was felt that there was some affinity between participants and policies were near enough for some give and take to emerge which would be less likely at a meeting where minutes were being taken.

The air of neutrality brought about by the lifting of the tight controls accompanying the arrival of Sir David Eccles at the Ministry did not last too long; or at least led to no relaxation on the part of the TUCEC's scrutiny of government education policy. In 1956 a stream of circulars were issued between April and June affecting a range of educational services; 301 limited the cost of new schools at a time of rising costs of materials, 302 milk in schools, 306 capital investment for school buildings, 307 fees for further education and 308 dealing with the school meals service. The TUCEC considered that taken as a whole they 'suggested an undesirable change in attitude on the part of the minister of education and that in particular circulars 301, 306 and 307 were likely to prejudice the educational services of the country'.[36] They disapproved of 301 which was designed to reduce the standard of school building. The TUC in turn were receiving resolutions critical of education cuts from affiliated trades unions such as USDAW (26 April 1956) and the National Youth Conference of the ETU. Vincent Tewson was moved to write on behalf of the General Council pointing out that much of the building programme outlined by him to TUC delegates in 1955 had since been delayed, a prospect the General Council considered to be 'very serious'.[37]

A note within the Ministry of Education from I.R. Fletcher to the Minister suggested the tactics to adopt in response to Tewson's letter. Delaying a reply was advisable 'until we know whether we are forced to hold Authorities back considerably more than their inevitable difficulties will hold them back in many cases'.[38] It was suggested the Minister

> follow the line taken up in Circular 298, and in his answer to supplementary questions put by Mrs Alice Bacon in parliament on the 8 March...These broadly justify the deferment of some projects in the programme by reference to the delay which is taking place in any case...I think I ought to say that discussions with the Treasury have the most restrictive possible results, it will not be possible to maintain this line for long...as we shall be forced to slow up the tempo of the building to a pace palpably less than what the Authorities are capable of.[39]

The ministry were under pressure, not just from the TUC and teacher unions but also from the Association of Education Committees representatives who were to be received by the minister to discuss Circular 301 'Limits of Costs for New Schools'. Briefing notes prepared for Eccles make it clear that they were aware that the policies being proposed had nothing to do with educational needs and everything to do with Treasury moves to contain inflation.

> We were bound to incur the charge of breaking our pledge over Circular 274. We had, however, a choice either of sticking to Circular 274 and contributing towards inflation, or of abandoning it in an attempt to combat inflation. We chose the latter as the lesser of two evils.

We cannot side-track the problem of the cost limits by retaining them at their present level while allowing some of the accommodation to be deferred. This is only a more expensive way of doing tomorrow what we do not do today. We could amend the present Building Regulations, thus accepting a lower basic standards, But

(a) We think the present standards are a reasonable minimum
(b) We could only reduce them in the face of more or less united and informed education opinion.[40]

. A page of methods by which standards could be reduced was provided; a reduction in space per pupil from 42 to 40 square feet in primary schools, 73 to 70 square feet in secondary schools; keeping building plans simple with straightforward shapes; not letting engineering consultants for services such as heating and electrical installations absorb more than a fair share of cost limits. Whilst not insisting on the cheapest, the most expensive of finishes to floors, walls and ceilings should not be approved. Then a phrase repeated so often down the years exposed the attitude towards schooling for the majority of ordinary children. Economies could be obtained 'By doing without frills' a view suggesting considerable ignorance of the conditions in which the majority of teachers and their pupils worked.

In dealing with the TUC Eccles was more conciliatory in his tone than Florence Horsburgh had been. 'I entirely agree with your Education Committee about the need for sufficient places in secondary schools to meet the pressure of the next few years,' he wrote to Tewson.[41] He went on to explain how he was dealing with the problems which had arisen over delays in school building and his tactics for dealing with the arrears which had built up. 'With the best will in the world they [the local authorities] could not start £89 million worth of work in a year. I have decided to recognise this fact and give authorities a provisional target of £105 million spread over 1956–57 and 1957–58; provisional because if more can be done next year as a result of defeating inflation we shall look at the programme again.'[42]

Part of the problem for local authorities was the increase in the rate of interest on loans which forced them to look again at building programmes. One way of coping with the increased costs was for them to slow down the rate of their rebuilding programme, an approach reinforced by government pressure in the form of circulars being issued, especially 298. Minor projects were to be deferred unless considered urgent. What incensed the TUC was that at their meeting the previous January the minister had told them that 'If the current rate of secondary school building could be maintained school places would be available for all children of secondary school age.'[43] This had been repeated approvingly to the 1955 TUC; now it was clear the minister had changed tack, or as trade unionists perceived it, gone back on his word. The suggestions which had been made within the Ministry of Education for ways of reducing expenditure had since emerged as advice to local authorities who would need 'to adjust to a certain degree their standards of space, design, construction and finish' for new primary and secondary schools. This was designed to save £4 million in taxes and rates during the year 1956/57; all to be gained at the expense of large numbers of pupils attending local authority schools. TUC pronouncements about 'the injustice to our children' and the 'disservice to the welfare and progress of the whole community' fell on stony ground.

A three-page letter expressing the frustration of the TUC with the manner education had been treated in recent years was sent from Tewson to Sir David Eccles:

> These measures will inevitably have the result that the children comprising the exceptionally large age-groups which will be entering the secondary schools in the next few years, having, in many cases, experienced a primary education characterised by overcrowded classes and inadequate school buildings, will be subject to similar educational disadvantages at the secondary stage also...All too frequently since 1951 have the General Council been compelled to protest at the interruption, slowing down or deferment of school building projects by government actions...The total effect of these successive circulars has been to create in the minds of the General Council disquiet as to the attitude of the Government at the present time towards the education service.[44]

ALL CHANGE AT THE MINISTRY – AGAIN AND AGAIN

The issue of funding would continue to plague the education system in spite of changes in prime minister and even more frequent changes in ministers of education. The Conservatives were to remain in power until 1964. General election victories in 1955 and 1959 meant that they would complete 13 years in office before Sir Alec Douglas-Home was defeated. Without jumping ahead to post-1960 years it is worth observing that during the years of Conservative rule there were eight changes of minister of education, three of whom held the office twice. At an average of 18 months per minister it does say something for the seriousness with which education was taken and of the status of the position as perceived by career politicians. If Eccles was able to avoid the continuing results of his programme of deferred school building and a degree of accepted decline in the standards set earlier it was partly because two years later, when the issue was raised again by the TUC he had left the ministry. Sir Edward Boyle was now in the post.

During the short period between Eccles and Boyle Lord Hailsham had come in January 1957 and left after all of eight months in September. His second spell from April to October 1964 was even briefer. He was one of many ministers lacking any experience of local authority schools attended by the majority of children; his education had been at Eton and Oxford. In his autobiography, in the brief chapter devoted to his first spell at the ministry, he states, 'I was Minister of Education between January and September 1957 – not long enough, one might think, to achieve much in the history of the department. Up to a point I agree.'[45] This is rationalised by his recording of the view of a 'senior civil servant' in conversation with Hailsham's wife. 'We reckon we have got everything out of a minister that he is capable of giving within eighteen months of his appointment.'[46] It would be difficult to think of any other profession or trade requiring a reasonable amount of knowledge and skill that this could be said of with any seriousness. Anthony Crosland in conversation with Maurice Kogan stated, 'I had four separate jobs in five and a half years, which was far too many.' He went on to explain that the rapid turnover of Cabinet posts had not always been the norm. 'In Baldwin's 1924–29 government 16 out 21 Cabinet Ministers held the same office throughout Parliament; 15 out of 20 did so in the 1931–35 government.'[47]

Hailsham was a maverick character in many ways but his views on education were in line with traditional Conservatism, restricted by his own social background – support for selective secondary schooling and fee-paying schools. His attitude towards teacher trade unions was perhaps less typical. 'One of the abiding weaknesses of the school educational scene, then ... was the number, quarrelsomeness and sheer vulgarity in the behaviour of the teaching unions.'[48] Yet when he did meet a deputation from the TUC who were once more following up several TUC resolutions on education sent to him earlier, including concern over the school building programme his manner was not at all confrontational. He suggested 'that there seemed to be no difference of opinion on what was required. But the problem was less of objectives than of ways and means, and of educating public opinion on the need for greatly improved educational facilities.'[49]

For the TUC it seemed that whoever was minister of education, the policy, if not the personality seemed to be monotonously similar. The month after Hailsham left the ministry Circular 331 was published dealing with educational building. As a result of the government's intention to limit capital investment in the public sector for the next two financial years 1958–1960 it was to be held to the same level as 1957/58. Schools needed to serve new housing developments would not be affected; those designed to replace all-age schools in rural areas together with plans for improvement in some primary and secondary schools would be 'deferred'. Minor building works so important in updating facilities to many older buildings were to be 'severely restricted'. Buildings for teacher training, special schools and school clinics would also be 'deferred'. Earlier assurances given to the TUC about LEAs having the freedom to carry out minor building projects at their own discretion were all forgotten.

In January 1958 to reinforce the message Circular 334 was issued declaring that it was 'imperative that the utmost economy in educational expenditure should be observed'. These demands for deferments, reductions and economies in school building began to sound like a repetitive mantra. Certain building programmes should be postponed rather than financed by borrowing. Hardly an element of education was not included in the demands for cutbacks: 'expenditure on the renewal and replacement of furniture and equipment in all educational institutions should be reduced to a minimum'. Whilst government could point to annual rises in educational expenditure most of this was devoted to attempts to keep pace with the growing school population. The General Council found themselves in a position which had hardly changed since the Conservatives had gained power in 1951; regular protests to government which seemed impotent in the face of increasing Conservative numbers elected with each post-war general election – 321 in 1951, 345 in 1955 and 365 in 1959. By contrast Labour watched its support in the House of Commons decline; 295, 277 and 258 respectively. The consumer boom arising from government economic policy was electorally successful; Peter Thorneycroft and Derick Heathcoat Amory were both skilful in producing tax-cutting budgets prior to general elections although the resulting short-term boom was usually followed by post-election deflationary measures. The financial rewards for investing in property at the expense of long-term investment in industry and the economic infrastructure of the country were to prove disastrous as the nation's share of manufactured goods declined and a series of balance of payments crises affected the strength of the pound internationally.[50] Small wonder that the education budget for capital projects was forced to replicate these stop–go policies.

The General Council could only report their feelings of despair to the 1958 Congress:

> The General Council have expressed on a number of occasions in recent years criticism of policies aimed at limiting expenditure upon education. They have met successive Ministers of Education to state their point of view, but with little success... the Council remain convinced that not only the interests of the nation's children but the vital interests of all our people are endangered by policies which restrict educational opportunities and so prevent the fullest development of individual abilities. Expenditure upon education represents an investment in the nation's future.[51]

They can have had few illusions as to how their call for the withdrawal of Circular 334 would be received. It seemed impossible to convince ministers that adequate provision for children in primary and secondary schools was vital if they were to be able to make the most of future opportunities in further and higher education. There was a glimmer of hope two years later when a circular in April 1960 raised the limit of cost per pupil in primary and secondary schools but even here a note of caution was added by the General Council because of subsequent announcements by Derick Heathcoat Amory, chancellor of the exchequer, that capital expenditure by public authorities, which naturally included school buildings, was to be held at the current level.[52]

NOTES AND REFERENCES

1. Thorpe, A. (1997) *A History of the British Labour Party*, p.134.
2. Beckett, F. (2000) *Clem Attlee: A Biography*, p.208.
3. Ibid. pp.251–2.
4. Marwick, A. (1982) *British Society Since 1945*, p.100.
5. Coxall, B. and Lynton, L. (1998) *British Politics Since the War*, p.22.
6. Gamble, A. (1990 edn) *Britain in Decline*, p.109.
7. See Gilbert, M. (1999) *A History of the Twentieth Century, Vol. III, 1952–1999*, pp.112–39 and Morgan, K.O. (1990) *The People's Peace: British History 1945–1999*, pp.147–56.
8. Clarke, P. (1996) *Hope and Glory: Britain 1900–1990*, p.242.
9. Morgan, K. O. (1990) *The People's Peace*, p.122.
10. Anthony Howard, Butler's biographer, is of the same opinion although his tone is more gentle:
    > Whether that was the design or not, it was, in effect, the way things worked

out. Rab's fourth budget, delivered to the House on 19 April, after Churchill's retirement and when the date of the election was already known, did have something of the flavour about it of being an electoral aperitif... but the subsequent history of the year was to demonstrate that the far wiser course for RAB would have been to produce an April Budget every bit as austere as his February statement.

Howard, A. (1987) *RAB: The Life of R.A. Butler*, p.214.

11. Gilbert, M. (1992) *Churchill: A Life*, pp.28–34.
12. Simon, B. (1991) *Education and the Social Order 1940–1990*, p.163.
13. Winstone, R. (1995) *Tony Benn: Years of Hope. Diaries, Papers and Letters 1940–1962*, 7 November 1951, p.160.
14. TUCEC to P.M., 11.12.1951, TUC 811/11.
15. *TUCEC Mins.*, 11.12.1951.
16. *TUC Report 1952*, p.163.
17. Ibid., p.164.
18. *TUCEC Mins.*, 10.2.1952.
19. *TUCEC Mins.*, 17.2.1953.
20. The *Observer* 8.2.1953 and *Daily Herald* 11.3.1953 were also critical of her approach.
21. Winston Churchill to TUC, March 1953, *TUCEC Mins.*, TUC 810/2622/1.
22. *TUC Report 1955*, p.183.
23. Ibid.
24. *TUC Mins.*, 12.1.1954.
25. *TUCEC Mins.*, 18.1.1954.
26. *TUC Report 1954*, p.315.
27. Ibid.
28. Simon, B. (1991), *Education and the Social Order 1940–1990*, p.168.
29. *TUC Report 1955*, p.333.
30. J.V. Stephenson, 3.2.1955, *PRO ED 147/445*.
31. Mr. A. Thompson to Mr. Part, 27.1.1955, *PRO ED 147/445*.
32. *TUC Report 1955*, p.55. and *PRO ED 147/445*.
33. Ibid., p.56.
34. A.T. 15.2.1955, *PRO ED 147/445*.
35. Reverse side of memo 26.2.1955 Ref.G795/4 *PRO ED 147/445*.
36. *TUCEC Mins.*, TUC 810/2622/1.
37. V. Tewson to Sir D. Eccles, 9.4.1956, *PRO ED 147/1035*.
38. I.R. Fletcher to Sir D. Eccles 24.4.1956. Ibid.
39. Ibid.
40. Briefing notes, Ibid.
41. Eccles to Tewson 26.6.1956, Ibid.

42. Ibid.
43. *TUC Report 1956*, p.167.
44. V. Tewson to Sir D. Eccles 13.8.1956 *PRO ED 147/1035*.
45. Hailsham, Lord (1990) *A Sparrow's Flight*, p.305.
46. Ibid.
47. Kogan, M. (1971) *The Politics of Education*, p.159.
48. Hailsham, Lord (1990) *A Sparrow's Flight*, p.308.
49. TUC Deputation to Min. of Educ., 20.3.1957, *PRO ED 147/1035*.
50. Boxer, A. (1996) *The Conservative Government 1951–1964*, pp.94–5.
51. *TUC Report 1957*, p.181.
52. *TUC Report 1960*, p.201.

CHAPTER 13

NURSERY EDUCATION AND SCHOOL WELFARE

NURSERY SCHOOLING – AN AREA OF CONTINUED NEGLECT

Of all the areas of education none suffered more during the post-war period than nursery schooling.[1] Whilst there were sound educational reasons for nursery schooling during the Second World War they were developed primarily to support mothers who were required to work. With the war over and the economic raison d'être removed, although the educational justification remained, successive governments ignored the need for their further development. There were many reasons for this neglect. There was initially a view that mothers should stay at home and be with their children. Then a traditional attitude that the younger the child the less important is their education and the less well-qualified a teacher needs to be, a belief reinforced by differences in pay scales between elementary and secondary school teachers in pre-war Britain which still continues in many countries. At its crudest the suggestion is that very young children can only play whereas older pupils deal with more difficult subject matter so their teachers need to have more knowledge. The reality as any experienced teacher knows is that different, rather than lower or higher, levels of skill are needed to cope with pupils of varying ages and abilities.

With attention focussed on the 'baby boom' entering primary schools to be followed later by similar pressures upon the secondary sector and the heated debate of selective secondary schooling, nursery schools remained outside the areas of education most frequently discussed. There was a failure to grasp the importance of the early years in the development of children emotionally and intellectually as well as physically. It was difficult to convince ministers of education that the provision of nursery schools for those parents who wished their children to attend one could provide a useful indicator of learning problems which might be apparent to a skilled teacher, and that it was easier, and cheaper to deal with them at that age rather than find out later in the primary or secondary school. This again would have required forward thinking and long-term investment, features it has been demonstrated were not central to the thinking of the Conservative governments which ruled from 1951–64.

The first resolution in support of nursery schooling in post-war Britain was passed in 1947. Miss B. Thom (Women Public Health Workers) whilst agreeing with a statement by the elderly trade unionist George Isaacs, now minister of labour, that mothers of young children should not be encouraged to go into industry, nevertheless, urged the government to 'facilitate the provision of more Day Nurseries for priority cases; for children whose mothers, for economic reasons, are obliged to be gainfully employed or during periods of a mother's illness or incapacity'.[2] Also included in the priority group were 'widowed mothers, the unmarried mother, and the mother who has been deserted by her husband'.

Miss Thom spelt out some of the virtues of nursery schooling: 'the benefits to the mental and physical development of the young child, the pleasure from the companionship of other young children'. In supporting the resolution Mr A. Harrison, (Confederation of Health Service Employees) added that nursery schools gave wives 'an opportunity, while keeping close contact with her child, to live a fuller life, which conforms with what we as men, and the rest of us, expect to live'. He wished nursery schooling to be considered as an essential part of the social system.

The economic reasoning of governments which would provide the main stumbling block to development was made clear in 1949 when Nancy Adams, woman officer of the TUC, wrote to the Ministry of Education requesting information on the number of nursery schools and plans for future building.[3] The answer given was that there had been an increase in the number of nursery schools from 353 in 1947 to 398 in 1948. However it was emphasised that:

> The building of new nursery schools can only be sanctioned where the Ministry of Education is satisfied after consultation with the Ministry of Labour, that such work is required to assist the employment of married women in industry. For this reason a large increase in the provision for children under five years of age is not expected during the year 1949.

Trade unionists soon learned to stress the economic rather than the educational advantages for nursery school provision. At a conference of Women Workers Miss. K. Ault (Tobacco Workers Union) suggested the TUC General Council should press the government to lay down a definite policy for day nurseries and give an adequate allowance to local authorities for this purpose. (The Ministry of Health had ceased to pay full grants to nurseries in 1946.) She drew attention to the fact that whilst many women were forced to work because of the increased cost of living 'some counties were without a single day nursery and there were still far too few in the London boroughs. Furthermore, as a result of the economy drive to reduce the cost of day nurseries, charges were being increased.' Miss MacNaghten (Musicians Union) told the conference that in Hammersmith there were so few places 'that practically only the children of widows and unmarried mothers were given places', whilst Mrs Mills (Blackpool Council Women's Advisory Committee) referred to the desire of Blackpool's Tory Council 'to abolish day nurseries although the cost...was equal to only a penny rate whereas the cost of the illuminations was equal to a seven and a half penny rate.'[4]

It was not easy to gain attention for nursery schooling but there was a steady pressure from women trade unionists in particular to force ministers to listen to their real concern. At the annual conference of representatives of unions catering for women workers a resolution was passed condemning the 'totally inadequate number of day nursery schools for children' and calling for a vigorous campaign from the labour movement on this question. This resolution was received by the TUCEC but whilst they were in favour of drawing the government's attention to the matter, they were probably reflecting public opinion when they decided 'nursery education could not be given priority at the present time'. Nevertheless Vincent Tewson wrote to Geoffrey Lloyd stating the TUC support for nursery schooling, stressing values other than economic which would emanate from a network of nursery schools.

> We believe that nursery schools and classes provide an invaluable social education and training for young children in the pre-school period and offer opportunities for constructive play and personal development which cannot be provided within any single family...We believe that the influence of nursery schools is wholly good, and we regret that in recent years some nursery schools and classes have been closed for reasons of economy.[5]

Lloyd's reply was predictable. He agreed with the value of nursery schooling but claimed that no progress could be made because of 'the extent of other claims on available staff and building resources'. Namely 'the bulge' as the higher post-war birth rate moved through the schools, the resulting larger classes and a shortage of secondary school teachers in particular. The most he could promise was that he would 'discourage any decline in nursery schooling', although by then there were already areas of the country which were devoid of such schools and classes.[6] The complete lack of progress in this area was admitted again in May 1960 by David Eccles, now in his second spell at the Ministry of Education, by the publication of Circular 8/60 which informed local education authorities that it had been found 'impossible to undertake any expansion in the provision of nursery education'.[7] The depressing contents of the circular were discussed by the TUCEC and Tewson wrote again to Eccles pointing out that the TUC disapproved not only of the message conveyed by the circular but also the suggestion that local authorities should think about running their existing nursery schools on a shift system. 'The TUC strongly condemned the negative policies as indicated by the circular.'[8]

One consistent policy of post-war education ministers of education was their neglect of nursery schooling. Some were willing to agree as to its importance, none would provide the necessary funding to provide a nation-wide service. The post-war birth rate was cited repeatedly as the reason, some might say the excuse, for refusing to expand nursery schooling. Eccles informed Tewson that he could not agree with the TUC view that it would be possible to allow some expansion of nursery education. A combination of half a million extra children in schools since 1956, 20,000 over-size classes and teacher shortage exacerbated by thousands of women teachers leaving annually to get married or raise families meant that the Ministry of Education believed resources should be focussed upon primary and secondary schools together with teacher training. It never seemed to occur to governments that more nursery classes would enable married women teachers to return to the classroom earlier if they knew their children were being well cared for and thereby help with the teacher shortage, a provision which would have helped married mothers in many occupations as had been only too well recognised by the government during the war. Eccles made it clear that the government had no intention of establishing an adequate nursery school system. 'There was certainly no scope at present for even a modest diversion of teachers from the primary schools for staffing additional nursery schools or classes.'[9] These answers always begged the question of government priorities in expenditure.

The TUC were dissatisfied with Eccles' reply. They expressed their doubts that recruitment of nursery school teachers would adversely effect the supply of teachers to primary and secondary schools for such a belief assumed that the interests, aptitudes and skills of teachers were almost the same regardless of the age group taught. Tewson wrote again emphasising that the 1944 Education Act required local education authorities to make provision for nursery education and wished to know when the minister would undertake these requirements in the Act. Eccles would not budge from his earlier stance and the vague assurance that he would 'seize the opportunity when it occurred' to expand nursery education left the TUC to conclude that in fact the government attached no real importance to this sector of education, either in educational or electoral terms.[10]

SCHOOL MEALS AND MILK

The labour movement had always been aware that there was a strong link between social welfare and education. Providing school places was obviously necessary but if children were undernourished they could not make the best of the opportunities provided for study. In 1893 a deputation from the Unemployed Committee including H.M. Hyndman visited A.H.D. Acland, the education minister, to ask for the government to provide funding for school meals. 'Acland declined to introduce any such measures stating that he was "reluctant to take any steps that would undermine parental responsibility or tend to weaken home ties".'[11] The TUC called upon parliament back in 1897 'to empower school boards to provide food for many thousands of starving and underfed children who are to be found in the people's schools throughout the country'.[12] Local voluntary schemes, often run by other sections of the labour movement such as the Independent Labour Party were already providing meals at breakfast or mid-day, or even both at the turn of twentieth century.[13] It allowed for up to a halfpenny in the pound rate to be raised by local authorities after authorisation by the Board of Education. Since that time improved standards of living had erradicated the worst aspects of child hunger but there was still evidence of undernourishment in the country up to the outbreak of the Second World War. Only half the local authorities were providing school meals in the 1930s, some claiming that in their areas there was no need. A small percentage of children in the poorest districts received free school meals, sometimes in premises which were not part of the school. Sir F. Freemantle, Conservative MP, echoed similar sentiments to those of Acland from the last century when he told the House of Commons in November 1936, 'Hunger, to a certain extent, is a very good thing' and the provision of school milk and dinners by the State may mean 'less is provided by bad or careless parents at home'.[14]

Government priorities change in war-time and the irony was that food rationing and the basic diet which followed as a consequence meant that Britain 'ended the war with a slightly better-fed and healthier population...British child mortality and sickness rates fell progressively during the war.'[15] During the war both school dinners and teas had been provided; the latter organised in some areas to allow children to stay on at school for an hour or more, when sandwiches, a cake and tea were provided as well as some form of supervised leisure, to give parents time to get home after their day's work. There were fluctuations in the service, partly as a result of evacuation.[16] After the war, teas were rapidly abandoned but mid-day school meals continued with one third of a pint of milk provided during the mid-morning break. Talk of making school meals and milk free, as part of Beveridge's Welfare programme to provide income in kind, was only partially successful. Milk was provided free in 1946, the money being found for it in Dalton's budget but meals were priced at the cost of the food provided although given free to children from low-income families.

During the 1949 financial crisis which led to devaluation of the pound the price of school meals was increased by one penny from five to sixpence. It soon became clear that there was no prospect of meals being made free for all children; on the contrary prices would rise whenever economies were called for in educational expenditure. In 1951 the link between the price paid by parents and the average cost of a dinner was broken by a new regulation which only referred to charges at 'an approved rate'.[17] By 1953 they had been raised to ninepence and, whilst low-income families were still absolved from payment, protests began to arrive at the TUC from trades councils and affiliated unions. For example Bethnal Green Trades Council passed a resolution condemning the reduction in food subsidies but pointed the finger of blame at the general cuts in the Education Bill. 'We feel this is a retrograde step and will have a detrimental effect on the children.'[18] Other trades councils protesting included those from Barry and District (19 February 1953), Manchester and Salford (29 February 1953), Barnes and District (3 March 1953) and Tonbridge (9 March 1953). The claim was that the increases were having an immediate effect upon the number of children taking meals. The TUCEC put the matter before the TUC Economic Committee who pronounced that less than half the increase of the price resulted from 'the reduction in food subsidies and that the greater part of the increase must be attributed to the Government's policy of educational economies'.[19]

Within the TUC there had been doubts as to the value of contacting the minister of education but a letter from Len Murray to D. Bowers disagreed, reinforcing the view that the ministry's economy drive was the larger factor in the increases. He wrote, 'I do not agree with the Education Committee's view that it would be "useless" to talk to the Minister of Education. It would probably be fruitless but it was within the Minister's competence to decide whether or not the extra charge or at least half of it should be levied, and she should be held responsible.'[20] Tewson's letter to the minister informing her of the decline in school dinners taken as depicted by information from 11 trades councils received a reply in which she promised to examine the situation after receiving the results of a return on the number of meals being provided in June. When the results of the count were known it became clear that numbers 'have declined by nearly 250,000. Count the extra children on the rolls this year and the number who might have taken school meals but did not must be bigger... With every reservation, however, it is clear that the rise in price has had serious repercussions... As the school medical officer for Smethick has just suggested in his annual report, good food is cheaper in the long run than medical treatment,' so reported the *Times Educational Supplement*. (24 July 1953). One by-product of the reduction in demand for school meals was revealed in a letter from Bromley (Kent) TC to the TUC expressing concern at 'the reduction of hours and wages of employees of Bromley's school canteen'.[21]

There was to be a repeat performance by the government in 1956. First Circular 302 was issued in May reducing the daily allowance of milk for nursery school children from two-thirds to one-third of a pint of milk with instructions to local authorities to exercise extreme care in ordering school milk. Schemes offering free school milk to some children at weekends and during holidays were abolished. The TUC estimated 'the total savings from this petty economy will be £125,000 ... [which] indicates a niggardliness of approach to educational provision'.[22] Then came Circular 308 announcing a further one penny rise in the price of school dinners to tenpence. A deputation from the TUC led by W. Beard and including Dame Florence Hancock (TGWU), J. Campbell (NUR), J. Crawford (Boot and Shoe Operatives), E.J. Hill (Boilermakers), W.E. Jones (Mineworkers) and Denis Winnard (TUCEC secretary) met with Sir David Eccles to discuss the issue of school meals and milk once more. He promised to look again at the effect on numbers taking meals following the price rises although an earlier promise by Florence Horsburgh to do so had led to no action being taken even when the fall had been dramatic. It was also obvious that no action would follow another significant fall.

Eccles stated that his personal view was that, 'he would like to get rid of family allowances and make school meals free to school children' but that was clearly not going to happen.[23] The TUC agreed with his view on school dinners but not with the abolition of family allowances. The Minister refused pleas to restore proposed cutbacks emphasising 'the necessity to show clearly that public expenditure was being administered with economy... it was necessary to concentrate educational expenditure on the most essential items'.[24] The idea that school meals were not 'essentials' in the education service had in any case been reinforced in February 1957 when the Chancellor had raised the prices again by a further twopence to one shilling; once more a rise above the cost of the food provided and a further indication of moves to economise in the welfare services.

SCHOOL TRANSPORT

There were three aspects of transport for children of school age which were raised in the 1950s: children walking beyond the statutory minimum distance, walking to school along roads considered dangerous due to traffic congestion and the lack of reduced fares for pupils staying on at school. The first two were raised with the Labour government as early as 1949. A question arose at the 18th annual conference of representatives of unions catering for women workers who passed a resolution urging 'an improvement in transport services in rural areas and drawing attention to the needs of school children'.[25] Local authorities were obliged to provide transport to and from school where the journey for children under eight years of age was more than two miles in walking distance and for older children more than three miles. They could provide transport for children walking a shorter distance if there were special circumstances, such as dangerous roads to be crossed on the journey. As with all discretionary powers some local authorities acted upon them, others did not. The minister of education expressed sympathy with the walking distances undertaken by some children but believed that to reduce these would place demands upon public transport services which the companies would find it difficult to meet.

The TUC decided to use their network of trades councils once more to gather information to see how the law on transport for school children was working out in practice. The results from this survey in which 70 trades councils submitted information showed that there were very few places in which local authorities were not providing transport for children according to the criteria of distance but there was growing concern about the increase in the volume of road traffic which was forcing large numbers of children to negotiate dangerous road conditions which could be partly countered if more school buses were provided for more children. This information was forwarded to the minister but no satisfaction was forthcoming because it was claimed there was neither spare bus capacity nor the necessary funding even had it been available. Far from expansion school transport was one of the areas which was to be reduced as part of the government's 'economies in the field of education'.[26] Given this policy, ministerial promises to 'examine all cases sent to him' were of little comfort. In fact he did act in a few isolated cases but then suggested these problems should be taken up with the individual local authority rather than submitted to him. Walking two or three miles to school had been the norm for many working-class children, distances dwarfed by those which had faced children a generation or so earlier, but these journeys whilst not necessarily a hardship when the weather was warm and dry presented a different experience in winter. Then, cold and wet weather combined with reduced hours of daylight leading to children going to and returning from school in the dark produced a particular problem for rural children. Past generations of children had walked long distances to school because there was no alternative means of transport. This was no longer the case since the development of bus, tram and train services. The main problem now was less the distance to school than the danger from increasing road traffic, a problem which would increase rapidly in the years ahead.

The idea of reduced fares for some school children was generally based upon the leaving age of 14 set by the 1918 Education Act. A combination of the raising of the school leaving age to 15 years and a move towards more pupils staying on beyond the statutory leaving age meant that an increasing number of young people did not qualify for reduced fares unless they were travelling to and from school. Families were faced with finding full fares for young people who earned no wage, a difficulty for those on low incomes. This led to a discussion at the annual conference of the Shop, Distributive and Allied Workers (USDAW) where a resolution was passed asking for legislation which would allow pupils up to 16 years of age to qualify for half-price fares on public transport. The Union asked the TUC General Council to comment upon the resolution.[27] Details were forwarded to the TUCEC who referred to an earlier study by the TUC Research Department and views expressed by the TUC Economic Committee. It appears that the TUCEC knew they could not win on this issue because although the moral argument was strong the key issue was an economic one, bus companies claimed they could not afford such a scheme to provide reduced fares for older school pupils when they were undertaking travel unrelated to school activities. The matter was also raised at the Annual Conference of Trades Councils who passed a resolution calling for legislation 'to allow all children of school age (up to 15 years) to enjoy reduced fares on public transport road and rail'. When they received this latest resolution the TUCEC explained that they had considered the issue three times during the last two years. Pupils going to and from school do get reduced fares, it is for other journeys that they do not. This reply was based on the fact that they had already sounded out the Ministry of Transport whose attitude was clear; the financial problems for transport companies made the idea impractical. The TUCEC concluded 'no practical purpose would be gained by pursuing the issue'.[28] Their explanation had already been passed to the Annual Conference of TCs which nevertheless passed a similar resolution again. The government were reluctant to concede to requests for reduced fares because they knew they could only be achieved if they were prepared to offer considerable subsidies to the transport companies. In the long run it might have proved cheaper nationally because high fares on public transport for family travel helped to persuade many to invest in the purchase of a car, a policy which appeared initially to be a cheaper alternative to road and rail travel when four or five people were travelling. One more example of a short-term financial decision which was to contribute to larger economic problems in the future, in this case road congestion and pollution.

SCHOOL UNIFORMS

By 1900 most private schools had adopted school uniforms and these were taken up by many state secondary grammar schools alongside traditions of houses, prefects and speech days.[29] Uniforms were comparatively expensive and a further disincentive for parents on low incomes during the inter-war period to support their children who may have passed an entrance examination in taking up their place at a secondary grammar school. In 1956 the Associated Engineering and Shipbuilding Draughtsmen enclosed a resolution passed by the National Tracers' Sub-Committee of the Association which, whilst approving the wearing of school uniform, 'deplored the fact that in a number of cases they were only available from certain firms in each district which resulted in higher expense than parents could afford'.[30] It was requested that the

TUC look into the question of monopoly in the manufacture and sale of school uniforms.

The TUCEC secretary reported that the matter had been raised in the House of Commons (4 December 1956) to which the secretary of state had replied he could find little evidence that this was really a problem. This complacent answer displayed incredible ignorance of the situation. The fact was that some schools chose elaborate coloured blazers and badges in order to signal to the local public that both the children and the school were distinctively different, usually implying better, than other pupils and schools. In general they marked out the pupils attending fee-paying and selective schools. As the orders for such uniforms were relatively small they were inevitably more expensive than the average school blazer. Many parents were only too willing to pay for a uniform which advertised the fact that their child did not attend the local secondary modern school. Such prices were a burden for many working-class pupils and some local education authorities did introduce a system of grants to help low-income parents to meet the costs involved. It was one more problem the TUCEC were asked to follow up to which they did not believe they could gain a satisfactory solution. The only advice they could offer was for trade unions to take up the matter with their local education authority. In the long run the problem for most parents would be solved by a combination of the move away from selective secondary schools and the adoption of more of them of uniforms which could be purchased from chain stores so that the only special cost might be the school badge and tie. In time blazers would give way to more practical garments such as sweaters and some schools abandoned uniforms – often only temporarily before changing attitudes encouraged their reintroduction.

MAINTENANCE ALLOWANCES

This had been a major item on the TUC education agenda in the pre-war years because it was realised that some parents could not afford the loss of earnings suffered by a child staying on at school instead of starting work. Maintenance allowances for children in these circumstances were seen as a means by which more working-class children would be able to stay on at school. A working party was set up by the Ministry of Education in the autumn of 1957 to examine this problem during the post-war period. It tried to establish 'what part of the expenses falling upon parents who allowed their children to stay at school would be beyond the resources of the poorest parents'. They concluded that: 'maintenance allowances of £55 at age 15, £65 at age 16 and £75 at age 17 should be paid in respect of children staying on at school where the annual net income of the parents did not exceed £300'.[31] A scaled system of lesser grants for parents earning more than the £300 was suggested with a cut-off of more than £480. These recommendations to the minister of education were rejected as too generous and he suggested they be reduced to £40, £55 and £65 respectively which he would be willing to authorise local education authorities to adopt as maximum allowances. The TUCEC believed the minister's recommended grants were inadequate and strongly criticised him for rejecting the findings of the working party. They believed the consequence would be that 'many children will continue to be deprived of the opportunity to remain at school beyond the statutory leaving age'.[32]

NOTES AND REFERENCES

1. For tentative steps towards support for nursery education during the inter-war years see Gordon, P., Aldrich, R. and Dean, D. (1991) *Education and Policy in England in the Twentieth Century*, pp.158–9.
2. *TUC Report 1947*, pp.413–14.
3. N. Adams to G. Tomlinson, 21.1.1949 and G. Tomlinson to N. Adams, 1.2.1949, TUC 815.1(1).
4. Women Workers' Conference 12/13 May 1950, TUC Archives, University of North London.
5. V. Tewson to Geoffrey Lloyd, 29.10.1958, TUC 815.1(1).
6. G. Lloyd to V. Tewson, 7.11.1958, ibid.
7. *TUCEC Mins.* 12.7.1960.
8. V. Tewson to D. Lloyd, 2.8.1960.
9. D. Eccles to V. Tewson, 8.11.1960, TUC 811/17.
10. *TUC Report 1961*, pp.181–2.
11. *Justice*,11 February 1893, Quoted in Manton, K. (1998) 'Socialism and Education in Britain 1883–1902', p.34, PhD (London).
12. *TUC Report 1897*, p.50.
13. Griggs, C. (1983) *The Trades Union Congress and the Struggle for Education 1868–1925*, pp.146–51; Simon, B. (1965) *Education and the labour movement 1870–1920*, pp.133–7.
14. Hansard 1936, 5th Series, Vol. 317, 1936–1937, Col. 157, 4, November 1936.
15. Hobsbawm, E. (1994) *Age of Extremes: The Short Twentieth Century 1914–91*, p.47.

16. See Gosden, P.H.J.H. (1976) *Education in the Second World War*, Ch. 9.
17. Garner, D. (1985) 'Education and the Welfare State; The School Meals and Milk Service 1944–1980' *Journal of Educational Administration and History*, Vol. XVII, No. 2.
18. Bethnal Green T.C. to V. Tewson, 12.2.1953, TUC 810.2623(1).
19. *TUCEC Mins.*, 10.3.1953.
20. L. Murray to D. Bowers, 14.4.1953, TUC 810.2623(1).
21. Mr Whitehart to V. Tewson, 11.6.1953, TUC 810.2623(1).
22. *TUC Report 1956*, p.169.
23. *PRO ED 147/1035.*
24. *TUCEC Mins.*, 8.10.1956.
25. *TUC Report 1949*, p.153.
26. *TUC Report 1950*, p.163.
27. USDAW to TUC, 26.4.1956, TUC 811/13.
28. *TUCEC Mins.*, 9.10.1956.
29. Griggs, C. (1985) *Private Education in Britain*, p.17.
30. AESD to TUC, 13.12.1956, TUC 811/14.
31. *TUC Report 1958*, pp.1–2.
32. *TUC Mins.*, 8.10.1957.

CHAPTER 14

THE 1944 EDUCATION ACT: UNFINISHED BUSINESS

In March 1956 the minister of education asked the Central Advisory Council for Education (England)

> to consider in relation to the changing social and industrial needs of our society, and the needs of its individual citizens, the education of boys and girls between 15 and 18, and in particular to consider the various levels of general and specialised studies between these ages and to examine the inter-relationship of the various stages of education.

The first sentence of the preface in volume 1 of the more than 500-page report from the council sets out the terms of reference for what was to become known as the Crowther Report. The 33 members of the Committee included two from the TUCEC, Miss B.A. Godwin and the secretary Denis Winnard. The detailed study, published in November 1959, looked at the system of secondary education recognising that by the age of 15 most of the children in the country were already at the end of their schooling. The report pointed out that 'one and three quarter million boys and girls aged 15–17 inclusive would all be receiving either full-time or part-time day education if the 1944 Education Act had been put fully into effect by raising the school-leaving age and introducing county colleges'.[1] This failure by governments to deliver the service promised more than a dozen years earlier was one which had been frequently criticised by the TUC. In effect the figure was about 40 per cent for both full and part time students; 80 per cent of pupils left school before they were 16.

The changing social conditions of post-war Britain were outlined: the increase in life expectancy; earlier marriages; smaller families and rise in divorce rates.[2] Also noted was an increase in the numbers and proportions of the occupations needing higher standards of education. This was a central theme of the report which went on to state that young people needed a longer period of education to cope with the move away from manual work in traditional industries to the growing demands related to the expansion in clerical and professional work arising from structural changes in the economy. 'If we are to have higher standards in life – we shall need a firmer educational base than we have today.'[3] So much of the report reads like a textbook covering social changes which were not only relevant to the 1950s but which in many ways would remain stubbornly true for decades to come. For example, juvenile delinquency 'still largely a male prerogative' was associated with 'specific neighbourhoods which are marked by a high concentration of about every social problem... typical of such areas are the inner, declining rings of impoverished districts near the centre of the great cities... But... a new housing estate, if left without appropriate provision for communal life and inadequate social leadership, can be as deadly as a decaying slum.'[4] The manner in which the housing on estates was related to the income of the occupants, and in turn the schooling provided, not so much in the quality as in the social composition of the pupils, gave greater prestige to some schools than others. A fact which in turn became associated with examination results and attractiveness or otherwise to good ambitious teachers. The result was a widening gap in the quality of housing, life-style and schooling of areas from the 1950s onwards.[5] Deprived social conditions were identified as a major contributory cause of delinquency and one change which was really significant compared with the pre-war period was that 'Whatever the reason, neither adults nor teenagers are willing nowadays to take very much on authority.'[6]

Many organisations provided evidence to the Council: Ten Associations of Education Committees; four Associations of Municipal Authorities; ten County Council Associations; the London County Council; Teachers organisations; Chief Education Officers and numerous other institutions from the FBI to the TUC, Institute of Bankers to the Standing Conference of National Voluntary Organisations; 34 individual witnesses representing organisations as diverse as Pitman's College to the Staff Training Department of Selfridges, Winchester College to the British Transport Commission – as well as several academics including Dr R. Pedley, Dr

Stephen Wiseman and Professor Sir Solly Zuckerman. In addition a further 43 organisations submitted memoranda including the Catholic Education Council and the Communist Party.

The TUC's six-page submission built upon Congress policy, recognised the changing industrial and social needs which must prepare young people for 'life and work in a society characterised by relatively rapid social and economic change'.[7] Their first priority was one they had been pursuing for 20 years; a rise in the school leaving age to 16 because 'a secondary course extending in many cases over a period of less than four years cannot be regarded as meeting satisfactorily the needs either of society or of the young people themselves'.[8] Their view on the importance of a sound general education as a basis for later specialisation was also repeated and this should include 'an adequate understanding of the methods and achievements of science, and should suitably reflect, and effectively prepare young people to appreciate, the significance of science and technology in society'.[9] As to the forms of secondary education the General Council's view was that 'it is educationally and socially undesirable that young people should be unduly segregated on the basis of their possession or otherwise of certain specific abilities, especially if such segregation is related also to different fields of future employment and consequently to different degrees of social studies';[10] a point which will be taken up further when the debate concerning comprehensive education is considered in the 1960s.

County colleges were the second priority for the TUC as the best way of providing part-time study. Voluntary staying on was welcomed but this was perceived as a slow method of increasing the numbers of post-16 students. They believed there was a case for decreasing the degree of specialisation in sixth form studies which was believed to commence at too early an age. As always caution was expressed towards vocational education and two other criteria were recommended to encourage more youngsters to continue with their studies – that day rather than evening studies should be provided for the 16 plus age group and adequate maintenance grants should be available. Furthermore, as more youngsters took advantage of day-release courses it would be necessary to examine the content and standard of some of the courses being offered to see how far they were appropriate.

All of these measures depended upon the supply of a sufficient number of teachers being trained. The TUC approved of the plan to increase teacher certificate courses from two to three years in 1960 but realised this would mean that no teachers would graduate from teacher training colleges in the year 1962 and the supply would be reduced in future years.

If the school leaving age was to be raised and class sizes reduced it would be necessary to expand the number of places available in teacher training colleges and institutes of education.

The thoroughness and detail of the Crowther Report when published in 1959 is illustrated by the fact that the summary of principal conclusions and recommendations covered 26 pages; hence it is necessary to make a further summary in order to pick out the key points: the raising of the school leaving age to 16 and the introduction of county colleges, both provisions of the 1944 Education Act should be fulfilled. The former to take place between 1965 and 1969 when there would be a trough in the secondary school population. The early leaving of pupils in maintained grammar schools was a worry as was the downward pressure of sixth-form A level subjects leading pupils to make subject choices by the age of 13 years. Whilst specialisation at sixth-form level had some advantages there was a need to bring arts and science pupils together for such subjects as religious studies, art, music and physical education. Complementary classes should be held to ensure the literacy of science students and the numeracy of arts students. These lessons could take place in what was described as 'minority time', much of which was wasted. A levels should be an assessment of the two or three years of work in the sixth form and not seen only as an entrance examination for higher education. Given the increased number of young people qualifying for higher education there was a need to expand the number of university places and simplify the variety of entry requirements among different universities and their faculties. Summarising the Crowther Report runs the risk of oversimplifying what was in effect a study showing the complexities of a secondary education system which had evolved almost piecemeal out of so many varied strands catering originally for different social groups. The report was met with the general approval of the TUC. Accordingly, Miss B.A. Godwin who had worked on the Council moved a composite motion at the 1960 TUC:

> This Congress welcomes, as a major contribution to educational advance, the Report of the Central Advisory Council for Education.
>
> It endorses particularly the recommendation that the Government should prepare now for raising the school leaving age to 16 by laying down a date for the implementation of this reform, and urges the Minister of Education to take the steps necessary to ensure that the size of classes can be progressively reduced, the school leaving age raised to 16 and compulsory part-time education introduced in accordance with the Council's timetable.[11]

No contentious debate followed because Congress found the Council's central arguments so convincing. Whilst not expecting Congress to agree with all the recommendations, Miss Godwin asked for 'support and endorsement for the major recommendations in regard to the school leaving age. This is of course existing Congress policy.' Mr C.T.H. Plant (Inland Revenue Staff Association) seconded the motion and spoke of the general support Crowther had received: 'The WEA and the London County Council both press for this reform. The Association of Education Committees welcome it, the teachers welcome it, the British Employers Confederation – hardly a body renowned for starry eyed idealism – have accepted it.'[12] He referred to a study of National Service recruits to the army and navy, details of which appeared in volume two of the report. The recruits were divided into six ability groups. 'The Committee found that two-thirds of those in the two top ability groups had left school at 15.'[13] This scale of wastage would arise again in the arguments over selective secondary schooling. Mr Plant finished with a quote from the Report:

> The education that is provided for the great mass of children is inadequate both in its quality and its duration. In the middle, between the brightest quarter and the great mass of ordinary children, the deficiencies, relative to the need, are greatest of all, for it is in this "second quartile" that the richest vein of untapped human resources lies, which will have to be exploited if this country is to keep a place among the nations that are in the van of spiritual and material progress.[14]

The General Council had published its response to the Crowther Report shortly after it was published, much of it repeating the ideas outlined in its earlier memorandum. Its general welcome to the findings arose from a belief that 'the recommendations of the report can provide the basis for a planned programme of educational advance which is urgently needed in the interests of the nation's children and young people, and in the interests of the nation itself'.[15]

The argument that education should be considered as an investment was gathering pace in the 1950s, a question the Crowther Report posed. 'Education can be regarded in two ways – either as a duty that the state owes to its citizens, and therefore as part of the "welfare state", or as a means of increasing the economic efficiency of the whole community, and therefore as a form of productive national capital investment.'[16]

Cost was bound to be a major question for the government. Crowther argued that the 'cost of our recommendations would not be very large when set against such other items of national capital investment or expenditure on dwellings or plant and machinery, or alternatively against such items as drink or tobacco'.[17] Mr Plant at the 1960 TUC made another comparison: 'In real terms we are spending little more of our national income on education than we were in 1938. These reforms...may cost £200 million a year extra but when set against what we are spending on other things, including armaments, it is a small amount.'[18]

Sir David Eccles had set up the Crowther Committe and by the time it reported three years later to him, two ministers had arrived and departed. There was a debate in the House of Commons in March 1960 before Macmillan's government 'announced that it would not take any immediate action on the key recommendations...Sir David Eccles, accepted the principle that these recommendations should be carried out at sometime in the future.'[19] This reference to some vague future time indicated a lack of real governmental concern for large numbers of secondary school children who left school at the earliest date, the bulk of whom were at secondary modern schools and most likely to be from relatively low-income families. This contrasts with the action taken in response to the Report's findings which showed that as a consequence of more pupils gaining the A levels required for entry to higher education 'more places for higher education will be required than are now envisaged'. Most of these pupils came from the socially and academically selective secondary school sector – the public schools, direct grant grammar schools and local authority grammar schools. Their parents were more likely to come from higher-income groups and it is difficult to avoid the suspicion that Macmillan's prompt announcement in 1960 of the setting up of the Robbins Committee the following year was partly because this was an issue which affected a higher proportion of vociferous middle-class parents compared to the raising of the school leaving age. To that extent there was a measure of electoral calculation in the decision. The bulk of the detailed findings of the Crowther Report which had taken more than three years to produce at a cost of over £10,000 were ignored. 'The Crowther Committee estimated their recommendations would put £200–£250 million on the education budget...Four years later the Robbins Committee recommended a ten-year development programme costing £3,500 million. It was accepted by the 1959–64 Conservative Government within 24 hours of being published.'[20]

WHAT THE TUC IS DOING – 1958

In 1957 Sir Thomas Williamson (General and Municipal Workers Union) in his presidential address to Congress had focussed upon the nature of investment which was required in the economy. 'We need it in the right places. We need machine tools rather than pin-tables, and good roads rather than road houses...The nation's needs, not profits for the few, must come first.'[21] In the year of Crowther's publication the TUC produced a substantial pamphlet entitled *What the TUC is Doing*, setting out their policies on a full range of matters, including education. The central theme of the section on education also reinforced the idea of productive investment. A contrast was made between the way in which trade unions were investing in the provision of education courses for their members whilst the government was failing to provide adequate resources for the education system.

> Education has been a major casualty in the Government's drive for false economy. Time and again in recent months the TUC has had to make forceful protests at Government action in lopping public spending on this vital service. To stunt education today is to risk jeopardising the prospect of the nation's prosperity tomorrow.[22]

A long catalogue of capital projects halted or deferred was listed: new buildings to replace all-age schools halted; some projects for new buildings in teacher training colleges delayed; provision for handicapped children and school clinics deferred; building for improved school meals service severely restricted; numerous proposals for playing fields and community halls had come 'under the axe'. It was a sorry litany of much needed educational infrastructure which the TUC kept pressing the government to provide only to be met by frequent pleas of the need to economise in education. The pamphlet enabled the programme of the TUCEC which had evolved over the years to become more widely known. It inevitably took the form of a summary of familiar proposals: raising the school leaving age to 16, part-time education for all to 18, maintenance grants for pupils from low income families who wished to stay on at school and reduced fares on public transport for children still at school. At the same time the response of the government to these proposals was recorded. The TUCEC programme was not dramatically radical, rather it expressed the desire for the government to provide for all children, at the very least, appropriate buildings in which to give the quality of service necessary for the time, and with an eye to the immediate and long-term future of the nation. To begin to obtain these relatively modest goals would have required a commitment to long term planning and investment from the government and perhaps a minister who stayed long enough at the Department to have a genuine interest in seeing such plans come to fruition. There was little evidence that this was the case in the 1950s.

In March 1958 a summary of the work of a TUC–Labour party study group on education was produced.[23] It covered the full range of education from nursery schooling to higher education and included fee-paying schools, maintenance grants, school meals and milk, and government proposals to change the method of financing local authority education. Most of the proposals were established TUC education policy and it would seem that there was common ground with the Labour party with the exception of two issues, if only in matters of emphasis – selective secondary schooling and fee-paying education. The differences here might have been based on a matter of political judgement; the Labour party was seeking electoral support from the voters in a way that the TUC was not. These points will be taken up later when both of these issues will be considered further in the next section. However, the new method of financing local government services arose a year earlier and was one to which the TUC responded with some energy.

In February 1957 the Ministry of Housing and Local Government had outlined changes to the system of exchequer grants in services provided by local authorities. The main change was to adopt a system of general grants to replace percentage grants made to specific services. The education service was likely to be seriously affected by these proposals. The TUCEC and Economic Committee considered these proposals with the result that a public statement was issued by the General Council in May criticising the plans. There were two major concerns. One, that education would suffer because so much of the Exchequer grant was scheduled for this service that when money was put into single pool there would be temptations to use part of it for other areas of local government provision which were suffering from underfunding. The other worry was that this was one more strategy in the government's economy drive to change the balance of local government support from central taxation to local authority rates.

In fact the proposals were more complex as the TUC's statement acknowledged. For example certain specific grants would remain, such as those for the police service, advanced technological education, school meals and milk. However whereas approximately one sixth of local government finance had been in the form of a block grant this proportion would now increase to two-thirds. The 60 per cent of funding for education from central government and the 40 per cent from local authority rates which had been the pattern so far was bound to change to the detriment of the education service, the result of which would be an indirect cutback in expenditure on education for which the government would escape any responsibility. This would be at a time when larger numbers of pupils were staying on at school in the more expensive stage of secondary schooling. It was suggested that the revaluation of rateable values scheduled for 1961 would provide extra revenue for local authorities to fund education services thereby reducing demand upon central government finances. Block grants were not a new idea but the political motives which lay behind what was suggested merely as a restructuring of finances made many wary, especially when viewed in the light of the chancellor's statement back on 19 February, that the proposals 'should introduce a stabilising influence in the Central Government's contribution to local expenditure'. This could be read as a fixed payment regardless of inflation or increased demands upon the education service. In plain words, an opportunity to cut back expenditure by central government on education. The GC's conclusion was that 'The government's proposals thus represent a direct threat to local government services, and particularly to the education service, while offering to local authorities no more than a semblance of greater freedom from central control.'[24]

The 1957 TUC passed a resolution proposed by Mr C.T.H. Plant (Inland Revenue Staff Federation) condemning government policy 'designed to restrict development in social services and impose a heavier burden upon working-class ratepayers'.[25] He pointed to the chancellor's (i.e. Peter Thorneycroft) claim that the scheme would stop 'extravagance and inefficiency'. It was not just teachers who found the idea of extravagance in local authority schools difficult to reconcile with reality, Mr Plant also referred to comments of Lord Hailsham who 'I think makes the best speeches on education of any Minister of Education since the war, though I think he has to prove he is the best Minister'. Hailsham he said had stated, 'Ever since I joined the Ministry I have been conscious of whispering campaigns that we are spending too much on education. Well, I am going to be airy about it. I propose to say in quite categorical terms that this assertion represents approximately the opposite of the truth. On this issue of extravagance I am spoiling for a fight, and I intend to win.'[26] How successful he might have been will not be known for within a few days of the September TUC he had left the ministry to become Lord President of the Council.

The TUCGC also wrote to the prime minister. Macmillan's reply claimed that he shared the TUC's opinion of the importance of developing the education service but before they had even received the letter his government had introduced a Local Government Bill which included provision for changing the system of financing local government services as they had proposed earlier. Accordingly the TUC produced a critical statement of the government's action which was issued to the press and the PLP. This outlined the objections which had been raised by the TUCEC and at the 1957 Congress. It was suggested,

> that it is not without significance that when 'block' grants for education were proposed by the Geddes and May Committees they were advocated as a means of economising in public expenditure upon the education service... [and it was believed]... that the present measure will operate to that end.[27]

There was widespread opposition throughout the trade union movement and most educational organisations but their protests could not prevent the key objectives of the changes to local government financial support being put into operation. Yet there was also evidence that the protests had made a difference for it was revealed a year later that the government had accepted minor adjustments to the local authorities' estimates of the expenditure to be paid to them during the two financial years 1959–61 and 'had decided to pay local authorities in the form of general grants amounts which were virtually equivalent to the total of specific grants which they had received in respect of the services under previous arrangements'.[28] The TUC realised there would be a need to monitor the future working of the new methods of financing local government and to take account of changes in costs which might occur in the education services. However the TUC could be reasonably satisfied with the part they had played in focussing attention upon government proposals which initially had threatened the measure of financial support going to the local authority education service.

NOTES AND REFERENCES

1. (1959) *15–18: Report of the Central Advisory Council for Education (England). (The Crowther Report)* Vol. 1. p.5.
2. Ibid.,Ch.3, 'Population changes and their educational consequences'.
3. Ibid., p.3.
4. Ibid., pp.38–9.
5. Lowe, R. (1988) *Education in the Post-War Years: A Social History*, p.128 and (1997) *Schooling and Social Change 1964–1990*, Ch. 4.
6. *The Crowther Report*, p.43.
7. *TUC Report 1958*, p.183.

8. Ibid.
9. Ibid., p.184.
10. Ibid.
11. *TUC Report 1960*, p.427.
12. Ibid., p.429.
13. Ibid., p.428.
14. Ibid., p.429.
15. Ibid., pp.186–7.
16. *The Crowther Report*. The thinking behind this approach was put forward in Ch.6, 'Burden and Benefits', pp.54–60.
17. Ibid., p.450.
18. *TUC Report 1960*, p.429.
19. Rogers, R. (1984) *Crowther to Warnock*, p.13.
20. Ibid., pp.21–2.
21. *TUC Report 1957*, p.80.
22. *What the TUC is Doing*, TUC, p.17.
23. *TUCEC Mins.*, 11.3.1958.
24. *TUC Report 1957*, p.179.
25. Ibid., p.396.
26. Ibid., p.397.
27. *TUC Report 1958*, p.178.
28. *TUC Report 1959*, p.185.

PART 4 – A TIME OF HOPE
1960–1970

CHAPTER 15

SOCIAL DEPRIVATION:
EDUCATION TO THE RESCUE?

PRINCIPAL AREAS OF TUC CONCERN

The 1960s were a decade of much activity in education, new hopes, new plans from a stream of reports which covered areas of education from pre-schooling to higher education, maintained schools to fee-paying secondary schools. The TUCEC responded to all of these developments giving oral evidence to some, written evidence to many and commenting upon every one. There were four areas central to TUC education policy; nursery education, discouragement of streaming and promotion of comprehensive schooling, raising the school leaving age to 16 and opposition to fee-paying schools. These core themes were raised at every opportunity throughout the 1960s whether through evidence submitted to a Commission investigating some aspect of education, deputation to a minister of education, resolution passed at Congress and worked on locally by trades councils or by close co-operation with organisations pursuing similar aims.

In addition, a whole range of educational issues were debated at Congress and addressed to ministers in departments other than education. These included school transport, maintenance allowances, child employment, provision of amenities for children during school holidays, vocational education and day-release for teenagers at work to attend college. The views of the TUC on many of these issues were frequently asked for and careful responses prepared which illustrated both their sound knowledge of the educational system and that of the lives of the majority of the working population. To this extent it can be said that more than any other organisation they had the interests of the majority of children at heart because the parents of so many of these children were represented by organisations affiliated to the TUC. It was this everyday experience which enabled them to suggest policies based upon the reality of the needs of the majority of the country's children and young people.

During the 1960s there was a theme, not new but increasingly recognised, sometimes central at other times less so, which could be detected within the major education reports of the decade; Crowther (1959), Newsom and Robbins (1963), Plowden (1967) and those on the fee-paying schools, Newsom (1968) and Donnison (1970). This theme was that there was a clear relationship between the social background of children and their academic attainment. It was supported by educational research from the inter-war period right through to 1970 and beyond.[1] The evidence was produced with monotonous regularity but the scale of the reorganisation necessary to tackle this widespread phenomenon was difficult to undertake, partly due to strong opposition from vested interests which benefitted from the unequal opportunities endemic in the educational system. This central problem of social class was compounded by disadvantages for many girls who left school at the earliest opportunity thereby curtailing their studies. There was also a significant number of children who had to make adjustments to cope with an education system with which they were unfamiliar because either they or their parents, had been born overseas in countries with cultural backgrounds which differed to varying extents from that of the United Kingdom. The latter is a complex area because variations were so wide from parents and children whose first language was not English, to those with different religions, customs and attitudes. Some measure of the challenge for the education system can be gauged from the incredible number of languages to be found among pupils within Inner London Education Authority Schools.[2]

It would be both naive and incorrect to imply that changes in the education system by themselves would have brought equality of opportunity in education to all pupils for the system which had evolved from Victorian times onwards inevitably reflected the society it served – mainly one in which disparities of wealth and income were manifested in the daily lives of every inhabitant. It was never necessary to be a social scientist to realise that marked differences could be observed in most areas in the quality and location of housing; in relation to industry; the quality of shops; how near the gas works were in some districts as opposed to the golf course; the density of housing. Just growing up in any area was enough to give most people a sense of the social geography of any town and this knowledge once gained could be applied to almost any area of the country. Education was no exception when it came to the location of schools with selective schools usually to be found in areas which were predominantly populated by the middle classes while working-class areas were largely served by elementary and later secondary modern schools. Most of the major fee-paying schools were more likely to be found in or near county and market towns; some of a poorer quality often located in leafy suburbs or seaside resorts. All of these descriptions are generalisations but they are substantially correct.

This pattern was continued with the suburban developments of the 1930s and those following the housing boom of the post-war period when housing estates rapidly developed, differentiated by price, and new accompanying schools reflecting the financial circumstances of families as well as their educational values and aspirations for their children.[3] Thus it was not the education system itself which was the prime cause of the lack of equality of opportunity but it was a contributory factor. The basic inequalities of income and wealth endemic to British society led to inequalities of all kinds including housing, working conditions, health, longevity, holiday entitlements and all areas of consumption. Education was no exception in this relationship between income and life opportunities. Numerous studies recorded such information in great detail and frequently led to much discussion but rarely to action on the scale necessary to eradicate many of these widespread inequalities.[4]

This was all clear to many trade unionists from the experiences they underwent daily in factories, coal mines, docks and offices as well as those of their spouses and children within the neighbourhood. They sought to improve the life chances of their children by working collectively for better incomes and conditions of work as well as better opportunities for their children at school. To do so meant that many of those who enjoyed the benefits resulting from tradition and privilege resisted the demands of the TUC for what can only be decribed in general terms as a 'fairer society'. Improvements came with the expansion of the welfare state which did so much to eliminate the worst excesses of poverty prevalent in many areas until the late 1930s. Yet at the same time the more affluent sections of society were able to maintain many but not all of the privileges money could buy, not least in the area of education. As departments within the TUC pushed for improvements in the areas with which they were concerned so the TUCEC worked to improve opportunities in schooling. They were able to point to significant improvements for which they could claim a considerable part of the credit. At the same time the forces ranged against the ideas they promoted were well organised and within key areas of power, including the civil service and parliament. Their priorities of expenditure rarely coincided with those of the labour movement.

Even allowing for the defence of vested interests it is possible to suggest that the social background and life-style of many of the men, for women were rarely in positions of power before 1970, meant that with the best will in the world they simply had no conception of the lives of the majority of people because most of them had been separated from them at home, school and university, and by their social circle, life-style and interests. This again is a generalisation but one amply substantiated almost alone by reference to their experiences of schooling and higher education. It is reinforced when their career opportunities and attitudes are contrasted with those working within the trade union world including the full-time officers of the trade union world. (See Appendices 1, 4, 5 and 6.)

The areas of education pursued by the TUC in the 1960s were sometimes those which were ongoing, such as nursery education, whilst others could be short-lived, such as school transport. Sometimes several were on the agenda of meetings with the education minister or evidence submitted to an investigating committee. It is convenient to examine the issues raised in turn even though they were sometimes being considered simultaneously and it would be misleading to think that the TUC worked on one issue until it was resolved before moving on to another, although they obviously had an order of priorities, and nursery education was one of the most long-running because it was probably the most neglected by successive governments.

NURSERY EDUCATION

With the refusal of education ministers in the 1950s to consider any expansion of nursery education the TUC put the issue on 'hold' waiting for some new initiative which might provide an opportunity to return to the matter. This presented itself in the form of the enquiry of the Central Advisory Council (England) appointed in August 1963 under the chairmanship of Lady Plowden 'to consider primary education in all its aspects, and the transition to secondary education'.[5] The membership of 25 was without any representative from the TUC but the General Council were invited to give evidence which they did so in a written submission which raised 27 points,[6] including the need to expand nursery education.

> The General Council would welcome a substantial increase in the provision of nursery schools and classes for 2 to 5 years olds ... [which] can offer a

more helpful environment for individual growth and social development than the home alone ... in the case of manual workers' children housing conditions and other restricting factors limit what can be done by individual parents.[7]

To counteract the retort of the education ministers that nursery schooling would take teachers from primary schools where they were desperately needed it was suggested that married women who were qualified teachers were deterred from returning to part-time or full-time work by concern for care of their children and in this respect 'the effects of a wider provision of nursery education should not be overlooked'. This point was at last taken up by Michael Stewart, the secretary of state for education, in response to a letter from the TUC in November 1964.[8] He wrote:

Since the war there had been a virtual embargo on the expansion of nursery school provision, partly because the resources made available for educational building had been concentrated on providing places for children of compulsory school age, but in recent years mainly because of the teacher shortage in primary schools. Since July 1964 local education authorities had been allowed to start nursery classes where such classes would clearly lead to an increase in their teaching force by enabling teachers with young children to return to the education service.[9]

However, whilst expressing personal sympathy with the TUC he made it plain that no action would be considered before the Plowden Committee had reported on all aspects of education. The TUCEC considered that providing nursery places only where it would encourage married women teachers back into schools was an unduly narrow approach because the inadequacy of places 'particularly handicapped the children of manual workers'. They decided to put forward their ideas on nursery expansion when they gave oral evidence to the Plowden Committee.

During the same year two resolutions on the subject were passed at the TUC Women's Conference; one proposed by the TGWU 'believed that nursery school places should be available to all children between the ages of two to five, as envisaged in the 1944 Education Act', linking this to a practical problem, that 'proper facilities should be available for the use of children of working mothers, during school holidays and the end of the school day'. The second resolution moved by the NUGMW hoped 'that the needs of working mothers with young children will receive attention from the Government' and supported the International Labour Organisation's recommendation, 'child-care preference of mothers with young children should be studied on a local level basis and service provided to meet these needs'.[10]

It was both the need for and wish of mothers to work which created the demands for child care met by the expansion of private nurseries. Because of their fees they were largely the preserves of the middle classes. In 1965 there were more than 18,000 3–4-year-olds in full-time private nurseries; nearly 10,000 attending part-time. The failure of local authorities to make adequate provision for under-fives also led to the setting up of play groups, the first in Marylebone in 1961, which inspired other enterprising parents to copy the idea and one year later Mrs Belle Tutaev helped to establish the Pre-School Play Group Association. They received a Nuffield Foundation Grant of £1,500 in 1962 and £3,000 per annum for three years in 1966 from the DES. In that year there were about 600 groups catering for 20,000 mainly 3- and 4-year-old children, mostly in London and the Home Counties. By 1971 the groups had grown to around 7,000 catering for 17,000 children and the social spread had widened to include significant numbers of working-class children. Successive governments were pleased with this self-help provision because it was so cheap compared with nursery schooling in terms of the quality of premises required and the fact that there was no structured career for helpers requiring salary and pension rights from local education authorities. Hence some of the pressure for pre-school care by fully trained and qualified staff was removed at virtually no cost to central government.[11]

In a meeting with Anthony Crosland, minister for education and science, in February 1966 the TUC pointed to 'the growing number of children being deprived of opportunity of nursery education as a result of the virtual stand still imposed by successive governments upon the expansion of facilities within this field'. They pointed to the decline in both total numbers and as a proportion of the relevant age group and went on to express concern at the resulting 'unsupervised growth of private nursery schools where standards were not always satisfactory'.[12] Crosland was clearly in an embarrassing situation for he fully recognised the justice of their case. Education resources were being absorbed by the continuing demand for primary school places and to cope with the pressures on future secondary school accommodation by the government's commitments to raising the school leaving age. He replied that whilst there was a 'reasonable allocation of resources to the education service' he could 'hold out no real prospect of any substantial expansion of nursery education in the foreseeable future'.[13]

At the 1966 Congress Mrs E. Beith (Health Visitors Association) put forward a resolution expressing, deep concern for those pre-school children whose mental development, emotional adjustment and sometimes even physical health are being impaired through circumstances of housing or social background, and including those who are suffering as a result of unsatisfactory child-minding.[14]

Congress urged the DES and the minister of health to 'take immediate steps to increase substantially the number of nursery schools, nursery classes and day nurseries' but they must have realised that Crosland's answer earlier in the year meant that there would be no positive response to their requests at the very least until some time after the Plowden Committee had reported. Even their suggestions for 'regulation and inspection of all private nursery schools by the DES...to enable minimum standards to be set' was only met by the answer that institutions catering for children under school age were the responsibility of the Ministry of Health.[15]

THE PLOWDEN REPORT 1967

The Plowden Report was submitted to the secretary of state at the DES in October 1966 and published in 1967. Chapter 9 was devoted to 'Providing for Children Before Compulsory Education' and began by stating that, 'The under fives are the only age group for whom no extra educational provision of any kind has been made since 1944.' They went on to tackle the reasons for failure in this area by successive governments. 'To meet the demand must cost much money, involve considerable building and employ many teachers. When all three are scarce, can we honestly recommend expansion; or must we, however reluctantly, agree with the inaction of successive governments.'[16]

The Report went on to consider the present position: 'In 1965, about 7 per cent of all children under five were receiving some form of education in a school or nursery class...The highest proportion came from professional and unskilled workers' homes – 25 per cent and 20 per cent respectively.' For working-class children a significant number of the places were given to children with some kind of social handicap – the middle classes had been forced to resort to private provision and out of a total of 1,585 nurseries in England and Wales 82 were in Orpington alone. The Report supported expansion of nursery education on educational, social, health and welfare grounds. Only two of the 175 individual witnesses questioned whether such expansion was desirable and educational institutions gave overwhelming support. Thirteen recommendations related to nursery education were made. The first was unequivocal: 'There should be a large expansion of nursery education and a start should be made as soon as possible.'[17] It was suggested that the responsibility for nursery education should be transferred from the health to education department and a survey undertaken by all local authorities to ascertain the net cost of the extra accommodation needed to provide nursery places in their area and to discover the number of teachers necessary.

Small wonder that in the report to the 1968 TUC it was pronounced that the 'General Council emphatically endorses recommendations for a large expansion of nursery education' reminding delegates of the long record of the TUC in campaigning for this provision which was 'especially important for the children of manual workers and those in unsatisfactory home conditions'.[18] At the same time they made it known that they were firmly opposed to the suggestion by some members of the Plowden Committee of fees being introduced for this area of schooling which was within the maintained sector of the education system.

There is little evidence to suggest that Patrick Gordon-Walker, minister at the DES, shared the level of enthusiasm of the TUC for Plowden's support for nursery education. In February of the same year a TUC deputation comprising J. Crawford, A. Roberts, G.F. Smith, R. Milson and Denis Winnard, secretary of the TUCEC, met with the minister, E. Morgan and N. Hardiment.[19] They were critical of the lack of government support in this area. J. Crawford reminded the minister that 'successive governments had failed to make any progress towards provision of adequate facilities for this purpose'. He wanted to know what the government's intentions were regarding the implementation of the Plowden Report's recommendations for nursery education. Mr Smith recalled persistent TUC representations to successive governments to end the comparative neglect of nursery education. He referred to the 'widespread extent of irregular and inadequate childminding' as well as asking that responsibility for nursery education be transferred from the Ministry of Health to that of Education as suggested by Plowden. Gordon Walker accepted that there were social as well as educational arguments for nursery education, indeed he thought the former were probably stronger but lack of money as usual was the reason given as to why the general recommendations of Plowden were unlikely to be met in this area of education: 'The cost of the Plowden recommendations would be at least £100 million, if applied over the whole country, and additional facilities for nursery education would not be staffed without worsening the staff situation in infant and junior schools . . . some public funds for the selective expansion of nursery education, would probably be concentrated in

Educational Priority Areas (EPAs). Denis Winnard asked about the £16 million allocated to school building and was frankly told, 'none of this special allocation would be applied to nursery facilities'. More surprising was the minister's qualified support for the suggestion by the two members of Plowden who had advocated fee paying for nursery schooling. He believed that 'more rapid progress would be made if fees were charged according to parents' means...since nursery education was, like further and higher education, outside the period of compulsory education, there might be justification for charging fees for it'. This view was anathema to the TUC. As for the unsatisfactory private arrangements for the care and education of young people, particularly the under-fives, and the solution that they should be brought within the public education system to ensure an adequate standard, the minister made it clear that there was no plan to change present arrangements. Gordon Walker's attitude adds to the doubts which have been raised as to his commitment to and suitability for the post of minister of education; doubts which would be reinforced over his approach to the raising of the school leaving age.

THE SEEBOHN REPORT

A year after the Plowden Report came out another report was published which also dealt with aspects of child care, the Seebohn Report, set up 'to review the organisation and responsibilities of the local authority personal social services in England and Wales, and to consider what changes are desirable to secure an effective family service'. This was not on the scale of Plowden, there were only ten members of the Committee and research was not on the extensive scale of the former although it necessarily ranged widely in an attempt to improve the co-ordination between a myriad of services from child welfare to home helps, adult training centres to certain aspects of housing. The main recommendation was for each local authority to establish a social services department with a similar department in central government for the overall planning of the services, as well as research to provide evidence to inform policy decision in relation to the care of children under 5 years of age. It proposed a direct statutory responsibilty upon local authorities to make provision for children under 5 because facilities were unevenly spread.

The scale of the problem was illustrated by the fact that there were about 450,000 working mothers with children under five 'some of whom had to work out of economic necessity'. The enormous growth in private nurseries and child minders was noted 'in some of which conditions endangered their health and safety, and impaired intellectual development'. This was precisely in line with arguments presented by the TUC,[20] who readily endorsed Seebohn's recommendations for greater provision and the part schools could play 'in the diagnosis of family social problems affecting children' and suggested local education authorities should supervise voluntary play groups, a responsibilty the DES had shown no interest in adopting. The Seebohn Report was well received by social workers and in general by both Houses of parliament. The main findings were implemented in the Local Authority Social Services Bill which was pushed through Parliament in May 1970 just before the General Election.[21] It clarified the obligation of different departments but by the very nature of some of the issues, such as juvenile delinquency and certain aspects of child care, it was not considered logical to place them all in one department, such as education, when other areas such as welfare or offences against the law, had to be taken into consideration.

Given the record of post-war governments on nursery education, when the DES asked the TUC for suggestions to a change in the law to education in preparation for a new education bill being prepared by Edward Short they included a paragraph on nursery education, more out of dogged hope than expectation of implementation. Their policy had become repetitive because the fundamental principles for them had not changed any more than the regular negation of governments. They wished for 'substantial expansion in nursery education on grounds [that it] would benefit nearly all children... particularly children of manual workers and children living in unfavourable social conditions... [and that] education should be available to children from two years of age whose parents want it'.[22] Unfortunately no British government was willing to give the financial priority necessary to fund education in its broadest sense to children in their most formative years, spending on which could have been justified as an investment for the future probably more than any other section of the service. One can only speculate how much educational and behavioural problems might have been diagnosed and remedies sought in the early years of childhood to the benefit of the individual child and the long-term interests of society.

Government ministers expressed a measure of sympathy for nursery education but not one was able to persuade Cabinet colleagues as to the importance of education tailored specifically to the needs of children under 5 nor of the long-term benefits to the country. They were probably aware that the initial expenditure would benefit many children but that benefits to society would not be apparent for some years to come. That future must have seemed to be far away to the government at the time but society would reap the results of the neglect of early learning facilities in a comparatively short time in historical terms.

Public opinion within the country, except perhaps among parents with young children, seemed to feel that the younger a child, the less demanding was the teacher's role and consequently the less important the provision of this form of education. There was in any case always a feeling among some people that young children should be looked after by their mothers exclusively in the home and that sending them to nursery school was in part a neglect of their responsibility. This view together with the evidence that in their earliest years most children should not be away from home for many hours led the Plowden Committee to recommend part-time nursery education, an approach readily endorsed by the TUC.

EDUCATIONAL PRIORITY AREAS

The one exception to this lack of progress of nursery schooling came within the Educational Priority Areas, soon known as EPAs, recommended by the Plowden Report. In January 1969 under the Urban Aid Programme more than 10,000 extra nursery places were approved in the first phase of expansion. This early attempt at positive discrimination to provide extra support in the earliest years to children in socially disadvantaged areas in order to break the cycle of under-achievement in local primary and secondary schools showed signs of real progress with enterprising schemes set up by among others A.H. Halsey and Eric Midwinter. In spite of the initial enthusiasm there was a failure to realise just how long it would take for tangible results to be seen and the necessary scale of funding which might have allowed this to be observed was not forthcoming. In addition there were criticisms of the whole philosophy from some on both the political Left and those on the political Right. Among the former was a decline in the belief in the power of education to bring about a fairer and more just society when its structure was intrinsically based upon such large inequalities in income and wealth.[23] By contrast some at the other end of the political spectrum argued for a return to traditional ideas in schooling which would maintain the status quo. In effect this meant not only accepting the social structure of the time but providing an education differentiated according to the demands of the market economy and all that this entailed.

The tragedy is that there is sound evidence to suggest that if the schemes of the EPAs had been fully funded and extended they would have brought substantial benefits. The two-volume Report on Educational Priority published in 1972 analysing the experience gained from several of the pilot schemes concluded that, 'Pre-schooling is the outstanding economical and effective device in the general approach to raising educational standards in EPAs.'[24] As well as the investment in such schemes parallel investment was needed in the areas of declining industry and urban decay which provided the depressing environment in which considerable numbers of children were living. Sound evidence for the decline in delinquency and increase in staying on rates at school among youngsters in the USA who participated in the comparable 'Head Start' programme showing that the scheme did pay off would also emerge later but way after the time for it to be widely recognised just what a good investment it had been.[25] Ted Short did claim in 1969 that in his Education Bill proposed for the following year, 'he was intending to include the universal provision of pre-school education'[26] but good intentions are not the same as achievements as the history of education demonstrates only too readily.

ROSLA – MORE SUPPORT FROM OFFICIAL REPORTS

Despite a rebuff from Sir David Eccles to implement the raising of the school leaving age as recommended in the Crowther Report the TUC never gave up their long-cherished ambition to see 16 as the common leaving age for all secondary school children. Whenever the opportunity arose they returned to this aim and proposals by the government in 1961 concerning technical education provided such an occasion. The government was seeking to clarify the routes from secondary schools into technical education against a background of changes within industry and high rates of failure among students entering certain technical courses. There was a need to relate entry to technical and national certificate courses more closely to the educational attainments of students and to differentiate to a greater extent education and training in the part-time courses of craftsmen, technicians and technologists. A White Paper entitled *Better Opportunities in Technical Education* was published in January 1961 and the TUCGC gave its approval to the proposals made in the belief that they could 'bring about needed improvements in the quality of technical education'.[27] One suggestion in the report they noted in particular was the inclusion of a statement which:

> emphasizes quite rightly in their view, the value of a 5 year course of secondary education to young people entering upon different technical

courses. They continue in their view that a proper foundation will be provided for technical education only when the minimum School Leaving age is raised to 16. The early implementation of that long-planned reform would not only ensure that many more young people were adequately equipped for further education, but would also assist in simplifying the necessary somewhat complex pattern of technical courses outlined in the statement.[28]

The TUC were given another opportunity to give their views the following year when requested to provide both written and oral evidence to the Newsom Committee. In their memorandum they claimed an 'essential prerequisite to the proper development of educational provision for children in this age group... would also make it clear that the community does not attach greater importance to the secondary education of some children to that of others'.[29] In fact certain sections of the community believed precisely that.

When Newsom reported in October 1963 the TUC were able to state, 'The views which had been put by the General Council in evidence to the Advisory Council were generally met by the findings and recommendations of the report.'[30] The Newsom Report stated: 'The pupils will need to have a longer period of full-time education than most of them now receive,' and went on to reason,

> There is, surely, something of an anomaly in the fact that whereas a five-year secondary course is regarded as an essential minimum both for our ablest children in the grammar schools and for those of very limited capacities indeed, in schools for the educationally sub-normal, less is demanded for the large majority of children who neither progress as quickly as the first group nor are as severely limited in their potential as the second.[31]

Whilst TUC support was unanimous of resolutions to raise the school leaving age there were at least a couple of occasions at Congress when a measure of concern was expressed. In 1964 Mr J.W. Jeffery (Association of Scientific Workers) proposed a motion which was seconded by Mrs C.E. Page (USDAW) 'Welcoming the decision to raise the school leaving age to 16, as recommended by the Newsom Report, believing that far more of the natural resources should be devoted to education of the children with whom the report was concerned.' The motion was carried but in his speech of proposal J.W. Jeffery did raise the concern of some teachers about 'the value of an extra year when those who believe they have failed under the system of streaming and selection believe the system has little to offer them.'[32] This was a relevant comment in relation to some pupils in schools which were strictly streamed so that forms would be labelled from A onwards in any one year. It takes little imagination to realise the low self-esteem engendered in children allocated to F onwards or at times the way in which the status of teachers could become unofficially graded if their work was mainly with examination classes as opposed to pupils who were already deemed to have 'failed'. By the time some pupils had reached 14 with a record of low academic achievement behind them, their last year could be spent in what became known as the 'leavers' form', often allocated to the poorest premises in the school. Small wonder that some of them were difficult to teach because they often recognised the low regard in which they were held by some members of staff within the school. This was one of the worst aspects of streaming in which children were graded like products based almost exclusively on their perceived future ability to pass examinations. This value attached to children was understood by the pupils themselves and at times some teachers approached classes with preconceived ideas according to the label given, whether it be A or F. It was for this reason that there were doubts in some areas as to the value of all children staying a further year in such situations. The challenge was to change the system to ensure that the extra time spent in school would be of value to all pupils.

At the same Congress Mr A.E. Hall (Amalgamated Society of Woodworkers) raised another concern about ROSLA unless attention was given to the present system of training craftsmen.[33] At the present time some pupils gained apprenticeships and spent time at College learning theoretical skills combined with day-release where they carried out practical work. Mr Hall pointed out that with a further rise in the school leaving age to 16 there would be pupils who would be nearly 17 before they would be able to consider such a career and by then, unless new arrangements were made, they would be considered too old for an apprenticeship.

A MANIFESTO COMMITMENT POSTPONED

During the last weeks of 1967 there was widespread public expectation that the Labour government was considering the postponement of ROSLA to 16, previously planned for the academic year 1970/71. This commitment had appeared in both the 1964 and 1966 Labour party manifestos. Richard Crossman recorded in his Diary on 15 December that 'George Brown has been complaining that people had been campaigning for postponement...But the decision has still to be taken.'[34] The TUC sought an urgent meeting with the minister, Patrick Gordon Walker, which was held on 8 January 1968. He was unable to clarify the government's intention stating that a final decision has yet to be made. This was true because although the issue had been raised in Cabinet on 17 December 1967 and discussion begun on 4 January 1968 it would be a week before an agreement would be reached – and then only by a narrow margin. The TUC representatives made it clear that having advocated a school leaving age of 16 since 1936 they would deeply resent any further postponement, especially because of the adverse effect on manual workers' children, in particular those in the north where voluntary staying on was lowest. They argued that delay in any case would be a false economy in the light of the need for a larger number of better educated and more skilled people.[35] As the minister had not been able to confirm that the promise made earlier in 1964 by the then government to implement this part of the 1944 Education Act which had been reaffirmed by successive governments would go ahead as planned, the TUCGC issued a General Statement describing briefly the attempts to increase the school leaving age by another year and focussing on the recommendations of recent reports by the Central Advisory Council from Crowther in 1959 to Newsom in 1963. They pointed out that the contribution of 15-year-olds to industry and commerce was marginal and that the voluntary system of staying on reinforced the selective process which discriminated against manual workers' children. They ended with a plea to the government, 'to adhere to the commitment to carry through this major educational advance by the date already announced.'[36]

The Cabinet met on 5 January to discuss a package of cutbacks proposed by the chancellor, Roy Jenkins. They covered defence and public expenditure. In defence proposed reductions in expenditure would come from cutbacks in armed services east of Suez and the cancellation of the United States F111 fighter plane; public expenditure cuts would be in health with the restoration of prescription charges (an issue the prime minister had resigned over in 1951) and the postponement of the school leaving age by two years from 1971 to 1973, although Jenkins proposed three years. This was the main education issue which would create the greatest anger, but the end to free school milk in secondary schools and reduction of capital grants to direct grant grammar schools were also included. Harold Wilson described the postponement as 'difficult, not to say repugnant' but justified it by claiming that this would save £33 million in 1968–69, and £48 million in the following year, mainly in the related school building programme...partly to help with the progress of comprehensive reorganization and partly to provide more funds for improving conditions in 'educational priority areas'...the [total savings would be] of £39 million in the first year and £58 million in the second.[37]

Clive Ponting gives a harsher explanation:

From late in December Wilson and Jenkins (though not the Cabinet) were agreed that the reintroduction of prescription charges and postponement of the raising of the school leaving age were necessary to appease the bankers (even though devaluation had been intended to cut Britain free from these influences over economic policy).[38]

There was an impassioned discussion over the postponement of the raising of the school leaving age which has been recorded by various participants.[39] Barbara Castle wrote that

George [Brown] said he would rather accept any cut at all from the Chancellor, than this. None of the rest of us, he said, know what it was like to be denied a proper education – not only at University but also at school. It rankled all one's life (no one would notice any deprivation in you Foreign Secretary, soothed Harold) Jim [Callaghan] and Ray Gunter argue on exactly the same lines.[40]

Richard Crossman's description of events was similar but his tone was otherwise. He was uncomfortable with the views expressed and showed little sympathy for their reasoning.

George Brown...came out with an attack before the feeble Gordon Walker could say anything. It was an unpleasantly class-conscious speech strongly implying that no one except the middle-class socialist who had never felt the pinch or never had a child at a state school could dare to suggest postponement of the school-leaving age. Ray Gunter and Jim Callaghan followed much the same working-class line while Tony Crosland and Gerald Gardiner spoke as socialist ideologists. Fred Peart and George Thomson provided the professional trade-union case as represented by the NUT. Gordon Walker sat through this debate speechless and obviously trembling.[41]

Crossman's views of people seem to lack feelings of charity: 'I don't know which I disliked more – the pathetic weakness of Gordon Walker or the outrageous cynicism of Callaghan, who as Chancellor of the Exchequer had urged the postponement and was now joining the working-class battle against it.' Although Denis Healey voted for postponement he showed greater respect for those who were opposed saying that the discussion 'produced moving protests from Jim Callaghan, George Brown and Ray Gunter, all of whom had been denied a university education by having to leave school too early to take the necessary examinations'.[42] From a dinner party at Dick Crossman's a few days earlier Barbara Castle was to record, 'On education Dick and Tommy were particularly vociferous about the importance of postponing the school leaving age, otherwise the quality of education would continually decline. I was inclined to agree with them, but Wedgie was adamant against.'[43]

Gordon Walker, in explaining his agreement to the postponement stated, 'I am suggesting this in place of the cuts in university expenditure because the universities represent such an influential body of opinion.'[44] George Brown challenged him over his preference to help the minority of university students as opposed to the 400,000 pupils who would now miss an extra year of schooling and links between the education of the members of the Cabinet and how they voted over this issue have been made since. It was clearly not a simple matter of social class for both Healey and Wilson came from ordinary circumstances, both winning scholarships to Oxford, the former from a direct grant grammar school, the latter from a county grammar school. What can be said from the voting results is that all four of those who had been denied a university education, Brown, Callaghan, Gunter and Thomson, voted against postponement, but so too did four who had attended Oxford University, Benn, Crosland, Longford, and Stewart together with Peart who had been at Durham University. (Stewart and Thomson were both ex-teachers.) However, all of those who voted for postponement were graduates, most of whom had studied at Oxford, including Richard Marsh who had been a student at Woolwich Polytechnic and Ruskin College.

Postponement:	For		Against	
Castle B.	Oxford		Benn T.	Oxford
Crossman R.	Oxford		Brown G.	
Gardiner G.	Oxford		Callaghan J.	
Gordon Walker	Oxford		Crosland A.	Oxford
Greenwood T.	Oxford		Gunter R.	
Healey D.	Oxford		Longford F.	Oxford
Hughes C.	Aberystwyth		Peart F.	Durham

Jenkins R.	Oxford	Stewart M,	Oxford
Ross W.	Glasgow	Thomson G.	Dundee
Shore P.	Cambridge		
Marsh, R.	Woolwich Polytechnic/		
	Ruskin College		
Wilson H.	Oxford		

Lord Longford resigned over the issue saying, 'I felt if I swallowed this, there was nothing I wouldn't swallow.'[45] Brown did not, but the decision was one which he always felt passionately about as he was to record later: 'I thought it was one of the greatest betrayals a Labour Government so overwhelmingly composed of University graduates, could make of the less privileged people who, after all, had elected it.'[46] Perhaps the most telling comment was made by Anthony Crosland when asked by Crossman just who would be affected by postponing the raising of the school leaving age: 'Only 400,000 children. But they're not our children. It's always other people's children. None of us in this room would dream of letting our children leave school at fifteen.'[47]

It could be argued that defence and public expenditure needed to be reduced because of the economic situation, but a stronger Labour education minister, would have been loathe to abandon a long-held pledge of the labour movement affecting the majority of the nation's children. Patrick Gordon Walker showed no such inclination. Crosland thought he had 'lost his nerve', Crossman castigated him for his 'weakness' and Benn believed his actions were 'disgraceful'. By April, Gordon Walker had been made to stand down in favour of Ted Short at education. He had been just one more example of a politician placed in charge of the nation's schools for a brief period of time, just over seven months, that, even if he had been closely involved with schools and local education authorities, could not possibly have achieved anything worthwhile. As it was, his experience of the education system was confined to Wellington Public School and Oxford University. He simply had no conception of pupils leaving school at 15. In parliament the cutbacks were attacked; the Conservatives protested about the defence cuts, those on the left in the Labour party were more concerned with cutbacks to welfare programmes including those suffered by education.

At the 1968 TUC delegates expressed disappointment at the action of the Labour government. In the education debate Mr W.A.G. Easton (ATTI) put forward a lengthy resolution deploring the cuts announced in January which would 'deny essential educational opportunities to the young people and hinder economic growth...Congress would take every opportunity of impressing upon the government of the day the need drastically to reduce armaments and overseas military expenditure if the education service is to meet the needs of the 1970s.'[48] He went on to remind delegates of the struggle in which the TUC had been engaged since its foundation 100 years earlier in both initiating and supporting reforms to the education system to improve opportunities for the majority of the nation's children, and of the real gains won after much hard work, patience and time.

Mr J.S. Davison (ASTMS) in seconding the resolution spoke out angrily against the recent cut backs:

> We have come a long way from the promise of the scientific and technical revolution, the white-hot promise of equal opportunity in education for everyone...Bill Easton...has just reminded you of the high hopes we had of raising the school leaving age, of the high hopes we had for comprehensive schools and comprehensive education. At the end of this month we have the end of the free school milk service; how mean can you get? What high hopes we had for working mothers of an extension of nursery schools and nursery education, and what hopes many of our youngsters had of further and higher education.[49]

He went on to paint an unfavourable picture of the education system; 'fewer than 1 child in 14 gets any nursery schooling, 1 out of 7 primary school classes and 1 out of 3 secondary classes oversize...only 5 per cent of age group in university – one of the lowest proportions in Europe and the Western World, many gaps in part-time education, adult education almost forgotten, the poor relation of the system'.

There was one more chance for progress in the last month of the year when the DES invited the TUCGC to suggest changes in the law relating to the government's intention to introduce a new Education Bill in 1969. Pointing out that the government are already committed to ROSLA to 16 by 1972/73 (although past experience cannot have encouraged full-scale optimism), the TUC in reply wrote, 'this minimum age will presumably be written into a new Education Bill', adding that they were cautious about suggestions that older pupils might take the extra year at a college of further education save under exceptional circumstances, fearing that vocational education might be offered when the real need was for five years of secondary schooling.[50]

The government were left in no doubt as to the annoyance of the TUC over the postponement of ROSLA, which the TUC continued to pursue even if it now seemed a lost cause. They considered a resolution passed at the 1968 TUC Women's Conference which urged the TUCGC 'to press for a reversal of the Government's decision to postpone ROSLA from 1970 to 1972 and [opposition to] narrowly conceived work experience schemes for children and any relaxation of child employment'.[51] As this was in accordance with TUC policy it was brought to the attention of Edward Short, the education minister. Short's reply reaffirmed the government's decision to raise the school leaving age, a pledge which had the conviction of a cabinet minister who had supported the move in the first place. It was now becoming apparent that issues relating to the extra year were being discussed, especially the curriculum for the final year and whether pupils would be able to leave at the end of the term in which they reached 16.

TUC policy was to have one leaving date for all whilst the government was proposing two, although initially in 1968 they had favoured one and asked for the TUC's views on the idea. Following a discussion within the TUCEC it was suggested the education minister be asked why the department's views had changed: 'This decision seemed to reflect a common element in recent Government approaches to questions affecting young people, in that consideration other than those of the welfare of young people concerned appeared to be given overriding weight.'[52] The secretary of state replied, 'that the difference of opinion between the General Council and himself was only one of timing...his aim was to work towards ensuring the best possible secondary education for all in terms of duration and depth, and that a great deal in that connection had already been achieved'.[53] The reasons given for having two leaving dates were that some youngsters might have difficulty in obtaining a job if all 15-year-olds left at once and that when the school leaving age was raised to 16 some pupils would be nearly 17 when they left school. A further letter from the secretary of state confirmed that the two leaving dates would be retained after 1972 and while the TUC disagreed they could see no purpose in pursuing the issue any further.[54]

WORK EXPERIENCE FOR 15-YEAR-OLDS

The Newsom Committee had asked the TUC their views on school leavers entering routine employment and what factors led to success at work, to which the reply had been that this was a difficult question to answer and should be the subject of 'systematic and objective study rather than subjective comment and opinion'.[55] Having said that, they provided a list of problems associated with young people entering certain areas of employment. There was the risk to their health as they were exposed to work hazards, dust, fumes, noise and evidence of an increase in industrial accidents of young people. Vocational guidance was inadequate due to a lack of staff in the youth employment service and a need for compulsory part-time day-release for young people. Their main doubts about the value of part-time work experience by school children was not only fear of the secondary schooling they would miss out on but a genuine belief that it served little purpose because 'the nature and conditions of work are subject to constant change'.[56] Hence the need to provide secondary education which would equip young people with the 'capacity to meet effectively whatever circumstances their entry into employment may bring'.[57] This was the reason for their insistence on an essentially general and liberal education as a foundation from which young people could go on to cope with the rapid changes they would meet with in industry and commerce.

In August 1969 the Department of Employment and Productivity informed the TUCGC that they and the DES had decided that when the school leaving age was raised to 16 the minimum legal age of entry to employment should not be raised accordingly in order for work experience schemes to be introduced during the last year of secondary school. The TUCEC prepared a paper for discussion concerning the numerous factors which might be involved in government proposals. They carried this out in the light of their earlier discussions with the Newsom Committee as to how 'experiments enabling some pupils over 15 to participate to a limited extent, under the auspices of the school, in the world of work in industry, commerce or in other fields, should be carefully studied'.[58] A joint TUC/CBI group had visited Sweden in 1965 to study a scheme started in that country back in 1940 but found it difficult to establish a meaningful criteria with which to assess the value of the scheme. The next year the National Youth Employment Council considered a study by youth employment officers of 137 schemes which concluded there was little value in relation to vocational guidance and only limited value in easing the transition from school to work.

The result of the deliberations of the TUC was that they had serious reservations about schemes of work experience for 15-year-olds for a variety of reasons arising from the central limitations of such schemes, that they could not afford children a wholly real experience of working life. Children involved could not experience the reality of industrial discipline, the effects of sustained monotonous repetitive semi-skilled work over a period of months or years and as the time allowed would only enable them to be involved with one job they lacked the maturity to gain a valid conclusion about work. Of considerable concern was the 'disturbingly high number of accidents of young people at work (to which the Chief Inspector of Factories has drawn attention in successive annual reports) that must compel anyone concerned about the well being of school children to hesitate in advocating their temporary employment'.[59]

They listed a series of criteria the DES would need to consider: all children should receive some instruction about safety aspects of the place in which they would work; they should be adequately insured against personal injury; the explicit consent of the parents would be needed; there should be provision for consultation with trade unions; and the DES should establish criteria by which educational evaluation of the schemes could be ascertained. The TUCEC met with DES officials in February 1970 to discuss the proposed scheme. For the DES Mr Beever believed work experience would develop communication skills of pupils through discussion, provide material relevant to social education and be particularly suitable for less able children 'who learned more readily by doing things than by abstract thinking'.[60] The TUC remained unconvinced. Mr Mitson referred to evidence from Sweden which found that in the opinion of the teachers such schemes did not stimulate pupils to take a greater interest in school work and as for increasing their interest in further education it was ironic that some young people who were interested in their work were denied day-release by their employers. While Mr Beever said he thought such schemes could benefit all children it was clear that the main thinking was targeted at children considered less academically able. Moreover, the kind of work experience offered would be in routine manual and clerical posts which may well reinforce the limited career aspirations which permeated much of working-class culture. It would be difficult to envisage pupils from fee-paying schools spending time away from school seeking to gain experience of life on the factory floor because their parents or teachers had been convinced that it would help to 'develop their communication skills'.

Mr Crawford expressed the worry which lingered about schemes which took children out of school, 'the major question concerned the educational value of schemes and whether time spent on them was better used than it would have been in promoting general education'.[61] The continued reluctance of the TUC to promote these schemes is best reflected in a statement in the report on the issue which had been prepared for the TUCEC. 'For most young people hitherto the period of secondary education has been too short to permit them to receive a satisfactory secondary education.'[62] With the promise of a full five-year secondary course being finally introduced in 1972 they were hardly likely to agree to plans which would reduce the time available thereby nullifying the very aims for which they had campaigned for so long.

When the TUCEC met in the summer to discuss the issue further some members suggested a properly planned work experience scheme could have value, including educational value, for secondary pupils in their last year of compulsory schooling and that agreement should be given to a limited legislative measure permitting 15-year-olds to participate in a scheme after the school leaving age had been raised. Other committee members continued to hold a contrary view doubting the educational benefits and loath to see the extra time gained for schooling eroded immediately by time spent at work.[63] They decided to await further consultation with the Home Office who were examining the situation in the light of the Children and Young Persons' Act.

One factor often overlooked by many civil servants who had stayed at school at least until they were 18 and usually continued their education at university was that considerable numbers of working-class children were not strangers to the world of work. There was widespread illegal work in towns, especially the growing demand for Saturday workers, helping in street markets, shops and small firms where they carried out routine tasks for payment, as well as the legal familiar paper rounds early in the morning and evening, largely undertaken by boys but increasingly by girls too. Not only would the practice of week-end jobs continue to expand as more children voluntarily stayed on at school beyond the minimum leaving age and sought money to buy items they could have afforded if they had gone straight into the world of work but the growing 'pop culture' in all its forms generated and stimulated by astute marketing created a teenage market which encouraged youngster to buy goods specifically designed for them, especially in clothing fashions and music. This 'teenage culture' penetrated ever further down the age groups through secondary school into the primary school. Some youngsters needed part-time work to earn the money for these items; younger children tried to persuade their parents of the need for them to have the goods they claimed were being enjoyed by 'all their friends'. Most parents found such pleas difficult to ignore and the growing influence of advertising, especially through television, which brought the advertisers' message into nearly every home meant that it would be working-class children who were more likely to undertake part-time work, especially when some of the coveted goods were beyond the means of their parents to buy alongside the necessary weekly expenditure for the family. The idea that this group of children would benefit from work experience as if they had no conception of the adult world was misleading.

It was far more likely at the time that it was those from higher-income groups attending selective schools who were without part-time work experience, sometimes because their parents could afford to purchase items associated with 'teenage culture' which were highly regarded by their children and sometimes because they would not agree to their children carrying out low-paid work which detracted from the time and energy they needed to devote to study if they were to succeed academically. Pupils at boarding schools had no possibility of undertaking part-time work, especially as schools often worked Saturday morning. Prosperous middle-class parents could afford to take the long-term view and deter their children from taking part-time work at least during the school term. Many trade unionists who had no option when they were young but to leave school at 14 years of age could look back with regret at the limitations to their career prospects which had often resulted from the lack of further years in formal education. It was a major reason they were unwilling to acquiesce to schemes which they believed might be to the detriment of the career opportunities of their own children.

DAY-RELEASE FOR YOUNG WORKERS

Whilst this area was outside the province of the years of compulsory education it was clearly linked to issues of work experience, ROSLA, further education and skills training at the place of work. Like many ideas in education it had a long history. The 1918 Education Act contained plans for Continuation Schools for pupils to study further part-time from the age of 14 when they left school until they were 18 years of age. In the harsh economic situation of the inter-war years and in the face of widespread opposition from the Federation of British Industries the proposals were gradually abandoned. Some enlightened employers supported the scheme, such as Bourneville in Manchester, Boots of Nottingham, Rowntree of York and Cross and Blackwell in London, names familiarly associated with the provision of good working conditions for their employees.[64] Several areas did establish Continuation Schools, especially the London County Council and Rugby but only the latter survived past 1921.[65]

In 1960 a letter was received from the minister of education inviting representatives from the TUC to discuss the possibilities of giving young persons a right to claim day-release for further education.[66] While welcoming this letter, doubts were expressed as to the seriousness of the minister, Sir David Eccles, as there was no evidence of the recruitment of the additional further education staff who would be needed. However uncertain they may have been over the minister's intentions, the publication of the Crowther Report in November 1959 concerning the education and training of 15–18-year-olds had brought the subject of part-time study for young people back on to the education agenda once more. Crowther rejected the suggestion that every young worker should have the right to day-release for further education, believing that the right would be illusory for some 15-year-old workers, a view with which the TUC agreed. The vocational education to be provided should contain an element of general education the TUC believed. They favoured block release for craft courses and a sandwich basis for technicians' courses. They welcomed the general findings of Crowther which were, in general, in sympathy with TUC education policy. The estimated costs of all the Crowther recommendations would be a further £200–£250 million to the annual education bill. Whilst Sir David Eccles accepted the principles in the report he regarded their implementation as something for the future. Perhaps the TUC's earlier scepticism had been justified.

A special committee was appointed by the minister of education in November 1962, to be chaired by Mr Henniker-Heaton, to which the TUC were invited to send representatives. Mr J. O'Hagan and Mr G.F. Smith were chosen with Dame Anne Godwin, Mr G.E. Green and Miss W. Buddeley sometimes attending. They reported in May 1964 and showed that in 1963, 555,000 boys and 694,000 girls aged between 15 and 18 received no day-time education. The question of granting the right to day-release had not been within the Committee's terms of reference but they did recommend that all young people under 18 should be enabled to continue education, at least part-time, as originally provided for in the Education Acts of 1918 and 1944. It was believed that targets needed to be set starting with an additional 250,000 young people to insure progress. The TUC were pleased with the outcome but doubted whether making the scheme voluntary would bring about the desired effect.

Progress was slow. By 1968 the TUCEC were complaining at the 'still limited haphazard day release schemes and the need for co-operation between the Ministers of Education and Labour'.[67] The education minister admitted to a slight fall in the numbers of 15–17-year-olds getting day release between 1963 and 1966 but during that last year there was an increase in the proportion of the age group included in these schemes. Some Industrial Training Boards were making grants conditional upon substantial day-release for further education as a financial incentive. Although the minister had accepted the Henniker–Heaton recommendations for 250,000 young workers getting day-release by 1970 the TUC did not believe this would take place unless he took more positive action to promote its expansion. They asked that trade union members of industrial training boards should provide them with information as to the extension of the scheme which they could use when arguing their case.

By the time it came to forward their suggestions for the new proposed Education Bill in 1969 the TUC's summary reflected the lack of progress in this area over the years. They wanted attendance for one day per week over a 44-week period. This policy compared to the reality showed just how far there was to go. They listed the missed opportunities: county colleges never established, two major reports concerned with this subject, Crowther and Henniker–Heaton never really acted upon with successive secretaries of state for education suggesting reliance for day-release being placed upon industrial training boards. Their conclusion was that 'the rate of progress does not inspire confidence'.[68]

NOTE AND REFERENCES

1. See Silver, H.(1973) (ed.) *Equal Opportunity in Education.*
2. The ILEA Report entitled *Improving Secondary Schools* published in 1984 found 147 different languages, p.45.
3. This pattern of development and the social consequences are well drawn in Lowe, R. (1997) *Schooling and Social Change 1964–1990,* Ch. 4.
4. For example Townsend, P. (1979) *Poverty in the United Kingdom*; Black, D. (1980) *The Black Report on Health.*
5. The title 'Chairman' is used here rather than chair/chairperson because that is how it appeared in the original report.
6. *TUC Report 1964*, pp.209–15.
7. Ibid., p.211.
8. TUCGC to Secretary of State, 10.11.1964; Secretary of State to TUCGC, 10.12.1964; *TUCEC Mins.* 12.1.1965.
9. Secretary of State to TUCGC, 12.1.1965; *TUCEC Mins.* 9.3.1965.
10. *TUCEC Mins.*, 9.11.1965.
11. See Whitbread, N. (1972) *The Evolution of the Nursery-Infant School,* pp.112–19.
12. Report of the meeting between the Secretary of State for Education and Science and members of the TUCEC, 14.2.1966, TUC 811/22.
13. Ibid.
14. *TUC Report 1966*, p.520.

15. *TUC Report 1967*, p.217.
16. (1967) *Children and their Primary Schools: Report of the Central Advisory Council (England) (The Plowden Report)* p.116, para. 291.
17. Ibid., p.132, para. 343.
18. *TUC Report 1968*, p.239.
19. *TUCEC Mins.* 12.3.1968.
20. *TUC Report 1969*, p.304.
21. Forder, A. (1971 edn) *Penelope Hall's Social Services of England and Wales*, pp.276–9.
22. *TUC Report 1969*, p.296.
23. For example Bowles, H. and Gintis H. (1976) *Schooling in Capitalist America.*
24. *Educational Priority Areas Vol. I*, p.180.
25. For detailed information on the EPAs and follow up to their progress see Halsey A.H. (ed.) (1972) *Educational Priority: EPA Problems and Policies*, Vol. I; Payne, J. (1974) *EPA Surveys and Statistics*, Vol. II; Silver, H. (ed.) (1983) 'Education Against Poverty; interpreting British and American policies in the 1960s and 1970s' in *Education as History*; Silver, H. (1991) 'Poverty and Effective Schools' *Journal of Educational Policy*, Vol. 6, No. 3; Smith, G. (1977) 'Positive Discrimination by Area in Education; the EPA Idea Re-examined' *Oxford Review of Education*, Vol. 13, No. 3.
26. Benn T. (1988) *Office Without Power; Diaries 1968–72*, p.168.
27. *TUC Report 1961*, pp.186–7.
28. Ibid.
29. *PRO ED 146/148*, 4.7.1962.
30. *TUC Report 1964*, p.215.
31. Ibid., pp. 6–7.
32. Ibid.
33. Ibid., pp.487–8.
34. Howard, A. (ed.) (1979) *Crossman Diaries – Selections 1964–1970*, p.378.
35. *TUC Report 1968*, p.242.
36. Ibid.
37. Wilson, H. (1974) *The Labour Government 1964–1970*, p.615.
38. Ponting, C. (1989) *Breach of Promise: Labour in Power 1964–1970*, p.304.
39. Benn, T. (1988) *Office Without Power*, p.17; Castle, B. (1984) *The Castle Diaries 1964–1970*, pp.350–1; Crosland, S. (1982) *Tony Crosland*, pp.194–5; Howard, A. (ed.) (1979) *Crossman Diaries*, pp.390–391; Wilson H. (1974) *The Labour Government*, pp.614–16.

40. Castle, B. (1984) *The Castle Diaries*, pp.350–1.
41. Howard, A. (ed.) (1979) *Crossman Diaries*, pp.390–1.
42. Healey, D. (1989) *The Time of My Life*, p.338.
43. Castle, B. (1984) *The Castle Diaries*, p.348.
44. Benn, T. (1988) *Office Without Power*, p.6.
45. Crosland, S. (1982) *Tony Crosland*, pp.195–6.
46. Brown, G. (1971) *In My Way: the Political Memories of Lord George Brown*, p.175.
47. Crosland, S. (1982) *Tony Crosland*, p.194.
48. *TUC Report 1968*, p.492.
49. Ibid., p.493.
50. *TUC Report 1969*, pp.297–8.
51. Ibid., p.309.
52. *TUCEC Mins.*, 26.8.1969.
53. Ibid.
54. Secretary of State to TUCGC, 10.12.1969, TUC 811/26.
55. *PRO ED 146/48*.
56. *TUC Report 1962*, p.170.
57. Ibid.
58. (1963) *Half Our Future: Report of the Minister of Education's Central Advisory Council (The Newsom Report)* p.75.
59. Report prepared for the TUCEC on Work Experience – *TUCEC Mins.* 10.2.1970.
60. DES – TUC Meeting 12.3.1970, Ibid.
61. Ibid.
62. TUC Report *TUCEC Mins.* 10.2.1970.
63. *TUCEC Mins.* 14.7.1970.
64. See Andrews, L.(1976) *The Education Act 1918*, pp.47–52, 72–5.
65. See Bernbaum, G. (1967) *Social Change and the Schools 1918–1944*, pp.30–3 and Simon, B.(1974) *The Politics of Educational Reform, 1920–1940*, pp.62–3.
66. Min. of Education to TUCGC, 19.7.1960, *TUC Report 1961*, pp.187–8.
67. *TUC Report 1968*, p.245.
68. *TUC Report 1969*, pp.300–1

CHAPTER 16

SECONDARY EDUCATION: ACADEMIC AND SOCIAL SELECTION

SECONDARY SCHOOL REORGANISATION

The provision of free primary and secondary schooling for all children had been a central theme in TUC education policy even if over time the wording had changed, as for example from multilateral to comprehensive. The issue of comprehensive education and selection were inevitably intertwined. It was illogical to suggest schools following these different approaches could co-exist in the same area for the former assumed all local children would attend their neighbourhood school whilst the latter only accepted children selected either by success in an entrance examination if it was a local authority school or parental fees together with an entrance examination if it was a fee-paying school. In fact for those schools at the bottom of the pecking order in the fee-paying sector if the parents could afford the fees they would take pupils almost regardless of academic ability as measured by an internal or external examination. The arguments in support of either form of schooling were numerous and by 1960 well known. The educational case for selective education based upon examinations was based upon the fact that people differ in their abilities and aptitudes. More controversial was the belief that it was possible to measure the intelligence of a child around 11 years of age and produce a score, referred to as the intelligence quotient (IQ), which not only accurately recorded the level of intelligence at this age but provided a sound prediction of her or his ability when they became an adult. This faith in the accuracy of IQ tests was based upon the conviction that intelligence was largely innate and did not vary over time.

Those opposing such a view believed that tests claiming to measure intelligence were flawed, that unintentionally they favoured the children of higher-income groups as compared to those from lower-income families and that they failed to take into account many other factors which contributed to the intellectual development of young people, from good teaching to parental support and encouragement. There were other circumstances less frequently expressed at first and they were to do with the social composition of the neighbourhood in which the school was located and attitudes taken towards schooling by parents and the general ethos of the area, including peer group pressure on children. Put frankly, some middle-class parents did not wish their children to attend schools in socially deprived inner city areas or on large local authority housing estates. Selection to a grammar school more or less guaranteed that the school would be in a pleasant area and that most of the pupils would come from middle-class homes. Such schools, neighbourhoods, parents and pupils were likely to be supportive of the formal education provided. This situation arose primarily from the way in which areas were socially divided in terms of the price and type of accommodation provided. If a child from a middle-class family did not succeed in gaining entry to a grammar school, faced with the alternative of attending a secondary modern school, the parents might opt for a fee-paying school. This was less possible as comprehensive schooling spread. There were, therefore, at least two issues behind arguments for a change in the secondary school system; one group could be classed as educational, others were more clearly linked to social attitudes. There were occasions when the former were put forward to obscure the latter.

Accurate evidence on social issues takes a long time to collect and produce, considerable time to permeate among the professionals and even longer to enter into public debate. Indeed, some research material never gets to the public arena because it is kept out by more popular simplistic views which certain sections of the media may find both more supportive of the political philosophy they espouse and easier to portray. In any case it would take several school generations after 1944 before the accuracy of the IQ tests as predictors of academic potential would be challenged in the light of the actual education experience of pupils, many of whom would defy the assessments made of them at 11 both later in school and in their future careers. Just like the pre-war generation of pupils from working-class homes forced to leave school at the end of an elementary schooling with all its consequences for their future adult lives so thousands of children now deemed to have 'failed' the 11-plus had their confidence often undermined for many years afterwards, even some who by other means, from attendance at evening classes to further study within a company had very successful careers. It is difficult to deny that at the height of the selection process in the 1950s to receive that slip of paper at school which told a child that they had 'failed' the test, and this was the experience of approximately 80 per cent of the school population, was akin to receiving the black spot among the pirates in *Treasure Island*.

During the 1950s two studies were published which were to have a major impact within the education profession. The first was by two men who had attended a grammar school in Huddersfield, Brian Jackson and Denis Marsden, both from working-class backgrounds who went on to study at Cambridge University. They set out to discover why the local grammar schools contained predominantly pupils from middle-class homes and what it was about the minority of pupils from working-class homes which allowed them to succeed in the system when most of their contemporaries did not. Their study was published as *Education and the Working Class* in 1962 and was reprinted many times by Penguin. One key factor which emerged was that pupils who gained grammar school places from working-class backgrounds and succeeded academically tended to readily adopt the middle-class cultural values of the school. Usually their progress ran parallel with a gradual disengagement with their past primary school friends and the general ethos of the neighbourhood. It demonstrated also that the families from middle-class homes and neighbourhood were at an advantage because their values were more likely to coincide with those of the school. Therefore they fitted in more easily. Working-class children who resisted the values of the school were more likely to pay the price by leaving before they were 16.

Whilst Jackson and Marsden's book became almost popular reading among educationists at the time, another report, this time an official publication, published several years earlier in 1954 entitled *Early Leaving*: (full title *Early Leaving: Report of the Central Advisory Council for Education (England)*) was slowly ticking away with its evidence gradually spreading throughout the world of education.[1] This report demonstrated clearly that although considerable numbers of working-class children entered grammar schools the majority of them did not get five passes at GCE ordinary level and of these more than half left before the end of their fifth year so that they did not even sit for the examinations. Most significant was what actually happened to children from different social backgrounds during their time in school. Graded originally into three bands according to ability measured by tests it was perceived that children from the working classes gradually sank down into the lower bands whilst those from higher income groups rose to the higher bands. Among the five socio-economic groups listed the correlation was clear – the higher the social background of the child the more likely they were to move upwards and vice versa. Something unintended was taking place within the school. It is worth reproducing the relevant table summarising the situation because it demonstrated clearly that it was not measured IQ at 11 years of age which was the best guide to the academic attainment of a child but her or his family background, as defined at the time by occupation of the father.

Table 2. Comparison of Pupils' Achievements at the Beginning and End of their Grammar School Life (Maintained Grammar Schools Only)[2]

Selection Group at 11	Academic Category at 16–18	Professional and Managerial	Clerical	Skilled	Semi-skilled	Un-skilled
		%	%	%	%	%
1	A B C	79.9	64.6	60.1	46.8	29.6
	D	10.2	16.8	13.6	15.4	16.3
	E F	9.9	18.6	26.4	37.9	54.0
	All	100	100	100	100	100
2	A B C	61.8	53.3	42.6	27.7	25.6
	D	12.8	15.2	16.5	14.6	12.0
	E F	25.4	31.5	40.9	57.7	62.4
	All	100	100	100	100	100
3	A B C	48.3	36.3	32.6	22.8	12.8
	D	18.2	21.5	15.6	15.1	10.7
	E F	33.5	42.2	51.8	62.1	76.4
	All	100	100	100	100	100

These statistics have been selected directly from the table produced in *Early Leaving Report*; they do not add up precisely to 100 in the report, even though 100 is given as the total. This is due to figures being rounded up/down to one decimal place.

As the table illustrated nearly 80 per cent of the children ranked in the top band ABC from professional and managerial parents were still in such bands by the time they were 16 but only 30 per cent of the children with parents who were unskilled workers similarly classified at 11 had retained their position in the top band. By contrast among those graded in the lowest band EF at 11 among the former social group only 33 per cent remained in this band whilst nearly 50 per cent were now in the top band but among the children of the unskilled only 13 per cent had worked their way into the top band whilst more than 75 per cent had remained in the lowest band. Moreover, as the chart shows, children from intervening socio-economic groups fitted in precisely between these two extremes showing a smooth gradation from one socio-economic extreme to the other. The findings illustrated the powerful influences of home background, neighbourhood, peer group pressure and the expectations of some teachers.

This was not a crude deterministic fact for it was clear that some children from poor circumstances overcame considerable obstacles and were successful academically; conversely some children with all the apparent social advantages did not succeed at school. However, the evidence for the importance of home background, and above all supportive parents whatever their social background was a key factor in the understanding of why success at school in terms of examination passes, and opportunities for further education and career prospects correlated more closely with these circumstances than IQ scores or teaching methods.

Within the same decade two further studies would confirm much of this research. One by J.W.B. Douglas looking at success in the 11-plus among primary schools showed that schools with the best results were to be found in the more affluent neighbourhoods.[3] Working-class pupils who did succeed tended to be living just inside the catchment area of a school populated by middle-class children and had supportive parents with values not always shared by their neighbours as to the importance of education. A follow-up study by a team led by Douglas a few years later looking at what happened to the earlier group of pupils who had now entered secondary school revealed that gaps in achievement between children tended to widen as the children moved through the school. The importance of success or failure during the early years of schooling showed once more the key role nursery education could play for it was easier to correct learning problems when children were very young than when they had reached their teens; by then years of comparative failure at school could turn learning difficulties into behavioural difficulties leading to general disenchantment with school among some children. The pattern of early leaving was also correlated with social class.

By the 1960s TUC policy on secondary schooling was clear. They were firmly against the 11-plus examination and from being in favour of comprehensive schools at least on an experimental basis in the post-1944 years they were now wholly supportive of a fully comprehensive system of secondary schooling. At the invitation of the Newsom Committee the TUC submitted a memorandum some 12 pages in length which addressed a wide range of issues dealing with secondary schooling. It began by questioning the assumption applied in the terms of reference attempting to cover 'average or less than average ability children'. The Advisory Council used the term 'ability' in the 'commonly understood sense of intellectual capacity as reflected in normal school attainment'. This was too narrow a view for the TUCGC because of their

> experience of the high level of capacity in practical and creative activities of many young people who have not revealed an 'intellectual' capacity in the form of academic attainment, and from the unquestioned achievements in many fields by men and women who have not experienced the type of secondary education held to be appropriate for the most able.[4]

Considerable numbers of people adjudged at 11 to average or less than average ability later succeeded in further education, adult education or higher education, demonstrating capacities for relatively high intellectual performance. Hence the distrust of the TUC in methods of selection for secondary school.

They also gave serious attention to social factors involved, making it clear they were familiar with the findings of the Early Leaving Report which highlighted how attendance and ultimate academic attainment at grammar schools were closely related to the social class of parents. The progress of children from higher-income groups almost regardless of the type of secondary school attended led them to suggest that the social forces at work needed to be studied and understood more fully. They had little doubt that 'the tests for selection had evolved primarily in the light of the social and vocational needs of children of a certain social background rather than necessarily of a certain type or level of ability'.[5] For the working-class families their world of work had been one demanding little in the way of formal eduation, 'dominated by economic insecurity and uncertainty and therefore primarily concerned with short term considerations...characterised by an essential preoccupation with practical affairs, and by an essential emphasis upon the working or neighbourhood group rather than upon the individual'.[6] This was a cultural phenomenon which had its strength in terms of co-operation and neighbourly support at times of crisis but seemed to be in some way detrimental to success in selective secondary grammar schools. This seemed to imply that individuality, even self-interest was necessary for academic success. The detailed document makes summary difficult but the TUCGC stressed the social factors working upon school success, their rejection of the segregation of pupils in secondary schools and the principles which should permeate the secondary school curriculum 'to live full and satisfying lives', an assumption which the TUCGC believed it was unnecessary to argue in the context of this inquiry.

Dame Anne Godwin was a member of the TUCEC from 1952 to 1963, a member of the Crowther Committee of 1959, the Donnison Committee of 1970 and president of the TUC in 1962. She used her opening address at this Congress to focus upon the area in which she was most knowledgeable, education. She was critical of the system:

> We spend a great deal of time arguing about the iniquities of the 11-plus system, whether its method of selection is right. What we should do is to reject, once and for all, the whole rotten conception of first-class and second-class citizenship that is involved, a conception which apparently begins to operate through the process of intellectual streaming when the child is somewhere about the advanced age of seven.
>
> We should leave off worrying about the opportunities available to the 20 per cent or 25 per cent of our children who 'succeed', to use the precisely correct word, in getting into grammar schools. Instead we should ask ourselves what we have done to those – the 75 per cent to 80 per cent – who in their earliest years have been labelled failures.[7]

This passionate speech was a good summary of the TUC's position on the 11-plus examination and selective secondary schooling even if the wording of official TUCEC communications was of a less emotive tone. As Mr E.D. Swift (Inland Revenue Staff Federation) would remind delegates the following year 'comprehensive schools were still a matter of bitter arguments and controversy',[8] a view recognised by the TUC in evidence to the Plowden Committee when they carefully voiced their wishes in more diplomatic tones:

> The GC believe that a radical reorganisation of secondary education upon a more comprehensive basis would greatly assist in freeing the later years of primary education from pressures tending to diminish their value, distort their purpose, and would enable primary schools to contribute more constructively to resolving the problem of transition to secondary education.[9]

The policy was repeated in similar manner to the Newsom Report in which they 'questioned the validity of current practices of segregating children according to their "measured" ability both within and between different types of school'.[10] Newsom's conclusion that 'excessively fine gradings of ability groups should be avoided' was too vague as far as the TUC were concerned. It was secondary organisation 'upon a more comprehensive basis' that they wished to see rapidly introduced.

CIRCULAR 10/65 AND ALL THAT

This seemed more likely when Tony Crosland introduced Circular 10/65 with the intention of ending selection at 11-plus by requesting local education authorities to submit reorganisation plans for secondary education in order to end selection to different types of secondary school. To some extent Crosland's role in Circular 10/65 was comparable to that of Butler with regard to the 1944 Education Act. The groundwork had already been prepared by others, in this case by Michael Stewart.[11] Like Butler before him he was the prime negotiator who dealt skilfully with conflicting interest groups in order to make progress. Another case of a minister receiving the credit for action for which he was only partly responsible.

Nevertheless, the TUC were pleased with the contents of the Circular and in their response made nine points, the first two dealing with the matter of selection. They were now satisfied that there existed,

> convincing evidence establishing beyond reasonable doubt that these practices [selection tests] are neither just to large numbers of individual pupils, nor effective in deploying educational resources to the maximum benefit of the nation ... [They were also] satisfied that the re-organisation of secondary education on comprehensive lines ... will make a major contribution to establishing a more genuine equality of educational, occupational and social opportunity for all.[12]

That Crosland did not take a harder line towards reorganisation was due to a mixture of pragmatism and ideology. His minister of state, Reg Prentice, wished for a tougher stance; rather ironic in view of his later defection in 1977 to the Conservative party. The reality was that changes to organisation were taking place in local authorities and there were insufficient funds being made available for faster change at the time. In addition, Crosland believed that changes from voluntary agreement would be more lasting.

Whilst comprehensive schools promised to bring benefits for the majority of children whose destination would otherwise be a secondary modern school the parents of the minority of children attending grammar schools realised these changes would affect their children too. Some supported the reorganisation believing that comprehensive schooling was a fairer system for all children; others resisted proposed changes, supporting the retention of grammar schools for various reasons such as that their children were gaining an advantage by being in a selective school which was better resourced than a secondary modern school and enjoyed higher status within the community. One interesting phenomenon was to note the change in support for selective schooling before and after the results of the 11-plus examination when some would transfer their allegiance to comprehensive schools if their child was not successful in the entrance examination. Similarly some parents faced with the news that their child had not gained a grammar school place would make efforts to send their child into another county which had abolished selection to attend a comprehensive school if the distance was not too far. This was true for example for some living in Kent in areas adjacent to East Sussex. The 11-plus examination system brought anguish to many parents and the majority of children who were faced with what had become a traumatic event in their schooling at such a young age.

Understandably, the grammar school lobby did its best to protect its privileged position of selecting pupils by a test claiming to measure potential academic ability which also resulted unintentionally in a considerable amount of social selection. Teaching well-motivated children in a pleasant district with strong parental support is an easier task than teaching disenchanted youngsters who have been labelled as failures in a socially deprived area, as any experienced teacher will testify. The shock to many teachers who went in to some inner city areas to teach in secondary modern schools in what would be considered challenging circumstances was recorded in a series of novels written by teachers, based upon their experiences, which later became films, such as Michael Croft's *Spare the Rod*, Edward Blishen's *Roaring Boys* and Leonard Braithwaite's *To Sir with Love*. Arguing that grammar schools could be retained whilst secondary modern schools were lumped together and renamed comprehensives denied the whole purpose of the desired change. It was frustration over this issue which led Crosland on returning from a meeting with four of the teachers' associations with membership largely in selective schools to declare to his wife: 'If its the last thing I do, I'm going to destroy every fucking grammar school in England and Wales. And Northern Ireland.'[13] Said in exasperation which turned to laughter when he realised he would not be able to see through complete comprehensivisation, it is a quote which is repeated often enough. Another oft repeated is the one attributed to Harold Wilson which seemed to contradict Crosland's outburst. While in opposition he is supposed to have said, although he denied having said so, 'that the grammar school would be abolished "over my dead body"'. In fact he took a lively interest in their destruction.[14]

It is likely had Boyle been appointed as education minister in the 1970 Heath administration that Circular 10/65 would not have been withdrawn. He suggested to Lord Vaizey that it would have been sufficient not to proceed with Short's Bill.[15] The new minister, Margaret Thatcher, however was a person of strong convictions, with few doubts and the first of the right-wing ideologues to take over at the DES. She withdrew Circular 10/65 and issued 10/70 cancelling the provisions of the former. Local authorities would now decide for themselves with parental choice being given priority as to the type of secondary school system to be followed in their area. In fact this policy was not followed consistently and almost immediately she found herself involved in a dispute at Barnet which had been working on a plan for a comprehensive system for several years and in a referendum of parents and teachers found that 79.4 per cent favoured reorganisation. Mrs Thatcher overturned the decisions.[16] In the long term her legacy would be somewhat different, as the minister who presided over the closure of the most grammar schools. The tide for reorganisation of secondary schooling was too strong to hold back except in a few Tory heartlands. There was hardly any support for the 11-plus examination although many parents paradoxically did favour the idea of grammar schools – a view which was to a large extent dependent upon whether their children were successful or not in the entrance examination which many had come to believe was so unfair.

POLITICAL PARTIES AND SELECTION

Public perception tends to suggest that Conservatives were opposed to comprehensive schools whilst Labour supported them. This is far too simplistic a view and is in any case inaccurate as has been shown through the policies of Labour ministers of education during the Attlee governments. It would be more accurate to say that after the 1950s the labour movement increasingly supported the abolition of the 11-plus and the reorganisation of secondary education but within the Conservative party opinion was more divided. Many Conservative MPs wished to see grammar schools retained, although when such schools were available locally they usually chose to send their own children to a fee-paying school. At local authority level considerable numbers of Conservative councillors were well aware of the hostility towards the 11-plus felt by significant numbers of their middle-class constituents and supported reorganisation for educational reasons. As for Conservative ministers of education they were by no means hostile to all secondary school reorganisation.

If one considers the four Conservative ministers of education between October 1959 and October 1964 one can ignore to some extent the last year when Hailsham and Edward Boyle each spent a few months in the post, far too short a period to make any effective change. Unlike Hailsham, who relished confrontation, David Eccles, at the Education Office from October 1959 to July 1962, and Edward Boyle, who took over until April 1964, acted in a relatively pragmatic way. Both were aware of the change in social conditions which had taken place during the 1950s and which entrenched past attitudes of their own party could no longer ignore. As other countries recovered from the Second World War and Britain faced increasing economic challenges for exports, Eccles was one minister who was willing to point out that the education system of some of these rivals was playing a major role in their success. Adding a Cold War element to the threat he was willing to tell Macmillan 'the Russians, since 1917, had now become the industrial rival even of the USA. "This has been done by education. Communism will surely triumph unless NATO allies outclass and keep a long lead over Russia and China in public education."'[17]

Education was a major item on the political agenda by the turn of the 1960s and attitudes began to change as the argument that it should be seen as a sound investment which would bring future economic prosperity gathered greater support. The demands on educational expenditure were increasing; as with all governments priorities would decide how money was allocated. Conservative governments were more enthusiastic about support for what was considered to be the most intelligent pupils and the need for more opportunities in higher education. They readily accepted much of the Robbins Report whereas they showed less enthusiasm in implementing the Newsom Report dealing with 'average and below average children'.

Eccles had to fight hard to raise the profile of education within the Cabinet to impress upon colleagues not only the importance of expanding opportunities in schooling for the country, but the electoral dangers if they did not. He told the Parliamentary Committee on Education, 'incidentally education was the open door for erstwhile Labour voters to enter the Tory middle class'.[18] He was also willing to threaten resignation to force the Cabinet to grasp how fundamental was the need to finance expanding education services to meet the increasing expectations of parents.[19]

Eccles and Boyle were aware that whatever the arguments might be about secondary reorganisation, the 11-plus was widely and increasingly unpopular. As early as 1955 Eccles had warned Eden, 'The most political problem in education is the ll+.'[20] They recognised the educational case made by some for the retention of grammar schools often supported by Conservative MPs and local grammar school pressure groups. They were equally aware that there was little local support for the retention of secondary modern schools which were part and parcel of the selective system. However vociferous Conservative party activists might be in their support for selection, both ministers knew that it was their more open-minded approach, which in general favoured decisions being made at local authority level that was a better reflection of public opinion nation-wide. The dilemma was how to cope with the dislike of the 11-plus, introduction of non-selective secondary schooling, whilst retaining a local grammar school with a long history and good reputation. They inevitably faced pressure from groups with policies which were clearly incompatible. Their common tactic was to argue that the decision on reorganisation should be taken locally and that they would make a decision based purely on educational criteria. This helped them to avoid the direct responsibility for much reorganisation. Boyle realised that reorganisation was underway nationally and was reluctant to become involved in defending selection when it was clear that only a minority wished the system to be retained.[21] He approved of the long-held plan of the LCC to go comprehensive in 1958 and told delegates at the Association of Education Committees annual meeting in that year that '11-plus selection has received a mortal blow'.[22] He was also willing to state that, 'not all grammar schools were good schools, and that their examination results were sometimes worse than those of the local secondary modern school'.[23]

These views were anathema to traditional Conservatives and towards the end of the decade opposition to these liberal and pragmatic views began to arise from a new emerging radical right element within the party. Eccles and Boyle had supportive prime ministers in Macmillan and Heath (Sir Alec Douglas-Home was only prime minister for a year and the fellow old Etonian he chose to be education minister was in that post for an even briefer spell). Boyle was retained by Heath as shadow education minister although it is doubtful whether he could have held on to the post in the light of changes taking place within the Conservative party. By the time they had returned to power with an increase in the number of MPs with right-wing ideological tendencies he had left to become Vice Chancellor of Leeds University.

The move to the political right within the party was the product of various embryonic groups earlier in the decade, stimulated by such personalities as Rhodes Boyson and Harry Greenway, both teachers in London, and Brian Cox and Anthony Dyson, professors of English Literature. Perhaps the main credit should go to Angus Maude, Chairman of the Conservative Education Committee 1954/55 and 1963 and member of the Conservative Teachers' Association National Advisory Committee in 1964. He was vehemently opposed to Edward Boyle's liberal approach to education and even more antagonistic to socialist ideas. His educational philosophy was expounded in an influential book entitled *Good Learning*, published in 1964, which promoted selective secondary schooling.[24] In this his views were mirrored by another Tory MP, Gilbert Longden, who was a member of the education committee and policy group of the party. If Maude's rhetoric enthused a growing band of supporters the more factual and better-argued publications of the Institute of Economic Affairs were to prove more valuable in suggesting a framework for the introduction of free-market principles into education policy.[25]

When political parties lose office a post-mortem usually follows and questions are asked as to the policies which had been pursued. In 1964 Douglas-Home's defeat provided an ideal opportunity for the New Right to question recent Conservative social policy, including education. They willingly seized the chance and within a few years were challenging the legacy of Eccles and Boyle. Educational pragmatism was out; its place taken by New Right ideology which would be promoted in the years ahead with a missionary-like zeal.

COUNCIL FOR EDUCATIONAL ADVANCE – MARK 2

The TUC were reluctant to join organisations pleading a special case because they were always aware that they had to represent the views of Congress where there may be individuals or groups who supported trade union policies in general but not those of external organisations. There were occasional exceptions, such as the Council for Educational Advance in 1942 when the views of those involved coincided with those of the TUC. Twenty years later another pressure group was formed to campaign for educational advance which took the same title as the 1942 organisation.

In October 1962 Denis Winnard, Secretary of the TUCEC reported to his committee that he had attended a meeting called by the NUT to consider a campaign for educational advance to be called the Council for

Educational Advance (CFEA), whose objective was to arouse general support for reforms widely acknowledged to be required in the education service.[26] The next month a letter arrived from the CFEA explaining that 22 educational organisations had declared support with another 19 other representatives attending an exploratory meeting. A discussion within the TUCEC raised doubts as to the capability of the organisation and whether it 'would contribute effectively to achieving the objects of the TUC's educational policy'.[27] It was decided that the TUC could not participate in the proposed scheme.

In spite of this answer, in December the issue arose again when the NUT asked if the TUC would reconsider as it might appear as if they disapproved of the campaign. They suggested it might be possible to have a category of membership for organisations sympathetic to the views of the CFEA but who did not wish for full membership. Once more the matter was discussed, this time Anne Godwin asked whether the NUT were seeking support for specific NUT campaigns dealing with recruitment, salaries and the status of teachers. This thought may have been partly a result of the reluctance on the part of some at the TUC to become involved in a campaign which dealt with matters specific to members of a trade union which still refused to affiliate to the TUC. It might have seemed like a one-way bargain. Other committee members disagreed, believing that the campaign should be supported because it favoured the 1944 Education Act which was also TUC policy. By 5:4 it was decided to invite CFEA members to the next meeting of the TUCEC.[28]

Early in the New Year representatives from the CFEA met the TUCEC. They were Mr E.J. Britten (general secetary of the ASTMS), Fred Jarvis (secretary of the NUT), Margaret Marsh (education officer of the WEA) Miss M. Mushoda (general secretary of the Council for Children's Welfare) and Mrs R. Remington (president of the Association of Divisional Executives). They stated their case admitting that different organisations would stress their own priorities in the campaign. In the discussion which followed the TUCEC expressed sympathy for the general aims but said they did not wish to become involved. They did offer to circulate affiliated trade unions and trades councils with information about the campaign should they wish to join whilst explaining priorities in TUC education policy.[29] CFEA campaigned strongly in support of state education. Another organisation with similar aims was the Confederation for the Advancement of State Education established in 1960 which later became the Campaign for State Education (CASE), pressing for smaller class sizes, resisting cuts in educational expenditure and supporting parent representation on governing bodies and improved salaries and conditions for teachers. They produced a journal several times per year entitled *Parents and Schools* the back numbers of which provide a record of the issues raised in education during past years.[30]

SCHOOL MEALS AND MILK

The 1960s were to witness a further undermining of the welfare services associated with education and laid down by the 1944 Education Act as part of the 'social wage' for families. School meals and milk became common targets for a number of reasons. Meals were an easy area in which to economise; prices could be raised above the cost of the food supplied, money saved by not providing planned dining facilities and making children eat meals at their desks or in general purpose halls. Governments and ministers could argue that the provision of meals and milk were not strictly educational matters and therefore cutbacks in these programmes would not damage education in the way reduced budgets for books might. In addition, by the 1960s there were growing numbers of people who were led to believe that poverty no longer existed and the provision of school meals and milk was no longer necessary. If they had to be provided it should be at an 'economic price' which it was suggested growing prosperity had made it possible for all parents to meet.

As studies published a few years later would show, poverty had not been eradicated although full employment and the welfare state had meant that the poor did not suffer the deprivation and squalor endured by large numbers during the inter-war years, let alone the wretchedness of Victorian times. Low-income families were to be found in the countryside and inner-city areas but the decline of living standards on some local authority housing estates in suburban areas was yet to come. Although the vast majority of the population had become more prosperous in the post-war years, in many aspects of life the gap between groups had remained the same. The escalator effect where everybody standing on a step moves upwards together but the space between them stays the same could be observed in many areas of society. Infant mortality rates for example had improved for all social groups yet those for social class 5 were only at the level that social class 1 had experienced a generation earlier and meanwhile social class 1 had improved even further so that a significant gap still remained between the two social groups. This was true in many other areas of health and life-style. Moreover, it gradually became apparent that not all groups of people had shared much in the nation's increased prosperity. Poverty was 'rediscovered' in the late 1960s and

1970s and documented in several studies.[31] These trends were to be subsequently confirmed by further research in later years.[32]

The mid-day school meal provided a vital source of nutrition for the children of many low-income families. Later it would be argued that they went some way in providing a balanced diet in the face of competition from increasing numbers of American franchised fast food outlets offering food rich in salt and saturated animal fats which were linked to obesity and heart disease. Promoted by expensive advertising campaigns these junk foods proved attractive to many youngsters and posed a threat to the future health of children which school dinners could help to counteract. The principles of the 1944 Education Act had been eroded in the 15 years following the war. Prices were routinely increased and TUC protests almost took on a ritualistic form as ministers promised to consider the long-term effects of the latest rise, the results of which they later ignored.

It was not just the health of children which was affected by the provision of school meals. Mr Alan W. Fisher (NUPE) proposed a motion to the 1966 TUC drawing attention to 'the sound value of the school meals service, [and] to the difficulties created by staffing problems, inadequate equipment and unsuitable premises'.[33] A review of the school meals service was called for by the government in conjunction with the local education authorities to see what could be undertaken to remedy these difficulties. He went on to describe the scale of the service with 781 million meals being taken every school year providing for two out of every three school children. This vital service was provided by part-time staff, largely by women, often working in poor conditions.

Fisher referred to a letter by Sir Edward Boyle in *The Times* (8 August 1966) referring to cuts in education made by the Labour government in 1965, in which he stated 'Many of us feel that a more rational attitude to subsidies on school meals and milk would have rendered last year's cuts unnecessary.' This statement meant Sir Edward, a noted progressive according to Fisher, had:

> raised his standard with the reactionary forces of the Tory Party who would like to destroy the school meals service by increasing the prices to a level that most people would be unable to afford. Gone was the inconvenient recollection, that it was the Conservatives themselves in the 1944 Education Act who suggested that there should be free meals in schools. Gone also was the knowledge the family allowances were deliberately fixed at a low level in 1946 because it was assumed that this was going to happen.[34]

Fisher spelt out the difficulties of the school meals staff as revealed in a survey carried out by the Inner London Education Authority which revealed,

> wood and untreated concrete and stone floors had to be scrubbed by hand in many cases in the interests of hygiene. Food had to be trolleyed across playgrounds in all kinds of weather. Some of it had to be hauled between floors on rope hoists, or carried up and down flights of stairs... [and] ... much of the furniture used had to be erected and dismantled every day.[35]

Most of the women were organised in NUPE, belying the belief that women would not readily join trade unions, and Congress passed the motion willingly, in support of them. The problems outlined by Fisher were to be increased a few months later in the provisions of a DES Circular 25/66 issued in December. Following up the TUC Resolution on school meals with Anthony Crosland at the DES, the TUCEC confirmed their belief that the school meals service had a social value, not just in the provision of food, but in the act of eating a meal with friends under the supervision of teachers. They referred to the change brought about by Circular 25/66 in the financing of the service, expressing their fear at the block grant system which from their experience 'had been invariably associated with attempts to effect economies in public expenditure'.[36] Crosland tried to reassure them, claiming that the DES would continue to advise LEAs on the nutritional standard of meals provided and telling them 'he retained statutory powers to compel – at last resort – local authorities to provide an adequate school meals service'.[37] He informed them that the House of Commons Estimates Committee had recommended that the school meals service should be reviewed. The General Council replied that they would watch closely any developments affecting this service but by August Crosland no longer had responsibility for education as he had moved on to the Board of Trade.

If the supine Patrick Gordon Walker had accepted the cutbacks to education in January 1968 it was his successor, Edward Short, who had taken over at the ministry in April, who had to face the TUC in June. Blaming the state of the economy for the necessity to abolish free school milk in secondary schools he tried to point out new measures aimed to compensate for education cutbacks. He referred to recent increases in family allowances and the introduction of free school meals for the fourth and subsequent children in all families. As for the abolition of milk it appeared the government had taken professional advice on the nutritional value of milk to secondary school children, 'but investigation on this point had proved "inconclusive"'. It was in any case obvious that the decision had been based upon financial factors rather than those associated with nutrition. The Labour government's abolition of free milk in secondary schools provided a lead which a Conservative government might follow. They were to do so through a White Paper issued in their first few months of office foreshadowing public expenditure cuts, which sought to confine free school milk to children under 8 years old and to other junior pupils for whom milk was recommended on grounds of health.[38] The Education (Milk) Act of 1971 led to the effective ending of milk in schools, which prompted a chant 'Maggie Thatcher, milk snatcher', but she was only completing a policy out of conviction to end the provision of free school milk which a Labour government had started with timidity.

SCHOOL HOLIDAYS

After a couple of weeks of the summer school holiday some children became bored and mothers in paid employment were concerned about the care of their children during these weeks. In 1967 the TUC passed a resolution by the Health Visitors Association suggesting that much delinquency among school children was the result of 'boredom and idleness' and suggested that greater provision of holiday camps and organised holiday programmes based on museums, libraries, parks and other local amenities should be provided for children to attend, if they so wished, during a part of the school summer holiday. Whilst the TUCGC considered that the causes of delinquency were more complex they did agree that amenities for children during periods of holiday should be extended and improved especially in socially deprived areas. Apparently no systematic survey had been carried out into the extent and need for school holiday amenities. The TUCGC suggested that this was principally the responsibility of the LEA and that trades councils should be asked to gather information about the present provision of such amenities in their localities.

The result was that the following year 120 trades councils provided information to the TUC which included 28 city boroughs, 5 London boroughs and 33 counties covering about 3 million out of a total of 7,250,000 school children in England and Wales. The picture provided was varied. Forty trades councils reported school playing fields in their areas were made available to some extent for organised groups of children and some playgrounds were open but most LEAs made it a condition for adequate supervision to be available. A few even provided staff for this role. Thirty-four trades councils reported some availability of swimming baths whilst others were closed for maintenance during the holidays, 24 trades councils were in areas where there were holidays abroad organised by schools and paid for by parents and 18 recorded school meals operating. There were also some play leadership courses available. Various schemes with voluntary helpers, such as students and parents, provided a wide range of activities including painting, drawing, model making, drama, film shows and visits to places of local interest which were considered to be helpful for parents and children.

It was believed that there was a need for a general improvement in the scale and quality of holiday amenities which would be of particular value in large urban areas where there was little open space available, heavy traffic and poor housing. A number of local authorities took the view that provision of playing fields during the holidays was not their responsibility. Properly organised provision had educational value according to the TUC and every LEA should have a policy for the provision of school holiday amenities with the possibility of grants given to recognised organisations. Moreover, school meals should be continued as about 500,000 children were entitled to free mid-day meals and some of these children missed out during the holidays.

Edward Short accepted the TUC report's findings but could offer no real hope of meeting their requests. He referred to a Circular sent out jointly by the DES and Ministry of Housing to local authorities in 1964 encouraging the planning of recreational facilities for use of the whole community, including children. There was evidence that some local authorities were pooling their resources to make better the provision of amenities. They were told that fewer than one-third of LEAs continued with school meals because of the difficulty of staffing during the holidays and the risk that food would be wasted – a risk less likely when provided in play centres. As this was the responsibility of the LEAs, Short suggested the TUC should get the trades councils to take up the matter with their respective authorities.

The TUC expressed their disappointment which brought a second response from the minister. He could not encourage LEAs to provide amenities in the holidays because there was a need for them 'to limit educational expenses'. Similarly, when the TUC wrote to a series of organisations including the Association of Education Committees, the Association of Municipal Corporations, the County Councils Association, the Welsh Joint Education Committee and the Inner London Education Authority, whilst agreeing to inform their members of the TUC's views on the development of holiday amenities, they also made the point that, 'it would be difficult for local authorities to expand in this field because of the current restrictions on educational expenditure'.[39] It was clear that once again the TUC were able to outline a range of services required to help children and parents which were accepted as valid in principle but in the main unlikely to be provided due to the continued economic stringency in public expenditure.

NOTES AND REFERENCES

1. (1954) *Early Learning: Report of the Central Advisory Council for Education (England).*
2. Ibid.,Table K.
3. Douglas, J.W.B. (1964) *The Home and the School: A Study of Ability and Attainment in Primary Schools.*
4. *PRO ED 146/48.*
5. Ibid.
6. Ibid.
7. *TUC Report 1962*, pp.77–9.
8. *TUC Report 1963*, p.434.
9. TUC Evidence to Plowden Committee, *TUC Report 1964*, pp.211–16.
10. Ibid., pp.216–17.
11. Dean, D. (1998) 'Circular 10/65 Revisited: The Labour Government and the Comprehensive Revolution', *Paedagogica Historica*, pp.68–9.
12. Circular 10/65, *TUC Report 1966*, pp.208–10.
13. Crosland, S. (1982) *Tony Crosland*, p.148.
14. Pimlott, B.(1992) *Harold Wilson*, p.512.
15. Crook, D. (1993) 'Edward Boyle; Conservative Champion of Comprehensives' *History of Education*, Vol. 22, No. 1, p.61.
16. Woods, R. (1981) 'Margaret Thatcher and Secondary Reorganisation 1970–74' *Journal of Educational Administration and History*, Vol. XIII, No. 2.
17. Dean, D. (1995) 'Conservative Governments, 1951–1964, and their Changing Perspectives on the 1944 Education Act', *History of Education*, Vol .24, No. 3, p.259.
18. Address to Conservative Parliamentary Education Committee, 25 November 1959. Dean, D., ibid., p.259.
19. Ibid.
20. Eccles to Eden, 14 April 1955, quoted in Dean, D. ibid., p.251.
21. Kogan, M. (1971) *The Politics of Education*, pp.77–8.
22. *Education, 122*, 17.7.1963, Quoted in Crook, D. (1993) 'Edward Boyle', p.52.

23. Ibid., p.53.
24. Knight, C.(1990) *The Making of Tory Education Policy in Post-War Britain 1950–1986*, p.23.
25. Chitty, C. (1989) *Towards a New Education System: The Victory of the New Radical Right*, Chs. 7 and 8; Griggs, C. (1989) 'The New Right and Secondary Education' in Lowe, R. (ed.) *The Changing Secondary School*.
26. *TUCEC Mins.*, 9.10.1962.
27. *TUCEC Mins.*, 13.11.1962.
28. *TUCEC Mins.*, 11.12.1962.
29. *TUCEC Mins.*, 8.1.1963.
30. The 100th issue of *Parents and Schools* (January 1999) records some of the campaigns which CASE has been involved in since the 1960s.
31. Townsend, P. (1979) *Poverty in the United Kingdom*, see Ch. 4 for the period 1938–68; Field, F. (1973) *Unequal Britain: A Report on the Cycle of Inequality*.
32. Townsend, P. and Davidson, N. (eds) (1982) *Inequalities in Health (The Black Report)*; Field, F. (1981) *Inequality in Britain; Freedom, Welfare and the State*.
33. *TUC Report 1966*, p.522.
34. Ibid.
35. Ibid.
36. *TUC Report 1967*, p.217.
37. Ibid.
38. Garner, D. (1985) 'Education and the Welfare State: The School Meals and Milk Service, 1944–1980'. *Journal of Educational Administration and History*, Vol. XVII, No. 2., p.66.
39. *TUC Report 1969*, p.309.

CHAPTER 17

HIGHER EDUCATION

TRAINING AND PROVISION OF TEACHERS

Traditionally there were two different routes into teaching. A training college course of two years, which was extended to three years in 1960, from which a Certificate of Education was awarded. These courses provided both tuition in a major and minor subject to be taught in schools and included the study of education as well as periods of teaching practice in schools. A second way was by taking a three-year degree course followed by a one-year postgraduate certificate which included professional training. It was also possible to go direct into a school as a graduate without any professional training and this was the norm for most teachers who entered fee-paying schools although this practice gradually declined. In general students who attended colleges of education, initially known as teacher training colleges, taught in elementary schools in the inter-war period, then primary or secondary modern schools after 1944. Graduates were destined for secondary grammar and fee-paying schools although increasingly they were also recruited to secondary modern and comprehensive schools during the 1960s.

The TUC took an interest in the training of teachers, their conditions of work, their salaries, subjects taught and methods of teaching. This area would probably have achieved an even higher profile had teacher trade unions affiliated to the TUC earlier. In fact a minority group, the National Union of School Teachers, led by the formidable Miss Walsh, largely composed of uncertificated and supplementary teachers who made up about one-third of the elementary teaching force and were denied membership of the NUT, were affiliated during the inter-war period.[1] She used her position as the only practising teacher representative to make speeches at Congress and be included on TUC delegations to the Board of Education. The Union declined in membership and folded with her death in 1945. TUC delegates were always supportive of teachers and argued for a long time that TUC membership would not compromise the political neutrality of teacher unions in negotiations with government. The Association of Teachers in Technical Institutions (ATTI) were the first to affiliate in 1966 possibly because many had entered teaching as craftsmen from industry where affiliation was the norm. It was the disputes with government over teachers' salaries during the 1960s, especially action in 1963 when the minister of education imposed a settlement contradicting the recommendation of the Burnham Committee which helped to encourage the belief that membership of the TUC would give them a stronger voice. The National Association of Schoolmasters joined in 1963 and the NUT in 1970.

The decade began with the TUC turning its attention to the teaching of science which it believed should have a more important place in the curriculum. The era of space travel had started with the launch of the first unmanned satellite by the Russians in October 1957, followed by a series of satellites containing dogs, all in preparation for Yuri Gagarin's pioneering manned flight in 1961. The news was received in Britain with a mixture of surprise, admiration at the achievement and a realisation that science would be increasingly important in future technological development. The TUC called for a greatly increased output of 'technicians, technologists and scientists' and believed a start needed to be made in schools to increase the scientific base of the country. Their four-point proposal to improve the situation suggested the need:

(i)   To improve the salaries and conditions of work of teachers and lecturers.
(ii) Drastically to improve the teaching of mathematics and science in the (Teacher) Training Colleges.
(iii) To initiate a special programme to encourage scientists and mathematicians from other fields of work, including many more married women, to teach in our schools.
(iv) To greatly increase the supply of science and mathematics teachers, particularly in secondary modern schools.[2]

Comparisons in higher education were made with both the USA and USSR.

> In America 35 per cent of the population go to university. In Britain the number is 6 per cent...We all know of the spectacular progress in recent

years of Russian scientists...Do we think of the percentage of the Soviet population which goes to university as compared with Britain, and how much education in science and the principles of science is given there compared with what is given here?[3]

A 1957 UNESCO survey of university education in 28 countries was quoted: 'In terms of university students per million of the population Britain came fourth from the bottom. Only Ireland, Turkey and Norway were below us...should this not make us think?'[4] Facts were given to delegates about the low number of science teachers in secondary modern schools compared to the better-staffed grammar and fee-paying schools, and the Federation of British Industries fund equipping schools with science laboratories, mostly directed towards schools in the private sector. Mr Wells ended with an example from the past for them to consider:

In London there is a building called the Royal Institution devoted to science, and there is a tablet on the wall which says that in 1813...a member of the Royal Institution gave four tickets for a series of lectures by Sir Humphrey Davy to a young apprentice book binder. This young apprentice book binder went to the lectures. His name was Michael Faraday...how many potential Michael Faradays are there in Britain today to whom nobody has given any tickets of any kind whatever?[5]

The promotion of science and technology was always strongly supported by the TUC. After all, large numbers of the delegates represented workers engaged in the manufacture of the goods demanded by a modern society. Their concerns were followed up with the minister, Sir David Eccles, together with a question as to why he had decided to expand the training of primary school teachers in training colleges at the expense of secondary school teacher numbers. Instead of the colleges training 37 per cent of their students as secondary teachers they had been requested to provide 85 per cent of their places to students training for primary schools. The remaining 15 per cent of secondary places were to be allotted almost entirely to specialist secondary teachers of mathematics, science, physical education and handicrafts. These plans were based on projections of the school needs by 1970 for which it was believed the training colleges should concentrate, namely the age groups and specialisations which were not covered by universities.

Having considered the minister's actions the TUCGC issued a public statement concluding that they were very 'concerned about certain implications of these policies'. They believed this urgent action had resulted from a failure to aniticipate national needs in relation to the supply of teachers and that 'The serious prospective shortage of primary school teachers reported by the Ministry, and the drastic nature of the measures by which it is proposed to meet it, are the inevitable outcome of failing to give sufficient priority and urgency to expanding the total supply of teachers.'[6] Moreover the move to a three-year certificate course for the new intake of student teachers in 1960, which was fully supported by the TUC, inevitably meant that there would be no newly qualified teachers graduating from these courses in 1962. The minister informed the TUC that he had taken several steps to minimise this short-fall by increasing recruitment of teachers who had left the service, especially married women, encouraging some secondary school teachers to move voluntarily to primary schools and to continue the employment of teachers beyond the age of retirement where they were willing to do so. (Upon reaching the age of retirement, 60 for women and 65 for men in the 1960s, teachers could stay on by returning to the basic pay scale and becoming a classroom teacher for a further five years. The writer remembers two teachers of mathematics doing just this in a large comprehensive school in the late 1960s. It is an indicator of the increased demands upon teachers almost a generation later that thousands were applying to leave in their fifties.) The TUC remained unconvinced at the time that sufficient numbers of teachers could be attracted by programmes of this kind.

The suggestion that universities could provide any short-fall in secondary schools was questioned for it was not believed that graduates, whose education had naturally been of a formal academic nature, without at the very least undertaking a post-graduate certificate, were likely to be able to meet the educational needs of children requiring a 'non-academic' approach to their studies. The aim of the progamme Eccles explained in his response to the TUC, was to get rid of oversize classes by 1970 and to double the teacher training system by 1966. As for the concentration on primary school teachers this was to cope with the increase in the wastage of women teachers, which had shown itself clearly for the first time in 1958. He claimed that he was aware that in the longer term there would be a need to review the future place of the training colleges in the higher education system, and the National Advisory Council on the Supply and Training of Teachers (NACTST) was already examining these concerns and would now do so in the interest of the enquiry into higher education generally.

The specific issue of the need for more qualified teachers of science led to a reply from the minister that this would be met from the 'continuing improvement of technical education and expansion of the universities', an assumption which, it will be seen, was too optimistic. The special advanced courses in colleges of education for intending secondary school teachers combined with the three-year course introduced for all student teachers, would provide more time to improve the quality of main courses in science and mathematics. Most of those qualifying would enter secondary modern or comprehensive schools. A three-year course had been recommended in 1919 by the Committee of Principals in Training Colleges, by the McNair Report of 1944 and in 1956 in the Fifth Report of the National Advisory Council on the Training and Supply of Teachers. The refusal of successive governments to implement these past recommendations gives some indication of the limited expectations for elementary school pupils.[7] Further fears expressed by the TUCGC were believed by the minister to be 'exaggerated'.

Another opportunity for the TUC and other organisations to voice their views on teacher training came with the Newsom Report to which they were invited to submit evidence. Their main contribution here was with regards to teaching methods suitable for the majority of children. The request for more teachers was familiar enough but the reason for this was primarily to change the approach in schools to make small group work possible because they doubted 'whether [the] present approach of academic teaching methods and subject division were appropriate for most pupils'.[8] One problem was that most teachers had experienced formal teaching methods themselves and therefore assumed this style was suitable for the pupils they then taught. Sometimes the lecturers training secondary school students only had experience of selective secondary schooling themselves as pupil and teacher. Professional training for graduates was essential if teachers were not to continue with methods which might have been suitable for a minority within selective secondary schools but were less so for many other children. This had implications for school buildings where more spaces of less than a full class were required for some of the group work envisaged. Schools offered many pupils the opportunity to be introduced to an environment which provided cultural material and objective study, if only for part of the day, which was unavailable in many homes and streets.

In July the report by the NACTST referred to earlier by Eccles was published. It made gloomy reading on the short-fall of teachers in varying future circumstances. If present policies continued the short-fall of teachers which had been 65,000 in 1960 would be 51,000 by 1965, 49,000 in 1970 and 56,000 in 1975. If the school leaving age was raised to 16 before 1970, the shortage of teachers would reach 70,000 in that year, whilst if promises to reduce primary class sizes to 30 pupils before 1975 was met the shortage would be 140,000 in that year. Should professional training become compulsory for university graduates there would be a further shortage of teachers by 1970. The primary schools would suffer in particular because of the continuing rise in the birth rate and the wastage among young women teachers due to earlier marriages. The TUC's response was to suggest that they believed their proposals to the Committee on Higher Education, namely the Robbins Report, would contribute to solving some of these long-term problems. In reality there were problems within the teacher training colleges which were renamed colleges of education in 1960. Many of the religious establishments from the Victorian era, often built in cathedral towns, were comparatively small, taking no more than about 300 students, most of whom boarded. They had been modelled in terms of their buildings and some aspects of life-style on Oxbridge colleges. This was true also to a lesser extent for some of the secular colleges. Given their sites and facilities rapid expansion would not be easy, although this would be easier at some of the newer post-war purpose-built colleges such as Brighton. Nevertheless, expansion was undertaken by several methods: increasing numbers by having more students living in accommodation outside the college; opening annexes in nearby areas; and reducing the three-year course of nine terms to eight so that in 1968 students qualified at Easter and were available to teach in the summer term, a new intake having taken their place in college. Thereby the three-year course introduced in 1960 was shortened once more although this new system did not last for long.

The Ninth Report of the NACTST in 1966 looked back to the situation in 1962 and in the light of educational developments since then tried to forecast the staffing requirements for primary and secondary schools 20 years ahead. Taking into account the rising birth rate and the assumption that the school leaving age would be raised to 16 in 1970 they estimated that 'the total number of teachers in all kinds of educational institutions in England and Wales would need to grow from the 1963 figure of 360,000 to 665,000 by 1986 in order to bring class sizes within the limits laid down some 20 years ago'. If other desirable educational reforms were introduced the number required would be even higher. To put this into perspective it was estimated that to reach such targets and maintain them 'would require the recruitment of about half the total annual output of the higher education system'. The TUCGC's reaction to these gloomy predictions was to recommend that 'as a minimum, the Robbins Committee proposal for expanding the annual intake of the colleges of education to 40,000 students by 1974 should be advanced by three years'.[9] Other suggestions were to use new building techniques to complete new colleges earlier, the acquisition of existing buildings to serve as annexes, further expansion of existing colleges and the use of colleges of further education for teacher training. There was concern over the government's response which had been a call for a 20 per cent increase in the number of students admitted in addition to increases already planned 'without extra buildings'. They attributed part of the pronounced necessity for these urgent measures to the 'past inadequacies of the higher education system' which had been unable to produce a sufficient number of trained and qualified staff. They stressed the need to 'maintain standards in teacher training courses'. Another suggestion from the TUCGC based upon their long association with Ruskin College, was to recruit mature persons as teachers,

> they were aware that larger numbers of mature students could be recruited for teacher training if sufficient facilities existed. In most cases mature teacher training students would not require as lengthy a period of training as younger trainees and an increase in the employment of older teachers would contribute to greater staffing stability in schools.[10]

They could point to a recommendation from the Newsom Report to confirm this suggestion and they were pleased to receive a reply from the minister not only explaining that he 'attached exceptional importance to increasing the number of mature students' but outlining some of the ways it was planned to accomplish this aim. When a shortage of teachers was raised again in the Plowden Report the TUC returned to their theme of recruiting more mature students but also suggested that the recommendations of Plowden concerning teacher aides should with the co-operation of teachers' organisations be seriously considered.[11]

The colleges of education did expand rapidly by some of the means already described. By acting upon the NACTST 1965 Report, Crosland was able to persuade them to accept a higher number of students than had been previously considered possible. As Brian Simon has stated, 'By this time [1967/68]...the colleges of education (in England and Wales) had in fact expanded to a total of 94,800 students as compared with the Robbins' target estimate of 75,200. This was achieved without any reduction in standards of entrants.'[12] The ongoing problem would be in retaining teachers, for apart from the loss of many women who left, if only for several years to raise a family, certain subject teachers, especially in the areas of mathematics and physics, would often be tempted to leave in favour of more financially remunerative careers in industry.

THE ROBBINS REPORT 1963

The TUC had taken a growing interest in higher education in England and Wales, although hardly any of the representatives at Congress or their children had been given a realistic opportunity to study beyond secondary school level. One of the most outstanding achievements had to be that of Alexander MacDonald (1821–81), who left school at 8 years of age and later as a coalminer studied for university entrance to Glasgow University, graduated, then worked as a school teacher before returning to the Scottish Miners and becoming their president. (Trade union graduates increased as more white collar unions affiliated to the TUC during the second half of the twentieth century.) A considerable number had studied further as adults on full-time courses at Ruskin College and the Central Labour College, or part-time at the NCLC or WEA. A certain amount of academic snobbery did not afford the same status to attendance at these institutions outside the formal system of higher education, although there could be little doubt about the ability of many of the Ruskin and CLC students who went on to fill many senior posts in the labour movement. Sometimes it was suggested the length of the courses were not equivalent to that of traditional universities, not a very strong argument given the three eight-week terms of Cambridge and Oxford Universities.

However, the 1960s were now a time when expectations were changing throughout the country in terms of access to better educational opportunities, including entry to higher education. Past assumptions that a university education in general was largely the preserve of children from higher-income groups or the comparatively few working-class children who had obtained a place at a prestigious secondary school were under challenge. At the 1963 TUC Conference Mr C.T.H. Plant (Inland Revenue Staff Federation) moved a resolution on education which included a reference to 'the serious shortage of places in universities' and expressed the hope that the Robbins Committee would call for developments in higher education to meet the needs of society for more scientists, technologists, planners and administrators. He claimed, 'There are at least 5,000 university places too few for young people qualifying for a place in a university.'[13] Plant was voicing his optimism with regard to the Robbins Report which was due for publication one month after the TUC annual conference. The Robbins Committee had been set up by Harold Macmillan, prime minister in 1960, in response to increased demands for higher education and the chaotic 'system' which had evolved in England and Wales between the range of organisations from teacher training colleges to universities, which varied in status according to differences in traditions, staffing, students and resources.

The Committee headed by Robbins, an economist at the London School of Economics, was composed of 11 members, of whom six came from universities. There were also two industrialists, the chairperson of the LCC Education Committee and two teachers from fee-paying schools, Dame Kitty Anderson from North London Collegiate College and Anthony Chevenix-Trench of Bradfield who was to be appointed headteacher at Eton whilst on the Committee.[14] Whilst Harold Shearman from the LCC was closely allied to the WEA it is noticeable that the Committee included no representatives from state schools which were responsible for the education of 90 per cent of the country's children and nobody from the TUC or any other part of the trade union movement. This implies an attitude at the time that such matters as higher education were beyond the experience or ability of people outside the university, business or fee-paying school world, to discuss in any depth. Surprising, given that the TUC had been involved with Ruskin since its foundation in 1899 by representation on the governing body, providing grants and supporting a number of students annually at the college. Moreover, representatives from the TUCEC had been appointed to the extra-mural boards of Cambridge and Oxford Universities before 1926, Hillcroft College for women (1948), the Joint Committee of the TUC and LSE (1952), colleges of advanced technology and would increasingly receive invitations to join the governing bodies of other universities, e.g. Southampton University in 1967. (See Appendix 3.)

While the Robbins Committee were deliberating Mr J.K. Dutton (Association of Scientific Workers) drew the attention of delegates to the refusal by Selwyn Lloyd, chancellor of the exchequer, to accept the advice of the University Grants Committee as to the level of grants required if the number of university places was to be increased by 150,000 by 1966/67. A resolution was passed in which Congress demanded 'the provision of the finances necessary to enable the universities to expand teaching and research and to pay salaries comparable with those paid elsewhere in the public sector'.[15] He pointed to the statement of the Committee of Vice-Chancellors and Principals that they were 'profoundly disturbed by the Government's announcement about the resources to be made available to universities during the coming quinquennium'. Dutton suggested that far from the target being too ambitious 'it can be condemned as totally inadequate' and went on to criticize 'years of Government neglect and Exchequer parsimony' which denied the creation of the scientifically educated population needed for the future.

He also drew attention to the level of salaries throughout the universities which he claimed had a tradition of low pay. The technicians had at least been able to go to the industrial tribunal with their claims and the court had recently awarded them a 10 per cent rise. 'The teachers had their own union, not affiliated to Congress, more's the pity, and unable to go to arbitration' but they had a right to expect reasonable treatment. Instead they had been caught up in the 3 per cent incomes policy of the government so that their new claim submitted in May 1961, accepted by the UGC, who forwarded it accordingly in July, was rejected as it stood. The long-term economic consequences of these policies were reiterated, referring to supporting statements from both sides in the House of Commons. When the Robbins Report was published it called for a planned system of higher education, for which the guiding principle for entry should be 'for all those who were qualified by ability and attainment'. This would mean large-scale expansion in the number of full-time students from about 216,000 in 1962 to around 390,000 in 1973/74. All sections of higher education would share in the expansion, including many colleges of education and institutions for technological education, and there would be six new universities and five special institutions for scientific and technological education research. Facilities for adult education were also to be expanded. The establishment of the Council for National Academic Awards (CNNA) was also recommended, to award degrees to students completing courses in non-university institutions. The estimated costs would mean more than a tripling of educational expenditure for higher education between 1962/63 and 1980/81 (£206 million to £742 million; a doubling of the Gross National Product (GDP) from 0.8 per cent to 1.6 per cent).

The findings of the report were well received nationally and the TUC issued a statement in December considering it 'to be a major contribution to the development of higher education in this country' with the expressed hope that it would be accepted and 'energetically acted upon'.[16] Many of the ideas they had submitted in evidence were accepted, including a desire to see integration between different sections into a coherent system, but they completely dissented from the idea of separating ministerial responsibility for higher education, a suggestion which Mr H.C. Shearman on the Robbins Committee had opposed. The TUCGC had a suspicion that the move seemed like an inclination 'to appease the universities' sense of privilege and their possible apprehension about the future developments in higher education foreshadowed by the Committee's Report'.[17] If this was the case, it was denied by the decision of Douglas-Home as prime minister, who decided that higher education would be the responsibility of the Ministry of Education and Science, although within the department there would be a minister for higher education but he or she would be responsible to the secretary of state.

The views of the Committee as to the necessity of long-term planning for higher education were fully endorsed by the TUC, in particular the emphasis on science and technology reflected in the recommendation for 'the transformation of the colleges of advanced technology (with some appropriate widening of their fields) into technological universities or university faculties'. There was also ready acceptance of the suggestion to incorporate colleges of education through their constituent membership of university schools of education. This would achieve two TUC objectives: a unified system of higher education and the conferring of the status of university onto the colleges of education. However, there was also a potential danger in this policy that the university departments of education, which had in the past trained students often for selective secondary schools, might carry on with teaching methods unsuited to teachers in the majority of primary and secondary schools. This apprehension of the TUC voiced earlier in evidence to the Newsom Report was repeated now in relation to the Robbins proposals to bring colleges of education into the university field.

> The GC are concerned that the distinctive approach to the training of teachers developed by the colleges, whereby the student's personal and higher education is pursued within a course centred upon the educational needs of children and young people, should not be subordinated to more narrowly conceived academic considerations.[18]

Another reservation was voiced over funding. They accepted the necessity to safeguard academic freedom but were critical of the administrative arrangements in the form of the UGC whereby public funds were made available to universities. They questioned 'whether the expenditure of increasingly substantial sums of public money should continue to be wholly exempt from parliamentary scrutiny'.[19] The major recommendations of the report, expansion and a unified system of higher education, both TUC policy objectives in higher education, ensured TUC support. The main findings were welcomed by the Conservative government as well as the Labour party. This bipartisan response in parliament, widespread support within the educational world and major organisations such as the TUC, combined to make sure that the main recommendations would be acted upon swiftly. Among the most visible signs of this activity were extensions to the colleges of advanced technology with three of them becoming universities, Brunel, Bath and

Guildford. In addition three new universities were approved in England, Essex, Lancaster and Sussex and one in Scotland at Stirling. In fact in the case of Sussex the town of Brighton had been considering the possibility of establishing a university long before the Robbins Committee was appointed. Other similar developments were to follow, such as the University of Strathclyde.

The bipartisan approach over the Robbins Report meant that with the change of government in 1964 most of the proposals were carried through although one of the key points, a unified system of higher education was already in danger of being lost. Michael Stewart, an ex-school teacher was appointed secretary of state at the DES and within a couple of months in office had decided to reject the idea of colleges of education being brought into the universities financially and administratively. This was probably in response to pressure from local authorities who were reluctant to lose areas of higher education with which they had been closely involved for so many years. Crosland, who was to succeed him the following month, reinforced this policy in his Woolwich speech in which he stated the government's aim was 'to create two sectors in higher education, one of autonomous institutions, which would include universities, and another of institutions subject to control by local bodies, which would include the colleges of education and some technical colleges'.[20] The proposed closer administrative links to bring about a single system of higher education had been rejected. Colleges of education it was believed could enjoy academic freedom without necessarily having financial freedom from local authorities.

There were those who disagreed with the expansion of the university sector believing that 'more means worse'. This theme was taken up by *The Times*[21] and pursued by those of the radical right, not just with reference to the quality of students but also of teaching staff. In *Black Paper Two*, published in 1969 Angus Maude wrote, 'I have no doubt – from what I have seen, as well as heard, in universities – that some of the junior staff employed in the last 15 years have been distinctly inferior',[22] whilst Rhodes Boyson a few years later was to decry the 'Over Expansion of the Universities'.[23]

BINARY SYSTEM OF HIGHER EDUCATION

For a second time, Crosland was to find himself associated with a policy he did not initiate but would defend, and later be seen as the prime mover of, because of his Woolwich speech which received so much publicity.

Crosland inherited a policy approved by Michael Stewart, who in turn had already taken up one prepared by the previous Conservative government and DES officials. The binary system of higher education with universities financially independent of government, funded through the UGC and the remaining higher education system funded directly by local and central government was one which had developed over many years. Crosland's actions in effect froze the system and from then onwards promoted rapid expansion of the latter a year later through a white paper, *A Plan for Polytechnics and Other Colleges*, which one year further on resulted in a provisional list of 28 polytechnics. He also proclaimed there would be no new universities for about ten years. He was rejecting an essential recommendation of the Robbins Report for a unified system of higher education favoured by many groups including the TUC.

He gave four reasons for this change in approach in the speech at Woolwich Polytechnic:

(1) Vocational, professional and technological courses should be provided in a sector separate from universities in institutions with different traditions and cultures.

(2) If universities take over other institutions and remain the only degree awarding institution all other areas of higher education would have an inferior status.

(3) A considerable part of the higher education system should be 'under social control and directly respond to social needs'. Local government should retain a considerable participation and influence in the development of this sector.

(4) It was necessary to promote technical and professional expertise in a highly competitive world – and by implication traditional universities could not achieve this aim.

The last part was reinforced by a statement he would later regret; 'let us now move away from our snobbish caste-ridden hierarchical obsession with university status'.[24] In discussion with Maurice Kogan in the autumn of 1970 he admitted, 'I began by making an appalling blunder, from which I learnt a lesson I shall never forget. I got the whole thing off on the wrong foot by breaking my own rule. I said to the press that I wouldn't make any pronouncements on major policy for the first six months and I broke the rule by making the Woolwich speech.'[25] Revealing too in this discussion is at least tacit admission that the system of changing ministers rapidly from one department to another, no matter how clever they might be, does not give them the opportunity to learn enough about the area for which they are responsible, unless, like Michael Stewart, they have had substantial background experience. As Crosland admitted, after only three weeks in the post, 'I then had only a superficial knowledge of the subject.'

Ten months later, according to Tony Benn, he was less certain about the policy:

> We broke for lunch and I sat opposite Tony Crosland who admitted that he now had some doubts about the binary system for higher education and rather regretted the philosophic speech he had made in defence of the binary system when he had only been at the Ministry a short time.[26]

These doubts had obviously evaporated later when at Lancaster University in 1967 he set out with greater clarity and less contention his reasons for developing further the binary system.[27] Later still he would tell Kogan, 'the more I thought about it subsequently, the more I became utterly convinced that the policy was right'.[28]

There are two major questions which surround the binary system. How far was it Crosland's policy and how valid were his reasons for dismissing the Robbins' aims of a unitary system of higher education. Just as Butler receives the credit for the 1944 Education Act when the policy had already been drawn up by civil servants before he became minister, so too, long before Crosland arrived at the DES, after initial public support, the Conservative government of Alec Douglas-Home was already preparing plans to abort a unified system of higher education.[29] Once more it would be the permanent officials at the DES who would be seen to be making policy by presenting proposals to what would be a succession of three ministers of education, taking over the department within a twelve-month period, Edward Boyle, Michael Stewart and Tony Crosland. In the circumstances it is not surprising that aspects of their manoeuvring have been seen as 'devious'.[30]

From the publication of the Robbins Report in October 1963 to Crosland's Woolwich speech in April 1965 a number of concerns and vested interests were at work to undermine the idea of a unitary system of higher education. The local authorities had historic links with non-university institutions and were loath to sever them, especially as they had invested money and the time of local representatives for many years. This relationship provided them with a certain amount of prestige and Boyle, conscious that local authorities already felt that government policy had lessened their influence and importance, reported to the Cabinet in October 1963 'there are undoubted political disadvantages in further exacerbating this feeling'.[31]

Two other key concerns of government were finance and control. Universities were funded more generously than other sections of higher education, not just in library facilities which they sometimes claimed were necessary for more advanced work, but also for items of expenditure such as the furniture in refectories.[32] The contrast in facilities provided for students in universities, colleges of education, and existing polytechnics were apparent to students and staff with experience of the different systems, much of it arising from the differences in the social status of students attending these institutions in the past and to a lesser extent during the 1960s. By contrast to Oxford and Cambridge Universities, the regimes of nineteenth-century teacher training colleges were harsh, with timetables which kept them occupied from the early hours of the morning until late into the evening, and whilst these had slackened by the inter-war period, they still covered a twelve-hour day.[33]

In general, there was a contrast between students in colleges of education and their counterparts in universities in terms of their social origins, qualifications and experiences, especially when compared to Oxford or Cambridge students. So too were their subsequent careers, earnings and life-style for most were destined for primary and secondary modern schools during the 1960s. Providing resources to students in colleges of education and those in urban polytechnics on the same scale as students resident in universities, however deserving as a matter of social justice, would be expensive. It would be difficult to resist in any unitary system because parity of resources would be expected. By keeping different sections of higher education separate comparisons could not be made so easily. It would be a cheaper solution especially as all were agreed on the need for rapid expansion of student numbers in all areas of higher education.

Governments realised that indirect control through the UGC was not as efficient for their purposes as the level of control they exercised over the non-university sector of higher education, although this would change somewhat when the Public Accounts Committee were encouraged to make the UGC more accountable. Control of colleges of education enabled governments to expand or contract student numbers at short notice; a policy they adopted vigorously with disastrous long-term results. The long-promised reduction in class sizes in primary and secondary schools, which successive ministers had claimed they desired, if only enough teachers could be supplied, was not achieved by 1970 or in the foreseeable future. The James Committee set up to enquire into teacher education and training in 1970, with just seven members, reported in 1972. It recommended the amalgamation of colleges of education with other institutions of higher education where possible so that student teachers would mix with students from other disciplines. It also provided the opportunity for the government to reduce the number of student teachers and use the places to accommodate other students. One consequence was a continuation of the shortage of teachers especially in certain subjects.

If the government believed that universities would wish to remain aloof from other sections of higher education they were to be proven wrong. Enquiries showed that most universities favoured the Robbins' proposals whilst others were not averse to the idea with only Kent and Sheffield directly opposed.[34] Some had already begun discussions in the belief that the Robbins' proposals for a unitary system would be accepted. Most universities stood to gain extra funding and students by amalgamation; colleges of education hoped to gain the prestige, salaries and conditions which would go along with becoming an integral part of a university. Sir Toby Weaver, deputy secretary at the DES, pointed out to the minister that any decision made about colleges of education would 'go far to determining the future shape of the whole of higher education'.[35] To that effect it was important for the DES to state their policy on the Robbins' proposals before a meeting of the UGC gave its verdict on the issue. This move, to forestall the colleges, was explained as being of help to the UGC if they 'could be given a lead by the government'. The policy was therefore in place before the general election of 1964.

When Stewart was appointed minister at the DES in the new Labour government in October 1964, he had to be persuaded against 'lingering doubts' that it was important to make it clear that the colleges of education should end thoughts of enhancing their status by closer links with universities.[36] Within weeks Crosland had taken over and delivered his Woolwich Polytechnic speech, giving his four reasons for enhancing the binary system in higher education. Not one of these really stood up to any serious examination. The hidden agenda was that in the binary system government could increase its control over the non-university sector of education and expansion of student numbers more cheaply than in the unified system of higher education. The assumption that they could thereby ensure that students followed courses more closely related to the needs of the changing economy was not borne out by later experience. If the crucial areas of finance and control were excluded, what was left were arguments related to social prejudice and tradition. The attitude that full-time residential university students were in some ways more deserving in the provision of resources than those studying part-time in polytechnics or full-time in colleges of education was a reflection of social snobbery.

Similarly, the view that students on a diploma as opposed to a degree course should not be studying in the same institution was a matter of academic snobbery. Moreover, there were examples in both the university and non-university higher education sector which contradicted such suggestions. Birkbeck College of London University provided almost solely for students studying degree courses during the evening, and the most well-known of the polytechnics, Regent Street, had been teaching both full- and part-time students for external London University degrees for a longer period than many of the country's universities had existed. In most other countries many of the large colleges of education and polytechnics would have been recognised as universities. Distinctions of status between subjects, methods of study and differences in the social composition of students could be traced back to the Victorian age and they were so engrained in society that it would take some time to overcome them. There was no logical reason why students following courses at different levels should not share the same buildings any less than under-graduate and post-graduate students did.

Even if it was believed that the polytechnics were more attuned to the needs of society there was no academic reason why they should not have been renamed universities at the time. Eric Robinson pointed out that Portsmouth College of Technology had over 2,500 full-time advanced students – 'larger than any of the CATs were at the time of the Government's decision to grant them university status'.[37] In reality the polytechnics, especially those established for decades, had been urban universities in all but name, offering a wide level of studies from RSA professional qualifications to post-graduate degrees. Moreover, the simplistic view that universities were not involved with professions, industry and commerce, was just not true – medicine, dentistry, law, mining and engineering were all to be found in universities; and the converse suggestion that polytechnics were only concerned with professional courses was equally untrue as languages, the sciences and social sciences could be found in many polytechnics. Neither was there ever any clear directive given to the new polytechnics established by Crosland. This may have turned out to be to their advantage.[38]

Crosland's remarks to Kogan provide a clear insight into his reasoning:

> The second fallacy was to believe that if you changed the organizational set-up from a binary to a unitary one, all the technical colleges would instantly achieve university standards of buildings, student residences, libraries, research and so on. But quite apart from whether or not this would be a sensible policy, it wouldn't depend on the organizational structure, but

on the total amount of money available and how this was to be distributed between the hundreds of different institutions in higher and further education.[39]

That the public would not accept that all had equal status was true, but this had been equally so for universities established in the nineteenth and twentieth centuries as opposed to those of an earlier period; a view based upon the assumption that the older the institution the better it must be, one that can only be entertained among those with little knowledge of the state Oxford had sunk into during the early nineteenth century.[40] All of the institutions could have been brought under the umbrella of the universities at the time and those polytechnics and colleges with extensive experience in higher education granted university status. If that policy had been followed the government knew they would have had to spend more money on education.

TUC OBJECTIONS TO THE BINARY SYSTEM

The policy of the government did not meet with the approval of the TUCGC for two reasons. It contradicted the idea of a unified higher education system which,

> while taking full account of the varied contributions which different types of institution can make, would establish a parity of esteem between them. Their view implies that all forms of higher education should, in time, be provided under the same general auspices and be equally subject to some degree of social control.[41]

They could already see the continuation of the gap in both independence and status between universities and other institutions of higher education being maintained to the detriment of the latter. Problems of the divisive secondary school system would now be repeated in higher education. 'This continuing division may well result in the same kind of disparities, in relation both to institutions and their students, as were manifest in the "tripartite" system of secondary education.'[42] The secretary of state promised to 'bear in mind' their views but in the years to come the TUC's fears would be realised as the divisions within higher education were firmly formalised.

While welcoming the expansion of student numbers and development of polytechnics which would encourage part-time study and provide more non-degree courses they were concerned over a lack of technical and vocational courses at the lower level which had received only a scant mention from the minister. In addition, the White Paper indicated the strength of the government's persistence in its policy of establishing the binary system thereby perpetuating the artificial distinctions of status and real inequalities of treatment between different types of institutions.

> In indicating that local education authorities will have responsibility for the constitution and development of polytechnics, the White Paper demonstrates that the polytechnics are to be included in the second rank of institutions comprising the sector of the Government's binary pattern which is to consist of institutions more directly subject to public control than the universities comprising the autonomous sector. A tripartite pattern of higher education – universities, colleges of education and polytechnics – will then be completed.[43]

This likening to the selective system of secondary education, which was gradually being abandoned in the country suggested that the battle for reorganisation to a comprehensive system of schooling would now have to be faced all over again in higher education. The TUCGC reiterated their beliefs in a unified system of higher education

> embracing a variety of institutions together providing the multiplicity of courses required to meet the multifarious needs of students and the community... The perpetuation of distinctions, based essentially upon the degree of their remoteness from public accountability, is incompatible with a coherent system of higher education, and distorts proper distinctions arising from academic achievement.[44]

The TUCGC did not let the matter go. They restated their policy which had been consistent before and since the publication of the Robbins Report:

> a unified system of higher education embracing a variety of institutions together providing the multiplicity of courses required to meet the multifarious needs of students and the community. They believed that the scale of demands upon public funds and the crucial significance of its contribution to the national well-being, required that higher education should be effectively integrated with the preceding stages of the public education system and should be subject as a whole to a proper degree of public accountability.[45]

There were two problems in the form of vested interests which these proposals challenged. The universities had enormous influence as so many of their past students were to be found in the top echelons of government, commerce and industry. By the 1960s a majority of MPs were graduates so any attempt to challenge the autonomy of the universities would have met with powerful opposition. In addition, the influence of the local authorities was also considerable as had clearly been recognised by Boyle's observation. However logical, fair and practical TUC policy might be it would find formidable powers confronting it.

Crosland did not accept the criticisms of the TUCGC. He argued that

> one of the purposes of the White Paper was to eliminate tendencies towards a hierarchical structure of higher education within the further education system. He disagreed with their views on local authority control of higher education and denied it was part of his policy that there should be distinctions of status between institutions based upon their remoteness from effective public accountability.[46]

His only point of agreement was that the development of higher education as a whole should be planned and he interpreted this as favouring a binary rather than a unitary approach to higher education. There was no meeting of minds between the minister and the TUC on higher education.

The TUCGC wrote back to Crosland suggesting it was doubtful whether the superior status accorded to all existing university institutions could be attributed solely to considerations of merit, and considered their virtual freedom from public accountability was a significant factor in the status accorded them.[47] They believed that the binary system being promoted provided no radical departure from the existing pattern of higher education 'which they regarded as unsatisfactory on educational and social grounds'.[48]

There was further correspondence but no suggestion of compromise or room for agreement. Crosland agreed that status should be based upon merit and promised to build up the polytechnics but would not designate them universities 'since the polytechnics would have responsibilities for many thousands of part-time students and a large number of full-time students taking courses below degree level'. The public would not accept such institutions as comparable to universities, and the best way to raise their reputations, in his opinion, was to organise them separately and to build upon their distinctive characteristics. A strange reply from a minister who was to tell Kogan, 'I myself am a convinced egalitarian.'[49]

The TUCGC continued to maintain that the education secretary appeared 'to draw an unduly rigid distinction between degree courses and other courses of higher education and between part-time and full-time students'.[50] They were however compelled to recognise that the government seemed fully committed to developing a binary system. Their one measure of success was a request to the minister that he consider the desirability of including trade union representatives in the governing bodies of the polytechnics, given their past contribution to similar bodies of institutions of further and higher education. This he was able to do and subsequently a note of guidance was issued to local authorities suggesting there should be strong representation of industry and commerce in the governing bodies of polytechnics and that 'trade unions as well as employers' representatives should be appointed in consultation with appropriate national, regional or local organisations'.[51] Two years later in cabinet, talking about his White Paper in which he sketched out the outlines of his proposed 1970 Education Bill, Ted Short said, 'He wanted to end the binary system by bringing further and higher education together; and he wanted more adult education as in the Open University.'[52] The general election result of 1970 would prevent any move in this direction for many years to come.

THE OPEN UNIVERSITY

The one new university which did open, with the exception of the private Buckingham University formally opened in 1976[53] was the Open University. Harold Wilson can take the credit for this because although ideas for broadcasting education have been traced back to 1926 when Mr J.C. Stobart suggested the idea within the BBC[54] and several others had given some thoughts to such an idea, visits by Wilson to both the Soviet Union and Chicago, provided him with models in terms of both degree level and correspondence courses and the use of teaching film. Although who thought up the idea is not relevant here there is some confusion. Tunstall suggests Wilson was inspired by his visits to the USSR and USA whilst Wilson's biographer writes,

> (Michael) Young had been stimulated by his own observation of correspondence teaching in the Soviet Union in 1962 to write an article for the educational journal *Where?* describing a possible 'open university' which would offer learning opportunities to adults studying at home. Young pointed to not only the success of Soviet correspondence courses which

provided 40 per cent of all graduates from higher education, but also to the use of television for educational purposes in the United States. Young's idea, which led to the foundation of the National Extension College in 1963, was much discussed in progressive educational and Fabian circles.[55]

Wilson introduced the idea on 8 September 1963 at a pre-election meeting of the Scottish Labour party:

> This new University institution, which will have its own Chancellor and Vice-Chancellor, governing body and full-time staff, will provide full degree courses with the help of radio and television combined with correspondence courses. We expect the first courses to be provided in 1970 and the rolls for students should be opened next year. The aim of the Open University is to widen the opportunities for higher education by giving a second chance to those who can profit from it, but who have been, for one reason or another, unable to go to University or a College on leaving school.[56]

It appeared in the Labour Party Manifesto of 1964 and when Labour won that election Jennie Lee was appointed minister of the arts and made responsible for the development of a system of higher education which would be accepted as a means of obtaining 'genuine' university degrees outside the established universities. Her friendship with the prime minister and freedom from the Treasury for this project provided her with the opportunity to ensure that it became a practical proposition. It was however a grim struggle with Wilson giving full support by pressing Callaghan to save it from Treasury cuts, whilst on occasions, he 'had to fight his own education minister, as well as the mandarins. The secretary of state shared the view of some of his advisers that there were better claims on educational money.'[57] Tony Benn gave it support but 'Crosland expressed no interest in the idea and Roy Jenkins was deeply sceptical'.[58]

Jennie Lee set up an all-male advisory committee of 12 dominated by academics from the university world. Ruskin College with its experience of providing adult education to students without formal qualifications, Birkbeck College known for specialising in teaching degree work to part-time students and London University with its long experience of external degrees were all excluded for some reason. It would seem that Lee believed the key to the success of this new form of university in Britain would be acceptance by the traditional established university sector. She was determined it would not be linked to past forms of adult education which enjoyed little status. University degrees would be the main area of focus and they were to be as rigorous as those obtained in other sectors of higher education. It was becoming clear, however, that this second-chance university would not be specifically aimed at working-class people but was more likely to appeal in general to the middle classes, and that certainly turned out to be the case in its early years when teachers were the biggest single group of students. There were special reasons for this early dominance of teachers. Thousands had been awarded Certificates of Education after attending colleges of education for two or three years full-time study, but not a university degree. The incentives for them to study with the Open University were numerous; they received credits from their past Certificates if they took education units, local authorities initially contributed towards their fees and on graduating their salary was increased to that awarded to degree or good honours degree categories. Added to that a degree enhanced their career opportunities, they were familiar with study methods and – like many OU students – they gained personal satisfaction from the achievement of successful study. Some of these factors were true for other public sector workers and in terms of career opportunities, for most people. This issue never worried Lee whose reply to such criticism was, 'I wish people would stop talking about the limited number of working-class men and women who have joined...I have said time and time again that the most insulting thing that could happen to any working-class man or woman was to have a working-class university.'[59]

The TUC gave consideration to the proposals in the White Paper, *A University of the Air*, which outlined the provision of radio and television lectures associated with correspondence courses, periods of residential study and regular tutorials. The lack of substantial cost was also mentioned. The TUC questions were not a challenge to the fundamental idea but rather about possible side effects and then later over the vital need for preparatory courses for students who had been out of formal education a long time – an area of which they were speaking from experience given their long association with Ruskin College.

They wondered whether the OU broadcasts at degree level might lead to a reduction of general educational broadcasting, particularly on television. There was lack of detail over this issue in the White Paper so a meeting was arranged with Jennie Lee to seek further clarification about the government's intentions. This took place in November 1966 at which she explained that the intention was to use the BBC2 channel, partly at peak viewing times as well as radio broadcasts. The co-operation of local education authorities and the library service were also being sought. Students would register with the OU and pay fees, 'though in cases of need local education authorities might assist students financially'. It was aimed to form local groups of students for tutorials in suitable premises. Generally these turned out to be in colleges and as the courses got underway the residential days would become established during the summer vacation on many university campuses.

Jennie Lee emphasised that the OU would be open to everyone which prompted the TUC representatives to welcome any proposal which would 'make educational opportunities available in later life to those who had left school at the minimum age,' and then proceed to the by now familiar issue.

> There was some evidence, however, that in adult education the existing responsible bodies were increasingly attracting those who already enjoyed more than the minimum of educational opportunity. If, as was possible, the Open University were subject to the same tendency, its contribution towards helping those where educational needs were greatest would be limited.[60]

This pattern had been common in most national adult education schemes throughout the century. The WEA had discovered within a decade of its foundation that unskilled manual workers did not participate regularly and gradually artisans, clerical workers and others in white collar jobs began to form the core of students. This was partly because after hours of tiring manual work it was difficult for all but the very committed to undertake serious study during the evening. There were other cultural factors at work too, such as the short period of formal schooling experienced by most working-class people which gave them few basic study skills and a life-style which provided little opportunity to participate in various cultural pursuits. There were of course exceptions, such as the miners' lodges in South Wales where regular donations contributed to the establishment of their own libraries.

Another anxiety of the TUC was whether tutors might be drawn away from other adult education provision. More fundamental was their experience with students undertaking courses at adult residential colleges which 'strongly suggested that adult students with minimum formal educational qualifications needed considerable individual help and guidance, especially in the early stages of sustained educational courses, if they were to succeed in their studies'.[61] Whether they were hinting that help from Ruskin College staff in this field could be useful is not clear but they were informed that their views on this matter would be borne in mind but details such as these would be a matter for the OU when it opened rather than governmental ministers. When the TUC met the education secretary the following year to protest about cutbacks in educational expenditure, especially the postponement of ROSLA to 16 he was on the defensive claiming that 'these economies had been forced upon the government by economic circumstances'. The one crumb of comfort came at the end when he announced that 'The Open University project, which he thought would be of great benefit to adult working people, had been exempted from the economies.'[62] The TUC continued to consult with the government over the OU in 1969 providing written evidence to a government committee of enquiry on the subject of adult education.[63] This new university of the air appeared to be safe and later when reflecting on his decade at the top Wilson placed it as one of the three 'most important achievements' of the government.[64]

However, it did face financial cuts from the new Conservative administration in 1970 from Ian Macleod 'who had fought for its demise' and from Mrs Thatcher who, according to Sir William Pile, then permanent secretary at the DES, claimed she 'was all for killing the Open University, which I managed to argue her out of on the grounds that their degrees cost only half of Oxbridge's'.[65] The OU became established as a university offering high-quality courses with well-produced written material, television and radio programmes, many of which were to be used by other universities in their courses.

The TUC fought for the implementation of a unified system of higher education and opposed the binary system which they saw as one other aspect of the hierarchical structure of British society. The forces working against a unified system, political, social and economic, certain areas of education – all combined to prevent the development of such a system. There can be no doubt that it would have been very expensive, have taken years to accomplish if the necessary buildings and resources alone are taken into account. On the other hand, it could be pointed out that until 1970 those who had gained the least from the nation's investment in higher education were daughters and sons from working-class backgrounds, especially those from families designated as 'unskilled' in the poor inner city areas. By contrast, as the Robbins Report clearly demonstrated, it was the children of the middle- and upper-income groups who gained the most in the amount of money spent on their education by the State and the rewards reaped later from better careers which afforded good working conditions, higher salaries and pensions. To that extent it could be argued that those in positions of influence denied the scale of expenditure which would have been necessary to provide more of the daughters and sons from lower-income groups with the well-resourced forms of education which their own children were able to experience. Having said that, it needs to be emphasised, that the expansion of the student population in higher education in Britain during the second half of the 1960s in particular, was not only unprecedented but surpassed that recommended by the Robbins Report. From 1962/63 to 1967/68 the number of students in full-time higher education in Britain grew from 217,000 to 376,000, and the increase over these five years was greater than over the preceding 25.[66] Moreover, it was reinforced by a policy of no tuition fees and a level of grants, albeit related to parental income, probably more generous than anywhere else in the world. So much so that there were questions being raised in some quarters about the scale of financial support being given to students. This led to the TUC, when submitting its statement to the government in December 1968 in relation to the proposed new education bill, to respond to these doubts by making it known they, 'strongly opposed suggestions to replace the present system of grants by a system of loans, on the grounds that a system of loans would create a further barrier to higher education for young people'.[67]

NOTES AND REFERENCES

1. Griggs, C. (1983) *The Trades Union Congress and the Struggle for Education 1868–1925*, pp.209–11.
2. *TUC Report 1960*, p.432.
3. Ibid.
4. Ibid., p.433.
5. Ibid.
6. *TUC Report 1961*, pp.183–4.
7. A three-year course was recommended in 1919 by the Committee of Principals in Training Colleges, by the McNair Report in 1944 and the Fifth Report of the National Advisory Council on the Training and Supply of Teachers in 1956. The resistance to an extended and improved course for teachers reflected the limited expectations for elementary and later secondary modern school pupils. Gordon, P., Aldrich, R. and Dean, D. (1991) *Education and Policy in England in the Twentieth Century*, p.256; Morrish, I. (1970) *Education Since 1800*, p.142.
8. *TUC Report 1962*, p.168.
9. *TUC Report 1966*, p.217.
10. Ibid., p.219.
11. *Plowden Report*, Ch. 26.
12. Simon, B. (1991) *Education and the Social Order 1940–1990*, p.256.
13. *TUC Report 1963*, p.163.

14. Simon, B. (1991) *Education and the Social Order 1940–1990*, p.233.
15. *TUC Report 1962*, p.354.
16. *TUC Report 1964*, p.222.
17. Ibid., p.225.
18. Ibid.
19. Ibid., p.225.
20. Simon, B. (1991) *Education and the Social Order 1940–1990*, p.247.
21. Layard, R., King, J. and Moser, C. (1969) *The Impact of Robbins*, p.26.
22. Cox, C.B. and Dyson, A.E. (eds) (1969) *Black Paper Two*, p.152.
23. Boyson, R. (1975) *The Crisis in Education*, Ch. 16.
24. Gosden, P.H.J.H. (1983) *The Education System Since 1944*, pp.178–83; Richmond, W.K. (1978) *Education in Britain Since 1944*, pp.125–30; Simon, B. (1991) *Education and the Social Order 1940–1990*, pp.247–50.
25. Kogan, M. (1971) *Educational Policy Making*, p.193.
26. Benn, T. (1987) *Out of the Wilderness: Diaries 1963–1967*, 10.2.1966, p.385.
27. The Lancaster speech is reproduced in full in Appendix C, Robinson, E. (1968) *The New Polytechnics*.
28. Kogan, M. (1971) *Educational Policy Making*, p.193.
29. The political machinations behind the rejection of Robbins' unitary system of higher education policy and its replacement by a cheaper binary system are revealed in a detailed article by Godwin, C.D. (1998) 'The Origin of the Binary System', *History of Education*, Vol. 27, No. 2, pp.171–91.
30. Ibid., p.187.
31. Ibid., p.176.
32. Hencke, D. (1978) *Colleges in Crisis*, pp.89–90.
33. Lawson, J. and Silver, H. (1976) *A Short History of Education in England*, pp.390–1.
34. Godwin, C.D. (1998) 'The Origin of the Binary System', p.177.
35. Ibid., p.179.
36. Ibid., p.182.
37. Robinson, E. (1968) *The New Polytechnics*, p.43.
38. For a detailed examination of subjects taught and the various arguments about the role of universities and polytechnics at the time see Silver, H. (1983) 'Education as History', pp.213–26 and Silver, H. (1990) *Education, Change and the Policy Process*, Ch. 4.
39. Kogan, M. (1971) *Educational Policy Making*, pp.194–5.
40. Simon, B. (1960) *Studies in the History of Education 1780–1870*, pp.84–94.

41. *TUC Report 1966*, p.220.
42. Ibid.
43. Ibid., pp.221–2.
44. Ibid., p.222.
45. *TUC Report 1967*, p.232.
46. Ibid.
47. Ibid., p.233.
48. Ibid.
49. Kogan, M. (1971) *Educational Policy Making*, p.194.
50. *TUC Report 1967*, p.233.
51. Ibid., p.234.
52. Benn, T. (1988) *Office Without Power: Diaries 1968–72*, 19.5.1969, p.168.
53. Griggs, C. (1985) *Private Education in Britain*, pp.115–19.
54. Tunstall, J. (1974) *The Open University*, p.3. Chapter 1 provides a brief history of early developments at the OU.
55. Pimlott, B. (1992) *Harold Wilson*, p.514.
56. Wilson, H. (1974) *The Labour Government 1964–1970*, p.175.
57. Pimlott, P. (1992) *Harold Wilson*, op cit. *or* p.514.
58. Hollis, P. (1997) *Jennie Lee – A Life*, p.315.
59. Ibid., p.311.
60. *TUC Report 1967*, p.236.
61. Ibid.
62. *TUC Report 1968*, p.68.
63. *TUC Report 1969*, p.282.
64. Pimlott, B. (1992) *Harold Wilson*, p.601.
65. Simon, B. (1991) *Education and the Social Order 1940–1990*, Footnote 64, p.464.
66. Layard, R., King, J. and Moser, C. (1969) *The Impact of Robbins*, p.13.
67. *TUC Report 1969*, p.302.

CHAPTER 18

THE PUBLIC SCHOOLS: STILL A FORCE TO BE RECKONED WITH

FEE-PAYING SCHOOLS: SAME ISSUES – DIFFERENT DECADE

If the initial spur for the Fleming Report came from fee-paying schools searching for public subsidies to come to their rescue in the face of falling numbers during the late 1930s, the Public Schools Commission arose from an entirely different situation. By the 1960s the fee-paying sector was not only under attack from financial problems but also from an increase in criticism of their role as schools working to retain and enhance the interests of the more privileged sections of society. When the Labour general election victory in 1964, albeit a narrow one, brought into government a party committed to the extension of comprehensive education, fee-paying schools seemed to be particularly exposed. Their's was a twofold system of selection, in part academic, in part social due to the high fees demanded by the schools.

Even by the 1960s, the influence of the fee-paying schools was enormous. This is not to suggest that every person attending one finished their schooling agreeing with the ideas which permeated most of the leading HMC schools, for it would take little effort to give examples of ex-pupils who rejected these values and were harsh critics of these institutions. However, the vast majority who attended these schools came from families with well above average incomes and wealth who readily accepted the values of the system either because they had no experience of the schools attended by the majority of the population or because they could readily see the benefits the schools bestowed upon those who had been pupils. Some measure of the influence can be gained from the numerous surveys concerning educational background of those in dominant positions in society. Some of the facts will be familiar enough, so much so that they were accepted as if they were the natural order of society in England and Wales. Yet this attitude runs the risk of failing to grasp just how truly distorted the situation had been during the years from 1926 to 1970.

INFLUENCE WITHIN THE CONSERVATIVE PARTY

For most of these years about 5 per cent of pupils attended fee-paying schools yet within the Conservative party the percentage of their MPs educated in such schools was never less than 72 per cent in 1959 and up to 85 per cent in 1945 and 1950. Even by 1966 when debates about the fee-paying schools were being stimulated by the Public Schools Commission, 80 per cent of Tory MPs had been educated outside the maintained sector. Of the 360 Tory MPs in 1961/62, 60 had been to the same school, Eton. All six of the Conservative prime ministers between 1923 and 1963 were educated at leading HMC schools, half of them at Eton. If one considers the Tory Cabinets between 1925 and 1955 no less than 92 per cent attended fee-paying schools; in the 1957 Cabinet the percentage had risen to 94 per cent, going down slightly to 91 per cent in 1963.[1] This was the reverse of the educational experience of the population. Given such overwhelming dominance it can be of no surprise that there was continued support for the fee-paying sector of schooling within the Conservative party.

When Edward Boyle was at the DES, his predecessor said to him, 'You will find it difficult to get the Cabinet to understand education because so few of them have been involved in maintained schools.'[2] Boyle, one of the many old Etonians in the Cabinet, tells how a former Conservative under-secretary, from a different social background, said to him in 1962, when both he and Keith Joseph had entered the Cabinet,'Good luck to both of you and I think you ought to do reasonably well, but it does seem almost too good a coincidence that you should both be baronets, one from Eton and one from Harrow.'[3] Boyle was willing to admit what must have seemed to most people obvious, 'Eton always has been well represented in the Cabinet. The average income of old Etonians is considerably higher than that of the nation at large and we probably do have more freedom to look around to consider what we'd like to do.'[4]

This goes some way to explaining why an analysis of the occupations of Conservative MPs which gave four categories, professional, business, unoccupied and workers found that on average between 1918 and 1945 only 4 per cent came in the last category with this figure remaining the average through to 1951 before dropping to zero until 1964 when it rose to 1 per cent. Approximately 50 per cent were from the professional category and about 30 per cent from business. More than half of Tory MPs had received a university education, increasing fairly steadily from 53 per cent in 1924 to 67 per cent in 1966. The lack of maintained school experience goes some way to understanding their inter-war indifference to the provision of secondary education for all. Even in the post-war period most Tory MPs simply had no experience of the maintained sector as pupil, parent or teacher.

INFLUENCE WITHIN THE LABOUR PARTY

A comparison with the Labour party during the same years provides a considerable contrast. Labour MPs attending fee-paying schools rose from 7 per cent in 1924 to 23 per cent in 1945 before falling to 18 per cent in 1966, whilst those with a university education rose steadily from 14 per cent in 1924 to 51 per cent in 1966, an illustration of the benefits of wider access to secondary schooling from the late 1930s onwards. Of the three prime ministers during these years only Attlee attended a fee-paying school, Haileybury, whilst MacDonald (Drainie, Lossiemouth) and Wilson (Wirral Secondary Grammar) attended maintained schools, with both Attlee and Wilson going to Oxford University. If one considers Labour Cabinets between 1924 and 1967 there was a rise in those educated privately from 17 per cent to 42 per cent, before it fell to 33 per cent in 1976, a fall which was not mirrored in Tory Cabinets. The occupational backgrounds also make for a contrast. Taking the same categories, between 1918 and 1935 72 per cent were workers, whilst 24 per cent were professional and these figures changed to 41 per cent and 49 per cent in 1945, 43 per cent and 47 per cent in 1950, 45 per cent and 46 per cent in 1951, respectively. After that the percentage from the workers category fell to 30 per cent in 1966 whilst that for professionals rose to 43 per cent. Business background never reached more than 11 per cent.

The fact that the political party which ruled in parliament for most of the period 1926–70 was represented overwhelmingly by members who attended fee-paying schools, and that this was even more true of the Cabinet where considerable political power was concentrated, provides at least circumstantial evidence that any attempt to introduce changes which might be seen in any way as detrimental to these schools would be fiercely resisted. Moreover, the resistance, regardless of the educational interests of the majority of the population, would take place both directly in the House of Commons and indirectly through the social network of the HMC schools in particular, from masonic lodges to London clubs.[5]

THE OLD SCHOOL TIE

Within other key influential areas of society, the top ranks of the judiciary, civil service (especially the Foreign Office) armed forces, Church of England, financial world, academia and industry were disproportionately dominated by ex-public school boys (hardly any women were in such positions by 1966) showing the close link between these educational establishments and the social background of their 'customers', a link so strong that it is difficult to explain fully in terms of ability or coincidence. The proportion had been falling in most categories, especially is this true for the armed forces during times of war, but as late as 1967, the relationship was still very evident, see Table 3.

Table 3. Percentage of Ex-Public School or Ex-Direct Grant School Boys Found in Key Influential Positions in Society[6]

Profession/Position 1967	Total	Total Whose School is Known	Ex-Public School %	Ex-Direct Grant %
Vice-Chancellors, Heads of Colleges, Professors of all English/Welsh Universities	1646	925	32.5	12.7
Heads of Colleges, Professors of Oxford/Cambridge	256	217	49.3	10.6
Admirals, Generals & Air Marshals	22	20	55.0	15.0
Physicians/Surgeons London Teaching Hospitals on GMC	244	232	68.0	12.5
Directors of Prominent Firms	102	96	70.8	11.4
C. of E. Bishops	45	36	75.0	5.5
Judges & QCs	78	77	79.2	7.7

Various explanations might be put forward for the close relationships between about 250 schools and the senior posts in so many areas of power and influence. The schools attract the most intelligent pupils, they have the best teachers, or is it a combination of both? There are two problems with this suggestion. The first is that in order to argue that it is merit alone which explains the situation, one has to imply that before the 1960s say hardly any girls were intelligent enough to compete for these senior posts, unless one is willing to admit that either bias in favour of the boys or prejudice against the girls played at least some part in the selection process. Once this is accepted then other areas can be legitimately explored. When the examination results at Oxford and Cambridge were surveyed in 1958, a reasonable date for the post-war record, it was found that boarders from HMC schools and direct grant grammar schools did not do as well as those from LEA grammar schools, in spite of the benefits of smaller class sizes, an extra year in the sixth form and supervised homework time, see Table 4.

Table 4. Oxbridge Degree Results by Type of Secondary Education: Men (1958)[7]

Type of Secondary Education	Good %	Poor %
HMC & Direct Grant:		
Boarders	32	49
Day Boys	45	30
LEA Grammar	50	33

In 1962 the percentage of public schoolboys entering colleges at Oxford ranged from 29.3 at St Peter's to 70.6 per cent at Christ Church and 80.6 per cent at Trinity. Again the suggestion that merit alone is responsible for the glittering careers which seem to follow from attendance at a fee-paying school is difficult to support when the colleges were ranked by the proportion of students obtaining firsts and seconds among the 23 colleges. Trinity and Christ Church were 18th and 17th respectively.[8] One is left with the question of why public schoolboys did so well in their chosen careers. Is it because they were interviewed by people who had also attended fee-paying schools and recognised the value and character of applicants who seemed to share those with their colleagues and themselves, and who would therefore fit in well within the department? The Foreign Office has been dominated by ex-fee-paying schoolboys. Anthony Sampson's 1962 study of ambassadors and senior officials found that 88 per cent had been to public school and 76 per cent to Oxford or Cambridge.

A survey in 1971 looked at the educational background of directors in clearing banks, merchant banks and discount houses, insurance companies and industrial firms.

Table 5. Results of 1971 Survey Looking at the Educational Background of Directors of Clearing Banks, Merchant Banks and Discount Houses, Insurance Companies and Industrial Firms[9]

Type of Business	Fee-Paying schools	Local Authority Schools
Clearing Banks, etc.	79	20
Merchant banks and Discount Houses	84	22
Insurance Companies	99	19
Industrial firms	173	87

Among bishops in 1960–62, 85 per cent had been educated at fee-paying schools and whilst their influence in the community declined during the twentieth century a number were still able to exercise a disproportionate amount of power through their membership of the House of Lords. C.B. Otley's study in 1968 showed that 82 per cent of army officers at the rank of lieutenant-general and above had attended such schools, a figure hardly different to that of some 20 years earlier.[10] Among 58 judges in the House of Lords and the Supreme Court almost 68 per cent had been privately educated.[11] By 1970, 62 per cent of top civil servants, 83 per cent of foreign ambassadors, 67 per cent of top rank Church of England clergy and 83 per cent of directors of clearing banks had been educated at public schools.[12] These 'old boy' networks were a fact of life among those in elite positions. This was consolidated by membership of London Clubs, most of which were exclusively male, in which nearly every leading company was represented, as Whitley demonstrates.[13] He provides a picture of the meeting places where the most powerful came together well away from public gaze. It is difficult to believe that the meals or daily newspapers are the main attractions of these old clubs which may be satirised in film and television but in effect serve as a valuable meeting place for those with considerable influence in society. The problem with the long-held assumption that ex-public school boys were in leading positions throughout much of the country during the twentieth century because they were, in general, much more able than the vast majority of other people is that it was during this time that the comparative economic decline of the nation took place. However suitable their talents and training may have been in past times, and even this is open to debate, it seems as if many of them were out of touch with the demands of a rapidly changing society struggling to maintain an important industrial base in the second half of the twentieth century.

THE TUC AND FEE-PAYING SCHOOLS

If much of the foregoing material is familiar that does not negate the scale of the influence of the fee-paying schools among the elite sections of society. In any case, these were the facts which faced those who were seeking to make England and Wales a fairer society. It is also a necessary picture to bear in mind when remarks are made about the power of the trade union movement, for although it is true that collective action among co-operating trade unions is a formidable force it is rarely used, if only because there is a considerable body of law which restricts trade union activity and because the interests of one union may conflict with those of another. Their potential power is visible. Their views are expressed in open annual conferences. What they do not possess is the more discreet power which has been exercised by the Establishment throughout the century and indeed long before then; 'the social network through common schooling, ancient university, entry to key professions, access to the higher ranks and the other connections from the formal boardroom to the informal London Club'. By contrast to the two major political parties of the time, it has not been possible to find any leading trade unionist at the TUC or member of staff who worked at the headquarters who attended a fee-paying school, especially an HMC school.[14] To that extent, the education they received was typical of the vast majority of the population. In general they were primarily concerned to see more resources put into the maintained schools and steps introduced to improve the educational opportunities of these children. They saw the fee-paying sector as an anachronism in a democratic society, especially during the 1940s, when they had made their views clear to the Fleming Committee. Soon they would be asked for their opinion once more.

Part of Dame Anne Godwin's speech as president of the TUC has been referred to concerning selection for secondary education (see p.279). She also told Congress at the time that the education system was,

> riddled with class distinctions and stratified by class assumptions, the influence of the public schools was all pervasive. They have established an enclave of privilege for themselves in our midst. They have created barriers of speech, of social habits and modes of thought that do great harm to the nation. But the real danger to the community is that they have imitators.[15]

It was not until 1966 that mention of fee-paying schools arose again and when it did it was in response to two diverse issues: admission to Oxford University and Circular 10/65 on secondary school reorganisation. The TUCGC enquired as to why no reference was made in the Circular to the government's views regarding the position of independent schools, other than direct grant and voluntary schools. Anthony Crosland, the secretary of state, replied that he intended to appoint a Commission 'to examine the best ways of integrating the independent schools with the State system of comprehensive secondary education'. The Commission was established in May 1966 and the TUCGC was invited to submit evidence to it.

OXFORD UNIVERSITY COMMISSION UNDER LORD FRANKS

The Oxford University Commission, with Lord Franks as chairperson, was set up to examine the role of the university in the UK system of higher education and reported in May 1966. Of particular interest to the TUC had been the admissions system. 'The Commission found that Oxford admitted a smaller proportion of maintained school pupils (41 per cent) and manual workers' children (estimated at little more than 13 per cent) than any other British university except Cambridge. The unduly low proportion of pupils accepted by Oxford from maintained schools was ascribed partly to the widespread belief that Oxford was academically and socially exclusive (and so likely to be uncongenial to most pupils from State schools); and partly to the differing length and content of sixth-form courses provided at different secondary schools, which materially affected candidates' chances in the Oxford Entrance Examination.'[16]

It was recommended that the responsibility for entrance should rest with the university and not the colleges and changes made to the examination system which favoured pupils undertaking extended sixth-form courses at independent schools in order to increase the proportion of pupils from other schools. All closed scholarships exclusive to public school pupils should be abolished and the number of open scholarships substantially reduced. These schemes would remove some of the special advantages enjoyed by pupils from fee-paying schools. However, the TUC proposal that 'specific action should be taken to increase the number of manual workers' children entering Oxford on the ground that their recommendation would secure an increase in the rate of applications from State secondary schools' was rejected.[17]

The TUCGC forwarded their comments on the report to Lord Franks making 11 points, agreeing with some recommendations such as the university being responsible for admissions rather than individual colleges, but, whilst accepting that 'academic promise' should be the main criterion for selection and that other non-academic interests should be taken into account, believed that the admission pattern was unsatisfactory and did not meet 'the principles which the Commission adopted'. Their main concerns were that the

> existing imbalance between the number of manual workers' children and those of children from other social classes is so severe, even in comparison with other British universities (except Cambridge), that a reformed entrance examination alone will certainly prove insufficient to correct it. The closed Oxford scholarships are certainly an anachronism, essentially because they have come to be awarded to candidates who would in any case almost certainly secure entry to Oxford by more conventional means, but the General Council cannot accept the view of the Commission that the financial obstacle to working-class children entering Oxford has entirely disappeared.[18]

Although the university would claim it was not responsible for the social and educational system it was believed that, given their status and power they could use their influence and resources to do more to help in overcoming the discrimination working-class pupils faced in seeking higher education. All the TUCGC could do in this instance was express the hope that the university would take radical action to secure in its undergraduate community more equality of opportunity for talented young people from all social classes.

THE PUBLIC SCHOOLS COMMISSION – NEWSOM

Sir John Newsom was appointed chairperson to the Public Schools Commission which reported in 1968. According to John Rae five people turned the post down before Newsom accepted.[19] He also suggests that Crosland wanted a Royal Commission similar to those reporting on the schools during the nineteenth century, the Clarendon and Taunton Commissions of 1864 and 1868 respectively, but had to be content with a smaller committee. It is possible that a Labour Cabinet wanted information more quickly than the four years taken by the Taunton Committee. Apart from Newsom there were 15 other members although one resigned within eight months. Among the well-represented fee-paying schools were Dame Kitty Anderson, ex-head teacher of North

London Collegiate College for girls, Mr J.C.V. Clancy, head teacher of Marlborough and Mr T.E.B. Howarth, headteacher of St Pauls. Two head teachers of comprehensive schools were also on the Committee: Mr W.S. Hill of Myers Grove in Sheffield and Dr H.G. Judge of Banbury School in Oxfordshire, as well as four academics, Lord Annan, Professor D.V. Donnison of the LSE, John Vaisez the economist and Mr B. William. John Davies represented the CBI and Dame Anne Godwin the TUC. Other members were Dr K. Bliss, Dr T.E. Faulkner and Mr G.H. Metcalffe.

Apart from the general aim of finding ways to integrate the fee-paying schools into the maintained sector other tasks were set: an assessment of the needs of boarding education, to 'ensure that the public schools should make their maximum contribution to meeting national educational needs' and to 'create a socially mixed entry into the schools in order to ... reduce the divisive influence which they now exert'. How serious the Labour government was about this Committee is not easy to say but Crosland's rather cynical view suggests that at the very least they had no serious plan by which any of this could be achieved although it is possible that this is what they were expecting the Commission to produce. Crosland said, 'The Commission will take a couple of years to complete its findings, but that's OK as there's no money currently available at Education to reform the public schools. The state sector must be strengthened so that it can match all but the very best fee-paying schools. Hence teacher supply is one of my priorities.'[20]

A year later the Newsom Committee had been established and the TUCGC submitted its evidence making it clear that while they had no direct acquaintance of the individual schools listed by the Commission they were warranted in commenting upon the public schools because of their effect upon the public educational system and society – and because of their willingness to participate in a similar manner to the Fleming Committee more than 20 years earlier. The statement they provided illustrated once more the principles upon which TUC education policy was formulated. As far as they were concerned nothing had changed fundamentally to alter views established during the Second World War concerning fee-paying education. This was not a matter of refusing to budge from attitudes which developments in education had rendered no longer applicable. On the contrary it was demonstrated that in spite of certain changes within the fee-paying schools, their privileged situation and undue influence in so many key areas of the dominant strata of British society had not changed significantly in any way. Familiar past suggestions of offering places to children other than those from high-income families were rejected because, as they had told the Fleming

Committee in the 1940s, the TUCGC 'are not concerned to transfer the privileges associated with public schools from one group of pupils to another group. They are concerned that the system of educational privilege, closely related to social and economic privilege, represented by the public schools considered as a whole, should be ended.'[21]

This clear statement really implied that there was therefore not much point in discussing all the tortuous attempts by the Commission to justify the system of fee-paying schools which were seen as contrary to the fair promotion of educational opportunity for all children. They were quick to point out that the terms of reference 'seem clearly to imply the continued existence of the public schools with some possible modification' but noted that talk of integration was 'with' not 'into' the state system of education.

They provided an analysis of the public schools which explained their objections to the system. Allowing for minor variations between them,

> a public school is a distinct form of secondary education. It differs from other forms of secondary education in the traditions and values upon which it is based, in the social purposes which it is intended to serve, in the scale of resources applied to it in relation to the numbers of pupils receiving it, in the conditions in which it is conducted. It is designed to equip its recipients to take their places in an occupationally and socially privileged elite. The public schools exist to provide it; their staff are concerned to assist in parting it; their pupils attend because their parents wish them to acquire it. It flourishes because the well-established connections between the public schools and the adjacent universities, the public service, certain professions and some sections of business management, enable educational privilege to be translated with a remarkable degree of certainty into occupational and social privilege. This factor is reinforced by its exclusive character, by the fact that it is not, and cannot be, available to more than a small minority of secondary pupils. These aspects of the functioning of the public schools seem to the General Council to be fundamental to their existence.[22]

The logic of this view was that 'If the public schools do not provide public school education in this sense they have no reason to exist.' There was therefore no point in the Commission 'considering means by which the public schools may be induced to desist from providing the form of secondary education which they exist to provide' because this was precisely what high-income parents were able and willing to pay for. Minor reforms would make no difference; major reform would mean they were no longer public schools in the sense that parents would not be willing to pay high fees for privileges no longer available.

The TUCGC replied to various other issues raised by the Commission. They found the schools 'damaging to the public education system' in that they have no responsibility with regard to national educational policies. They opposed selective secondary education, especially the 'essential criterion of selection' used by the schools to recruit the majority of their pupils according to the parents' capacity to pay fees. Subsidies to enable some pupils to enter the schools were also dismissed. 'The General Council are opposed to the application of public funds to private enterprise unless accompanied by an effective degree of public control.'[23]

The TUC were uncompromising in their views of fee-paying secondary schools. They believed 'that public school education, inseparably related as it must be to the perpetuation of occupational and social privilege, is socially undesirable as well as damaging in its effects upon the public educational system'.[24] In effect private education should be ended. They recognised that this policy 'would meet with influential opposition' but believed it was in the best national interest.

As to the question of boarding they did not believe it was necessarily related to the issue of fee-paying schools as there were boarding facilities in some local authority schools. They had two main thoughts regarding boarding education. The first was that it could be beneficial for the majority of older pupils to experience a short period, perhaps about a week, in residential education. A different environment could stimulate new interests. However, the view that children from socially disadvantaged backgrounds would gain from residential education was more doubtful. Indeed,

> the removal of children from their familiar surroundings, however unsatisfactory those surroundings may appear to be, for long periods during their formative years, may well have damaging effects upon the children's personal and social development far outweighing any gains in the improved academic attainment and opportunities which might result from attendance at boarding schools.[25]

There was nothing of encouragement to the Commission from the TUCGC's statement of evidence and when they sent a copy to the minister of education, suggesting that little useful progress could be made by the Commission until the government gave a clear declaration of its policy he replied that he 'hoped that such a basis would emerge in the Commission's report' and did not wish to jeopardise developments by making a statement until he had seen it.

The Public School Commission's First Report under Sir John Newsom was published on 22 July 1968. A week earlier it was before the Cabinet for discussion yet none took place! Tony Benn wrote

> Caroline had done a great deal of work on this and given me a big brief but Harold didn't want to discuss it. It was agreed that it would be published without comment. It was a terrible report suggesting that 50 per cent of public schools should be opened to ordinary boys, but that would in fact limit intake to those of reasonably high ability – a ghastly document.[26]

Having delayed the question of the fee-paying schools by setting up a Committee, the report had now allowed the question to emerge once more and it seems that Harold Wilson saw nothing but potential trouble ahead if a debate ensued, and even worse if any attempt was made to take any action which might adversely effect the privileges of the schools. Knowing full well that he would be criticised within the Labour party if he gave support to fee-paying schools, and realising the danger he would face from the powerful lobby within the Establishment if he suggested serious reform he chose to do nothing. He probably saw it as a digression from more important matters as well as a certainty of sparking off a mass of hostility from influential sections in society which he could well do without. His interest in the matter is reflected in the attention he gave it in his 1,000-page account of the Labour government between 1964 and 1970 when mention of setting up the Commission appears as a list of items in the Queen's speech but no mention is made of the report published later.[27] Pimlott's analysis is that:

> The Labour Government remained oddly indifferent to the private sector in education. In place of more definite action, Crosland merely set up a Public School Commission ... to consider what to do. Newsom's half-baked proposals for integrating independent schools into the state system ... were shelved and quickly forgotten. The Government's line on private education continued to be that it would simply wither away once state secondary schools had become so good that everybody would want to send their children to them.[28]

One interpretation of this view could be that it was extremely naive. The more likely explanation was that already mentioned – concern at the furore which would follow any action taken perceived as detrimental to the interests of the private sector.

The Report found few friends. The fee-paying schools believed suggestions of a 50 per cent intake of pupils from the maintained sector would be too restrictive and would completely change the nature of the schools. Neither were they willing at this time any more than they had been at the time of the Fleming Report to surrender control over admissions. As usual, they would be pleased to accept subsidies from central or local government in the form of fees paid for some pupils but only on their own terms. These were in general a willingness to take in a minority of children from the maintained sector who had shown academic promise and would thereby enhance the reputation of the schools. By contrast no enthusiasm was displayed for taking children of average or below average ability from such schools who might at least benefit from the smaller class sizes enjoyed in the private sector. The only real significance of the report was the information it provided which confirmed the special part the schools played in the education of dominant sections within British Society; information which would be quoted freely in future education debates. The divisiveness of so many aspects of fee-paying schools was spelt out in considerable detail. 'They belong, in a remarkable degree, in a world of their own.' This summed up so many of the features, such as the fact that public schools played games chiefly with other public schools, the teachers even if they move schools remain within the private sector, whilst 'The segregation of boys and girls in boarding schools for ten of their most formative years must have a socially divisive effect.'[29] Tables and charts documented the continued dominance of ex-public school boys in senior posts comparing their success with pupils from maintained schools. The pattern was a familiar one.

TUC RESPONSE TO NEWSOM REPORT

Just as the TUCGC's statement of evidence to the Commission had provided no support for the tentative avenues of enquiry set by the terms of reference, so too the Commission's report provided no satisfaction to them. They responded with detailed comments to the points made in the report actually commencing with a measure of agreement:

> They concur in the Commission's general conclusion that independent schools are a divisive influence in society. However, they regret that the doubts which they expressed in evidence to the Commission, as to whether its terms of reference would enable it to make consistent and radical recommendations concerning the public schools, are confirmed by the report.[30]

To a great extent the TUC document only reiterated points made in its original statement of evidence. They believed that the Commission's recommendation concerning integration was 'incompatible with the present efforts of the community to establish a system of non-selective secondary education as a means of a more genuine equality of educational opportunity than has existed previously'.[31] It seemed that having established certain facts the Commission could not admit to their cause and consequences. Referring to the nature of the public schools the Commission had confirmed, 'That purpose is clearly the transmission of educational, occupational and social privileges from those who currently enjoy them to their children.' The statistics supplied substantiated this conclusion. 'Yet having accepted these facts, the Commission appears to regard them as incidental, rather than as central, to the nature of the public school system.'[32]

Another contradiction was the Commission's suggestion that 'public schools themselves have no responsibility for the effects of the public school system' and it was time we helped them to change 'a situation not of their own making'. It was claimed that 'they deplore their social exclusiveness and privilege-conferring role'. Yet as the TUC had pointed out in its original statement to the Commission, 'these attributes of public school education are mainly what fee-paying parents pay for, and if the public schools did not possess them the main reason for their existence would disappear'.[33] As far as the TUCGC were concerned recommendations by the Commission could only be judged by 'their contribution to ending the public school system'. They were able to support the Commission on one matter of substance, 'the withdrawal of financial subsidies from public funds (in the form of tax relief and the like) at present available to schools for providing private education'. Even this minor reform was never acted upon. The conclusion of the TUCGC was encompassed in one last key sentence: 'In the light of all these reservations the General Council cannot support the principal recommendations of the commission's report.'[34]

THE PUBLIC SCHOOLS COMMISSION – DONNISON

The Public School Commission's membership changed slightly for their second task, to consider how independent day and direct grant grammar schools could participate in the move towards comprehensive secondary education. Sir John Newsom made way as chairperson for D.V. Donnison, Professor of Social Administration at the LSE. Two head teachers of

HMC schools, J.C. Dancy and T.E.B. Howarth left whilst the former independent day school headteacher C.R. Allison and three direct grant grammar school head teachers were appointed, Bruce McGowan (Solihull), Roger Young (George Watson's, Edinburgh) and Jean Wilks (King Edward VI School for Girls, Birmingham), as well as Robin Wood, Dean of Windsor.

The direct grant grammar schools were a mystery to most of the population, including many concerned with education. Their origins lie in the 1926 Hadow Report which recommended that all schools taking pupils over 11 years of age should be regarded as secondary. Grant aided secondary schools were given a choice in their source of funding: either by the local education authority or by a direct grant from the central authority, namely the Board of Education. For the minority of 235 schools which chose the latter system they had to reserve 25 per cent of their places free to pupils selected by the LEA. Whilst the 1944 Education Act abolished fees in all local authority secondary schools an exception was made concerning the direct grant grammar schools although their numbers were reduced to 164.[35] They were selective schools which had much in common with HMC day schools. Among the boarding pupils 85 per cent had fathers of professional and managerial backgrounds – Social Classes 1 and 2. For day schools the percentage was 58 per cent. Those with semi-skilled and unskilled fathers were 1.3 per cent and 8 per cent respectively. In 1964 the schools received approximately 75 per cent of their income from local authority and central government funds with the remaining 25 per cent coming from parental fees.

Among the direct grant grammar schools were 57 Roman Catholic and seven Methodist. Neither of these two groups was hostile to the idea of non-selective secondary schooling. Just over half were girls' schools. In effect, whether schools were or were not direct grant was largely an historical accident rather than evidence that they all achieved high academic results. The best-known were those with good reputations for examination successes, the most famous of which was probably Manchester Grammar, but such schools were atypical; only about ten came in this category of super-selective schools although their reputation rubbed off on all the other schools categorised as direct grant grammar schools, just as the reputations of the HMC schools gave the impression that all fee-paying schools provided excellent facilities, tuition and good academic results. There were towns where direct grant grammar schools obtained better examination results than the maintained grammar schools; but there were also examples where the maintained grammar schools outperformed the direct grant grammar school. The explanation was to be found in the social intake of the school as Sir Alec Clegg, chief education officer for the West Riding demonstrated with reference to Sheffield, Bradford and Leeds.[36]

The question for the Labour government was how they could follow a policy of integrating maintained grammar schools which catered for approximately 20 per cent of the school population, into a system of non-selective secondary schooling whilst ignoring the 3 per cent attending selective direct grant grammar schools in which the fees of some parents were subsidised by the State whilst 25 per cent of free-place pupils were paid for by local authorities. In short how could they justify a system in which some children had more money spent on their education than others? Whilst the Commission which reported in March 1970 could agree that the schools should participate in local authority reorganisation schemes and that fees should be abolished in day schools which were largely financed by central and local government they could not agree on the best way that this might be achieved. Those with direct grant grammar school connections suggested a scheme by which the schools could retain full grant status receiving money from a centrally financed School Grants Committee which would preserve their greater degree of independence without giving them more influence than local authority schools. An equal number of the Committee, seven, suggested the direct grant status should go and they should be 'controlled or aided maintained schools' as was the case with religious schools. Professor Donnison and Lord Annan were willing to support either scheme. Mr Allison and Robin Woods wished to retain fees on a means-tested basis and at least some of the schools as selective grammar schools. One recommendation was for the governing bodies to be made more representative of the local communities, including representatives from trade unions and employers, a move which was bound to find favour with the labour movement.

TUC RESPONSE TO DONNISON REPORT

The government welcomed the report, the Conservatives opposed it. Mrs Thatcher, shadow minister of education, promised to reverse any decision which would integrate the schools into the local education authority if the Conservatives won the next general election. The TUCEC believed it 'contributed a modest step towards' comprehensive reorganisation and agreed a note of comment should be produced and sent to the secretary of state at the DES.[37] In contrast to the Public Schools Commission's First Report the note issued by the TUCGC gave it a general welcome:

The conclusions while in some respects less radical than the General Council have advocated, are generally acceptable to them as constituting a constructive contribution to the diminution of educational privilege and the development of an effective system of comprehensive secondary education for all.[38]

They agreed with the analysis made of the direct grant system which provided 'a good academic education for a minority of children (selected according to estimated academic ability and, in effect, by social class) at the expense of the majority, including most working-class children, who receive an inadequate minimum education'. This fitted in precisely with trade union views regarding the hierarchical situation of the tripartite secondary school system. They supported desires for the direct grant schools to participate in local authority reorganisation schemes for non-selective secondary schooling and the elimination of school fees.

However, they were unhappy about suggestions that direct grant schools could join the private sector because this clearly implied 'the continued existence of a private sector of education'.[39] Integration would bring about a 'modest, though not insignificant diminution of educational inequality' but the 'continued existence of other private secondary schools, even integrated boarding schools, is incompatible, unless those schools admit pupils of all levels of ability'. They also rejected proposals for super-selective schools put forward by two members of the Commission but not supported by the majority. The TUCGC concurred with the Commission's general conclusion about the education of gifted children:

> For the sake of gifted and ordinary children alike, gifted children should be educated with their less gifted contemporaries in comprehensive schools ... because there is no certain way of identifying such children, and partly because such segregation would diminish the quality of the general education both of those children in the 'super-selective' schools and those excluded from them.[40]

FEE-PAYING SCHOOLS AND THE TUC: INCOMPATIBLE EDUCATIONAL AIMS AND OBJECTIVES

It was clear that the objectives of the fee-paying schools and their supporters were incompatible with those of the TUC. The former inevitably wished to retain the features of their system which made them attractive and affordable to the more affluent sections of society. For the TUC all of these schools stood for a measure of privileged education and social networking which combined to reinforce inequality of opportunity in education, future careers and the quality of life in almost every social sphere at the expense of the majority of the population. The two sides were therefore diametrically opposed. There were no grounds for a compromise which would not either have destroyed the special features and benefits for which parents were willing to pay high fees, nor moves which might diminish some of these features whilst retaining others which the TUC could accept.

The TUC rejected any moves which might allow a few more children to be offered access to the advantages fee-paying schools could offer because this would do nothing to help the vast majority of children. They objected to any system which reinforced a belief that some children were more deserving of greater expenditure on their education than others. Those in families with above average wealth and incomes already enjoyed the advantages afforded by superior purchasing power. Could it be right that they should also be able to buy more of the scarce educational resources available nationally as well? There was no way that the TUC representing the majority of working families could accept such a philosophy. The Labour government intended to act upon the main recommendations of the report through the education bill introduced by Edward Short into parliament in which it was intended to make reorganisational planning for non-selective secondary schooling a statutory requirement. Before this bill could make much progress a change of government was accompanied by a change in education philosophy which gave strong support to the fee-paying sector which had evolved in the country. This helped to ensure that the two major reports of the Public Schools Commission published in 1968 and 1970 achieved no visible change in the fee-paying secondary school sector. Secondary schools would remain divided into fee-paying and maintained schools, for some a sign of continued independence in education, for others a symbol of and contributor to the wide differences in wealth, income, power and quality of life within society.

NOTES AND REFERENCES

1. Butler, D. and Butler , G. (2000) *Twentieth Century British Political Facts 1900–2000*, p.190.
2. Kogan, M. (1971) *Educational Policy Making*, p.90.

3. Ibid., p.72.
4. Ibid.
5. Rich, P.J. (1991) *Chains of Empire: English Public Schools, Masonic Cabalism, Historical Causality and Imperial Clubdom*, and (1993) *Elixir of Empire: English Public Schools, Ritualism, Freemasonry and Imperialism.*
6. *Public Schools Commission*, First Report 1968, Vol. II, Appendix 8, Section 4, p.236.
7. Quoted in Glennerster, H. and Pryke, R. (1966) *The Public Schools*, p.22.
8. Ibid., p.23.
9. Whitley, R. (1974) 'The City and Industry; the Directors of Large Companies, their Characteristics and Connections' Table 2, p.70 in Stanworth, P. and Giddens, A. (eds) *Elites and Power in British Society.*
10. Quoted in Boyd, D. (1973) *Elites and Their Education*, p.55.
11. Ibid., p.54.
12. McCulloch, G. (1991) *Philosophers and Kings*, p.39.
13. Whitley, R. (1974) 'The City and Industry: the Directors of Large Companies, their Characteristics and Connections', in Stanworthy, P. and Giddens, A., *Elites and Power in British Society*, p.70.
14. It has not been possible to locate any privately educated leading trade unionist after searching through volumes of *Who's Who*, all ten volumes of the *Dictionary of Labour Biography*, and the obituaries appearing in the Annual TUC Reports or numerous autobiographies/biographies of trade unionists.
15. *TUC Report 1962*, p.79.
16. *TUC Report 1966*, p.226.
17. Ibid., p.227.
18. Ibid., p.228.
19. Rae, J. (1981) *The Public School Revolution*, p.38.
20. Crosland, S. (1982) *Tony Crosland*, p.149.
21. TUC Statement of Evidence to the Public Schools Commission, May 1967. *TUC Report 1967*, p.218.
22. *TUC Report 1966*, p.67.
23. *TUC Report 1967*, p.220.
24. Ibid.
25. Ibid., p.223.
26. Benn, T. (1988) *Office without Power: Diaries 1968–72*, 18.7.1968, p.91.
27. Wilson H. (1974) *The Labour Government 1964–1970*, p.230.

28. Pimlott, B. (1992) *Harold Wilson*, pp.512–13.
29. *Newsom Report 1968*, Ch. 3, pp.55–8.
30. *TUC Report 1969*, p.313.
31. Ibid., p.314.
32. Ibid.
33. Ibid.
34. Ibid., p.316.
35. Allsopp, E. and Grugeon, D. (1966) *Direct Grant Grammar Schools*. This booklet provides a concise history and analysis of the schools during the mid-1960s. See also Davis, R. (1967) *The Grammar School*, pp.210–20.
36. Allsopp, E. and Grugeon, D. (1966) *Direct Grant Grammar Schools*, p.9.
37. *TUCEC Mins.* 9.6.1970.
38. *TUC Report 1970*, p.302.
39. Ibid., p.303.
40. Ibid.,p.304.

CONCLUSION

The TUCEC enjoyed good relationships with the CBI, successive education ministries, teachers' unions, the University Grants Committee and WEA. Their strength lay partly in the fact that they were not seen to be making a special plea for self-interest which might be an accusation aimed at professional bodies. They recognised that within the government for most of the time the Board of Education and its successors were not in a very powerful position. This meant they tended to be reactive and cautious over certain issues although on other occasions, such as the manoeuvrings at the Board of Education (BOE) during the Second World War, this had been far from true. The Board were slow to become involved with crucial areas such as the curriculum, examinations and teaching methods until late in the day when the Schools Council was established in 1964. The Council had a balance of politicians and professional members, including a representative from the TUC. Later the Council's work began to be seen as an irritant by Conservative administrations and it was duly abolished by Sir Keith Joseph in 1984.

The TUC was in the vanguard of reform in education. Matters often dismissed at the time as inappropriate or too expensive would later become readily accepted. They advocated decimalisation in 1905 which was finally introduced in 1971 and teacher–parent councils in 1944 which were introduced in the 1980s, albeit in a different form from the one they had proposed. Other examples would be the raising of the school leaving age from 14 to 15 years of age, and later to 16; access to free secondary schooling for all children and wider opportunities for more young people to receive higher education. They maintained support for school medical services and school meals, working hard to resist the moves of various governments to increase the price of school dinners and reduce the hours and therefore the pay of the thousands of part-time staff working within the service. Their arguments were politely listened to but ignored when it came to cutting back on these areas of educational expenditure. Similarly they lost the battle to retain free school milk in secondary schools under Harold Wilson's Labour government and to prevent abolition of milk in primary schools by Margaret Thatcher when she was minister of education in Ted Heath's Conservative administration of 1970. In both cases the amount of money involved was small, the motivations for abolition by both governments varied ranging from a view that education must be seen to share in cutbacks in public expenditure to a belief that it was not the responsibility of the state to provide a free nutritious drink to children. An unintentional by-product of this policy was the introduction into schools of cola drinks of dubious nutritional benefit.

From the 1920s onwards they campaigned for maintenance grants and resisted suggestions in 1968 to substitute student loans for grants in higher education. Maintenance grants would appear for some children nearly 70 years later; student loans in half that time. They were involved in campaigns to end the 11-plus entry examination to secondary schools which were successful in most areas of the country but they had less success in fighting to prevent the standards governing the quality of school buildings being reduced to make economies in education. Just as they argued for the abolition of the divisive tripartite system of secondary schooling so for the same reasons they argued in vain against the development of the binary system in higher education, which lasted almost 25 years before being abandoned.

Some ideas were overtaken by events. Esperanto was one such example.[1] During the inter-war period, the idea of an international language which would allow ordinary people from different countries to converse freely was promoted, partly in the belief that it might contribute to making another war less likely. Dialogue between citizens would lessen the opportunity for governments to make decisions which could plunge countries into the kind of European War of 1914–18. Some schools introduced Esperanto, especially in London. International conferences were held promoting the 'new' language. The TUC supported the spread of Esperanto and as late as 1947 the NUR introduced a resolution at Congress for 'Esperanto to be taught in all schools in Britain and the Commonwealth'. The extent of interest within the TUC is born out by the existence of two files in the TUC Archives at Warwick University (MSS 292/903/1-2) covering the years 1927–60. Yet in spite of considerable enthusiasm for many years Esperanto did not become the international language hoped for by its supporters for a variety of reasons. English in its various forms, especially as a second language, was to take over that role. Esperanto ceased to be of interest to the TUC. Perhaps one of the strangest aspects of Esperanto is that today it seems to have almost vanished from the recorded history of the period.[2]

The resistance to their demands for greater progress in education from different governments was based to a large extent upon the cost of their proposals. During the inter-war years Conservative or Conservative-dominated national governments followed a policy of low public expenditure in order to keep taxation down. In the immediate post-war period, education was competing for funds in the first place with every other area in which investment was desperately needed, from housing and the health service to industry and agriculture; from the 1950s onwards it would be competing with a massive armaments programme which took a disproportionate amount of the nation's resources. The TUC rarely commented upon social inequalities within the country during formal meetings with ministers or in their evidence to official committees. At Congress it was a different matter and there delegates were willing to be more critical of the situation in which they found themselves confronted by those who had benefitted from extra years in full-time education at school and university and who expected their own children to enjoy the same privileges, denying such opportunities to the majority of other people's children because they argued the country could not afford the expenditure involved.

The TUC was aware that resistance to reforms in education were due to special interest groups who enjoyed particular advantages and privileges by maintaining the status quo. The fee-paying schools were the major group in this area; Oxford and Cambridge universities to a lesser extent. The TUC objected to academic and social advantages being purchased by those with well above average incomes. The only reform the fee-paying schools were willing to consider was an increase in the entry of above average intelligent children from lower-income families if local authorities or central government would meet the school fees. Such a scheme would bring public subsidies to the schools and the good results of those carefully chosen would enhance the academic reputation of the schools, inevitably at the expense of local authority schools. For the TUC, the idea of making it possible for a few more children to enjoy these privileges was no solution. They believed no group of children whether through claims to above average intelligence, greater wealth of parents or a combination of the two should be entitled to purchase a greater share of the nation's scarce resources in education. In plain words these children were no more deserving or of greater worth to society than any others. They believed the only solution was to end the existing fee-paying system of schooling, a considerable part of which had been originally founded for poor local scholars.

Such a view was anathema to any Conservative government for, given the educational background of Tory MPs, these were 'their' schools which were being criticised. Their instinct and practice was to protect and support the fee-paying sector. Within Labour governments there may have been considerable sympathy and support for TUC policy, they may have believed that it was necessary to undermine a system which promoted a whole series of attitudes throughout society which reinforced Conservative values but they knew too well the strength of the fee-paying lobby. Any attempt at serious reform would find them faced with a well-organised special interest group with power out of all proportion to its numbers which could and would create serious electoral damage to any Labour government. The media might point to trade union power during an industrial dispute but this was nothing compared to the old boy network which was as powerful in 1970 as it had been in 1926[3] and one which has been very successful in preventing any serious challenge to their privileged position in education throughout the twentieth century. If the TUC did not push the issue it was because they believed other areas impinging more directly upon the majority of children, such as raising the school leaving age, were more important.

Two unrelated events during 1970 would bring changes to education. The first was the affiliation of the NUT, the largest and oldest teachers' union, to the TUC. J. Crawford, chairperson of the TUCEC welcomed them, stating they 'can speak with great authority as to the need for improvements in the terms and working conditions of schools and college teachers'.[4] When Edward Britton, the secretary of the NUT, moved the resolution on education he told delegates that his union was celebrating its centenary that year and that 'Very soon after the formation of the National Union of Teachers a resolution to affliate to the TUC was very narrowly defeated and it is a matter of regret to many of us that it has taken so long to rectify that mistake.'[5] The addition of the NUT to the other ranks of teachers' unions affiliated to Congress would strengthen the weight of educational practioners within the organisation although the different traditions of these unions would not always prove harmonious.

The second significant event of 1970 was the appointment of Margaret Thatcher to the post of secretary of state at the DES. Her first action was to scrap Circular 10/65 and replace it with 10/70. She then announced a programme of expansion for education covering nursery schools, primary schools in particular and the polytechnic side of higher education. In addition, the long-promised raise in the school leaving age to 16, delayed so frequently in the past, (the last time by Roy Jenkins' 1968 cuts in public expenditure) was finally introduced in time for the beginning of the school year in September 1972. Apart from this action, many of the other promises would be diluted when the Heath government was faced with the economic crisis of 1973. One hint of future Conservative party thinking was the increase in funding for direct grant grammar schools, the highly selective grammar schools at which most entrants were fee-payers.

A change in post-war Conservative party ideology was witnessed as the radical right began their counter-offensive with the launch of the first of the *Black Papers* in 1969 denouncing the 'Egalitarian Threat' resulting from the wider access to all forms of education which had taken place.[6] The 'free market' was back and in time would be applied to education as to any other area of society. With the much publicised criticisms from radical right groups education would find itself increasingly under attack.[7] Whereas education had been promoted in the past as an investment which would help the country to cope successfully in an increasingly competitive world it would now become one of the scapegoats for the comparative failure of the economy. From now on education was under attack, or more precisely the public sector of education for, by contrast, fee-paying schools were generally praised by radical right wing pressure groups and much of the parliamentary Conservative party which had moved politically to the right. The impact would go well beyond the Conservative government and the way was paved for a return to some of the policies and structures of the past, even if they came wrapped in new terminology, such as increased parental choice. Some would call it a return to basics; other would see it as a means by which the more privileged groups regained some of their privileges. What was certain was that any assumption that the story of education in Britain during most of the twentieth century could be described as a period of steady and inevitable access to improved school facilities and progress would need to be questioned. The education system was always subject to the economic prosperity of the country and rarely considered the top priority for national investment. Moreover, schools always had to work within the social setting in which they were located; some in prosperous areas with well-educated, supportive, above average income parents whilst others worked hard to serve areas of social disadvantage in which there were high levels of unemployment, poor housing and a decaying infrastructure. All had to cope with the pressures of a commercial age in which values promoted by some areas of the media were anti-intellectual and contrary to the values being promoted by most schools. Teachers would find themselves increasingly criticised by government ministers and newspapers as a particular problem in one school was turned into a generalisation for many schools. Even so, most parents remained supportive of the schools their children attended.

Affiliated TUC membership would decline as widespread unemployment returned in the 1980s in just the same way as it had during the inter-war depression. The suggestion that trade unions were no longer necessary in the changing economic circumstances accompanying the de-industrialisation of many parts of Britain seemed to reflect this fall in membership before the impact of privatisation, short-term contracts, part-time working and contracting out work for the lowest tender brought the reality home to people of the deterioration in the working conditions which accompanied so many of these changes. Schools would also find themselves confronted with these changes, initially as the provision of services such as school meals and cleaning were privatised but later in areas directly involved with teaching through hybrid schemes such as schools opting out of local authority control and supply teachers provided by commercial agencies.

There were conflicting signs concerning progress in education towards the end of the twentieth century. There was still a relationship between social class and academic attainment, but compared to a generation ago, a majority of all pupils now stayed on beyond compulsory school-leaving age and gained formal qualifications, whilst about 25 per cent of 18-year-olds went on to higher education. These marked improvements in educational opportunities and achievements which had been campaigned for consistently by the TUC would still have seemed beyond the expectations of trade unionists in the first half of the century. Moreover, by the end of the century, the comparative failure of girls in gaining educational qualifications compared to boys had been reversed as on average they out-performed boys from the start of primary schooling to the end of secondary schooling. Under-achieving boys was the new challenge for the twenty-first century.

After 1997 an extensive refurbishment programme in schools and colleges was undertaken, and the long haul to make amends for years of neglect in the maintenance of buildings began to get underway. New premises and equipment to improve both basic accommodation and rapid changes in information technology brought much needed development to institutions which had seen little change to major resources for 25 years.

By contrast, and this would have both surprised and dismayed the TUC in 1970, the suggestion that there would be a re-introduction of selection in secondary schooling, a known cause of so much personal misery a generation earlier, albeit now under the guise of specialist schools, would have been considered impossible. The encouragement of more religious schools, in spite of the evidence of their contribution to the divisiveness in Northern Ireland, (an issue raised by Bob Smillie of the Miners' Federation at Congress back in 1907) would have seemed unthinkable. An increase in schools separating children primarily upon religious and cultural differences, given the growing number of conflicts in urban areas with a 'racial' dimension, hardly seemed to be a positive way of creating harmony in a multicultural society.

Battles once thought won would need to be fought again and there were the first signs emerging by the early twenty-first century that public attitudes towards privatisation were changing in the light of reality. It was becoming clear that the interests of private companies in pursuit of profits were not the same as those whose primary concern, through their professional training, was to provide services to the general public. A litany of privatised disasters from the mis-selling of private pensions by insurance companies to the disastrous chaos inflicted upon the railway network raised doubts as to whether these changes had been for the better. In education too, the moves towards privatisation weakened after the electoral defeat of the Conservative party in 1997. School vouchers advocated by the Institute of Economic Affairs in 1975, considered and reluctantly rejected by Keith Joseph in 1983 on the grounds of administrative impracticability faded as a serious idea, although still harboured by some such as Iain Duncan-Smith, the new leader of the Conservative party. Similarly, the abolition of local education authorities as desired by Kenneth Baker in the 1980s had not taken place on the scale predicted, although private companies had made inroads in the provision of schooling in some areas. Even the system of opting out to become a grant maintained school did not make the progress predicted by the Conservative government of 1987 in spite of substantial extra funding to schools which agreed to take this route.

Slowly, well-resourced public services, including schools and colleges, were regaining public support, even if the willingness to pay the required taxes lagged behind. The rejection of privatisation of the school system by the NUT Conference from 1999 onwards suggested a new-found confidence among trade unions. Once more it was time for the TUC to take their place in the vanguard among those organisations seeking to protect and promote an educational system which regarded all as worthy of equal consideration regardless of their social circumstances. Anyone who believed the TUC had outlived their purpose would need to think again.

NOTES AND REFERENCES

1. Esperanto was invented by Dr Zamenov (1859–1917) of Warsaw and the first book was published in 1887. The British Esperanto Association, now based at Wedgewood Memorial College, has approximately 500 members with about another 1,000 people in the UK who are Esperanto users. They publish several journals and the Annual World Congress attracts around 3,000 delegates from many countries. The total Esperanto bibliography now stands at over 20,000 volumes.
2. There must be references to Esperanto in some books dealing with the period 1926–70 but it has not been possible to locate one in the present bibliography which includes most of the recent well-known studies of the history of education.
3. Paxman, J. (1990) *Friends in High Places*, Ch. 6.
4. *TUC Report 1970*, p.69.
5. Ibid.
6. See Musgrove, F. (1987) 'The Black Paper Movement' in Lowe, R. (ed.) *The Changing Primary School*; Wright, N. (1977) *Progress in Education*.
7. See Chitty, C. (1989) *Towards a New Education System: The Victory of the New Radical Right*; Griggs, C. (1989) 'The New Right and English Secondary Education' in Lowe, R. (ed.) *The Changing Secondary School*.

APPENDIX 1

TRADES UNION CONGRESS EDUCATION COMMITTEE 1926–70

Years in Office	Chairman	Education	Relevant Comments
1926–36	Arthur Pugh (1870–1955) Pres. TUC 1926	Elementary Educ to Standard IV Left School at 12	Iron & Steel Trades Confederation Member TUCEC Chairperson WETUC
1937–39	George Hicks MP Pres. TUC 1927	Elementary	SDF, originally bricklayer, supporter of PLEBS, NCLC, 1st Sec. AUBTW. Wrote foreword to 1927 edn of *The Ragged Trousered Philanthropists*
1940–46	G.W. Thomson Pres. TUC 1947		Draughstman
1947–50	H. Bullock (1885–1967) Pres. TUC 1950		General & Municipal Workers Union
1951–67	W.B. Beard (1892–1967) Pres.TUC 1956		United Patternmakers Association
1968–70 on	J. Crawford Pres. TUC 1973	Elementary School Left School at 14	Coalminer

Years in Office	Secretary	Education	Relevant Comments
1926–31	Alec S. Firth (1892–)	Shelley Elem.Sch. Penistone Gram.Sch. Huddersfield Tech.Col. B.Sc.(Econ) Univ. London lst Class Dip. Commerce	Tutor WEA, Lecturer Huddersfield Tech. Col.; Stats. Officer Dept. Wool Textile Prod., War Office; Labour Cand. Cambridge Univ. 1923/24 Fellow Royal Stats. Soc. Secretary WEA 1931–34
1932–56	J.V.C. Wray (1896–1982)		
1957–74	Denis Winnard (1916–1986)	Grammar School, Rochdale. Univ. of Oxford	Tutor WEA, Lancashire.

Note: In spite of considerable correspondence and searches on the internet it has been impossible to provide complete details of the schooling/further education of several trade unionists. Their names seldom appear in dictionaries of biography (*Who's Who*, *DNB*) or the obituary columns of papers such as *The Times*. *The Dictionary of Labour Biography* has helped to remedy this problem and the increase in IT in general means that more is now on record but details of the lives of some of those who were born in the early 20th century have not survived, at least not in any published form known to the author.

APPENDIX 2

EDUCATION COMMITTEE OF THE GENERAL COUNCIL OF THE TUC 1926–70
(SELECTED YEARS[+])

Year[*]	Chairman	Secretary	Other Members (Mr unless otherwise stated)
1928	Arthur Pugh	Alec S. Firth T. Richards	J. Beard, J.W. Bowen, H.H. Elvin, G. Hicks,
1938	George Hicks MP	J.C.V. Wray W. Stott, G.W. Thomson	H.H. Elvin, Miss F. Hancock, J. Jones,
1948	H. Bullock	J.C.V. Wray L. Evans, C.J. Geddes, Miss F. Hancock, G.W. Thomson	W.B. Beard, J. Bowman, Sir G. Chester,
1958	W.B. Beard	Denis Winnard A. Hallworth, Dame F. Hancock, E.J. Hill, J. O'Hagan, L. Poole, L. Sharp, R. Smith, B. Walsh, W.P.J. Webber, R. Willis	J. Campbell, Miss B.A. Godwin, S.F. Greene,
1968	J. Crawford	Denis Winnard R.W. Briginshaw, L. Cannon, S.F. Greene, S. Hill, D. Hogarth, T. Jackson, Mrs M. Patterson, C.T.H. Plant, A. Roberts, G.F. Smith	W.C. Anderson, Miss W. Baddeley, D. Basnet,

[*]Refers to past academic year.
[+]Full details of Committee Membership are given in Section E of each TUC Annual Report.

APPENDIX 3

TUCGC REPRESENTATIVES ON EXTERNAL 'EDUCATIONAL'
ORGANISATIONS 1926–70 (SELECTED YEARS)

Year	Organisation	TUCGC Representatives
1928	Oxford Delegacy for Extra Mural Studies	J. Beard, Arthur Pugh
	Cambridge Board of Extra Mural Studies	J. Beard, H.H. Elvin
	National Advisory Council for Juvenile Employment	Ben Turner, A. Conley, H.H. Elvin,W.Kean, Miss J. Varley
1938	Ruskin College	H. H. Elvin, W. Stott
	Joint Consultative Committee – on the After Careers of Extra Mural Students	G. Hicks, H.H. Elvin, G.W. Thomson
	Oxford Delegacy for Extra Mural Studies	Miss F. Hancock, J.V.C. Wray
	Cambridge Board of Extra Mural Studies	H.H. Elvin, J. Jones
	NCLC	G. Hicks
	WEA	G.W. Thomson
	WEATUC	G.W. Thomson
1948	Nat. Co-operating Body for Educ. (UNESCO)	H. Bullock
	Nat. Co-operating Body for the Social Services (UNESCO)	W.B. Beard
	Nat. Foundation for Adult Education	H. Bullock, G.W. Thomson
	Joint Committee of TUC and LSE for course in TU Studies	H. Bullock, Sir George Chester, L. Evans, Miss F. Hancock
	NCLC	W.B. Beard
	WEA	H. Bullock
	WEATUC	C.J. Geddes
	Ruskin College	J. Bowman, Sir George Chester, Miss F. Hancock
	Oxford Delegacy for Extra Mural Studies	H. Bullock, J.V.C. Wray
	Cambridge Board of Extra Mural Studies	Sir George Chester
	Council for Educational Advance	H. Bullock, W.B. Beard, G.W. Thomson, J.V.C. Wray
	Central Advisory Council for Adult Education in H.M. Forces (Home Service)	C.J. Geddes
	National Association of Boys' Clubs	H. Bullock
	Campaign Committee for the Expansion of	H. Bullock,

Year	Organisation	TUCGC Representatives
	Higher Education	A.Winterbottom
	Hillcroft College for Working Women	Miss F. Hancock
	National Juvenile Employment Council	H. Bullock,
		Sir George Chester,
		Sir L. Fawcett,
		Miss F. Hancock
1958	UK Committee for UNESCO	W.B. Beard
	Nat. Co-operating Body for Educ. (UNESCO)	W.B. Beard
	ICFTU European Advisory Committee on Education	W.B. Beard,
		Dame F. Hancock,
		Miss B.A. Godwin
	Nat. Institute of Advanced Education	Miss B.A. Godwin,
		W.J.P. Webber
	British Association for Commercial & Industrial Education	J. O'Hagan
	Jt. Comm. of TUC and LSE – Trade Union Studies	W.B. Beard,
		Dame F. Hancock,
		W.J.P. Webber, R. Willis
	NCLC	G.B. Thorneycroft
	WEA	J. Crawford
	WETUC	F. Hayday
	Ruskin College	W.B. Beard,
		Dame F. Hancock,
		R. Willis
	Hillcroft College for Working Women	Dame F. Hancock
	Oxford Delegacy for Extra Mural Studies	G.B. Thorneycroft,
		J.V.C. Wray
	Cambridge Board of Extra Mural Studies	W.B. Beard
	National Youth Employment Council	W.B. Beard, A. Hallsworth,
		Dame F. Hancock,
		R.Willis
	National Association of Boys' Clubs	H.L. Bullock
	Boy Scouts	H.L. Bullock
	Army Cadets	H.L. Bullock
1968	Jt. Comm. of TUC and LSE - Trade Union Studies	S.F. Greene
	Ruskin College	J. Crawford, D. Basnett,
		L. Cannon
	Hillcroft College for Working Women	Mrs C.M. Patterson
	WEA	J. Crawford, D. Winnard
	Consultative Group of TU Officials - Education	D. Basnett
	The Schools Council	D. Winnard
	National Youth Employment Council	W.B. Beard, J. Crawford,
		S.F. Greene,
		Mrs C.M. Patterson,
		D. Winnard

APPENDIX 4

EDUCATIONAL BACKGROUNDS OF CHAIRPERSONS OF MAJOR EDUCATION
COMMITTEES/REPORTS 1926–70

Report	Chair	School	University	Position
Hadow Report (Pub. 1926)	Sir W.H. Hadow (1859–1937)	Malvern	Oxford	Vice Chanc. Sheffield University
Consultative Committee BOE Primary School (Pub. 1931)	Sir W.H. Hadow	Malvern	Oxford	Chair Consultative Committee BOE
Sec. Educ. with Special Ref. to Gram./Tech. Schools	Will Spens (1882–1962)	Rugby	Cambridge	Fellow/Tutor Cambridge 1927–52
Norwood Report (Pub.1943)	Sir Cyril Norwood (1875–1956)	Merchant Taylors	Oxford	Head Marlborough/ Harrow. President St Johns Oxford
Fleming Report (Pub. 1944)	Lord Fleming (1877–1944)	Glasgow High School	Glasgow & Edinburgh	Solicitor General for Scotland 1921, MP Dumbarton 1924.
McNair Report (Pub. 1944)	Sir Arnold McNair (1885–1975)	Aldenham & Gonville	Cambridge	Prof. of Law Cambridge Vice Chanc. Liverpool Univ.; Judge International Court, Hague
Education Act (1944)	R.A. Butler (1902–82)	Marlborough	Cambridge	Minister of Education Master Trinity Coll. Cambridge 1965–78
Higher Technological Education (Pub. 1945)	Lord Eustace Percy (1887–1958)	Eton	Oxford	Minister of Education Pres. BOE 1924–29

Report	Chair	School	University	Position
Early Leaving (Pub. 1954)	Sir Samuel Gurney-Dixon (1878–1970)	Leys School	Cambridge	Pres. Union of Educational Institutions
Crowther Report (Pub. 1959)	Geoffrey Crowther (1907–1972)	Leeds G.S./ Oundle	Cambridge	Editor *Economist* Director various companies
Newsom Report – Half Our Future (Pub.1963)	John H. Newsom (1910–1971)	Imperial Service College (I.S.C.)	Oxford	Chief Educ. Officer Hertfordshire Governor: Haileybury/I.S.C.
Committee on Higher Education (Pub. 1963)	Lord Robbins (1898–1984)	Southall County Sch.	London	Prof. Economics LSE 1st Chancellor Stirling Univ.
Children and Their Primary Schools (Pub. 1967)	Lady Plowden (b.1910)	Downe House		Gov. BBC/Pres. Cent. Adv. Council for Educ. (Eng.) 1963–66
First Report Public Schools (Pub. 1968)	Sir John Newsom	Imperial Service College (I.S.C.)	Oxford	Chief Educ. Officer Hertfordshire Governor: Haileybury/I.S.C.
Second Report Public Schools (Pub. 1970)	David Donnison (b. 1926)	Marlborough	Oxford	Prof. Social Administration LSE 1961–69

APPENDIX 5

EDUCATIONAL BACKGROUND OF PRESIDENTS/MINISTERS OF EDUCATION
1926–70

Date	Pres./Min. of Education	School Attended	Further/Higher Education
1924–29	Lord Eustace Percy (Con)	Eton	Oxford
1929–31	Sir Charles Trevelyan (Lab)	Harrow	Cambridge
1931	H.B. Lees-Smith (Nat. Lab)	Aldenham	Cadet RMA Woolwich/ Oxford
1931–32	Sir Donald Maclean (Lib)	Haverfordwest GS	
1932	Edward Wood (Lord Irwin) (Con)	Eton	Oxford
1934–35	Lord Halifax (formerly Lord Irwin) (Con)	Eton	Oxford
1935–37	Oliver Stanley (Con)	Eton	Major 1914–18
1937–38	Earl Stanhope (Con)	Eton	Oxford
1938–40	Earl De La Warr (Nat.Lab)	Eton	Oxford
1940–41	Herwald Ramsbotham (Con)	Uppingham	Cambridge
1941-45	R. A. Butler (Con)	Marlborough	Cambridge
1945	Richard Law (Con)*	Shrewsbury	Oxford
1945–47	Ellen Wilkinson (Lab)	Stretford Rd Sec.Sch.	Manchester Univ.
1947–51	George Tomlinson (Lab)	Rishton Weslyan Sch.	
1951–54	Florence Horsburgh (Con)**	St Hilda's Folkstone	
1954–57	Sir David Eccles (Con)	Winchester	Oxford
1957	Quintin Hogg (Lord Hailsham) (Con)	Eton	Oxford
1957–59	Geoffrey Lloyd (Con)	Harrow	Cambridge
1959–62	Sir David Eccles (Con)	As above	
1962–64	Sir Edward Boyle (Con)	Eton	Oxford
1964	Quintin Hogg (later Lord Hailsham) (Con)	As above	
1964	Sir Edward Boyle (Con)	As above	
1964–65	Michael Stewart (Lab)	Christs Hospital	Oxford
1965–67	Anthony Crosland (Lab)	Highgate	Oxford
1967–68	Patrick Gordon Walker (Lab)	Wellington	Oxford
1968–70	Edward Short (Lab)	Secondary	Durham

*Not in Cabinet
** Not in Cabinet until September 1953

APPENDIX 6

EDUCATIONAL BACKGROUNDS OF RECONSTRUCTION COMMITTEE –
BOARD OF EDUCATION 1940[*]

Name	School Attended	University	Further Information
Bosworth-Smith, N. (1886–1964)	Harrow	Cambridge	'Public School' teacher
Cleary, W.C. (1880–1944)	Bedford	Cambridge	Principal Asst. Sec. Elem Branch 1940–45, Dep. Sec. Min. Educ. 1945–50
Wallis, H.B. (1882–1956)	King Edward, B'ham	Oxford	Lecturer Manch. Univ. 1906–09, Princ. Asst. Sec. Tech Branch.
Williams, G.G. (1890–1974)	Westminster	Oxford	Teacher Wellington/ Lancing. Princ. Asst. Sec. Second. Branch 1940–46, Dep. Sec. Min. Educ. 1946–53
Wood, S.H. (1884–1958)		London	Princ. Asst. Sec. Teacher Training
Charles, R. (1882–1951)	Aysgarth/ Kings, Canterbury	Oxford	HMI 1906, Chief Inspect. Elem. Schls 1933–46
Duckworth, F. (1881–1964)	Rossall	Oxford	HMI 1906, Chief Inspect. Second Schls, Sr. Inspect 1941
Elliot, W. (1910–)	St Pauls	Oxford	1936–48 Staff Inspect. Chief Inspect. Sec. Educ. 1959–66
Miss Hammonds[+]	?	?	Senior Woman Inspect.

[*]Based upon biographical notes in Gosden, P.H.J.H. (1976) *Education in the Second World War: A Study in Policy and Administration*, pp.434–42.

[+]It has been impossible to find out any information concerning Miss Hammonds. The unsorted archives on the Inspectorate at the Institute of Education, London University, which may contain information were not available at the time of writing.

BIBLIOGRAPHY

Minutes/Correspondence
1926–70 *Minutes of the General Council of the Trades Union Congress.*
1926–70 *Minutes of the Education Committee of the Trades Union Congress.*
1926–70 *Minutes/Papers concerning TUC Deputations to the Board/ Ministry of Education/Department of Education & Science* at the Public Record Office. Specific references provided where relevant.

Theses
Manton, K. (1998) 'Socialism and Education in Britain 1883–1902', PhD (London).
Wallace, R.G. (1980) 'Labour, the Board of Education and the Preparation of the 1944 Act', PhD (London).

Reports
1905 *Report of the Interdepartmental Committee on Medical Inspection and Feeding of Children Attending Public Elementary Schools.*
1926–70 *Annual Reports of the Trades Union Congress.*
1926–28 *Report of the Committee on Education and Industry (The Malcolm Committee)*, HMSO.
1926 *Report of the Consultative Committee on the Education of the Adolescent (The Hadow Report)*, HMSO.
1933 *Report of the Consultative Committee on Infant and Nursery Schools*, HMSO.
1936–37 *Hansard, 1936*, 5th Series, Vol. 317, 1936–1937.

1938   *Report of the Consultative Committee on Secondary Education with Special Reference to Grammar Schools and Technical High Schools (The Spens Report)*, HMSO.

1943   *Report of the Committee of the Secondary Schools Examination Council on Curriculum and Examinations in Secondary Schools (The Norwood Committee)*, HMSO.

1944   *Report of the Committee on Public Schools Appointed by the President of the Board of Education (The Fleming Report)*, HMSO.

1954   *Early Learning: Report of the Central Advisory Council for Education (England)*, HMSO.

1959   *15–18: Report of the Central Advisory Council for Education (England) (The Crowther Report)*, HMSO.

1963   *Half Our Future; A Report of the Central Advisory Council for Education (England) (The Newsom Report)*, HMSO.

1963   *Report of the Committee on Higher Education Appointed by the Prime Minister (The Robbins Report)*, HMSO.

1967   *Children and Their Primary Schools: A Report of the Central Advisory Council for (Education) (The Plowden Report)*, HMSO.

1968   *First Report of the Public School Commission (The Newsom Report)*, HMSO.

1970   *Second Report of the Public School Commission (The Donnison Report)*, HMSO.

1984   *Improving Secondary Schools: A Report of the Commitee on the Curriculum and Organisation of Secondary Schools*, ILEA.

Articles/Papers

Alexander, A. (2002) 'The Soviet Threat was Bogus', *The Spectator*, 20 April.

Allen, V.L. (1960) 'The Re-organisation of the Trades Union Congress 1918–27', *British Journal of Sociology*, Vol. XI, No. 1.

Andrews L. (1972) 'The School Meals Service', *British Journal of Educational Studies*, Vol. XX, No. 1.

Bailey, B. (1995) 'James Chuter Ede and the 1944 Education Act', *History of Education*, Vol. 24, No. 3.

Barber, C (1980) 'The Exemption System: 1833–1944', *Journal of Educational Administration and History*, Vol. XII, No. 1.

Betts, R. (2001) 'We've Got to Live Here After You've Gone', *Journal of Educational Administration and History*, Vol. 33, No. 1.

Brooks J.R. (1972) 'The Politics of Secondary School Reorganisation:

Some Reflections', *Journal of Educational Administration and History*, Vol. IV, No. 2.

Brooks, J.R. (1977) 'The Council for Educational Advance during the Chairmanship of R.H. Tawney, 1942–49', *Journal of Educational Administration and History*, Vol. IX, No. 2.

Burgess, K. (1993) 'Education Policy in Relation to Employment in Britain 1935–45; a Decade of "Missed Opportunities"', *History of Education*, Vol. 22. No. 4.

Carpenter, P. (1985) 'Churchill and His "Technological" College', *Journal of Educational Administration and History*, Vol. XVII, No. 2.

Chitty, C. (1988) 'Central Control of the School Curriculum 1944–87', *History of Education*, Vol. 17, No. 4.

Collins, J.M. (1969) 'The Labour Party and the Public Schools; a Conflict of Principles', *British Journal of Educational Studies*, Vol. XVII, No. 3.

Crook, D. (1993) 'Edward Boyle; Conservative Champion of Comprehensives', *History of Education*, Vol. 22, No. 1.

Dean, D. (1969) 'The Difficulties of a Labour Educational Policy: The Failure of the Trevelyan Bill 1929–1931', *British Journal of Educational Studies*, Vol. XVII, No. 3.

Dean, D. (1970) 'Problems of the Conservative Sub-Committee on Education 1941–1945', *Journal of Educational Adminstration and History*, Vol. III, No. 1.

Dean, D. (1986) 'Planning for a Postwar Generation: Ellen Wilkinson and George Tomlinson at the Ministry of Education 1945–1951', *History of Education*, Vol. 15, No. 2.

Dean, D. (1992) 'Presentation or Renovation? The Dilemmas of Conservative Educational Policy 1955–1960', *Twentieth Century British History*, Vol. 3, No. 1.

Dean, D. (1992) 'Consensus or Conflict? The Churchill Government and Education Policy', *History of Education*, Vol. 21, No. 1.

Dean, D. (1995) 'Conservative Governments 1951–1964, and their Changing Perspectives on the 1944 Education Act', *History of Education*, Vol. 24, No. 3.

Dean, D. (1998) 'Circular 10/65 Revisited: the Labour Government and the "Comprehensive Revolution" in 1964–1965', *Paedagogica Historica*, Vol. 34, No. 1.

Demaine, J. (1992) 'The Labour Party and Education Policy', *British Journal of Education Studies*, Vol. XXXX, No. 3.

Doherty, B. (1964) 'The Hadow Report, 1926', *The Durham Research Review*, No. 15.

Fieldhouse, R. (1981) 'Voluntaryism and the State in Adult Education: The

WEA and the 1925 TUC Education Scheme', *History of Education*, Vol. 10, No. 1.

Fieldhouse, R. (1994) 'The Labour Government's Further Education Policy 1945–1951', *History of Education*, Vol. 23, No. 3.

Garner D. (1985) 'Education and the Welfare State: The School Meals and Milk Service, 1944–1980', *Journal of Educational Administration and History*, Vol. XVII, No. 2.

Godwin C.D. (1998) 'The Origin of the Binary System', *History of Education*', Vol. 27, No. 2.

Gosden, P (1995) 'Putting the Act Together', *History of Education*, Vol. 24, No. 3.

Griggs, C.(1981) 'The Trades Union Congress and the Controversy over the National Society's Standard of Reading Book', *British Journal of Educational Studies*, Vol. XXIX, No. 3.

Hurst, J. (1999) 'The 1936 Education Act and Special Agreement Schools: An Example from Berkshire', *History of Education Society Bulletin*, No. 63.

Hyndman, M. (1976) 'Multilateralism and the Spens Report: Evidence from the Archives', *British Journal of Educational Studies*, Vol. XXIV, No. 3.

Jeffereys, K. (1984) 'R.A. Butler, the Board of Education and the 1944 Education Act', *History*, Vol. 69.

Le Quesne, L. (1970) '1919–1945 The Headmasters' Conference Between Two Peaces', *Conference*, Vol. 7, No. 1.

Lowe, R. (1998) 'Constant Elements in Educational Policy: Morant, Butler and Baker Compared', *History of Education Society Bulletin*, No. 61.

Marsden, W.E. (1990) 'Rooting Racism into the Educational Experience of Childhood and Youth in the Nineteenth and Twentieth Centuries', *History of Education*, Vol. 19, No. 4.

McCulloch, G. (1993) '"Spens *v.* Norwood": Contesting the Educational State', *History of Education*, Vol. 22, No. 2.

McCulloch, G. and Sobell L. (1994) 'Towards a Social History of the Secondary Modern Schools', *History of Education*, Vol. 23, No. 3.

Middleton, N. (1972) 'Lord Butler and the Education Act of 1944', *British Journal of Educational Studies*,Vol. XX, No. 2.

Parker, D. (1998) '"Convenient Dispensary;" Elementary Education and the Influence of the School Medical Service 1907–39', *History of Education*, Vol. 27, No. 1.

Silver, H. (1991) 'Poverty and Effective Schools', *Journal of Education Policy*, Vol. 6, No. 3.

Simon, B. (1986) 'The 1944 Education Act: A Conservative Measure?', *History of Education*, Vol. 15, No. 1.

Simon, B. (1985) 'The Tory Government and Education, 1951–60 Background to Breakout', *History of Education*, Vol. 14, No. 4.

Simon, J. (1977) 'The Shaping of the Spens Report on Secondary Education 1933–1938; an Inside View', Part I and Part II, *British Journal of Educational Studies*, Vol. XXV, No. 1 and No. 2.

Smith, G. (1977) 'Positive Discrimination by Area in Education: the EPA Idea Re-examined', *Oxford Review of Education*, Vol. 13, No. 3.

Stevens, R. (1997) 'Containing Radicalism: the Trades Union Congress Organisation Department and Trades Councils 1928–1953', *Labour History Review*, 62.1.

Swinnerton, B. (1996) 'The 1931 Report of the Consultative Committee on the Primary School; Tensions and Contradictions', *History of Education*, Vol. 25, No. 1.

Wallace R.G. (1981) 'The Origins and Authorship of the 1944 Education Act', *History of Education*, Vol. 10, No. 4.

Wann P. (1971) 'The Collapse of Parliamentary Bipartisanship in Education, 1945–1952', *Journal of Educational Administration and History*, Vol. III, No. 2.

Watson D. (1998) 'Relations Between Education and Employment Departments, 1921–45: an Anti-Industry Culture versus Industrial Efficiency?', *History of Education*, Vol. 27, No. 3.

Wilmot F. (1999) 'Birmingham and the Open Air School Movement', *History of Education Society Bulletin*, No. 64.

Woods, R. (1981) 'Margaret Thatcher and Secondary Reorganisation', *Journal of Educational Administration and History*, Vol. XIII, No. 2.

Books/Pamphlets

Addison, P. (1985) *Now the War is Over; a Social History of Britain 1945–51*, BBC/Jonathan Cape.

Addison, P. (1994) *The Road to 1945: British Politics and the Second World War*, Pimlico. (First published by Jonathan Cape 1975).

Aldrich, R. and Gordon, P. (1989) *Dictionary of British Educationists*, Woburn Press.

Allsopp, E. and Grugeon, D. (1966) *Direct Grant Grammar Schools*, Fabian Society.

Andrews, L. (1976) *The Education Act 1918*, Routledge and Kegan Paul.

Arnold-Forster, M. (1983 edn) *The World at War*, Thames Methuen.

Bagwell, P.S. (1963) *The Railwaymen: a History of the National Union of Railwaymen*, George Allen and Unwin.

Bamford, T.W. (1967) *The Rise of the Public Schools: A Study of Boys' Public Boarding Schools in England and Wales from 1837 to the Present Day*, Nelson.

Banks, O. (1955) *Parity and Prestige in English Secondary Education*, Routledge and Kegan Paul.

Barber, M. (1994) *The Making of the 1944 Education Act*, Cassell,

Barker, E. (1983) *The British Between the Superpowers 1945–50*, University of Toronto Press, Toronto and Buffalo.

Barker, R. (1972) *Education and Politics 1900–51: A Study of the Labour Party*, Clarendon Press.

Baron S. *et al.* (1981) *Unpopular Education: Sociology and Social Democracy in England since 1944*, Centre for Contemporary Studies/ Hutchinson.

Beckett, F. (2000) *Clem Attlee: A Biography*, Pimlico.

Bellamy, J. and Saville, J. (eds) *Dictionary of Labour Biography, Vol. 1 (1972); Vol. 2 (1974); Vol. 3 (1976); Vol. 4 (1977); Vol. 5 (1979); Vol. 6 (1982); Vol. 7 (1984); Vol. 8 (1987); Vol. 9 (1993); Vol. 10 (2000)*, Macmillan.

Benn, C. and Simon, B. (1972) *Half Way There: Report on the British Comprehensive School Reform*, Penguin.

Benn, T. (1988) *Out of the Wilderness: Diaries 1963–67*, Arrow. (First published by Hutchinson 1987.)

Benn, T. (1988) *Office Without Power: Diaries 1968–72*, Arrow.

Black, D. (1980) *The Black Report on Health*, HMSO.

Blake, R. (1985) *The Conservative Party from Peel to Thatcher*, Fontana.

Blum, A.A. (1969) *Teacher Unions and Associations: a Comparative Study*, University of Illinois Press.

Bourne, R. and MacArthur, B. (1970) *The Struggle for Education 1870–70*, Schoolmaster Publishing Company.

Bowles, S. and Gintis, H. (1976) *Schooling in Capitalist America*, Routledge and Kegan Paul.

Boxer, A. (1996) *The Conservative Government 1951–1964*, Longmans.

Boyd, D. (1973) *Elites and Their Education: the Educational and Social Background of Eight Elite Groups*, NFER.

Boyson, R. (1975) *The Crisis in Education*, Woburn Press.

Branson, N. and Heinemann, M. (1973) *Britain in the Nineteen Thirties*, Panther. (First published by Weidenfeld and Nicolson 1971.)

Briggs, A. (1979) *Governing the BBC*, BBC.

Brivati, B. and Heffernan, R. (eds) (2000) *The Labour Party: a Centenary History*, Macmillan.

Brown, G. (1971) *In My Way: The Political Memories of Lord George*

Brown, Gollancz.

Brown, K.D. (ed.) (1985) *The First Labour Party 1906–1914*, Croom Helm.

Brockington, W.A. (1916) *Elements of Military Education*, Longmans, Green & Co.

Bullock, A. *The Life and Times of Ernest Bevin Vol. 1 – 1881–40* (1960) *Vol.II – 1940–45* (1967), Heinemann.

Butler, D. and Butler, G. (2000) *Twentieth Century British Political Facts 1900–2000*, Macmillan.

Butler, R.A. (1971) *The Art of the Possible*, Hamish Hamilton.

Calder, A. (1996) *The People's War: Britain 1939–45*, Pimlico (First published 1969.)

Carr, F. (1993) 'Cold War: The Economy and Foreign Policy', in Fyrth, J. (ed.), *Labour's High Noon*, Lawrence and Wishart.

Castle, B. (1984) *The Castle Diaries 1964–70*, Weidenfeld and Nicolson.

Chitty, C. (1989) *Towards a New Education System: The Victory of the New Radical Right*, Falmer Press.

Citrine, W. (1937) *The Trades Union Congress at Work*, TUC.

Citrine, W. (1937) *Education and Democracy: TUC Aspirations and Activities*, TUC.

Citrine, W. (1964) *Men and Work: an Autobiography*, Greenwood Press, Westport, Connecticut.

Clarke, P. (1996) *Hope and Glory: Britain 1900–1990*, Penguin.

Clegg, H.A. (1994) *A History of British Trade Unions since 1889, Vol. III 1934–1951*, Clarendon Press.

Cole, G.D.H. (1948 edn) *A Short History of the British Working Class Movement 1789–1947*, Allen and Unwin

Cole, J. (1996) *As It Seemed to Me*, Phoenix. (First published by Weidenfeld and Nicolson 1995.)

Cole, M. (ed.) (1989) *The Social Contexts of Schooling*, Falmer Press.

Conley, F. (1990) *General Elections Today*, Manchester University Press.

Corfield, A.J. (1969) *Epoch in Workers' Education*, WEA.

Cox, C.B. and Dyson, A.E. (eds) (1969) *Black Paper Two*, Critical Quarterly Society.

Coxall, B. and Robins, L. (1998) *British Politics Since the War*, Macmillan.

Craik, W.W. (1964) *The Central Labour College*, Lawrence and Wishart.

Crookham, A. (1998) *The Trades Union Congress Archive 1960–70*, Modern Records Centre, University of Warwick Library.

Crosland, S. (1983) *Tony Crosland*, Coronet Books/Hodder and Stoughton.

Cruickshank, M. (1963) *Church and State in English Education: 1870 to the Present Day*, Macmillan.

Davies, A.J. (1992) *To Build a New Jerusalem: the British labour movement from the 1880s to the 1990s*, Michael Joseph.

Davis, R. (1967) *The Grammar School*, Penguin.

Dent, H.C. (1957) *The Education Act 1944*, University of London Press (First published 1944.)

Douglas, J.W.B., (1964) *The Home and School*, MacGibbon and Kee Ltd.

Duberman, M.B. (1989) *Paul Robeson*, Pan Books.

Duffield, S. and Storey, R. (1992) *The Trades Union Congress Archive 1920–60*, Modern Records Centre, University of Warwick Library.

Eatwell, R. (1979) *The 1945–1951 Labour Government*, Batsford Academic.

Edwards, B. (1974) *The Burston School Strike*, Lawrence and Wishart.

Field, F. (1973) *Unequal Britain: A Report on the Cycle of Inequality*, Arrow Books.

Field, F. (1981) *Inequality in Britain: Freedom, Welfare and the State*, Fontana.

Field, J. (1992) *Learning Through Labour: Training, Education and the State 1890–1939*, University of Leeds Press.

Fieldhouse, R.T. (1985) *Adult Education and the Cold War*, Leeds.

Foot, M. (1975) *Aneurin Bevan, Vol. 1 1897–1945; Vol. 2 1945–1960*, Paladin.

Ford, B. (ed.) (1992) *Early 20th Century Britain: The Cambridge Cultural History*, Cambridge University Press.

Forder, A. (ed.) (1971 edn) *Penelope Hall's Social Services of England and Wales*, Routledge and Kegan Paul.

Fox, A. (1958) *A History of the National Union of Boot and Shoe Operatives 1874–1957*, Basil Blackwell.

Francis, H. and Smith, D. (1980) *The Fed: A History of the South Wales Miners in the Twentieth Century*, Lawrence and Wishart.

Fyrth J. (ed.) (1993) *Labour's High Noon: The Government and the Economy 1945–1951*, Lawrence and Wishart.

Fyrth J. (ed.) (1995) *Labour's Promised Land? Culture and Society in Labour Britain 1945–51*, Lawrence and Wishart

Gamble, A. (1990 edn) *Britain in Decline: Economic Policy, Political Strategy and the British State*, Macmillan.

Gardiner, J. and Wenborn, N. (eds) (1995) *The History Today Companion to British History*, Collins and Brown

Gathorne-Hardy, J. (1972) *The Rise and Fall of the British Nanny*, Hodder and Stoughton.

Gathorne-Hardy, J. (1979) *The Public School Phenomenon*, Penguin (First published by Hodder and Stoughton 1977.)

Gilbert, M. (1992) *Churchill: A Life*, Minerva.

Gilbert, M. (1998) *A History of the Twentieth Century, Vol. Two 1933–1951*, Harper Collins.

Gilbert, M. (1999) *A History of the Twentieth Century, Vol. Three 1952–1999*, Harper Collins.

Gilbert, M. and Gott, R. (2000) *The Appeasers*, Phoenix Press.

Glennerster, H. and Pryke, R. (1964) *The Public Schools*, Fabian Society

Gordon, P. (1980) *Selection for Secondary Education*, Woburn Press.

Gordon, P., Aldrich, R. and Dean, D. (1991) *Education and Policy in England in the Twentieth Century*, Woburn Press.

Gosden, P.H.J.H. (1972) *The Evolution of a Profession: A Study of the Contribution of Teachers' Associations to the Development of School Teaching as a Professional Occupation*, Basil Blackwell.

Gosden, P.H.J.H. (1976) *Education in the Second World War: A Study in Policy and Administration*, Methuen.

Gosden, P.H.J.H. (1983) *The Education System Since 1944*, Martin Robertson.

Griggs, C. (1983) *The Trades Union Congress and the Struggle for Education 1868–1925*, Falmer Press.

Griggs, C. (1985) *Private Education in Britain*, Falmer Press.

Hailsham, Lord (1990) *A Sparrow's Flight*, Fontana.

Halsey, A.H. (1995 edn) *Change in British Society: From 1900 to the Present Day*, Oxford University Press.

Halsey, A.H. (ed.) (1972) *Educational Priority: EPA Problems and Policies, Vol. 1. Report of a Research Project Sponsored by the DES and SSRC*, HMSO.

Halsey, A.H., Heath, A.F. and Ridge, L.M. (1980) *Origins and Destinations: Family, Class and Education in Modern Britain*, Clarendon.

Hattersley, R. (1996) *Who Goes Home? Scenes from a Political Life*, Warner Books (First published by Little, Brown & Co. 1995.)

Hattersley, R. (1997) *Fifty Years On: A Prejudiced History of Britain Since the War*, Little, Brown and Co.

Healey, D. (1990) *The Time of My Life*, Penguin (First published by Michael Joseph 1989.)

Hencke, D. (1978) *Colleges in Crisis: The Reorganisation of Teacher Training 1971–1977*, Penguin.

Hennesey, P. (1992) *Never Again: Britain 1945–1951*, Jonathan Cape.

Hill, D. (1977) *Tribune 40: the First Forty Years of a Socialist*

Newspaper, Quartet Books.

Hobsbawm, E. (1994) *Age of Extremes: The Short Twentieth Century 1914–1991*, Michael Joseph.

Hobsbawm, E. (1997) *On History*, Weidenfeld and Nicolson.

Holford, J. (1994) *Union Education in Britain: A TUC Activity*, University of Nottingham.

Hollis, P. (1997) *Jennie Lee – A Life*, Oxford University Press.

Horn, P. (1989) *The Victorian and Edwardian Schoolchild*, Alan Sutton.

Howard, A. (ed.) (1979) *The Crossman Diaries – Selections 1964–1970*, Book Club Associates.

Howard, A. (1987) *RAB: The Life of R.A. Butler*, Jonathan Cape.

Humphrey, G. (1989) *Wartime Eastbourne: The Story of the Most Raided Town in the South East*, Becketts Features.

Hutt, A. (1962) *British Trade Unionism: A Short History 1800–1961*, Lawrence and Wishart.

James, L. (1995) *The Rise and Fall of the British Empire*, Abacus.

James, L. (1998) *RAJ – The Making and Unmaking of British India*, Softback Preview.

Jones, J. (1986) *Union Man; An Autobiography*, Collins.

Jones, M. (1994) *Michael Foot*, Victor Gollancz.

Kirkham, P. and Thoms, D. (eds) (1995) *War Culture: Social Change and Changing Experience in World War Two*, Lawrence and Wishart.

Knight, C. (1990) *The Making of Tory Education Policy in Post-War Britain 1950–1986*, Falmer Press.

Kogan, M. (1975) *Educational Policy Making: A Study of Interest Groups and Parliament*, Allen and Unwin.

Kogan, M. (1971) *The Politics of Education*, Penguin.

Labour Party (n.d., *c.*1928/29) *Children First*, The Labour Party.

Labour Party (1933) *Labour and Education*, The Labour Party.

Labour Party (1958) *Learning to Live*, The Labour Party.

Labour Party/TUC (1928) *Nursery School to University*, The Labour Party/TUC.

Lawn, M. (1987) *Servants of the State: The Contested Control of Teaching 1900–1930*, Falmer Press.

Lawson, J. and Silver, H. (1973) *A Social History of Education in England*, Methuen.

Layard, R., King, J. and Moser, C. (1969) *The Impact of Robbins*, Penguin.

Laybourn, K. (1988) *The Labour Party 1881–1951*, Alan Sutton.

Leff, S. and Leff, V. (1959) *The School Health Service*, H.K. Lewis and Co.

Lewis, R. (1993) *Leaders and Teachers: Adult Education and the Challenge of Labour in South Wales 1906–1940*, University of Wales Press.

Lowe, R. (ed.) (1987) *The Changing Primary School*, Falmer Press.

Lowe, R. (1988) *Education in the Post-War Years: A Social History*, Routledge.

Lowe, R. (ed.) (1989) *The Changing Secondary School*, Falmer Press.

Lowe, R. (1997) *Schooling and Social Change 1964–1990*, Routledge.

Lowe, R. (1993) *The Welfare State in Britain Since 1945*, Macmillan.

Maclure, S. (1970) *One Hundred Years of London Education 1870–1970*, Allen Lane, Penguin Press

MacKenzie, J.M. (1984) *Propaganda and Empire: the Manipulation of British Public Opinion 1880–1960*, Manchester University Press.

McCulloch, G. (1991) *Philosophers and Kings: Education for Leadership in Modern England*, Cambridge University Press.

McCulloch, G. (1994) *Educational Reconstruction: The 1944 Education Act and the Twenty-First Century*, Woburn Press.

M'Gonigle, G. and Kirby, J. (1936) *Poverty and Public Health*, Victor Gollancz.

Martin, R. (1980) *TUC: The Growth of a Pressure Group 1868–1976*, Clarendon Press

Marwick, A. (1996 edn) *British Society Since 1945*, Penguin.

Marx, K. and Engels, F. (1968) *Selected Works in One Volume*, Lawrence and Wishart.

Mellors, W. and Hildyard R. (1992) 'The Cultural and Social Setting: the Edwardian Age and Inter-War Years', in Ford, B. (ed.) *Early 20th Century Britain*, Cambridge University Press.

Middlemass, K. (1986) *Power, Competition and the State, Vol.1. Britain in Search of Balance*, Macmillan

Middleton, N. and Weitzman, S. (1976) *A Place for Everyone: a History of State Education from the end of the 18th Century to the 1970s*, Victor Gollancz

Millar, J.P.M. (1987) *The Labour College Movement*, NCLC Publishing Society Ltd.

Mitford, N. (1978) *A Fine Old Conflict*, Quartet.

Morgan, K.O. (1985) *Labour in Power 1945–51*, Oxford University Press.

Morgan, K.O. (1992) *Labour People*, Oxford University Press.

Morgan, K.O. (1992) *The People's Peace: British History 1945–1990*, Oxford University Press.

Morris, M. (1939) *The People's Schools*, Victor Gollancz.

Morrish, I. (1970) *Education Since 1800*, George Allen and Unwin.

Morton, A. (1997) *Education and the State from 1833: Public Record Office Readers' Guide No. 18*, PRO Publications.

Musson, A.E. (1968) *The Congress of 1868*, TUC.

Parkinson, M. (1970) *The Labour Party and the Organization of Secondary Education 1918–1965*, Routledge and Kegan Paul.

Paxman, J. (1990) *Friends in High Places*, Penguin.

Payne, J. (1974) *EPA Surveys and Statistics*, Vol. 2, HMSO.

Pelling, H. (1971 edn) *A History of British Trade Unionism*, Penguin.

Pimlott, B. (1992) *Harold Wilson*, Harper Collins.

Pimlott, B. and Cook C. (eds) (1982) *Trade Unions in British Politics*, Longman.

Pollins, H. (1984) *The History of Ruskin College*, Ruskin College.

Ponting, C. (1989) *Breach of Promise: Labour in Power 1964–1970*, Hamish Hamilton.

Prochaska, A. (1982) *History of the General Federation of Trade Unions 1899–1980*, Allen and Unwin.

Rae, J. (1981) *The Public School Revolution, 1964–1979*, Faber and Faber.

Rich, P.J. (1991) *Chains of Empire: English Public Schools, Masonic Cabalism, Historical Causality and Imperial Clubdom*, Regency Press.

Rich, P.J. (1993) *Elixir of Empire: English Public Schools, Ritualism, Freemasonry, and Imperialism*, Regency Press.

Richmond, W.K. (1978) *Education in Britain Since 1944*, Methuen.

Robinson, E. (1968) *The New Polytechnics*, Penguin.

Roderick, G. and Stephens, M. (eds) (1982) *Where Did We Go Wrong? Industry, Education and Economy of Victorian Britain*, Falmer Press.

Roderick, G. and Stephens, M. (eds) (1982) *The British Malaise: Industrial Performance, Education and Training in Britain Today*, Falmer Press.

Rogers, R. (1984 edn.) *Crowther to Warnock: How Fourteen Reports Tried to Change Children's Lives*, Heinemann.

Rubinstein, D. and Simon, B. (1969) *The Evolution of the Comprehensive School 1926–1966*, Routledge.

Saran, R. (1973) *Policy Making in Secondary Education – A Case Study*, Clarendon Press.

Seifert, R.V. (1987) *Teacher Militancy: A History of Teacher Strikes 1896–1987*, Falmer Press.

Shinwell, M. (1981) *Lead With The Left: My First Ninety-Six Years*, Cassell.

Shirer, W. (1964) *The Rise and Fall of the Third Reich: A History of Nazi Germany*, Pan Books Ltd.

Silver, H, (1983) *Education as History*, Methuen.

Silver, H, (1990) *Education, Change and the Policy Process*, Falmer Press.

Silver, H. (ed.) (1973) *Equal Opportunity in Education*, Methuen.

Simon, B. (1960) *Studies in the History of Education 1780-1870*, Lawrence and Wishart. (Republished later under the title *The Two Nations and the Educational Structure*.)

Simon, B. (1965) *Education and the labour movement 1870–1920*, Lawrence and Wishart.

Simon, B. (ed.) (1968) *Education in Leicestershire 1540–1940*, Leicester University Press.

Simon, B. (1974) *The Politics of Educational Reform, 1920–1940*, Lawrence and Wishart.

Simon, B. (ed.) (1985) *Does Education Matter?* Lawrence and Wishart.

Simon, B. (ed.) (1990) *The Search for Enlightenment: The Working Class and Adult Education in the Twentieth Century*, Lawrence and Wishart.

Simon, B.(1991) *Education and the Social Order 1940–1990*, Lawrence and Wishart

Simon, B. (1994) 'The Student Movement in the 1930s' in Simon, B. (ed.) *The State and Educational Change*, Lawrence and Wishart.

Simon, B. (1998) *A Life in Education*, Lawrence and Wishart.

Sked, A. and Cook, C. (1993 edn) *Post-War Britain: A Political History 1945–1992*, Penguin

Sparrow, G. (1965) *'R.A.B.': Study of a Statesman*, Odhams Books Ltd.

Stanworth, P. and Giddens, A. (eds) (1974) *Elites and Power in British Society*, Cambridge University Press.

Stevenson, J. (1984) *British Society 1914–1945*, Penguin.

Stevenson, J. and Cook C. (1994 edn) *Britain in the Depression: Society and Politics 1929–1939*, Longman.

Stocks, M. (1953) *The Workers' Educational Association*, George Allen and Unwin.

Tapper, T. (1997) *Fee-Paying Schools and Educational Change in Britain*, Woburn Press.

Tawney, R.H. (1922) *Secondary Education for All: A Policy for Labour*, Allen and Unwin

Tawney, R.H. (1934) *The School-Leaving Age and Juvenile Unemployment*, WEA.

Taylor, A.J.P. (1965) *English History 1914–1945*, Oxford University Press.

Taylor G. and Ayres, N. (1969) *Born and Bred Unequal*, Longman.

Taylor, R. (2000) *The TUC: From the General Strike to New Unionism*, Palgrave.

Thomas, H. (1965) *The Spanish Civil War*, Penguin.

Thorpe, A. (1997) *A History of the British Labour Party*, Macmillan.

Tiratsoo, N. (ed.) (1998) *From Blitz to Blair: A New History of Britain Since 1939*, Phoenix (First published by Weidenfeld and Nicolson 1997).

Titmuss, R.M. (1963 edn) *Essays on 'The Welfare State'*, Unwin University Books.

Townsend, P. (1979) *Poverty in the United Kingdom*, Pelican.

Townsend, P. and Davidson, N. (eds) (1982) *Inequalities in Health (The Black Report)*, Penguin.

Tressell, R. (1927 edn) *The Ragged Trousered Philanthropists*, Grant Richards.

TUC (1937) *Education and Democracy*, TUC.

TUC (1944) *Interim Report on Post-War Reconstruction*, TUC.

TUC (1942) *TUC Memorandum on Education After the War*, TUC.

TUC (1958) *What the TUC is Doing*, TUC.

Tunstall, J. (ed.) (1974) *The Open University Opens*, Routledge and Kegan Paul.

Webster, C. (1988) *The Health Services Since the War, Vol. 1. Problems of Health Care – The National Health Service before 1957*, HMSO.

Wedge, P. and Essen, J. (1982) *Children in Adversity*, Pan Books.

Wedge, P. and Prosser, H. (1973) *Born to Fail*, Arrow.

Whitbread, N. (1972) *The Evolution of the Nursery/Infant School: A History of Infant and Nursery Education in Britain 1800–1970*, Routledge and Kegan Paul.

Whitley, R. (1974) 'The City and Industry: The Directors of Large Companies, their Characteristics and Connections', in Stanworth, P. and Giddens, A., *Elites and Power in British Society*, Cambridge University Press.

Wilkinson, E. (1939) *The Town That Was Murdered*, Victor Gollancz.

Wilson, H. (1974) *The Labour Government 1964–1970*, Penguin. (First published by Weidenfeld and Nicolson and Michael Joseph 1971).

Winstone, R. (ed.) (1995) *Tony Benn: Years of Hope. Diaries, Papers and Letters 1940–1962*, Arrow. (First published by Hutchinson 1994.)

Wright, N. (1977) *Progress in Education*, Croom Helm.

Wright, P. with Greengrass, P. (1987) *Spycatcher*, Heinemann, Australia.

Yorke, P. (1997) *Ruskin College 1899–1909*, Ruskin College.

INDEX

SUBJECT